Communications
in Computer and Information Science   1217

More information about this series at http://www.springer.com/series/7899

Markus Helfert · Cornel Klein ·
Brian Donnellan · Oleg Gusikhin (Eds.)

Smart Cities, Green Technologies and Intelligent Transport Systems

8th International Conference, SMARTGREENS 2019
and 5th International Conference, VEHITS 2019
Heraklion, Crete, Greece, May 3–5, 2019
Revised Selected Papers

 Springer

Editors
Markus Helfert
Dublin City University
Dublin, Ireland

Brian Donnellan
School of Business, Innovation
Value Institute
Maynooth University
Maynooth, Kildare, Ireland

Cornel Klein
Department of Corporate Technology
Siemens AG
Munich, Germany

Oleg Gusikhin
Ford Research and Advanced Engineering
Dearborn, MI, USA

ISSN 1865-0929   ISSN 1865-0937   (electronic)
Communications in Computer and Information Science
ISBN 978-3-030-68027-5   ISBN 978-3-030-68028-2   (eBook)
https://doi.org/10.1007/978-3-030-68028-2

This Springer imprint is published by the registered company Springer Nature Switzerland AG
The registered company address is: Gewerbestrasse 11, 6330 Cham, Switzerland

Preface

This book includes extended and revised versions of a set of selected papers from SMARTGREENS 2019 (8th International Conference on Smart Cities and Green ICT Systems) and VEHITS 2019 (5th International Conference on Vehicle Technology and Intelligent Transport Systems), held in Heraklion, Crete, Greece, from 3 to 5 May, 2019.

SMARTGREENS 2019 received 44 paper submissions from 22 countries, of which 11% were included in this book.

VEHITS 2019 received 90 paper submissions from 29 countries, of which 13% were included in this book.

The papers were selected by the event chairs and their selection is based on a number of criteria that include the classifications and comments provided by the program committee members, the session chairs' assessment and also the program chairs' global view of all papers included in the technical program. The authors of selected papers were then invited to submit a revised and extended version of their paper having at least 30% innovative material.

The purpose of the 8th International Conference on Smart Cities and Green ICT Systems (SMARTGREENS) was to bring together researchers, designers, developers and practitioners interested in advances and applications in the field of Smart Cities, Green Information and Communication Technologies, Sustainability and Energy Aware Systems and Technologies.

The purpose of the 5th International Conference on Vehicle Technology and Intelligent Transport Systems (VEHITS) was to bring together engineers, researchers and practitioners interested in advances and applications in the field of Vehicle Technology and Intelligent Transport Systems. This conference focused on innovative applications, tools and platforms in all technology areas such as signal processing, wireless communications, informatics and electronics, related to different kinds of vehicles, including cars, off-road vehicles, trains, ships, underwater vehicles and flying machines, and the intelligent transportation systems that connect and manage large numbers of vehicles, not only in the context of smart cities but in many other application domains.

The papers selected for inclusion in this book contribute to the understanding of relevant trends in the scope of the different areas of SMARTGREENS and VEHITS. The two papers in the area of Energy Aware Systems and Technologies deal with energy efficiency in the industrial manufacturing domain and with a "CCU label" to foster awareness and trust for Carbon Capture and Utilization. The selected paper for Smart Homes presents a system for reducing energy consumption, based on detection of repeated usage consumption patterns. With regards to Smart Grids, the paper included in this book proposes a "regional load shaping" approach as a market-based solution to resolve current challenges within the mid-voltage grid. The published keynote, which was presented by Prof. Dr. Rudolf Giffinger from Vienna University of

Technology, discusses the different concepts of innovation in Smart Cities and the corresponding role of urban planning.

In the area of vehicle technology and intelligent transport systems two papers address novel vehicle routing problems; two papers discuss efficient vehicle network infrastructure; two papers discuss development toward autonomous driving including infrastructure-supported connected automated driving and novel approaches in perception; 5 papers address intelligent transportation infrastructure including vision damage assessment, efficient parking support, accident data analytics, road assessment for safe cargo transportation and information communication technology for railway networks.

We would like to thank all the authors for their contributions and also the reviewers who have helped to ensure the quality of this publication.

May 2019

Cornel Klein
Brian Donnellan
Markus Helfert
Oleg Gusikhin

Organization

SMARTGREENS Conference Chair

Markus Helfert   Maynooth University, Ireland

VEHITS Conference Chair

Oleg Gusikhin   Ford Motor Company, USA

SMARTGREENS Program Co-chairs

Cornel Klein   Siemens AG, Germany
Brian Donnellan   Maynooth University, Ireland

VEHITS Program Chair

Markus Helfert   Maynooth University, Ireland

SMARTGREENS Program Committee

Javier M. Aguiar	Universidad de Valladolid, Spain
Carlos Antunes	DEEC - University of Coimbra/INESC Coimbra, Portugal
Mehdi Bagheri	Nazarbayev University, Kazakhstan
Simona Bernardi	Universidad de Zaragoza, Spain
Lasse Berntzen	University of South-Eastern Norway, Norway
Nik Bessis	Edge Hill University, UK
Riccardo Bettati	Texas A&M University, USA
Lorenzo Bottaccioli	Politecnico di Torino, Italy
Blanca Caminero	Universidad de Castilla-La Mancha, Spain
Lin Chen	Chinese Academy of Sciences, China
Ken Christensen	University of South Florida, USA
Calin Ciufudean	"Stefan cel Mare" University of Suceava, Romania
Georges Da Costa	IRIT, Paul Sabatier University, France
Wanyang Dai	Nanjing University, China
Cléver Ricardo de Farias	University of São Paulo, Brazil
Venizelos Efthymiou	University of Cyprus, Cyprus
Rania El-Gazzar	University of South-Eastern Norway, Norway
Tullio Facchinetti	University of Pavia, Italy
Adrian Florea	Lucian Blaga University of Sibiu, Romania
Hossam Gaber	University of Ontario Institute of Technology (UOIT), Canada

Béla Genge	University of Medicine, Pharmacy, Science, and Technology of Târgu Mureş, Romania
Christopher Gniady	University of Arizona, USA
André Gradvohl	State University of Campinas, Brazil
Adriana Grigorescu	National University of Political Studies and Public Administration, Romania
Piyush Harsh	Zurich University of Applied Sciences, Switzerland
Muhammad Hasan	Texas A&M University, USA
Nikos Hatziargyriou	National Technical University of Athens, Greece
Kerry Hinton	Centre for Energy Efficient Telecommunications University of Melbourne, Australia
Hartmut Hinz	Frankfurt University of Applied Sciences, Germany
Seongsoo Hong	Seoul National University, Korea, Republic of
Iskandar Ishak	Universiti Putra Malaysia, Malaysia
Bo Jørgensen	University of Southern Denmark, Denmark
Jai Kang	Rochester Institute of Technology, USA
Stamatis Karnouskos	SAP, Germany
Essam Khalil	Cairo University, Egypt
Nicos Komninos	Aristotle University of Thessaloniki, Greece
Sesil Koutra	Université de Mons (UMONS), Belgium
Mani Krishna	University of Massachusetts Amherst, USA
Sisil Kumarawadu	University of Moratuwa, Sri Lanka
Faa-Jeng Lin	National Central University, Taiwan, Republic of China
Marco Listanti	Sapienza University of Rome, Italy
Michela Longo	Politecnico di Milano, Italy
Marcin Luckner	Warsaw University of Technology, Poland
Zheng Ma	University of Southern Denmark, Denmark
Giovanni Maccani	Maynooth University, Ireland
Rabi Mahapatra	Texas A&M University, USA
Annapaola Marconi	Fondazione Bruno Kessler – FBK, Italy
Giaoutzi Maria	National Technical University of Athens, Greece
Daisuke Mashima	Advanced Digital Sciences Center, Singapore
Jean-Marc Menaud	École des Mines de Nantes, France
Daniel Mosse	University of Pittsburgh, USA
Elsa Negre	Paris Dauphine University, France
Carlo Nucci	University of Bologna, Italy
Edoardo Patti	Politecnico di Torino, Italy
Marco Pau	E.ON Energy Research Center - RWTH Aachen University, Germany
Cathryn Peoples	Ulster University, UK
Vítor Pires	Escola Superior de Tecnologia de Setúbal - Instituto Politécnico de Setúbal, Portugal
Philip Pong	The University of Hong Kong, Hong Kong
Evangelos Pournaras	ETH Zurich, Switzerland
Gang Quan	Florida International University, USA

Ana Carolina Riekstin	Kaloom, Canada
Eva González Romera	University of Extremadura, Spain
Enrique Romero-Cadaval	University of Extremadura, Spain
Javad Sardroud	Azad University Central Tehran Branch, Iran, Islamic Republic of
Huasong Shan	JD.com American Technologies Corporation, USA
Bo Sheng	University of Massachusetts Boston, USA
Nirmal Srivastava	Dr. B. R. Ambedkar National Institute of Technology Jalandhar, India
Norvald Stol	Norwegian University of Science and Technology (NTNU), Norway
Afshin Tafazzoli	Siemens Gamesa Renewable Energy, Spain
Paolo Tenti	University of Padova, Italy
Dimitrios Tsoumakos	Ionian University, Greece
Alexandr Vasenev	ESI (TNO), The Netherlands
Silvano Vergura	Polytechnic University of Bari, Italy
Sanjeewa Witharana	Max Planck Institute for Solar System Research, Germany
Igor Wojnicki	AGH University of Science and Technology, Poland
Qiuwei Wu	Technical University of Denmark, Denmark
Chau Yuen	Singapore University of Technology and Design, Singapore
Yayun Zhou	Siemens AG, Germany
Sotirios Ziavras	New Jersey Institute of Technology, USA

VEHITS Program Committee

Carlos Abreu	Instituto Politécnico de Viana do Castelo, Portugal
Felix Albu	Valahia University of Târgovişte, Romania
Aníbal T. De Almeida	ISR-University of Coimbra, Portugal
Florina Almenares	Universidad Carlos III de Madrid, Spain
Konstantinos Ampountolas	University of Glasgow, UK
Paolo Barsocchi	National Research Council (CNR), Italy
Marcel Baunach	Graz University of Technology, Austria
Sandford Bessler	Austrian Institute of Technology (AIT), Austria
Neila Bhouri	IFSTTAR, France
Gergely Biczók	Budapest University of Technology and Economics, Hungary
Bastian Bloessl	Trinity College Dublin (TCD), Ireland
László Bokor	Budapest Univ. of Technology and Economics, Hungary
Jean-Marie Bonnin	IMT Atlantique, France
Christine Buisson	Université de Lyon, France
Cătălin Buiu	Universitatea Politehnica din Bucureşti, Romania
Roberto Caldelli	CNIT, Italy
Pedro Cardoso	University of Algarve, Portugal

Hocine Imine	French Institute of Science and Technology for Transport, Development and Networks (IFSTTAR), France
Sheng Jin	Zhejiang University, China
Govand Kadir	University of Kurdistan Hewlêr, Iraq
Markus Kampmann	Koblenz University of Applied Sciences, Germany
Tetsuya Kawanishi	Waseda University, Japan
Seok-Cheol Kee	Chungbuk National University, Korea, Republic of
Sousso Kelouwani	Université du Québec á Trois-Rivières (UQTR), Canada
Hakil Kim	Inha University, Korea, Republic of
Xiangjie Kong	Dalian University of Technology, China
Anastasios Kouvelas	ETH Zurich, Switzerland
Zdzislaw Kowalczuk	Gdańsk University of Technology, Poland
Francine Krief	University of Bordeaux, France
Yong-Hong Kuo	The University of Hong Kong, Hong Kong
Peter Langendörfer	IHP, Germany
Deok Lee	Kunsan National University, Republic of Korea
Ruidong Li	National Institute of Information and Communications Technology (NICT), Japan
Mingxi Liu	University of Utah, USA
Gabriel Lodewijks	University of New South Wales, School of Aviation (UNSW Sydney), Australia
María del Carmen Lucas-Estañ	Universidad Miguel Hernández de Elche, Spain
Salim M. Zaki	Dijlah University College, Iraq
Michael Mackay	Liverpool John Moores University, UK
S. M. Hassan Mahdavi	VEDECOM, France
Zoubir Mammeri	Irit Laboratory - Paul Sabatier University, France
Barbara Masini	Italian National Research Council (CNR), Italy
José Manuel Menéndez	Universidad Politécnica de Madrid, Spain
Lyudmila Mihaylova	University of Sheffield, UK
Evangelos Mitsakis	Centre for Research and Technology Hellas, Greece
Antonella Molinaro	Mediterranean University of Reggio Calabria, Italy
Wrya Monnet	University of Kurdistan-Hewlêr, Iraq
Jânio Monteiro	Universidade do Algarve, Portugal
Juan Muñoz-Gea	Universidad Politécnica de Cartagena, Spain
Daniela Nechoska	Sofia University St. Kliment Ohridski, Republic of North Macedonia
Otto Nielsen	Technical University of Denmark, Denmark
Marialisa Nigro	Università degli Studi Roma Tre, Italy
Alfredo Núñez	Delft University of Technology, The Netherlands
Mohammed Obaidat	Jordan University of Science and Technology, Jordan
Dario Pacciarelli	Roma Tre University, Italy
Brian Park	University of Virginia, USA
Cecilia Pasquale	Università degli studi di Genova, Italy

Fernando Pereñiguez	University Centre of Defence, Spanish Air Force Academy, Spain
Mark Perry	Brunel University London, UK
Valerio Persico	University of Naples Federico II, Italy
Vassilis Prevelakis	Technische Universität Braunschweig, Germany
Paraskevi Psaraki-Kalouptsidis	National Technical University of Athens, Greece
Hesham Rakha	Virginia Polytechnic Institute and State University, USA
José Santa	Technical University of Cartagena, Spain
Oleg Saprykin	Propzmedia, Samara State Aerospace University, Russian Federation
Sanjay Sharma	University of Plymouth, UK
Shih-Lung Shaw	University of Tennessee, USA
Uwe Stilla	Technische Universität München, Germany
Todor Stoilov	Bulgarian Academy of Sciences, Bulgaria
Wai Yuen Szeto	The University of Hong Kong, Hong Kong
Elia Vardaki	Technical University of Crete, Greece
István Varga	Budapest University of Technology and Economics, Hungary
Francesco Viti	University of Luxembourg, Luxembourg
George Yannis	National Technical University of Athens, Greece
Kyongsu Yi	Seoul National University, Korea, Republic of

VEHITS Additional Reviewers

Iyas Alloush	DCU, Ireland
Ariyan Bighashdel	TUE, The Netherlands
Graziana Cavone	Polytechnic University of Bari, Italy
Zahra Ghandeharioun	ETH, Switzerland
Benjamin Gravell	The University of Texas at Dallas, USA
Mohammad Hamad	Technical University of Braunschweig, Germany
Alexander Hanel	Technische Universität München, Germany
Narsimlu Kemsaram	Eindhoven University of Technology, The Netherlands
Mirco Marchetti	University of Modena and Reggio Emilia, Italy
Antonio Meireles	ISEP, Portugal
Floris Remmen	Eindhoven University of Technology, The Netherlands
Fenglin Zhou	The University of Texas at Dallas, USA

Invited Speakers

Norbert Streitz	Founder and Scientific Director, Smart Future Initiative, Germany
Rudolf Giffinger	Institute of Spatial Planning, TU Wien, Austria

Jeroen Ploeg   2getthere B.V., Utrecht and Eindhoven University
                                            of Technology, The Netherlands
Anna Nikina-Ruohonen   Grenoble École de Management, France
Simona Sacone   University of Genova, Italy

Contents

Smart Cities and Green ICT Systems

Energy Efficiency Indicators for Textile Industry Based on a Self-analysis Tool

Samuele Branchetti[✉], Carlo Petrovich, Gessica Ciaccio, Piero De Sabbata,
Angelo Frascella, and Giuseppe Nigliaccio

ENEA – National Agency for New Technologies, Energy and Sustainable Economic
Development, Via Martiri di Monte Sole 4, 40129 Bologna, Italy
`samuele.branchetti@enea.it`

Abstract. Energy efficiency in the industry sector represents a crucial issue for the sustainable development, but manufacturing companies are not still implementing, on a mass scale, energy saving actions. One of the most important barriers is that many companies are scarcely aware about their consumptions and need reference values to compare their energy performances with similar factories. Nevertheless, since the enterprises are very heterogeneous and the production chains is often fragmented, these values have a high variability. The dispersion of these data has to be decisively decreased, but keeping generality to be representative. This goal is pursued here for the textile sector analysing datasets regarding 140 European factories. The datasets were retrieved by means of a self-analysis software tool, collecting energy consumption data in a simple and homogeneous way. The analysis of the data was performed using energy efficiency indicators and by clustering the factories. The method is here applied to textile industry and the outcomes show a correlation with some production variables, such as the raw materials, the kind of process and the price of the final products. The approach based on a regression analysis between energy consumptions and production has allowed to reduce the relative errors of the energy performances of different categories of factories from more than 100% to about 25–40% in many cases. In this way, energy efficiency indicators can be adopted as acceptable and representative references.

Keywords: Energy efficiency · Specific energy consumption · Benchmarking sustainable economy · Textile industry · Manufacturing · Yarn · Fabric finishing

1 Introduction

In European Union (EU-28) there are more than 2,000,000 of manufacturing enterprises for a whole turnover of about 7,500,000 million Euro.

The textile and clothing industry, including leather and related products, accounts for more than 10% of EU manufacturing enterprises and about of 9.5% of total turnover (EUROSTAT, 2016). This sector is based on small businesses: the companies with less than 50 people employed account for more than 95% of the total companies and 50% of the total people employed.

M. Helfert et al. (Eds.): SMARTGREENS 2019/VEHITS 2019, CCIS 1217, pp. 3–27, 2021.
https://doi.org/10.1007/978-3-030-68028-2_1

In 2016, the textile sector accounted for 62,100 companies, 78,000 million Euro of turnover and about 608,000 people employed.

More than 2/3 of EU textile production is located in the most populated countries: 26% in Italy, 17% in Germany, 9% in United Kingdom, 9% in France and 7% in Spain. The whole amount of production in EU turns out to be about of 1,800,000 tonnes of yarn and 4,000,000,000 m^2 of fabric.

The data concerning the energy consumption are the following: the total energy consumption in textile and leather industry sector has been of 4,236,211 tonnes of oil equivalent (toe). This consumption was mainly composed of electricity (1,785,313 toe, i.e. 20,763,192 MWh) and natural gas (1,971,482 TOE, i.e. 82,541,941 GJ), with lower contributions from other sources (EUROSTAT, 2016).

These values point out in a clear way that, even if textile are not considered energy intensive sectors, their consumption accounts for a significant amount of energy (and consequently of greenhouse gases). Nevertheless, there is no systematic analysis and collection of data about the typical energy consumption values for the textile sector. This is a key problem and these data were needed for the activities of the European project ARTISAN[1], whose aim was to provide tools and services for helping textile companies to capture, communicate and incorporate in their decision-making process the energy characteristics of their operations. This was envisaged to be achieved by utilizing innovative ICT modules in their enterprise management systems.

The available energy consumption data were scattered and fragmented and could be classified in the following way:

- data from European (EUROSTAT, 2016) and National statistics, covering only very broad, high-level and mainly economic indicators (e.g. sector energy consumption divided by sector turnover) and not for all European country areas;
- data from the unique available previous European project (EMS-Textile, 2007), developed under the Intelligent Energy program, but referring only to 4 countries (Greece, Portugal, Spain, Bulgaria) and not in a uniform way;
- data collected from the Italian Sectorial Association (specific for one country only) (SMI, 2013);
- some interesting data from the "Reference Document on Best Available Techniques for Textile Industry" (IPPC, 2003). Here, the energy consumption data are partial and incomplete because the focus was on environmental aspects in general.

Other data were found in the following papers:

- In (Hasanbeigi, 2012), the energy consumptions of 13 textile plants in Iran have been analyzed and audited, regarding five different sub-sectors (spinning, weaving, wet-processing, worsted fabric manufacturing and carpet manufacturing). This means that just two or three plants were analyzed in each sub-sector. Hence, the resulting indicators are deduced from a very limited number of factories;
- In (Lin, 2016), Chinese regional differences in the total energy efficiency of the textile industries are analyzed for the period 2000–2012. Considering the distance from the frontier technology, a huge energy saving potential is highlighted for the Chinese textile sector, but it results scarcely significant for the European situation.

Therefore, a path of projects and activities has been established in the European framework programs in order to achieve a more complete understanding of energy efficiency performances in textile industry (and related benchmarks) and to develop tools, best practices and supports for improving energy efficiency in textile companies.

These projects were ARTISAN[1] (FP7 project in 2011–2013), SESEC[2] (Intelligent Energy project in 2012–2015), and SET[3] (Intelligent Energy project in 2014–2017) which were collected under the activity called ENERGY MADE-TO-MEASURE campaign (EM2M)[4]. This had the goal of developing a coherent path acting on European scale, of collecting the needed data and sharing the results with the textile companies.

During the EM2M campaign, different actions were implemented in order to collect the energy data:

- analysis of the literature data;
- 28 energy audits performed by skilled experts, in order to get an understanding of the textile processes;
- Development of a self-evaluation tool, which is composed of a standalone application (SET Tool) and a web application (SET Web). In particular, the web application collects data from each standalone tool, validates and clusters them; moreover, it generates benchmarks, making them available to standalone tool users (Branchetti 2016);
- selection of six SMEs representative of different kinds of companies as SET pilot users and a comparison, performed for each of them, between the SET outcomes and the results of the visits by ENEA experts (Branchetti 2016);
- promotion of the use of the SET tool by textile companies, through about 20 international events.

At the end of this path, a very interesting set of data (more than 200 datasets) has been collected, which will be discussed in the following sections.

In Sect. 2, energy consumptions in textile manufacturing are discussed, together with a literature review. In Sect. 3, the SET Tool, the SET Web and the related database are outlined, whereas the main results are presented and discussed in Sects. 4 and 5.

In a previous paper (Branchetti, 2019), the SET database was introduced and the energy consumption data for yarn manufacturing were analyzed and discussed. In this paper, the literature review and the data analysis are extended also to the fabric and finishing manufacturing, broadening the discussion in a more comprehensive way for the whole textile sector.

2 Energy Consumption in Textile

The textile is one of the most complex manufacturing industries because of the wide range of textile products, processes, raw materials and technologies. It is difficult to

---

[1] https://cordis.europa.eu/project/rcn/100895/factsheet/en.

[2] https://ec.europa.eu/energy/intelligent/projects/en/projects/sesec.

[3] https://ec.europa.eu/energy/intelligent/projects/en/projects/set.

[4] https://em2m.eu/.

define boundaries among the processes and among the final products, considering also the ongoing evolution of non-traditional textile products.

The textile production processes combine a lot of sequential and/or alternative steps, all interrelated in producing a finished fabric. The main processes are shown in Fig. 1. The whole supply chain is often composed by different companies, each of which can execute one or more production steps within one or more factories.

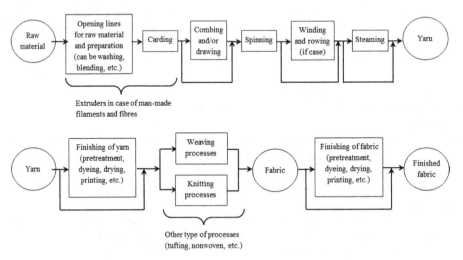

Fig. 1. Typical textile processes.

The combination of products and undertaken processes has a considerable influence on the energy efficiency and therefore, it is fundamental to define the framework within which the energy consumptions of the textile companies can be analyzed.

A first level of categorization, based on the NACE rev. 2 classification and on the "factory" as basic unit for the analysis, was adopted. This allowed to group three main kinds of production: the yarn production, the fabric production, the finishing of yarn and fabric (Table 1).

Table 1. Matching between SET project categorization and NACE rev. 2 classification.

SET project (Level 1)	NACE rev.2	Group
Yarn production	Preparation and spinning of textile fibres	13.1
Fabric production	Weaving of textiles	13.2
Finishing	Finishing of textiles	13.3

Two more specific levels were adopted to define the phases and the sub-phases of the processes for each kind of production as reported in Tables 2, 3 and 4 (Deliverable D2.3, 2014).

2.1   Energy Consumption in Yarn Manufacturing

The main production phases and sub-phases for yarn manufacturing are reported in Table 2. The dyeing, drying and other finishing processes are not included here in the "yarn production" category, because they are included in the "finishing" category.

Table 2.   Phases and sub-phases of the production processes for yarn production.

Phase (Level 2)	Sub-phase (Level 3)
Spinning preparation for cotton fibers	Opening for cotton
	Cards
	Drawing machines for cotton
	Lap winders
	Combing machines for cotton
	Roving frames
Spinning preparation for wool fibers	Opening lines for raw wool
	Raw wool scouring lines
	Carbonising lines
	Opening for wool
	Worsted cards
	Semi-worsted cards
	Woollen cards
	Drawing machines for wool
	Combing machines for wool
	Back washing machines
	Finishers
	Roving frames for worsted yarn
Production of man-made filaments and fibres	Extruders
	Winding
Spinning	Ring-spinning
	Compact spinning
	Rotor spinning
	Air-jet spinning
	Other Spinning machines
Winding, reeling and covering	Winding machines
	Reeling machines
	Covering machines
Yarn steaming, setting, moistening and coating	Autoclaves for steaming
	Heat-setting machines
	Moistening machines

(continued)

Table 2. (*continued*)

Phase (Level 2)	Sub-phase (Level 3)
	Yarn coating machines
Texturing, bulking and crimping	Texturing machines
	Bulking and crimping machines
Doubling and twisting	Doubling machines
	Twisting machines

In yarn production most of the energy consumption is due to electricity for the spinning processes (Hasanbeigi, 2012). Based on (Koç, 2007) the spinning processes represent about 55–80% of the energy consumption per kg of single yarn, with the percentage value being related to the kind of spinning machine. In general, the scientific literature on the energy consumption in yarn manufacturing is not systematic, often outdated and not well documented (Van der Velden, 2014). The spinning systems were classified here according to different technologies into ring spinning, compact spinning, rotor spinning, air-jet spinning and other spinning machines, which are characterized by different energy consumption behaviors.

Table 3. Main literature data about energy consumptions in yarn production (Branchetti, 2019).

Description	Electrical energy consumption [kWh/kg]	Thermal energy consumption [MJ/kg]	Reference
Spinning (1972)	5.4		(Kim, 1983)
Spinning (1980)	4.9		(Kim, 1983)
Range for spinning mills	2.7–4	1.1–4.7	(Tarakçıoğlu, 1984)
Range of spinning plants	0.55–7.3	0.14–0.73	(Visvanathan, 2000)
Ring yarn (combed) 20 tex	3.5–3.6		(ITMF, 2003)
Spinning of cotton (1997)	5.1		(Dahllöf, 2004)
Spinning of cotton	11.6		(Ellebæk Larsen, 2007)
Spinning of cotton (mix)	3.2–3.8		(Kaplan, 2010)
Open-end spinning 20 tex	3.0		(Kaplan, 2010)
Specific spinning plant	3.2–3.5		(Palamutcu, 2010)
Spinning plant	3.2–3.5		(EMS-Textile, 2007)
Ring spinning mills	6.6, 4.7	12.4, 7.1	(Hasanbeigi, 2012)
Open-end spinning mills	3.6	8.1	(Hasanbeigi, 2012)

A more comprehensive literature review concerning yarn manufacturing has been already reported in a previous paper (Branchetti, 2019). There, different studies are recalled, discussing energy consumption in different countries with important textile manufacturing (Iran, China and Turkey) and concerning different approaches and boundaries (e.g. LCA). A summary of this literature review is reported in Table 3.

These values confirm the wide distribution of the energy consumption data, but also a general consistency among them. The data spans in the range 0.5–11.6 kWh/kg and the average turns out to be 4.5 kWh/kg. Van der Velden (2014) claims that the wide range of these values is mainly due to the mixture of data coming from very different textile product characteristics, the most relevant of which is the yarn count. The values vary by a factor of 20 and the range is too high to be useful for benchmarking purposes.

2.2   Energy Consumption in Fabric Manufacturing

As far as energy consumption in fabric manufacturing is concerned, a similar fragmented situation as to yarn manufacturing occurs. Even so, it is possible to identify two main process categories: weaving and knitting. These categories are alternatives to each other and both of them include, at phase level, the preparation of the process and the fabric production at phase level, while many different technologies and production processes can be defined at sub-phases level, as shown in Table 4.

Table 4. Phases and sub-phases of the production processes for fabric production.

Phase (Level 2)	Sub-phase (Level 3)
Weaving preparation	Sectional warping
	Beam warping
	Draw-warping
	Beaming machines
	Sizing/slashing
	Indigo warp dyeing lines
Weaving	Rapier weaving
	Projectile weaving
	Air jet weaving
	Water jet weaving
	Shuttle looms
	Circular weaving
	Narrow fabrics weaving
Preparation for knitting	Beam warping
	Sectional warping
Knitting	Circular knitting machines
	Flat knitting machines
	Warp knitting machines
	Knitting machines for special purposes

After yarn manufacturing, the mills producing woven fabrics use processes such as warping, sizing and weaving. In weaving preparation, energy consumption changes according to the yarn and the fabric characteristics and the properties of the preparation machines (such as the sizing of the warp, the weft and warp yarn quality, the weight and the width of the fabric and the climate conditions) (Hasanbeigi, 2012). In weaving processes, the electrical energy consumption represents on average about 85% of the total energy consumption of the factories (UNIDO, 2010).

A literature review concerning fabric manufacturing is reported in Table 5.

Table 5. Main literature data about energy consumptions in fabric production.

Description	Electrical energy consumption [kWh/kg]	Thermal energy consumption [kJ/kg]	Reference
Weaving (1972)	4.76		(Kim, 1983)
Weaving (1980)	3.86		(Kim, 1983)
Weaving	2.15		(Ellebæk Larsen, 2007)
Air-jet weaving (200 dtex)	4.38		(ITMF, 2010)
Air-jet weaving (300 dtex)	2.97		(ITMF, 2010)
Warping, sizing, drawing, weaving	5.06	9.85	(Koç, 2010)
Air-jet weaving	1.15		(Koç, 2010)
Weaving	2.1–5.6	8.3–17	(Tarakçıoğlu, 1984)
Weaving	5.7–5.8	2.2–25	(Visvanathan, 2000)
Range for weaving machines	1.7–4.2		(Koç, 2010)
Rapier Weaving	2.2	17.3	(Hasanbeigi, 2012)
Projectile weaving	1.2	10.7	(Hasanbeigi, 2012)
Weaving + sizing	2.65		(van der Velden, 2014)
Weaving	1.82–4.19		(van der Velden, 2014)
Weaving (cotton)	3.03–7.08		(van der Velden, 2014)
Knitting (1972)	1.75		(Kim, 1983)
Knitting (1980)	1.29		(Kim, 1983)
Circular knitting (synthetic yarn)	5.01		(Ellebæk Larsen, 2007)
Knitting	2.32		(Ellebæk Larsen, 2007)
Circular knitting 200 dtex (cotton)	0.19		(ITMF, 2010)

(continued)

Table 5. (*continued*)

Description	Electrical energy consumption [kWh/kg]	Thermal energy consumption [kJ/kg]	Reference
Circular knitting 300 dtex (cotton)	0.16		(ITMF, 2010)
Circular knitting (synthetic yarn)	0.35		(ITMF, 2010)
Flat knitting - large panels (cotton)	1.16		(van der Velden, 2014)
Flat knitting - normal panels (cotton)	1.17		(van der Velden, 2014)
Flat knitting - thin sweater (cotton)	4.59		(van der Velden, 2014)
Seamless flat knitting (cotton)	5.42		(van der Velden, 2014)
Flat knitting t- hick sweater (cotton)	2.29		(van der Velden, 2014)
Knitting machine (cotton)	0.85		(van der Velden, 2014)
Circular knitting (synthetic yarn)	1.22		(van der Velden, 2014)

According to (van der Velden, 2014), the uncertainty in electrical energy consumption in weaving processes is about a factor of 4. The uncertainty is reduced taking into account the yarn count, but still remains at 2. Considering only the unit production part, (Palamutcu, 2010) reports a value of 1.25 kWh/kg for woven fabric production.

2.3 Energy Consumption in Finishing

The finishing of textile products is composed of various production processes which can be applied to yarn or fabric. There are some main categories (phases) and many specific processes (sub-phases), in sequence or alternative to each other (Table 6).

Table 6. Phases and sub-phases of the production processes for finishing.

Phase (Level 2)	Sub-phase (Level 3)
Pretreatment	Carbonising
	Singeing
	Crabbing
	Desizing
	Bleaching batch

(*continued*)

Table 6. (*continued*)

Phase (Level 2)	Sub-phase (Level 3)
	Continuous Bleaching
	Yarn washing
	Rope washing
	Open-width washing
	Solvent washing
	Milling/fulling
	Yarn Mercerising
	Fabric Mercerising
Dyeing	Yarn continuous dyeing
	Fabric continuous dyeing
	Autoclaves
	Hank
	Jet
	Overflow
	Winch becks
	Jiggers
	Other dyeing machines
Water extraction and drying	Centrifugal hydro-extractors
	Stenter
	Yarn Dryers
	Fabric Dryers
	Other Dryers
	Tumblers
Finishing machines	Mechanical finishing
	Decatising
	Calenders
	Singeing machines
	Knitwear ironing presses
	Tumblers
	Sanfor
	Other finishing machines
Printing	Top and yarn printing
	Flat screen printing
	Rotary screen printing
	Inkjet Printing
	Other printing machines

The finishing of textile is composed of a wide range of processes and consequently also of energy uses (van der Velden, 2014).

In wet textile processing, the thermal energy prevails with respect to electricity, because of high temperature processes (Hong, 2010), and it accounts for more than 50% with respect to the sum of electrical and thermal consumption (UNIDO, 2010).

A literature review concerning fabric manufacturing is reported in Table 7.

Table 7. Main literature data about energy consumptions in finishing.

Description	Electrical energy consumption [kWh/kg]	Thermal energy consumption [MJ/kg]	Reference
Dyeing - 80% cotton	1.15	31.3	(van der Velden, 2014)
Reactive Dyeing	3.36		(Ellebæk Larsen, 2007)
Dyeing – 65% cotton	2.85		(Ellebæk Larsen, 2007)
Finishing – fabric	1.97–2.5		(Ellebæk Larsen, 2007)
Dyeing	1–1.25	28.8–33.75	(van der Velden, 2014)
Wet processing - finishing	0.6–0.75	28.8–33.75	(van der Velden, 2014)
Wet processing - total	2.1	14.26	(van der Velden, 2014)

Electrical energy consumption in finishing ranges up to 3.36 kWh/kg (Ellebæk Larsen, 2007). Based on the kind of process, thermal energy consumption can vary from 3.96 to 9.38 kWh/kg (van der Velden, 2014).

3   Methods

3.1 Proposed Methodology

In order to encourage and facilitate the enterprises to obtain a pre-diagnosis on energy efficiency of their production processes, the SET Tool has been developed. This is a self-analysis standalone tool providing feedback on energy efficiency measures and energy indicators to the textile mills. The SET Tool was designed together with a web-based application, named SET Web, which is able to retrieve and filter the data provided directly from the enterprises. Enterprises can access SET Web and its services and are invited to insert data on: the yearly and monthly production amount (kg), the electrical and thermal consumptions of the mill (kWh and MJ), the number and the type of processes involved, the turnover (euro), the number of employees, the main used raw materials (e.g. wool, cotton, etc.), the product market segment (from low to luxury) and the market segment application (e.g. clothing, home textile, technical textile).

The data are recorded in an anonymous way and then are filtered by a faithfulness check. After that, performance comparisons with energy benchmarks are provided, in a customized way.

All these data are provided by the textile factories themselves and are automatically recorded and organized to build up a centralized and growing SET database. With respect to other benchmarking methodologies (Andersson, 2018), the SET Tool provides energy benchmarks dynamically, which are built by company self-profiling. Therefore, the companies themselves are involved to improve the quality of the benchmark.

3.2 Energy Efficiency Indicators

The energy efficiency indicators in industry measure "how well" energy is used in order to produce an output. Therefore, they can be calculated starting from the amount of energy used and production data at different levels of aggregation such as sectorial, sub-sectorial, factory or operational unit (APEC, 2000).

In general, the indicators can be expressed in economic or physical terms, depending on the input and the output considered (Patterson, 1996). Indicators calculated in monetary units measure the quantity of energy used in relation to the economic value of industrial activity generated and they are usually applied to the analysis of the energy efficiency at a macro-economic level (APEC, 2000).

Instead, the energy efficiency indicators referring to physical quantities are more suited to detailed sub-sectorial analysis and they are appropriate for the present study. In particular, the Specific Energy Consumption (SEC) is the main physical indicator to express the energy efficiency of an industrial activity and it is calculated as a ratio of energy used for producing a product. Taking the factory as level of aggregation, the SEC represents the energy consumption of the whole factory for each unit of product (Palamutcu, 2010; Branchetti, 2016; Lawrence, 2019):

$$SEC = \frac{Energy\ used}{Product\ amount} \tag{1}$$

Where, SEC is the specific energy consumption for industrial activity calculated as a ratio of energy used for manufacturing a specific amount of product.

The energy used can be expressed by different unit of measure interchangeable with each other (e.g. kWh, GJ, toe, and so on), while the unit of product is often in relation to the kind of production.

In textile industry the unit of product can be expressed in length/weight for yarn, area/weight for fabric, numbers of garments/weight for garment, and so on. Nevertheless, the kg results suitable to measure directly or by transformation the output of different production processes in yarn, fabric and finishing mills, and it has been chosen here for homogeneity in data analysis.

Moreover, the SEC can be calculated in relation to the total energy consumption or the single energy carrier, such as electricity or natural gas. In this study we refer to the "electrical SEC" and "thermal SEC" when representing electrical and thermal energy consumption respectively.

Further information about how companies use energy can be obtained investigating the relationship between monthly energy consumption and the monthly production. The variation of energy use is expected to be related to the factory production (Palamutcu, 2010; Branchetti, 2016). This relationship can be evaluated by regression analysis method, such as:

$$y = m \cdot x + q \tag{2}$$

Where, y is the whole energy consumption [kWh], m is the energy consumption to produce each additional unit of product [kWh/kg], x is the production amount [kg], q is the consumption when the production is zero [kWh].

The square of Pearson correlation coefficient of (2), usually named R^2, allows to evaluate the strength of the relationship between the energy consumption and the production. If the relationship is strong then R^2 appears close to 1 and it is possible to evaluate further indicators: energy consumption for each additional unit of product, consumption when the production is zero and the "base energy consumption", that is the percentage of the total energy not related to the production (Branchetti, 2016).

The energy consumption to produce an additional unit of product is an energy and physical indicator introduced as Incremental Energy Consumption (IEC) in (Branchetti, 2016). It is able to represent the energy efficiency of a factory, together with the SEC indicator, but focusing on the energy consumption directly related to the production. This indicator corresponds to m of (2) and it is identifiable as the slope of the linear regression.

The "base energy consumption" represents instead the energy auxiliary uses of the factory, such as lighting, air conditioning, heating, ventilation, etc. It contributes to the increase of the SEC, whereas it does not affect the IEC indicator of the company.

3.3 The Factory Database

The SET database concerns 4 main textile areas (the three categorization previously introduced and a combination of them): yarn production, fabric production, finishing processes and the factories involving a composition of these three kind of productions (yarn and finishing of yarn, fabric and finishing of fabric or the overall production processes).

At the end of 2017, the factory database was composed of 204 datasets, which were provided by 136 companies in relation to 140 factories. Excluding the data being inconsistent or not complete and the data referring to different years (even if to the same production), 124 datasets have been selected.

The database has the following properties and characteristics:

- for each of the 3 textile sectors (yarn, fabric, finish) it involves about 25–50 factories and 20–45 mills;
- it refers to the years 2012–2015;
- it involves the following European countries: Belgium, Bulgaria, Croatia, Czech Republic, France, Germany, Hungary, Italy, Lithuania, Portugal, Romania;
- it belongs to factories with up to 1000 employees and turnovers up to 115 millions of Euro;
- the annual product amount ranges from 5 up to 33,000 tonnes/year;
- as product market segment, it includes from low target market to luxury market;
- as market segment application, it involves: clothing, home textile, technical textile, underwear, protective textile;

- as main raw materials, it includes: cotton, wool, polyester, polyamide, polypropylene, acrylic, linen, acetate, silk, besides other natural fibres and synthetic fibres.

Other information on the database are provided in (Branchetti, 2019).

From the SET datasets it is possible to provide a quite general view of the energy consumption in yarn production, fabric production and finishing in Europe.

The range and the spread of the electrical and thermal energy consumption values are still very high, even excluding some outliers and incomplete datasets, as reported in Table 8, Fig. 2 and Fig. 3. This is due to the great variety of textile factories which have been collected.

Table 8. Energy consumptions for each unit of product in SET datasets (Branchetti, 2019). Primary energy (*) is expressed by kilogram of oil equivalent [kgoe] using a conversion factor of 0.000215 toe/kWhe (Table 4 of Commission decision 2007/589/CE and Annex II of directive 2006/32/CE).

	Yarn (min. – max.)	Fabric (min. – max.)	Finishing (min. – max.)	Yarn + Finishing Fabric + Finishing Yarn + Fabric + Finishing (min. – max.)
Electrical energy consumption [kWh$_e$/kg]	0.44–14.55	0.49–25.14	0.49–32.98	1.11–17.87
Thermal energy consumption [kWh$_t$/kg]	0.01–20.30	0.00–44.40	2.43–109.69	2.39 – 54.24
Total energy consumption [kgoe/kg]*	0.088–3.89	0.11–9.22	0.560–16.52	0.61–7.35

In textile industry, both electrical energy and thermal energy are used, but according to the different types of processes and products, electrical energy or thermal energy can prevail. The electricity is used mainly for operating machines (e.g. spinning, weaving and knitting) and facilities such as air compressors, air conditioning and lathing, while the thermal energy is used mainly for heating and production processes such as fixation of yarns, steam for autoclaves and hot water for dyeing.

In yarn and fabric manufacturing the use of electrical energy prevails, while in finishing thermal energy prevails (UNIDO, 2010; Hasanbeigi, 2012; Hong, 2010). The analysis of SET datasets confirms the prevalence of electrical energy consumption on thermal energy consumption for both yarn and fabric production, with an average of 85% and 73% respectively, while the thermal energy consumption prevails in finishing factories, where the electrical energy consumption has an average value of 28% (Branchetti, 2019).

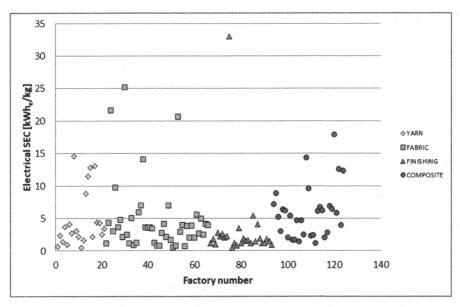

Fig. 2. Electrical SEC for different kind of production.

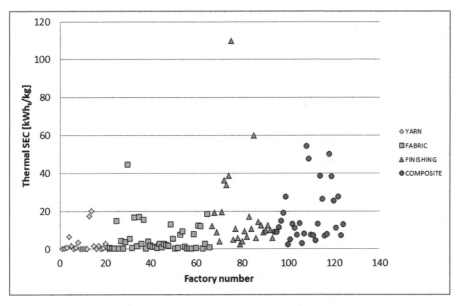

Fig. 3. Thermal SEC for different kind of production.

4   Results

All the available factories of the SET database were analyzed by calculating the SEC indicator and the regression parameters. The strength of the relationship between energy consumptions and production for all datasets has been checked by means of the correlation coefficient R^2.

The analysis of energy consumptions was realized for each factory in relation to the production process focusing on the electrical and thermal components, independently from the energy supply used (renewable, inner cogeneration, external suppliers, etc.) and only when $R^2 \geq 0.5$.

4.1   Energy Efficiency Indicators in Textile

Considering separately the dataset of factories involved in the different kind of production (yarn, fabric and finishing), the average of electrical SEC is respectively: 4.8 kWh$_e$/kg for yarn production, 4.7 kWh$_e$/kg for fabric production and 3.0 kWh$_e$/kg for finishing, with a relative error higher than 100%.

On the other hand, analyzing a subset of dataset composed of factories with electrical R^2 greater than or equal to 0.5 the average of electrical SEC is respectively: 5.5 kWh$_e$/kg for yarn production, 3.3 kWh$_e$/kg for fabric production and 2.1 kWh$_e$/kg for finishing, with a relative error within 85% (Table 9). Similarly, the average of electrical IEC provides an estimation of the incremental energy consumptions with an acceptable relative error limited within 65% (Table 10 and Fig. 4).

Table 9. Electrical SEC for different kind of production.

Electrical SEC	Average	Std	Relative error
YARN	5.5 kWh$_e$/kg	±4.6	84%
FABRIC	3.3 kWh$_e$/kg	±1.7	52%
FINISHING	2.1 kWh$_e$/kg	±1.3	62%

Table 10. Electrical IEC for different kind of production.

Electrical IEC	Average	Std	Relative error
YARN	3.5 kWh$_e$/kg	±2.3	64%
FABRIC	2.3 kWh$_e$/kg	±1.3	59%
FINISHING	1.2 kWh$_e$/kg	±0.7	58%

The thermal SEC of the initial group of factories is on average: 2.9 kWh$_t$/kg for yarn production, 5.2 kWh$_t$/kg for fabric production and 18.3 kWh$_t$/kg for finishing, with a relative error higher than 100%.

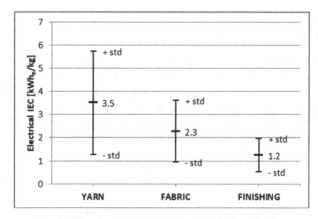

Fig. 4. Electrical IEC for different kind of production.

The thermal energy consumptions are mainly related to the finishing processed and then the correlation with the monthly amount of product is available only for this kind of production. Therefore, analyzing the subset of finishing factories with R^2 greater than or equal to 0.5 the average of thermal SEC is 10.8 kWh$_t$/kg, with a relative error of about 83%, while the average of thermal IEC is 8.5 kWh$_t$/kg, with a relative error of the same order (Table 11).

Table 11. Thermal SEC and IEC for finishing.

Finishing	Average	Std	Relative error
Thermal SEC	10.8 kWh$_t$/kg	±9.0	83%
Thermal IEC	8.5 kWh$_t$/kg	±7.1	83%

4.2 Energy Efficiency Indicators by Clustering of Textile

The value of energy efficiency indicators could be related to different features of products or production processes in textile industry. Therefore, we have investigated which of the following factors have a clear effect on the average SEC and/or IEC of the factories:

- main raw material (cotton, wool, polyamide, polypropylene, acrylic, linen, silk, other natural fibers, etc.);
- mix of production processes based on schemes of Table 2, 3 and 4;
- type of final product (yarn, fabric, non-woven fabrics, knitted fabric, etc.);
- product market segment (low, medium, top, luxury);
- market segment application (clothing, underwear, home textile, protective textile, technical textile);
- price of final product, calculated as a ratio of the factory turnover for producing one kilogram of product.

The analysis was made separately for each kind of textile production, clustering the factories based on single factor and considering the dataset with $R^2 \geq 0.5$.

Clustering by Raw Materials. In yarn production, clustering by raw material, the group of factories producing wool yarn shows an electrical SEC ranging between 6 to 14 kWh$_e$/kg, which is higher than the same indicator measured in factories producing yarn starting from cotton or "other materials" (i.e. linen, polyamide, acrylic and polypropylene). Indeed, the electrical SEC of the latter ranges between 2 to 4 kWh$_e$/kg (Table 12 and Fig. 5).

Table 12. Electrical SEC clustered by raw material for yarn factories (Branchetti, 2019).

Electrical SEC	Average	Std	Relative error
WOOL	10.4 kWh$_e$/kg	±4.0	39%
COTTON	2.3 kWh$_e$/kg	±0.6	26%
OTHER	2.7 kWh$_e$/kg	±1.0	37%

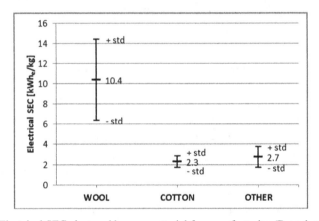

Fig. 5. Electrical SEC clustered by raw material for yarn factories (Branchetti, 2019).

Similar results are obtained for electrical IEC. The group of factories producing wool yarn shows an electrical IEC ranging between 4 to 8 kWh$_e$/kg, higher than the other clusters, which ranges between 1 and 3 kWh$_e$/kg (Table 13 and Fig. 6).

Applying this kind of clustering for fabric production and for finishing processes, respectively, the energy indicators (electrical SEC and electrical IEC) show an overlapping of ranges.

Clustering by Production Processes. The clustering based on processes does not allow to obtain useful results for yarn production and finishing, due to the large amount of processes and products with different features treated by the factories.

Table 13. Electrical IEC clustered by raw material for yarn factories (Branchetti, 2019).

Electrical IEC	Average	Std	Relative error
WOOL	5.8 kWh$_e$/kg	±1.7	29%
COTTON	1.8 kWh$_e$/kg	±0.7	38%
OTHER	2.2 kWh$_e$/kg	±0.8	37%

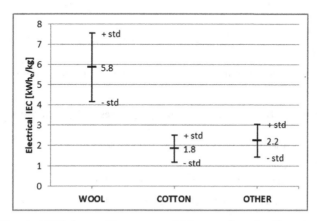

Fig. 6. Electrical IEC clustered by raw material for yarn factories (Branchetti, 2019).

Anyway, it is possible to evaluate two main process categories in fabric production (weaving and knitting) separately, because they are alternatives to each other in the available datasets.

Even if these two categories have overlapping values, the separation allows to provide indicators for comparison of energy performances of similar factories.

The group of factories undertaking weaving processes shows an electrical SEC ranging between 2 to 5 kWh$_e$/kg, while for factories undertaking knitting processes it ranges between 1 to 4 kWh$_e$/kg (Table 14 and Fig. 7).

Table 14. Electrical SEC clustered by processes for fabric factories.

Electrical SEC	Average	Std	Relative error
WEAVING	3.4 kWh$_e$/kg	±1.5	43%
KNITTING	2.6 kWh$_e$/kg	±1.5	57%

In the same way, factories undertaking weaving processes show an electrical IEC ranging between 1 to 4 kWh$_e$/kg, while for factories undertaking knitting processes it ranges between 0.5 to 3 kWh$_e$/k (Table 15 and Fig. 8).

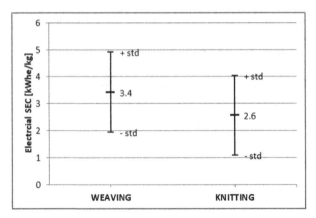

Fig. 7. Electrical SEC clustered by processes for fabric factories.

Table 15. Electrical IEC clustered by processes for fabric factories.

Electrical IEC	Average	Std	Relative error
WEAVING	2.5 kWh$_e$/kg	±1.5	58%
KNITTING	1.7 kWh$_e$/kg	±1.0	60%

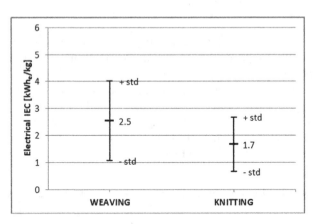

Fig. 8. Electrical IEC clustered by processes in fabric factories.

Clustering by Price of Final Product. In yarn production, the clustering based on the price of final product (Fig. 9) shows that the group of factories with a low price of final product has an electrical SEC ranging between 0.5 to 4 kWh$_e$/kg, which is lower than the same indicator measured in factories with a high price of final product (considering one standard deviation). The latter ranges between 4 to 14 kWh$_e$/kg.

A similar behavior is obtained for electrical IEC (Fig. 10).

The same kind of clustering is obtained for electrical and thermal energy indicators applied in finishing processes. The group of finishing factories with a low price of the final product shows energy indicators lower than those with higher price. The statistic in this case has to be improved to confirm this behavior.

In fabric production this trend does not appear.

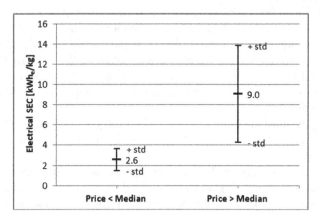

Fig. 9. Electrical SEC clustered by price in yarn factories.

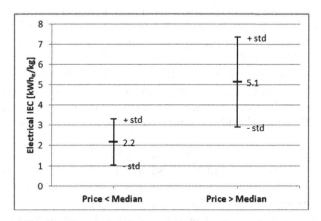

Fig. 10. Electrical IEC clustered by price in yarn factories.

5   Discussion

The dataset extracted from the SET database for yarn and fabric production confirms the prevalence of electrical energy consumption with respect to thermal consumption and shows an average electrical SEC respectively of 5.5 kWh$_e$/kg (relative error of 84%) and 3.3 kWh$_e$/kg (relative error of 52%). These values and its spread are compatible with ranges found in literature and they are due to many factors and choices already outlined in Sect. 2.1 and 2.2.

As far as finishing is concerned, the analysis of the dataset confirms the prevalence of thermal energy consumption with respect to the electrical energy consumption and shows an average thermal SEC of 10.8 kWh$_t$/kg with relative error of 83%, higher than the average electrical SEC of 2.1 kWh$_e$/kg with relative error of 58%.

The regression analysis method applied to the monthly data of each textile manufacturing dataset allowed to calculate the electrical and thermal energy consumption per each additional produced unit (i.e. the electrical and thermal IEC respectively).

The electrical IEC for yarn manufacturing shows an average value of 3.5 kWh$_e$/kg with a relative error of 64%, whereas for fabric manufacturing it is of 2.3 kWh$_e$/kg with relative error of 59%.

Concerning the finishing processes, the thermal IEC has an average of 8.5 kWh$_t$/kg with a relative error of 83%, whereas the electrical IEC is about 1.2 kWh$_e$/kg with the same relative error.

The relative error of electrical IEC for yarn manufacturing (64%) results lower with respect to those of electrical SEC (84%) and this difference can be explained considering that the auxiliary energy uses in SEC adds a further variability in the electrical consumptions.

Anyway, the relative error turns out to be 50–60% for both electrical SEC and IEC in fabric production and finishing, whereas it rises to 83% for the thermal indicators in finishing dataset.

Clustering by raw materials, we have found that the production of yarn starting from wool fibers is more energy consuming than the production of yarn based on cotton or other fibers. This result has been verified with a relative error that turns out to be 25–40% for both electrical SEC and IEC.

In fabric production, the values found for weaving and knitting are compatible with the ranges reported in literature. On average, the results confirms that is more energy consuming to undertake weaving processes respect to knitting and this is verified for both electrical SEC and IEC, with a relative error for the energy indicators that turns out to be 40–60%.

Clustering by price of the final product, we have found that the factories with a high price of final product results more energy consuming than the factories with a lower price of final product on average. This is true for yarn manufacturing and also for finishing, while it is not verified for fabric production.

The analysis based on other factors, such as type of product or market segment, does not provide satisfactory results about energy consumption clusterization, due to an overlapping of ranges for both SEC and IEC indicators.

6 Conclusion

Reference indicators would be useful in order to provide a fast and easy method to the factories to preliminary evaluate their own energy consumptions and to compare their energy efficiency performances. The methodology to provide these indicators should be deliver a fair trade-off between too general or too specific approaches and between too naïve or too demanding requests.

Concerning the textile production, as other industry sectors, unfortunately the companies have many different features: the production chains and the sub-sectors segments combine very heterogeneous and fragmented processes and a wide range of products. Consequently, the energy efficiency indicators for this sector appear highly variable and poorly representative.

The difficulties were tackled using a factory self-analysis approach which allows to profile the company and to compare performances against benchmarks and evolution across the years based on data provided by the factories themselves, automatically recorded and organized. This approach has allowed to retrieve and analyze a wide and detailed sets of data included in the SET database, obtained by the SET tools (Branchetti, 2019). In this paper the dataset have been analyzed with the final goal of obtaining valuable references for energy consumptions in textile industry.

The value of energy efficiency indicators and their spread we have obtained for yarn production, fabric production and finishing, are complementary and consistent with respect to the available literature and public data. The results confirm a high variability of SEC values within the textile sector, but also a correlation with different features of products or production processes, such as raw materials, the kind of process and the price of final products.

The electrical energy consumption prevails respect to thermal energy consumption in yarn and fabric manufacturing and, on average, the production of yarn is more energy consuming than production of fabric.

Clustering the datasets by raw materials the relative error in yarn manufacturing decreases from 83% to 25–40%. Moreover, the calculation of the energy consumption per each additional unit of product (IEC) can be useful to evaluate different energy contributions, separating the auxiliary energy uses from the production process energy consumption and providing a further energy efficiency indicator to compare the performances among similar factories.

In fabric manufacturing, considering separately the weaving and knitting processes, the electrical energy indicators show that, on average, the production by weaving is slightly more energy consuming than knitting, with a difference of about 1 kWh_e per kg of product. The values of these indicators have been provided in Sect. 4 with a relative error of about 40–60%.

The group of cluster based on the price of final products (ratio between turnover and amount of product) shows that the companies producing yarn or finished products with a higher price are more energy consuming.

The approach based on self-analysis and self-profiling of companies has allowed to create a textile database (actually composed of 204 datasets regarding 140 factories) which produce indicators becoming more and more representative along with increasing factory involvement.

The methodologies depicted in this paper and the developed tools can be adopted also in other manufacturing sectors, verifying case-by-case the framework for the production processes, the kind of clusters and their usefulness to achieve indicators about energy consumptions and performances.

References

Andersson, E., Arfwidsson, O., Thollander, P.: Benchmarking energy performance of industrial small and medium-sized enterprises using an energy efficiency index: results based on an energy audit policy program. J. Cleaner Prod. **182**, 883–895 (2018)

APEC (Asia Pacific Energy Research Centre). Energy Efficiency Indicators – A Study of Energy Efficiency Indicators for Industry in APEC Economies. Tokyo: Asia Pacific Energy Research Centre (2000)

Branchetti, S., Ciaccio, G., De Sabbata, P., Frascella, A., Nigliaccio, G., Zambelli, M.: Energy saving and efficiency tool - a sectorial decision support model for energy consumption reduction in manufacturing SMEs. In: SMARTGREENS: Proceedings of the 5th International Conference on Smart Cities and Green ICT Systems, Rome, Italy, SCITEPRESS, pp. 330–339. 23–25 April (2016)

Branchetti, S., Petrovich, C., Ciaccio, G., De Sabbata, P., Frascella, A., Nigliaccio, G.: Energy consumption characterization based on a self-analysis tool: a Case study in yarn manufacturing. In: SMARTGREENS: Proceedings of the 8th International Conference on Smart Cities and Green ICT Systems, 3–5 May 2019, Heraklion, Greece, SCITEPRESS, pp. 40–50 (2019)

Dahllöf, L.: LCA methodology issues for textile products [Licentiate thesis]. Chalmers University of Technology, Göteborg (2004)

Deliverable D2.3, SET - Production Processes and Efficiency Measures, Deliverable of SET project (2014)

Larsen, S.E., Hansen, J., Knudsen, H.H., Wenzel, H., Larsen, H.F., Møller Kristensen, F.: EDIPTEX — Environmental assessment of textiles. Danish Ministry of the Environment, Environmental Protection Agency. Working Report No. 24, Denmark (2007)

EMS-Textile "Results Oriented Report" - July 2007. https://ec.europa.eu/energy/intelligent/pro jects/sites/iee-projects/files/projects/documents/ems-textile_result_oriented_report_en.pdf. Accessed 08 Jan 2019

EUROSTAT, 2016. http://ec.europa.eu/eurostat/data/database. Accessed 04 Jul 2019

Hasanbeigi, A., Hasanabadi, A., Abdorrazaghi, M.: Comparison analysis of energy intensity for five major sub-sectors of the Textile Industry in Iran. J. Cleaner Prod. **23**, 186–194 (2012)

Hong, G.B., Su, T.L., Lee, J.D., Hsu, T.C., Chen, H.W.: Energy conservation potential in Taiwanese textile industry. Energy Policy **38**, 7048–7053 (2010)

IPPC, Integrated Pollution Prevention and Control - Reference Document on Best Available Techniques for the Textiles Industry. European Commission (EU), Seville? (2003)

ITMF (International Textile Manufacturers Federation), International Production Cost Comparison - Spinning/Weaving/Knitting. Zürich (2003)

ITMF (International Textile Manufacturers Federation), International Production Cost Comparison - Spinning/Texturing/Weaving/Knitting. Zürich (2010)

Lawrence, A., Thollander, P., Andrei, M., Karlsson, M.: Specific energy consumption/use (SEC) in energy management for improving energy efficiency in industry: meaning. Usage Differ. Energies **12**, 247 (2019)

Kaplan, E., Koç, E.: An investigation of energy consumption in yarn production with special reference to open-end rotor spinning. Fibres Text. Eastern Eur. **18**(79), 7–13 (2010)

Kim, S.Y., Grady, P.L., Hersh, S.P.: Energy consumption and conservation in the fibre-producing and textile industries. Text. Prog. **13**(3), 1–14 (1983)

Koç, E., Kaplan, E.: An investigation on energy consumption in yarn production with special reference to ring spinning. Fibres Text. Eastern Eur. **15**(63), 18–24 (2007)

Koç, E., Çinçik, E.: Analysis of energy consumption in woven fabric production. Fibres Text. Eastern Eur. **18**(79), 14–20 (2010)

Lin, B., Zhao, H.: Technology gap and regional energy efficiency in China's textile industry: A non-parametric meta-frontier approach. J. Cleaner Prod. **137**, 21–28 (2016)

Palamutcu, S.: Electric energy consumption in the cotton textile processing stages. Energy **35**, 2945–2952 (2010)

Patterson, M.G.: What is energy efficiency? Concepts, indicators and methodological issues. Energy Policy **24**, 377–390 (1996)

SMI, SMI IL SETTORE TESSILE-MODA ITALIANO NEL 2012–2013 (2013)

Tarakçıoğlu, I.: Energy Consumption and Conservation of Textile Finishing Mills. Uludag University Press, Bursa, Turkish (1984)

UNIDO (United Nations Industrial Development Organization), Global Industrial Energy Efficiency Benchmarking - An Energy Policy Tool Working Paper. Vienna (2010)

Van der Velden, N.M., Patel, M.K., Vogtländer, J.G.: LCA benchmarking study on textiles made of cotton, polyester, nylon, acryl, or elastane. Int. J. Life Cycle Assess. **19**, 331–356 (2014)

Visvanathan, C., Kumar, S., Priambodo, A., Vigneswaran S., 2000. Energy and environmental indicators in the Thai textile industry. In: Hu, X, Yue, P.L., (eds.) Sustainable Energy and Environmental Technologies. Proceedings of the Third Asia-Pacific Conference. Hong Kong, 3–6 December 2000, China, pp. 524–528 (2000)

Smart City: The Importance of Innovation and Planning

Rudolf Giffinger[✉]

Department of Spatial Planning, Centre of Urban and Regional Studies, TU Wien, Vienna, TU, Austria
rudolf.giffinger@tuwien.ac.at

Abstract. Smart Cities are in particular focusing on the implementation of new technologies with the purpose to tackle urban challenges like climate change, urban competitiveness and other problems of sustainable development. During the last years the ways of collecting data, of computing and using big data and of communicating evidence had been improved significantly. Smart Cities show a wide range of new technical facilities and services which are the outcome of specific concepts of innovation and urban planning approaches.

With respect to urban transformation processes coping with mentioned challenges, technical innovations are important. They enable the realization of energy efficiency, reduction of energy use or mitigation of emissions. At the same time technically-driven transformation processes in mobility conditions and communication are supporting the attractivity of cities. Smart cities very often claim to provide a 'better life' and sustainable development. In front of these developments it becomes obvious that technical innovations play a crucial role but at the same time we can assume a mutual relation with specific approaches of urban planning beyond such transformation processes.

The main objective of this contribution is to elaborate these different concepts of innovation and the corresponding role of urban planning. Based on a short description of the technical core of a Smart City which enables a more comprehensive data collecting, a more precise analysis of bigger and better integrated data sets and a faster communication, three different forms of innovation and their mutual relation with planning approaches are elaborated. Doing so, special attention is given to the basic understanding what is a city, who are the crucial actors, and which role do planning approaches have. Finally, it is shown that the concept of 'open innovation' can be used in a technical and in particular in a predominantly socially integrative way through the enforced co-creation of 'urban innovation'. The corresponding planning tool for its identification, conceptualization and implementation is the concept of an 'urban Living Lab' which enables and supports a smart and evidence-based understanding of urban planning.

Keywords: Smart City · Innovation · Triple and quadruple helix · Urban Living Labs

© Springer Nature Switzerland AG 2021
M. Helfert et al. (Eds.): SMARTGREENS 2019/VEHITS 2019, CCIS 1217, pp. 28–39, 2021.
https://doi.org/10.1007/978-3-030-68028-2_2

1 Introduction

Cities are facing different challenges like growth, competition between cities or climate change. Related to these challenges, the most crucial question is how to meet problems of sustainable urban development and to enable corresponding urban transformation processes increasing their respective resilience. In particular, Smart Cities with their main focus on implementing new technologies are expected to foster a better quality of life and to strengthen sustainable urban development. [1] Generally, the introduction of new technologies into the urban fabric is not new [2], but in particular the progress of information and communication technology (ICT) provoked the idea of the 'Smart City' considering specific technical qualities and different relevant components. Since some years this issue is discussed intensively based on former concepts like the 'information city', 'wired city' or similar labels. [3] Along with this discussion of the Smart City understanding, city-specific concepts with special focus have been implemented, realized or even changed; for instance, in Barcelona, Amsterdam, Vienna, Tallinn, Graz and many others.

Specific requirements of transformation processes are provoking a wide range of technical innovations. Komninos, Kakderi,, Panori and Tsarchopoulos [4] showed the evolutionary character of technical innovations and identified several innovation circuits having an impact on urban development conditions. Considering these new technologies, planners and urban researchers successively emphasized and demonstrated the new possibilities and options for planning. For instance, Balducci [5] underpinned the new possibilities of participatory metropolitan planning; Batty et al. [6] elaborated in a comprehensive perspective the role of new data and the importance of better ICT-technologies for measuring, calculating and simulating in urban planning. Very obviously, the new technical conditions offer new options for specific planning approaches. Accordingly, in this contribution the main objective is to demonstrate that certain planning approaches come along with technical innovations as they are mutually enabling each other. Facing this development, it is finally concluded that the character and the quality of technical innovations is changing towards a new form of 'urban innovation' which comes along with an increasingly place-based understanding of integrative planning enforcing the concept of 'open innovation'. [7]

Hence, the basic objective in this contribution is to show the interrelation of specific concepts of innovations with planning approaches and corresponding understandings of Smart City development. These different interrelations are elaborated by answering following questions: What is the core of the Smart City discussion? Which concepts of innovation can be distinguished? How do planning approaches support respective concepts of innovation? From a planning point of view the question is dealt with which actors are involved predominantly? Specific attention is finally given the quadruple helix understanding discussing the city as a complex system which asks for 'open innovation' and demands for new forms of planning approaches.

In Sect. 2 the complexity of urban challenges is elaborated. In Sect. 3, on the background of the Smart City discussion specific concepts of innovation are decribed in combination with distinct planning approaches – with a special focus on the quadruple helix model as base for open innovation and related planning tools. Section 4 is concentrating on specific features of urban Living Labs and discusses corresponding options for their implementation using more or less new technology. Section 5 concludes with some requirements of integrative planning supporting adaptive capacity as pre-condition of resilient urban development.

2 Challenges of Urban Transformation Processes

Regarding climate change, the increase of CO_2-emissions is identified as one of the driving factors of global warming. This increase of CO_2-emissions is caused through anthropogenic activities starting in the period of industrialization. Until now, human activities are estimated to have an impact of appr. $1,0°$ [8, p.6] Due to the evidence of higher climate-related risks, IPCC proposes in particular the limitation of CO_2-emissions effecting an increase of temperature by not more than $1,5°$ latest until 2052. This evidence led to the definition of the 17 SDGs which are defined in the 2030 Agenda for Sustainable Development. [9] Even though most countries committed themselves mitigating their emissions, total emission of CO_2 is still growing.

In this climate change contexts, the increase of urbanization becomes very important. On the global level the urbanization process is very strong: since appr. 2008 more than 50% of world population lives in urban agglomerations and it is an on-going trend. However, the degree of urbanization will increase during next decades differently [10]: since some decades these trends are very strong in China or some countries in Africa and Southeast Asia. Countries in Europe, Latin America or North America already show a high degree of urbanization, but reduced increase goes on at a high level within next decades. According to estimations of UN, in well-developed countries of OECD the urbanization degree will increase from 78% in 2015 to appr. 85% in 2050; in less developed countries the degree increases from 49% to 63% in the same period. Both trends indicate the need of transformation of the mechanism of the 'urban fabric' and as a follow-up the 'production of places' regulating growth and enforcing mitigation and adaptation strategies.

Besides, cities are experiencing strong changes for urban development through globalization and economic integration processes. Since some decades technological progress in transportation technologies and ICT as well as the decrease of national barriers through politically induced integration processes the meaning of certain components of territorial capital lost in importance on the national level but increased on the urban and city level. Thus, ICT and transportation infrastructure as well as cooperative and strategic planning approaches have become important to make cities more competitive and more attractive than others. [11, 12] Therefore, cities are increasingly challenged to identify, assess, activate and use their potentials aiming at the goals of competitiveness and attractivity. But these goals are strongly conflicting with goals and interventions aiming to strengthen sustainable and inclusive urban development. [13] Approaches of strategic planning enforcing cooperation between different stakeholders and aiming at mitigation and adaptation, have become crucial.

3 Innovation and Planning: A Mutual Relationship

Cities intend to enforce transformation processes through policies triggering the reduction of emissions, increasing energy efficiency or adapting to climate change and at the same time strengthening a city's competitiveness in the European or even global context. [1, 14, 15] Smart City initiatives come up and enforce the implementation and use of new technologies in order to cope with urban growth, a better life in a more efficient or even sustainable way. Several publications are demonstrating that the Smart City development changed its character in terms of goals and instruments and in particular of the implementation of technology. [3, 4, 16–18] In this contribution in a next step it is discussed how the concept of innovation and certain planning approaches evolved in a mutually influencing way.

Innovations in Smart City

Progress of ICT and in particular the change of web technology from 1.0 towards 2.0 supported the idea of the Smart City built on new technical facilities for a more effective steering of urban development. [19, 20] These new technologies provide increasingly more powerful and differentiated possibilities

- to collect information about recent trends and provide evidence in recent urban situations and to integrate information from different sources;
- to compute (big) data in three different ways: to create situational awareness in a descriptive way, to optimize real-time-decisions in a prescriptive way and to provide analytical results in a predictive way; and
- to communicate evidence, partly in real-time.

In front of changing possibilities of data production and collection, computation and analysis of integrated big data sets from different sources (including social media) and communication, now it is elaborated which concept of innovation is applied in interplay with certain planning approaches.

In general, urban development and technological progress always triggered cities as 'places of innovation' – in a technical and social way. [21, 22] Already 40 years ago Nelson and Winter [23] stated that innovation is a purposive but inherently stochastic activity which underlies selective mechanism driving urban competitiveness but also change and growth. In these contexts, innovations are therefore regarded as result of the complex urban system which is challenged permanently over time. Lambooy [24] already stated that cities or urban agglomerations offer effective contexts for evolving innovations meeting respective challenges through its cognitive and organizational competences.

On that background, Komninos et al. [4] argue that in the meantime three different 'innovation circuits' (IC) approached asking for and enabling a specific form of planning: IC1 is characterized by the creation of the digital space. "The overall smart urban system is made of heterogenous and uncoordinated initiatives by the public administration, global social media companies, national telecom companies, IT developers, e-service providers, and users; each actor adding some digital component to a common pool of resources, and each one offering new modes of user engagement, participation, and empowerment.". [4, p.4] Besides, these authors distinguish between the IC2 and IC3. IC2 provides more informed decision-making for different stakeholders of a city driving its development. IC3 finally, "guides the use of urban space and infrastructure through intelligent systems …", [4, p.4] In a Smart City all three Innovation Circuits ICs are existing at the same time and allow for the authors a smart planning which is based on these technical innovations.

Accepting that innovations do not only have a technical or social character [2, 25], it should be acknowledged that cities have certain competences for learning, assessing and also governing urban systems. This means that the design of the 'urban fabric' and the respective production of 'urban space' is not only outcome of the technical innovation but interlinked with further components which are responsible for transformation processes through the introduction of 'urban innovations'. Thus, innovations are not only differentiated by its technical or social characteristics, but also through its feature of being a 'product- and process innovation' or a 'systemic innovation' which is based on the general implementation of the first one. They are called innovation of first and second order. Suitner, et al. [26, p.10] based on Fagerberg's argumentation [2] underpin following important components for the production and introduction of innovations in general: cognitive-intellectual and physical-economic resources in order to implement planning strategies; creative and technical facilities and competences for the adaptation and design of planning processes; cognitive and analytical competencies and facilities for the assessment of spatial trends; and place-based knowledge on global trends and local conditions for its assessment and decision making.

Smart City Planning and Innovation

The basic idea was originated from the 'information city' using new ICTs innovatively and the ICT-centered smart city which is highly instrumented for optimizing decision making in the short and long term as well as for better managing and controlling city systems in about real time functioning. In that early stage of Smart City-development the basic understanding on innovation was a techno-economic one. Corresponding planning activities supported this concept of techno-economic innovation in a rather strict top-down understanding of planning as many new problems of procurement, implementation, organization and management had to be tackled by the city administration. The basic idea was – similar to IC1 – the increasing use of smart technology in order to produce the digital twin city in order to reduce their environmental impact and offer citizens better lives. Smart urban planners elaborated concepts how to establish, use and integrate new data sources in a technocratic evidence-based planning which predominantly is aiming at the efficiency of urban systems. This Smart City regards the city exclusively as a technical system in which a top-down planning approach is fostering the efficiency in different urban domains. [6] Citizens are not involved directly in this approach. According to Barcelona's first strategy [27, 28] the plan was to catch the anatomy of the city by 12 different domains and to translate it into digital space through 24 different layers. The 'digital twin city' should enable the integration of differently produced information as well as the simulation and communication of several trends and information in order to improve citizens' welfare and quality of life. [29] Due to its character of a data driven understanding of the Smart City which is clearly supported by a technocratic top-down approach of planning in which cities are regarded as technical platforms, we call this approach Smart City 1.0 (SC1.0).

In a different Smart City understanding a specific concept of innovation is combined with a changed planning approach. It is based on the triple helix and its enhancement towards the multiple helix. Basically, innovation is assumed from a systemic view as outcome of the collaboration of industry, science and governments. This collaboration of actors with their specific competences, facilities and expertise is more effective if corresponding processes between them are established. This means the processes of knowledge production and exchange (university – industry), of mutual learning (university – governments) and of market entrance (industry – governments). Caragliu, et al. [1] as well as Leydesdorff et al. [16] underpin the importance of smart technology for implementing the multiple helix and at the same time the changing role of city's governance and planning. Cities' representatives (planners and other stakeholders) are at the same time user but also participating producer resp. driver and customer of 'urban innovation'. DG Internal Policies [30, p.24] sum up *"Smart City' initiatives as multi-stakeholder municipally based partnerships aimed at addressing problems of common interest with the aid of ICTs"*. Correspondingly, many Smart City projects are implemented based on this understanding of innovation through the active involvement of city planning in a place based smart solution finding process. For instance, several projects had been initiated by FP7 or HORIZON2020 of the European Commission aiming at the energy transition through increase of energy efficiency, reduction of emissions and restructuring the energy delivery in favor of renewable energy sources. Projects like PLEEC [31] had been based on a sound definition of domains with potentials for energy transformation, of weaknesses and strengths of urban performance and of collaboration between city stakeholders from the different domains. Hence, innovation becomes a new character because of the changed role of planning. The evidence-based outcome of a local solution finding process is now governed by an integrative planning approach involving small and medium-sized enterprises (and not exclusively a global player of technology provision), corresponding experts within domains and the local planners. However, it is still technically dominated as citizens can be involved but participation is considered in a relative late moment of the project initiative. Caragliu [1, p.70] defines SC „... *when investments in human and social capital and traditional (transport) and modern (ICT) communication infrastructure fuel sustainable economic growth and a high quality of life, with a wise management of natural resources, through a participated governance.* Due to its triple helix-based understanding of innovation and a corresponding stakeholder-oriented conceptualization of the Smart City planning approach, this approach is called Smart City 2.0 (SC2.0).

Usually, urban problems and challenges are perceived and assessed on the local level in different ways because of an increasingly heterogenous urban society. Thus, the ways of solution and decision finding are increasingly based on local evidence and, in particular, on the involvement of local actors in a co-creative way. Hence, the concept of innovation is enhanced in form of the so-called 'open innovation' which is regarded as the interplay of the quadruple helix. This is an enhancement of the triple helix, explicitly considering residents as important actors similar to the other groups of actors. Basic idea of this concept of 'open innovation' is the outside-in-process which means the integration of external knowledge which helps an organization to become more innovative in a highly competitive environment or more effective in problem definition and solution finding. [7]

The city is regarded as a complex system which needs a multi-level planning perspective for understanding urban transformation processes. This process will take place through interaction processes within and between three urban levels: niches (micro level), regimes (meso level), and a socio-technical landscape (macrolevel). [32] In this perspective a new instrument of 'living labs' has been conceptualized for steering urban transformation processes in an increasingly complex environment. Generally Living Labs are defined as a user-centric innovation milieu which combines every-day practice and research. Correspondingly, this innovation concept needs a planning approach which enables this outside-in process of all engaged partners in real-life contexts and which enforces creating sustainable values. [33, 34]

Based on this understanding of a Living Lab, an urban Living Lab (uLL) in addition is embedded in a smart technical environment. It is defined as "*a physical region in which different stakeholders form public-private-people partnerships of public agencies, firms, universities, and users collaborate to create, prototype, validate, and test new technologies, services, products, and systems in real-life contexts. … Urban Living Labs are oriented on 'urban' or 'civic' innovation. This means that Urban Living Labs are often supervised by (or have a close relation with) the local government and have a strong focus on social value creation and civic engagement.*" Juujärvi et al. [35, p.22] Thus, ULLs may start as a niche-approach but will evolve as a driver transforming regimes and systems. From this point of view, urban planning becomes a crucial role in a smart technical environment. In place-based evidence, it is enforcing the transformation of cities in a bottom-up way. In comparison to former understandings this approach involves citizens in a co-creative way in an early stage and is even using smart technologies in order to bring outside knowledge through web based or direct communication into local smart activities. Because of its strong differences to former approaches, we call it Smart City 3.0 (SC3.0).

4 Smart City and Open Innovation

In the Smart City 3.0 exist different ways applying the concept of open innovation. Compared to the SC2.0, the character of innovation again is changing due to the involvement of additional actors (most of all residents) in an early stage of decision finding processes. [36] From a technical point of view Komninos et al. [7] argue that cities are now able to evolve the IC3: they are increasingly providing interactive open concepts for any user. This reaches from open data concepts to those of open source concepts including problem specific hackathons, until the use of collective intelligence [37] in algorithm-based decision finding processes, for instance in automated car driving or other domains applying artificial intelligence approaches.

A well-known way of enforcing collective intelligence is the involvement of citizens as experts on the local level. This has become prominent through the concept of urban Living Labs. They activate external knowledge through their implementation at the neighborhood level and integrate it into bottom-up organized initiatives. In this quadruple helix perspective, Smart City development explicitly considers the role of citizens with their value systems, creativity and local evidence as important components in open solution finding processes. [34] Thus, initiatives are strongly resident centered, technology is regarded as an instrument supporting processes, but not as a goal. In a real-life setting, communities are established at the level of quarters.

However, uLL have become a prominent project approach funded by different institutions (European, national, urban) for instance in the domain of mobility or the domain of energy transformation. SINFONIA is an example of a HORIZON2020 funded European project in collaboration with the City of Innsbruck and Bolzano and with local actors focusing on energy transformation through local production and use of wasted heat or renewable energy or through thermal renovation of buildings. In some parts these projects show the features of open innovation although its enrollment into the whole urban system is still limited because of its complexity of decision making of different stakeholders involved. [38, 39]

Another project that is enforcing uLL as instrument for an open innovation process, is E_profile [40] a project in Austria by FFG and in collaboration with the City of Linz. This project aimed at the energy transformation process in local quarters with support of a web-based communication tool. This tool enables the description and modeling of the recent energy demand of buildings and allows the simulation of future energy demand reduced through thermal renovation activities, use of solar energy or wasted energy as well as the calculation of renovation costs. As the transformation process has to consider the recent local physical conditions of buildings but also social conditions and expectations of involved actors (citizens as house owners or renters) a web-based tool for simulation and communication was established.

Figure 1 shows the basic idea of an open innovation approach supporting the activities of an uLL in any urban quarter. In this approach a mutual flow of knowledge is considered empowering and enhancing an open innovation concept: First, the flow of knowledge from outside into the Lab is triggered as local actors have expertise on their conditions, preferences and expectations. Second, a flow of knowledge from inside-out (scientists, technicians and planners towards the neighborhood) is enabled and communicated through simulation of preferred future energy solutions and visualization of effects in terms of reduction of energy use, change towards renewable energy sources

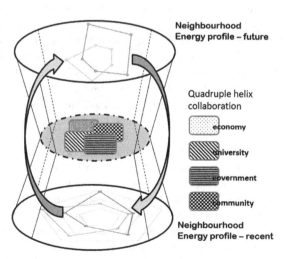

Fig. 1. quadruple helix approach for energy transformation of quarters. Own design based on Kolehmainen, et al. [41].

and costs of rehabilitation investments. Hence, the planning approach conceptualized as an urban Living Lab has a clear mutual understanding of knowledge production in planning and decision finding processes: technical support of monitoring, simulation, visualization and communication of relevant knowledge supporting fosters a bottom-up process of decision finding and at the same time a top-down process of communicating the impacts on the energy transformation process of a quarter.

5 Conclusions

The differences of Smart City understanding for urban development become obvious when looking at the concept of innovation and corresponding planning approaches. In a technical perspective they vary remarkably regarding their changing possibilities determined by web1.0, web2.0 and the establishing of collective or artificial intelligence for decision making. In a planning perspective one can distinguish between different approaches: top-down, bottom-up or counterflow principles, data driven against inclusive or integrative understanding.

As described above, technical innovations show a certain evolutionary character. This implies that there is a certain path dependency which concept of innovation can be realized depending on the existing urban technical standard. At the same time, it becomes evident that the application of a specific innovation concept needs a corresponding planning understanding for its effective implementation into the urban fabric. Obviously, there is an intrinsic logic regarding the combination of a certain concept of innovation with a corresponding planning approach.

Cities following the SC1.0 understanding predominantly improve their technical 'smartness'. In comparison, the SC2.0 and SC3.0 combine concepts of innovation in a much smarter way with recent planning approaches including three resp. four different groups of actors. In particular, the SC3.0 expects the inclusion of local evidence (monitoring and local expertise) which supports place-based decision making but also inclusive learning processes. In that case of SC3.0, the pure technical innovation is replaced by the concept of an 'urban innovation' which is characterized by the integration of technical and social innovation on the local level and through its replication it is likely to change urban development in a more profound and comprehensive way. Of course, all these concepts are usually not applied in a strict and exclusive way but in mixed combinations. However, these differences indicate that cities have the option to decide in advance which innovation concept in combination with certain planning approaches should be implemented.

Facing these different options, cities are challenged to decide how to handle technology and how to enforce a distinct concept of innovation as it will become important for the design of a certain planning approach impacting urban development. In particular, in the SC3.0 the concept of open innovation based on smart technical standards, can be used in different ways for learning processes: in a more technical way for algorithm-based decision finding or in a more socially inclusive and creative way. So, this open innovation concept needs for its implementation an integrative planning approach in form of urban Living Labs: it uses smart technology for the support of collective intelligence or the co-creation in solution finding processes.

However, smart urban development is designed by the mutual relation of innovations and respective planning approaches. Smart City understandings as described above will improve each of the four components (cognitive-intellectual and physical-economic resources; creative and technical facilities; cognitive and analytical competencies/facilities and place-based knowledge on global challenges and local conditions) using technology in more or less specific ways; i.e., it's specific combination of the concept of innovation and respective planning approach. It is obvious that that SC1.0 enforces in particular the 'product- and process innovation' making the 'urban fabric' and 'production of places' more efficient. Thus, SC1.0 improves the existing mechanism of efficiency of the urban systems, but the question remains open whether technical innovations alone will meet the urban challenges in an effective and adaptive way increasing the city's resilience? SC2.0 and in particular SC3.0, both combined with a strong integrative and place-based planning approach can also enforce technical innovation, but they have the chance to predominantly encourage the 'systemic innovations' through mutual learning processes as well as through its strengthening of a city's adaptive capacity. In that contexts, technology enables both innovation of first and second order. But what is even more important, is the conclusion that in particular SC3.0 will strengthen the more a city's resilient development the more it is producing and integrating knowledge of global trends and local conditions in a co-creative way.

References

1. Caragliu, A., Del Bo, Chiara, Nijkamp, P.: Smart cities in Europe. J. Urban Technol. **18**(2), 65–82 (2011)
2. Fagerberg, J.: Innovation: a guide to the literature. In: Fagerberg, J., Mowery, D.C., Richard, R. (eds.) The Oxford Handbook of Innovation, pp. 1–27. Oxford University Press, Oxford (2005)
3. Nam, T., Pardo, T.: Conceptualizing smart city with dimensions of technology, people, and institutions. In: The Proceedings of the 12th Annual International Conference on Digital Government, pp. 282–291 (2011)
4. Komninos, N., Kakderi, C., Panori, A., Tsarchopoulos, P.: Smart city planning from an evolutionary perspective. J. Urban Technol. **26**(2), 3–20 (2018). https://doi.org/10.1080/10630732.2018.1485368
5. Balducci. A.: Smart planning for smart cities. disP. Plann. Rev. **48**(2), 4–5 (2012). https://doi.org/10.1080/02513625.2012.731823
6. Batty, M., et al.: Smart cities of the future. Eur. J. Phys. Spec. Top. **214**, 481–518 (2012)
7. Chesbrough, H.W.: Open Innovation. The New Imperative for Creating and Profiting of Technology. Harvard Business School Publishing Corporation, Boston (2003)
8. IPCC: Global Warming of 1.5 °C. Summary for Policy Makers (2018). https://report.ipcc.ch/sr15/pdf/sr15_spm_final.pdf. 5 August 2019
9. United Nations, Sustainable Development Goals – SDG (2015). https://sustainabledevelopment.un.org/sdgs. 7 August 2019
10. WBGU-Wissenschaftlicher Beirat Globale Umweltveränderungen, Der Umzug der Menschheit: Die transformative Kraft der Städte. Hauptgutachten. Berlin: WBGU (2016). file:///C:/Users/giffinger.SRF/Downloads/wbgu_hg2016.pdf. 17 August 2019
11. Begg, I.: Cities and competitiveness. Urban Stud. **36**(5–6), 795–810 (1999)

12. Camagni, R.: Territorial capital and regional development. In: Capello, R., Nijkamp, P. (eds.) Handbook of Regional Growth and Development Theories, pp. 118–132. Edward Elgar, Cheltenham / Northampton (2009)

13. Campbell, S.: Green cities, growing cities, just cities ? urban planning and the contradictions of sustainable development. J. Am. Plann. Assoc. **62**(3), 296–312 (1996)

14. Acatech – Deutsche Akademie der Technikwissenschaften (Hrsg.) Smart Cities - Deutsche Hochtechnologie für die Stadt der Zukunft. Nr. 10, Springer, Berlin (2012)

15. Caragliu, A., Del Bo, Ch.: Smart cities: is it just a fad? Scienze Regionali. Italien J. Reg. Sci. vol. 17, 1/2018; Special Issue: Smart Cities. In: Caragliu, A. and Del Po, Ch. (eds.) Past Achievements and Future Challenges, pp. 7–14 (2018)

16. Leydesdorff, L., Deakin, M.: The triple helix model of smart cities: a neo-evolutionary perspective. J. Urban Technol. **18**(2), 53–63 (2011)

17. Giffinger, R., Lyu, H.: The Smart City Perspective: A Necessary Change from Technical to Urban Innovations. Fondazione Giangiacomo Feltrinelli, Milano (2015). ISBN 978-88-6835-104-5

18. Fernandez-Anez, V.: Smart Cities: Implementation vs. Discourses. Dissertation at Departamento de Urbanística y Ordenación del Territorio. Escuela Técnica Superior de Arquitectura, Universidad Politécnica de Madrid, Spain (2019)

19. Schaffers, H., et al.: Smart cities as innovation ecosystems sustained by future internet. Technical report (2012). https://hal.inria.fr/hal-00769635/. 30 Jun, 2018

20. Berst, J. (Smart Cities Council) Smart Cities: by the numbers; for the people. APA American Planning Association. Creating Smarter Cities: Augmenting the Collaboration between Cities and Technology Industries. Webinar: 25th of October 2016 (2016)

21. Mumford, L.: [1938] The Culture of Cities. Harcourt Brace & Company, San Diego (1970)

22. Simmie, J. (ed.): Innovative Cities. Spon Press, London (2001)

23. Nelson, R.R., Winter, S.G.: In Search of Useful Theory of Innovation. Research Policy, 6, 1/1977, 36–76. Research: Digital Government Innovation in Challenging Times, 12–15 June 2011, College Park, MD, USA (1977)

24. Lambooy, J.G.: Knowledge and urban economic development: an evolutionary perspective. Urban Stud. **39**(5–6/2002), 1019–1035 (2002)

25. Schumpeter, J.: Kapitalismus, Sozialismus und Demokratie. Francke, München (1972)

26. Suitner, J., Giffinger, R.: Nichts Neues in der Raumproduktion? Innovation in Raumentwicklung und Planung. In: Suitner, J., Giffinger, R., Plank, L. (eds.) Innovation in der Raumproduktion. Jahrbuch Raumplanung 2017, vol.5, pp. 7–14, Wien, Graz: NWV (2017)

27. Barcelona (2014). http://de.slideshare.net/fullscreen/citybrandinggr/barcelona-smartcity-strategy/21. 17 May 2014

28. Barcelona (2019). http://www.urban-hub.com/de/cities/barcelona-macht-seine-smart-city-noch-smarter-2/. 5 August 2019

29. CISCO: Digital Barcelona. http://www.cisco.com/assets/global/ZA/tomorrow-starts-here/pdf/barcelona_jurisdiction_profile_za.pdf. 26 August 2019

30. DG Internal Policies: Mapping Smart Cities in the EU. European Union (2014). http://www.europarl.europa.eu/RegData/etudes/etudes/join/2014/507480/IPOL-ITRE_ET(2014)507480_EN.pdf

31. PLEEC: Planning Energy Efficient Cities. European Commission, FP-7; DG Energy (2013–2016). http://www.pleecproject.eu/. 7 August 2019

32. Geels, F., Schot, J.: Typology of sociotechnical transition pathways. Res. Policy **3**(36), 399–417 (2007)

33. Bergvall-Kareborn, B., Eriksson, C., Stahlbröst, A., Svensson, J.: A milieu for innovation – defining living labs. In: 2nd ISPIM Innovation Symposium – Stimulating Recovery – The role of Innovation Management. New York, December 2009

34. Bergvall-Kåreborn, B., Ståhlbröst, A.: Living lab: an open and citizen-centric approach for innovation. Int. J. Innov. Reg. Dev. **1**, 356–370 (2009). https://doi.org/10.1504/IJIRD.2009. 022727
35. Juujärvi, S., Pesso, K.: Actor roles in an urban living lab: what can we learn from Suurpelto, Finland? Technol. Innov. Manage. Rev. **3**, 22–27 (2013)
36. ENoLL – European Network of Living Labs. https://enoll.org/about-us/. 23 June 2019
37. Lévy, P.: Collective Intelligence – Mankind's Emerging World in Cyberspace. Perseus Books, Cambridge (1997)
38. Sinfonia Innsbruck. https://www.uibk.ac.at/bauphysik/forschung/projects/sinfonia/
39. Sinfonia Bolzano. http://www.eurac.edu/en/research/technologies/renewableenergy/projects/ Documents/Sinfonia_BZ_IT-DE.pdf. 26 April 2019
40. E_Profile Quartiersprofile für optimierte energietechnische Transformationsprozesse (2017). https://nachhaltigwirtschaften.at/de/sdz/projekte/e-profil-quartiersprofile-fuer-optimierte-energietechnische-transformationsprozesse.php; or http://www.eprofil.at/home. 2 April 2019
41. Kolehmainen, J., et al.: Quadruple helix, innovation and the knowledge-based development: lessons from rural and less-favoured regions. J. Knowl. Econ. **7**, 23–42 (2016). https://doi.org/ 10.1007/s13132-015-0289-9

Making CCU Visible: Investigating Laypeople's Requirements for a Trusted, Informative CCU Label

Anika Linzenich[1]([✉]), Katrin Arning[2], and Martina Ziefle[1]

[1] Chair of Communication Science and Human-Computer Interaction Center (HCIC), RWTH Aachen University, Aachen, Germany
{linzenich,ziefle}@comm.rwth-aachen.de
[2] Ansbach University of Applied Sciences, Rettistrasse 52, 91522 Ansbach, Germany
katrin.arning@hs-ansbach.de

Abstract. Carbon Capture and Utilization (CCU) refers to CO_2 being used in the production of, e.g., plastic products to replace fossil feedstocks. Thus, CCU can lower CO_2 emissions and the use of fossil resources. But the novel CCU products are still unfamiliar to the public. One way to raise public awareness and trust for CCU products could be a CCU label. Still, laypeople's requirements for a trusted, informative CCU label are largely unknown. Thus, the present study follows two aims: 1. Exploring trust in a CCU label and uncovering which label characteristics are most relevant. 2. Investigating the potential of involving laypeople in the development of a CCU label and identifying requirements and preferences for the specific design of the label. These aims were addressed by combining a design workshop with laypeople (n = 6) with an online survey (n = 147). In the workshop, participants had to develop CCU label drafts. In the subsequent online survey, demands and preferences for an informative and trust-building CCU label were quantified. Results showed that information sources that inform the public about the label were vital for building CCU label trust. Also, trust- and design-related label characteristics were important for the overall positive evaluation of a CCU label draft. Based on the findings, specific recommendations for the development of a CCU label are derived.

Keywords: Carbon capture and utilization (CCU) · Product label design · Trust

1 Introduction

To address the mega-challenges of climate change and fossil resource depletion, Carbon Capture and Utilization (CCU) technologies are developed to reduce CO_2 emissions and fossil resource use (Thonemann and Pizzol 2019): CO_2 emissions are captured at industrial sites, e.g., at power or chemical plants, and then used for example in the production

The original version of this chapter was revised: To enable a proper understanding of the content the link "CCU-Label – www.ccu-reduction.org" has been added in Fig. 5. The correction is available at https://doi.org/10.1007/978-3-030-68028-2_18

of plastic products or fuels (von der Assen et al. 2016; Zimmermann and Schomäcker 2017). Previous research has found that social acceptance is crucial for the successful roll-out of novel technologies (Feindt and Poortvliet 2020). Thus, understanding how the public perceives CCU and which factors can drive or hamper the roll-out of CCU technologies and products is vital. Studies on the public perception of CCU have revealed a positive general acceptance of the CCU technology and products (Arning et al. 2019; Perdan et al. 2017), but a low awareness of CCU among laypeople and trust issues related to the stakeholders involved in the roll-out of CCU (industry and policy) were identified (Arning et al. 2017; Offermann-van Heek et al. 2018). Moreover, it was found that laypeople demand to be informed if a product was produced using CO_2 as feedstock (Offermann-van Heek et al. 2018; van Heek et al. 2017).

Carefully developed communication concepts tailored to the information needs of the public can help to make the public familiar with the concept of CCU and related products. One possible information source to be integrated in an overarching communication strategy could be a product label that transparently marks CCU products. The label could enable laypeople to make an informed choice whether they want to use a CCU product (D'Souza et al. 2019). The label could also increase the public awareness of the novel CCU products and help to foster trust in the products and their manufacturing through transparency of information. It is critical however that the CCU label is well-designed to avoid possible misunderstandings, confusion, or evoking distrust in the public (as identified as serious issues in product label perceptions, e.g., Feindt and Poortvliet 2020; Gadema and Oglethorpe 2011; Thøgersen et al. 2010). Thus, it is vital to involve laypeople in the development and evaluation of a CCU label as they are the ones that have to understand, trust, and use the label in their purchase decisions.

So far, no study except for the previous research by Linzenich et al. (2019) has explored laypeople's demands for a trusted and informative CCU label. Following up on the first exploration of CCU label trust and trust-relevant label factors, which zoomed in on the effect of user factors on trust-building for a CCU label, the present work extends the view on CCU label trust and additionally explores requirements for the specific design of a CCU label. The results of a design workshop with laypeople and an online survey are analyzed to examine the suitability of a CCU label as decision help for consumers, to identify focal points for fostering label trust, and to explore perceptions and preferences for the design of a CCU label.

2   Theoretical Background on CCU Acceptance and Requirements for Product Labels

2.1   CCU Approach to Limit Fossil Resource Use in Industrial Production

There is a large variety of products that can be manufactured by CCU technologies, such as chemicals, minerals, and fuels (Zimmermann and Schomäcker 2017). One innovative approach is the use of CO_2 in the manufacturing of plastic products: By using CO_2 as a feedstock for producing polyols, a raw material needed in the production of, e.g., foam mattresses, $13-16\%$ reductions in fossil resource use and $11-19\%$ in CO_2 emissions can be achieved compared to conventional production (von der Assen et al. 2014). Although the contribution of CCU for saving fossil resources has been acknowledged, the contribution to fighting climate change was estimated differently: Whereas Thonemann and Pizzol (2019) identified a negative Global Warming Impact for several CCU technologies, Kätelhön et al. (2019) found that the effect of CCU for tackling climate change was limited compared to, e.g., electromobility. Currently, CCU technologies are still at an early stage of deployment (Zimmermann and Schomäcker 2017) and as for other innovative technologies (Feindt and Poortvliet 2020), the roll-out will depend on their acceptance (Jones et al. 2017).

2.2 Public Awareness and Perceptions of CCU Products

The social acceptance of an innovative energy technology encompasses a positive attitude towards and the active support (in the case of product technologies also the use) or passive tolerance of this technology (Schweizer-Ries 2008; Upham et al. 2015).

The current state of research on CCU acceptance points to a positive general acceptance of CCU technologies and products (e.g., Arning et al. 2019). Still, the public has been found to know very little about CCU technologies and to be largely unaware of CCU products (e.g., Perdan et al. 2017). Also, a comparatively low level of trust towards CCU industry and governmental institutions was revealed (Offermann-van Heek et al. 2018). It is thus important to find out how to increase awareness and trust related to CCU products. Information concepts providing laypeople with comprehensible information tailored to their information requirements are a possible lever for increasing CCU awareness. If the relevant information is displayed already on the CCU product, laypeople do not have to actively search for information but can see at a glance if a product was manufactured using CO_2 as a feedstock. That can be realized in terms of an internationally applied CCU label used on the range of available CCU products to improve transparency and understanding. This information strategy could then also help to build trust in CCU products and industry. Next, the state of research on the potential of product labels as decision help for consumers and on influence factors on product label trust and comprehensibility are summarized.

2.3 Information, Design, and Process Characteristics for a Trustful Product Label

Previous investigations of product label perceptions revealed that a trusted, comprehended label can positively influence the purchase intention and decision for a labeled product (e.g., in case of organic food production, Schouteten et al. 2019, and carbon labeling, Feucht and Zander 2018). This highlights the potential of well-developed product labels as useful decision help for informed purchase decisions (D'Souza et al. 2019). Since a product label offers limited space and it is to expect that laypeople only pay short attention to the label information in spontaneous purchase choices (Hong et al. 2004), it is all the more important that this information is self-explanatory and comprehensible. Also, it is crucial that the label is not conceptualized as a marketing tool aimed at selling products but as a transparent and user-centered information tool.

Past studies have identified some challenges for the comprehensibility and trustworthiness of product labels. Trust in another person or institution contains different dimensions (McKnight and Chervany 2001): The actual trusting behavior (deciding to depend on the person or institution because one expects a positive outcome) is preceded by the intention (=willingness) to trust the person or institution. This intention is influenced by one's beliefs whether the person or institution is truthful, reliable when it comes to keeping promises, competent, and acting in one's interest and predictably. Because trust and its opposite – distrust – can occur in the same situation referring to different evaluation aspects related to the person or institution, trust and distrust should be treated as separate constructs (McKnight and Chervany 2001; Ou and Sia 2009).

Trust issues are a serious obstacle for the successful introduction of a CCU label because of the double-relevance of trust. On the one hand, a product label can only build trust in a product if the label is accepted and on the other hand, label acceptance has been found to depend on the trust in the label (Darnall et al. 2018). Feindt and Poortvliet (2020) showed that trust in a product label can increase trust in a novel technology or product. At the same time, a label might be seen more skeptical if the product technology is not trusted. Another reason that makes trust so integral for the CCU product label development is that the CCU product label would refer to differences in the production process (CO_2 replacing fossil feedstocks) which are not discernable in the final product. Therefore, laypeople need to trust the CCU label even if they have no possibility for checking it. Label claims not verifiable by consumers are called "credence claims" (Bleda and Valente 2009). These claims are often found on eco-labels, which refer to environmental qualities of labeled products. Thus, eco-labels (e.g., the Blue Angel and the Nordic Swan) and the CCU label alike share the function of making production-related characteristics visible (Atkinson and Rosenthal 2014).

Label Information. A lack of understanding and misinterpretations of the provided information (both visual and verbal) are crucial barriers for the successful label adoption (Grunert et al. 2014) and have been revealed for several product labels (e.g., nanotechnology, Feindt and Poortvliet 2020; sustainability labels, Annunziata et al. 2019). Past research has identified insufficient information (D'Souza 2004) but also an excess amount of information ("information overload", Moon et al. 2017) as barriers for label comprehensibility. Further obstacles according to Moon et al. (2017) are the similarity to other existing labels (e.g., different eco-labels using a similar design and wording, which makes them difficult to distinguish), and unclear information, in particular ambiguous terms, for which no uniform definition exists across the variety of product labels (e.g., terms related to the concept of recycling, Taufique et al. 2019). Also, highly abstract concepts and figures (e.g., carbon footprints) have been found to be difficult to grasp (Upham et al. 2011). An unequivocal specificity of arguments on the product label (Atkinson and Rosenthal 2014), meaning details about the environmental benefits, and information available about the label (Emberger-Klein and Menrad 2018) and the certification process can build trust in the label and increase its use as decision help.

Label Design. The visibility of the label is another important factor, which can be increased by using logos on the label instead of pure text (e.g., Rihn et al. 2019). Also, the chosen label color can have an effect on the attention to product labels and the decision between products (Shen et al. 2018). Still, the design and used pictures need to be carefully chosen in order to be understood and not to trigger misinterpretations (Polonsky et al. 2002).

Label Certification. The acceptance of and trust in a product label do also rely on factors related to the awarding process. It was found that the certifying organization is a relevant trust-influencing aspect (with independent and known organizations often preferred to a self-awarding by product sellers or manufacturers) alongside approved awarding criteria (Atkinson and Rosenthal 2014; Offermann-van Heek et al. 2018).

Summarizing, the development of a successful (i.e., informative and trusted) CCU label is challenging and requires research. A promising approach to make sure that the label fulfills laypeople's requirements and to reveal barriers for trust and comprehensibility is the integration of laypeople in the label development process. In this process, laypeople's role should not be limited to the evaluation of possible label designs but should be involved in the creation of the label. This allows to uncover which mental representations of the CCU concept are prevailing among laypeople and in which "pictures" and "terms" they think the CCU concept. Compared to purely top-down developments, where label experts and technical experts create the label, this bottom-up approach reduces the risk of developing a label that neglects what laypeople care about.

2.4　Research Aims

The aims of the current paper are twofold: (1) Exploring trust in a CCU label and identifying the label characteristics which are trust-relevant. (2) Investigating perceptions, requirements, and preferences for the specific design of the CCU label and examining the potential of involving laypeople in the development of a CCU label.

To address the first aim, the data already published in Linzenich et al. (2019) will be re-used. To explore the second goal, results on specific CCU label design perceptions are derived from a design workshop with laypeople and additional data from the online survey. In the following section, the methodology for tackling the research goals will be described.

3　Methods and Materials

3.1　Methodological Approach

We chose a mixed methods approach that combined two steps: a design workshop with six laypeople and a subsequent online survey with 147 participants (see Fig. 1).

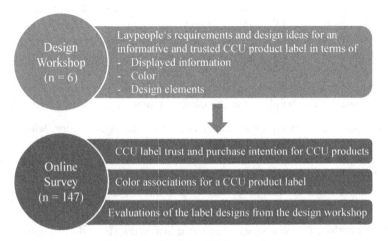

Fig. 1. Logic of empirical procedure.

3.2 Design Workshop

In the design workshop, the participants were asked to collaboratively develop their preferred designs for a CCU label to transparently inform the public about CCU products. This task included the displayed label information, label shape and color, and the chosen design elements (icons). Preceding the design task, participants were asked for their general color, shape, and symbol associations with the CCU process and a CCU label and they discussed on information requirements for a CCU label. The design workshop was audio-recorded with participants' consent and then transcribed for data analysis. The analysis of the design workshop transcript will focus on the task of developing the CCU label designs and not on the general discussion on associations with CCU and the CCU label. Six laypeople (three women and three men, aged between 19−61 years) participated. Participants came from different educational and job backgrounds to capture a variety of opinions and attitudes on the CCU label. The respondents volunteered to take part in the workshop and were not financially rewarded.

3.3 Online Survey

Following up on the design workshop, an online survey was conducted in fall 2017 to analyze and quantify the requirements of the public for a trusted and informative CCU label. The survey had two main aims:

1. On a general level, the goal was to explore trust in a CCU label and identify which label characteristics are relevant for trust and distrust in the CCU label.
2. On a more concrete level, the aim was to uncover laypeople's perceptions of and preferences for the label design concepts developed in the design workshop to derive recommendations for the specific realization of the CCU label.

Questionnaire. The questionnaire used in the online survey was structured in five parts. The questionnaire structure is displayed in Fig. 2 (for an overview of the constructs and questionnaire items analyzed in this paper see Table 3 in the Appendix and Fig. 7, the full set of questionnaire items can be found in Linzenich et al. 2019).

The first part included questions on participants' demographic and personality characteristics (e.g., age, gender, education, and respondents' self-assessed knowledge about CCU). The self-assessed knowledge about CCU was measured by four items (Cronbach's alpha = 0.92), on which respondents rated their perceived level of knowledge regarding different process steps of the CCU technology lifecycle (CO_2 storage, utilization, CCU products). The items were specifically developed for the CCU context and partly originated from the study by Arning et al. (2019).

The second and third section of the questionnaire dealt with respondents' requirements for a trusted CCU label. In the second part, participants' perceptions of a label for CCU products were assessed. Trust in a CCU label was measured by five items (Cronbach's alpha = 0.81) that were specifically developed for the topic of a CCU label. Items were derived from Moussa and Touzani (2008) and an interview study conducted prior to this research. The items addressed essential trust dimensions of McKnight and Chervany

(2001): the dimensions of trusting beliefs (related to belevolence and integrity) and trusting intentions. Furthermore, participants were asked to indicate their purchase intention for CCU products marked by the CCU label by answering five items (Cronbach's alpha = 0.87): There were two items on the active search for CCU products while shopping, two items on the preference of CCU products compared to conventionally produced alternatives, and one item on the intention to purchase novel and unknown products. All items were specifically developed for the present study.

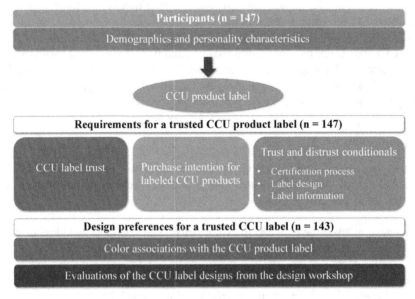

Fig. 2. Structure of the questionnaire.

The third part aimed at identifying ways for fostering CCU label trust: Participants were asked under which conditions they would trust or mistrust the CCU label, i.e., which label characteristics (label information, design, and certification process) would build (dis)trust in the label. 14 trust and 15 distrust conditionals were included (see Linzenich et al. 2019). All items on self-reported knowledge about CCU, trust, and purchase intention for a CCU label, and the (dis)trust conditionals were answered on six-point Likert scales (1 = "do not agree at all," 6 = "fully agree"). Mean values > 3.5 are regarded as positive response and values < 3.5 as negative response to an item.

The fourth and fifth section of the questionnaire dealt with respondents' design preferences for a CCU label. In the fourth questionnaire part, participants were asked which color they associated with a CCU label to identify their color preferences for the label. They could choose between eight colors that were presented to them as colored squares (for an overview of the selected colors see Fig. 6).

In the last part of the questionnaire, the two CCU label designs ("triangle" and "circle") developed in the design workshops were presented to the participants and they were asked to evaluate the label designs on a semantic differential (Osgood et al. 1957) containing 13 adjectival scales. Each adjectival scale consisted of a pair of bipolar adjectives and was answered on a six-point scale with the lower scale pole (=1) signifying the negative and the higher scale pole (=6) signifying the positive adjective. An overview of the adjective pairs used in the study can be found in Fig. 7. The adjective pairs were related to the overall affective evaluation (positive/negative) of the label draft (1 adjective pair), to the label information (5 adjective pairs), label design (4 adjective pairs), and label trustworthiness (3 adjective pairs). The adjectival pairs were derived from the discussions on CCU label requirements in the design workshop and on findings from past research on product label perceptions summarized in Sect. 2.3.

Sample. The online survey was conducted in fall 2017. Participants were recruited via e-mail and social media and they volunteered to take part. 147 data sets were used for further analysis. The sample consisted of 51.0% men and 49.0% women. The mean age of the sample was 33.3 years ($SD = 13.2$, range: $17-70$ years). 14.3% of the sample had a secondary school diploma or lower secondary school leaving certificate. 27.9% reported to hold a university entrance certificate and 56.5% had achieved a university degree or a higher qualification. The remaining 1.4% reported another type of qualification. Asked for their perceived level of knowledge about CCU (technology and products), the sample reported a rather low familiarity with the topic ($M = 2.27$, $SD = 1.17$).

Data Analysis. In a first step, mean values were calculated for all constructs assessed by multiple items. Data analysis was based on descriptive and inference statistics. *For investigating requirements for a trust-building CCU label,* mean values of CCU label trust and the purchase intention for labeled CCU products were compared using t-tests for paired samples. To investigate the relationship between trust in the CCU label and the purchase intention for labeled CCU products, a correlation analysis was run. In order to identify (dis)trust-building factors for the CCU label, a principal component analysis was used, followed by a regression analysis to examine the impact of the identified (dis)trust factors on CCU label trust. *For investigating perceptions and preferences of CCU label designs,* evaluations of the label designs ("triangle" and "circle") were compared applying a repeated–measures analysis of variance (ANOVA) to the mean values of the 13 adjectival scales for the label designs. A regression analysis was run to uncover which evaluation dimensions contributed significantly to the overall affective evaluation of a label draft. To check model analysis assumptions, regression diagnostics were analyzed. VIF values < 10 and tolerance values > 0.2 for all predictors included in the model indicated that there was no multicollinearity (Hair 2011).

4 Results

In Sect. 4.1, results on requirements for a trusted, informative CCU label are presented. In Sect. 4.2, the CCU label drafts from the design workshop are described and in Sect. 4.3 the results of the color associations with the CCU label and the evaluations of the label designs are presented.

4.1 Requirements for a Trusted, Informative CCU Label (n = 147)

CCU Label Perceptions. First, mean values for trust in a CCU label and the purchase intention for CCU products were calculated. A rather positive trust in the CCU label (*M*

$= 4.04, SD = 0.74$) was found. The purchase intention for CCU products marked by the label was significantly lower ($M = 3.47, SD = 0.86; t(146) = -8.75, p < 0.001$). CCU label trust and the purchase intention were positively correlated ($r = .53, p < 0.001$), meaning a higher label trusted was related to a higher purchase intention.

Trust-Building CCU Label Characteristics. Next, it was investigated whether there are ways for fostering CCU label trust: Which label characteristics related to label information, design, and the certification process can increase trust or distrust in the CCU label? To answer this question, a principal component analysis (PCA) was run to examine the factorial structure of the 29 trust and distrust conditionals (Linzenich et al. 2019). In line with Field (2009), only factors were selected that matched the following criteria: (1) The scree plot was visually analyzed and the characteristic point of inflexion was used as selection criterion. (2) Factors with eigenvalues > 1 were retained (Kaiser's criterion). (3) Items with a factor loading < .512 were excluded from further analysis. To check the quality criteria of the principal component analysis, Bartlett's test of sphericity was performed ($p < 0.001$). The data matrix was found to be adequate, and the Kaiser-Meyer-Olkin criterion (KMO = .775) indicated a good sampling adequacy.

The PCA identified five factors related to trust or distrust in a CCU label (Table 1), which explained together 46.5% of the total variance. Four of the factors were solely

Table 1. (Dis)trust factors identified in the PCA.

Factor	Definition	Trust/distrust factor?	Cronbach's alpha
Certifying organization	The factor is related to whether the certifying organization is a **private, dependent,** and **unfamiliar** organization, about which no information is provided.	Distrust factor	0.82
Certification process	The factor is related to whether the awarding criteria for the label and the guidelines and timeframe of the product controls are made **transparent** and whether an **independent** organization is in charge of awarding the label.	Trust factor	0.76
Information sources	The factor refers to the **information sources** that inform the public about the label (How do people get in contact with the label, e.g., via the media, politicians, or friends?).	Trust factor	0.76
Label information	The factor comprises the information displayed **on the label** (amount of information and links to additional information) and the background information available **about the label** (e.g., on the certifying organization).	Trust/ distrust factor	0.66
Label design	The factor refers to whether an **unusual shape or design** is used compared to existing product labels.	Distrust factor	0.80

trust factors or distrust factors. However, the "label information" factor was a mixed factor containing both trust and distrust conditionals.

To find out which of the five (dis)trust factors are most important for building trust in the CCU label, a two-stage procedure was chosen: First, respondents' self-evaluations how important these factors were for fostering their (dis)trust in the CCU label were analyzed and mean values were computed for each of the (dis)trust factors (Linzenich et al. 2019). The mean values for the (dis)trust factors are displayed in Fig. 3.

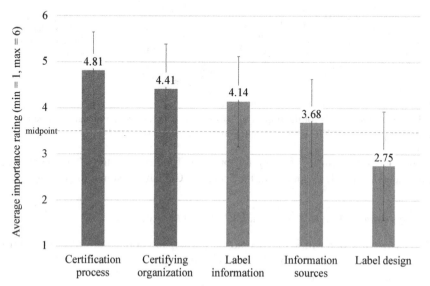

Fig. 3. Importance ratings of label (dis)trust factors for building (dis)trust in the CCU label (n = 147). Mean values on top of the bars, error bars indicate standard deviations.

The two certification-related factors (certification process and certifying organization) were seen as most relevant for CCU label (dis)trust, followed by the information-related factors (label information and information sources). All four factors were rated as (rather) important for fostering trust or distrust in the label. In comparison, the label design was not evaluated as germane to label (dis)trust. The relevance ratings differed significantly for all five factors with $p < 0.001$ (the only exception was the difference between the certifying organization and the label information with $p < 0.01$).

So far, only participants' self-evaluations have been considered. However, it is still unclear if those factors also had a statistically significant impact on CCU label perceptions. This was analyzed using stepwise regression analyses, in which the (dis)trust factors were entered as independent variables and trust in the CCU label and the purchase intention for labeled CCU products as outcome variables. The resulting regression models are found in Fig. 4.

CCU label trust was solely affected by the "information sources" factor ($\beta = .50$, $p < 0.001$), whereas all other (dis)trust factors had no significant impact. The "information sources" accounted for 24.4% of variance in CCU label trust ($F(1,145) = 48.08$, $p <$

0.001). The purchase intention for labeled CCU products was also influenced by the "information sources" ($\beta = .36$, p < 0.001) as biggest driver alongside the "certification process" factor ($\beta = .16$, p < 0.05). Both factors explained 16.1% in the purchase intention ($F(2,144) = 15.01$, p < 0.001).

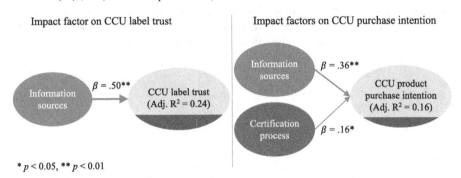

*p < 0.05, ** p < 0.01

Fig. 4. Regression models for the impact of information sources and a transparent, independent certification process on CCU label trust and purchase intention (n = 147).

After having identified factors for building (dis)trust in the CCU label, now requirements for the development of the specific CCU label design will be examined.

4.2 Laypeople's Design Ideas for a CCU Label (n = 6)

In the design workshop with six laypeople, the participants collaboratively created drafts for a suitable label for CCU products. The resulting two label designs "circle" and "triangle" are shown in Fig. 5.

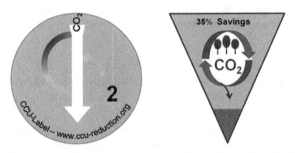

Fig. 5. CCU label designs developed in the design workshop (n = 6). Left: the "circle" label. Right: the "triangle" label. (The label designs displayed here are the electronically generated version of participants' hand-drawn label designs, which were used for the evaluation task in the online survey).

In the following, the label drafts and the underlying thoughts and arguments mentioned by the participants while developing the labels will be analyzed.[1]

---

[1] As the design workshops contained different stages of label development, also statements and argumentations of the participants were analyzed that were mentioned in earlier discussion stages in relation to the label color, shape, and design elements later chosen for the two label designs "circle" and "triangle."

Circle Label. The "circle" label had a circular shape which was associated with the CCU label by the participants out of two reasons: 1. It was linked to the shape of the earth: *"Also like the earth. With this I link something positive"* (female, 47 years). 2. The circular shape was associated with a *"cycle"* (male, 21 years) or recycling. The idea was to display the *"recycling sign"* (male, 61 years) to refer to the CCU process where CO_2 is re-used. A light-blue or turquoise color for the label was used. Turquoise was mentioned as an alternative to a green color as green was thought to be already overused by existing organic labels and turquoise was associated with *"particularly clean water"* (male, 51 years). The "circle" label design consisted of three main elements:

1. **A "phi-shaped" circle** with a color gradient from black to white ending in an arrow tip: This *"phi"* (male, 51 years), as it was called by respondents, was chosen because it resembled the shape of the term CO_2: *"Well, the beginning of the phi is the C, the swirl is the O and then we have just written 2 next to it and have added the white arrow below"* (male, 51 years). But it was also recognized that this might not be self-explanatory. At the same time, the phi shape symbolized a closed cycle for the respondents and was conceptualized as a spiraling *"circle arrow,"* which resulted in a phi shape or vortex *"that sucks in something"* (male, 51 years). This should visualize the capture and storage of CO_2 and the recycling character of CCU. Therefore, the shape was also referred to as *"funnel phi"* (male, 61 years).

   The color gradient from black to white was chosen to visualize that something bad was turned into something useable. Black was linked to CO_2 and carbon and white to something clean and the combination of these colors then illustrated *"that one uses exactly this pollution for something new and clean"* (female, 19 years).

2. **The term "CO_2"** entering the phi-shaped circle was used to emphasize that CO_2 *"runs into"* the funnel (male, 51 years), i.e., to make clear that CO_2 is the substance being captured and re-used. As it was considered important that a CCU label in general displayed which contribution to sustainability was achieved (*"Well, what good did I for the environment now? Did I save CO_2, or did I buy an organic product from organic farming or I don't know?"* (female, 19 years)), participants chose to display the term CO_2. The term CO_2 was used instead of CCU due to its higher popularity: *"Most people think: What is CCU? That's too much"* (female, 47 years).

3. **The text line "CCU Label** – www.ccu-reduction.org" at the bottom of the label, as a reference to where consumers could get additional information on the label and the label product: *"So that people who don't know where to put it can get respective information"* (male, 51 years). Here it was decided to display the URL of the label website. Another idea was to name the certifying organization that awarded the label.

Triangle Label. A triangle shape was perceived as an unusual and therefore eye-catching shape for a product label and the triangle was seen as emphasizing the idea of CO_2 capture (male, 51 years). The predominant label color was green, but it contained also blue elements and the triangle tip was colored in grey. Green was linked to the CCU label because the color was associated with the *"earth"* (female, 47 years). Also, it was thought that due to the many existing organic and eco-labels using a green color the association with organic and ecological was established (female, 25 years). Blue was also suggested for the label because it was associated with water (female, 47 years). The "triangle" label design contained five elements:

1. **A recycling circle** with an arrow leading out of it was placed in the center of the label. The icon was called "*circle arrow*" (male, 51 years) and was chosen to visualize the recycling of CO_2. The arrow leading out of the cycle should illustrate CO_2 being captured and stored: "*Just because of recycling, but I have also considered whether it would be useful to illustrate the removal of CO_2 out of the cycle by an arrow pointing down*" (male, 51 years).

2. **The term CO_2** in the center of the recycling circle to make clear that the label was about the re-use of CO_2: "*We have then also thought that it makes sense in any case to write CO_2 inside so that you directly know what it's about*" (female, 25 years).

3. **Three trees** were placed inside the recycling circle below the term CO_2. Unfortunately, no explanation was given why this element was chosen. One reason why this element might have been chosen could be the connection to the color gradient from green to grey used in the label design (see point 5), where green was associated with nature and trees that naturally process CO_2 (male, 21 years).

4. **The percentage of CO_2 savings** was written above the recycling circle. In the context of the label development it was not specified what was meant by the CO_2 savings. Sometimes, it was unclear whether the idea of giving a percentage for the CO_2 was linked to the amount of captured CO_2 that is stored in the product or the CO_2 savings related to the production process ("*give in percentage what the process would normally have and then the figure that it has now after being (...) specially processed*" (male, 21 years)), or even to the CO_2 source (with the percentage of the "*CO_2 amount coming from sustainable sources*" (female, 19 years)).

5. **A color gradient from grey to green** was used to further illustrate the CO_2 savings: The triangle tip was colored in grey, while the larger part of the triangle was green. The reasoning behind this color choice was given: One participant (male, 21 years) mentioned the idea of a color gradient from grey to green because he associated grey with "*smog, cloud or something like that,*" which would in case of CCU "*be processed to something green (...) like in nature, trees (...) that reprocess CO_2.*" The respondents suggested to have the larger part of the triangle in green color and the other part (the triangle tip) in grey. But there was a discrepancy between the allocation of the triangle parts to the CO_2 savings and the remaining emission of CO_2 in participants' statements. On the one hand, it was stated that the smaller percentage referred to the CO_2 savings and the larger part would then be the remaining CO_2 (male, 21 years). On the other hand, it was explained: "*Well, the grey then kinda stands for the CO_2-emission and the green then for that it was recycled*" (female, 25 years). As the grey part of the label was the smaller triangle tip, these explanations contradicted each other (in the first explanation the grey tip would be the savings, in the second it would be the remaining emissions). Another respondent said that

the association of the grey tip referring to the CO_2 savings would result in the label being more grey for higher CO_2 savings (male, 51 years).[2]

4.3 Color Associations and Evaluations of the CCU Label Designs (n = 143)

Color Associations. Both label designs from the design workshop predominantly included green, blue, and turquoise colors. As the number of workshop participants was very small, we aimed at quantifying the preferred colors for the CCU label in the online survey. Therefore, we asked the respondents in the online survey which color they associated with a label for CCU products. Results are displayed in Fig. 6.

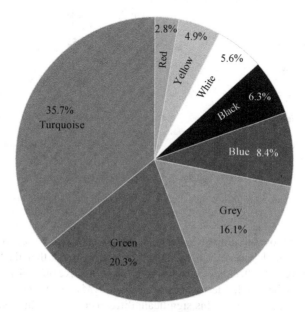

Fig. 6. Color associations for a CCU label (n = 143).

The majority of the 143 respondents associated turquoise (35.7%) or green (20.3%) with the label. The third most frequently chosen color was grey (16.1%). All other colors were rather occasionally linked to the CCU label. The results show that the chosen range of colors was quite similar in the design workshop and the online survey.

Evaluations of the CCU Label Designs "Circle" and "Triangle". Next, we examined how the label drafts from the design workshops were perceived and evaluated by laypeople. It allows to derive design recommendations for the development of a CCU label and investigate the potential of involving laypeople in the label development. To this aim, mean values for the 13 adjectival scales were calculated for each label design. Then, mean values for the "triangle" and the "circle" design were compared using a repeated–measures analysis of variance (ANOVA). Results are displayed in Fig. 7.

---

[2] However, despite this inconsistency it was decided to keep the original color segmentation for the use of the label design in the online survey to avoid distorting results.

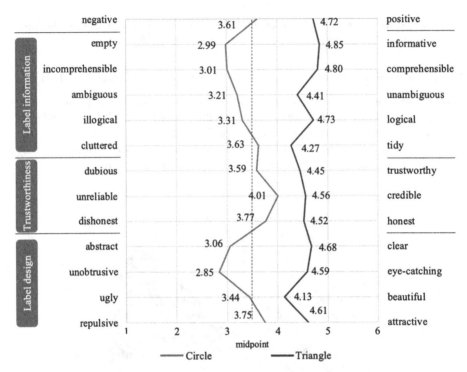

Fig. 7. Evaluation profiles of the label designs "circle" and "triangle" (n = 143).

Results for the overall affective evaluation (adjective pair "negative-positive") showed that the "triangle" label was evaluated significantly better than the "circle" label ($p < 0.001$): Whereas the "triangle" design was rated as positive ($M = 4.72, SD = 1.34$), the attitude towards the "circle" design was rather neutral ($M = 3.61, SD = 1.47; F(1,142) = 71.28, p < 0.001, \eta_p^2 = .33$). This significant difference was not limited to the overall affective evaluation, but the "triangle" was seen significantly more positive on all 13 adjectival scales ($p < 0.001$, see Table 2): According to respondents' judgments, the "triangle" provided a better information function, had a more appealing design, and was also more suited for building trust compared to the "circle" design.

On a descriptive level, the evaluation profile of the "triangle" label showed that all three label aspects (information-, design-, and trust-related label characteristics) were evaluated similarly positive so that there was no identified "weak spot." In contrast, the evaluation profile for the "circle" label was more pronounced, which gives a clue to relative strengths and weaknesses of the design: All mean values for information-related characteristics (except for "cluttered-tidy") and label design characteristics (except for "repulsive-attractive") were below the midpoint of the scale, whereas mean values for trust-related evaluations were above the midpoint (Fig. 7).

Having a look at the "top 3" label characteristics from the positive and negative side (Fig. 7), it can be seen that the "circle" design was perceived as rather credible, honest, and attractive but at the same time as rather unobtrusive, "empty," and incomprehensible. Although the differences in mean values were slight, this indicates that the "circle" label had a weakness in providing clear and comprehensible information and in its abstract label design. But even as the "triangle" label was preferred over the "circle" label, note that the "triangle" was perceived as rather positive to positive. Thus, this label still did not perfectly fulfill the requirements of an informative and trusted CCU label.

Table 2. ANOVA results for differences in the label evaluations between the "triangle" and "circle" label designs (n = 143, min = 1, max = 6, df1 = 1, df2 = 142).

Evaluation dimension	F	p	η_p^2
Negative-positive	71.28	0.001	.33
Empty-informative	129.35	0.001	.48
Incomprehensible-comprehensible	120.14	0.001	.46
Ambiguous-unambiguous	61.45	0.001	.30
Illogical-logical	91.12	0.001	.39
Cluttered-tidy	23.56	0.001	.14
Dubious-trustworthy	45.63	0.001	.24
Unreliable-credible	16.18	0.001	.10
Dishonest-honest	35.27	0.001	.20
Abstract-clear	117.83	0.001	.45
Unobtrusive-eye-catching	170.07	0.001	.55
Ugly-beautiful	24.18	0.001	.15
Repulsive-attractive	39.41	0.001	.22

Having found that the "triangle" label was preferred over the "circle" design, it would be insightful to know which evaluation dimensions contributed most to the overall positive affective evaluation of the "triangle" label. To unveil which label evaluations significantly affected the positive judgment, a stepwise regression analysis was run with the adjectival scale "negative-positive" as outcome variable. All other scales were entered as independent variables. The resulting regression model is shown in Fig. 8.

The model explained 67.4% of variance in the positive affective evaluation related to the "triangle" label ($F(4,138) = 74.55$, $p < 0.001$). It included the four adjectival scales "dubious-trustworthy," "unreliable-credible," "repulsive-attractive," and "unobtrusive-eye-catching." All other evaluative dimensions did not contribute significantly to the positive label evaluation and were excluded from the model. As can be seen in Fig. 8, a higher associated trustworthiness ($\beta = .29$, $p < 0.001$) and credibility ($\beta = .23$, $p < 0.01$) with the label were linked to a more positive label evaluation. Also, the more attractive ($\beta = .28$, $p < 0.001$) and eye-catching ($\beta = .17$, $p < 0.01$) the label was in respondents' eyes, the more positive the "triangle" was rated. It gets apparent that only aspects related to label design and to building label trust contributed significantly to the positive affective evaluation of the triangle label, whereas characteristics related to the information function of the label had no significant impact.

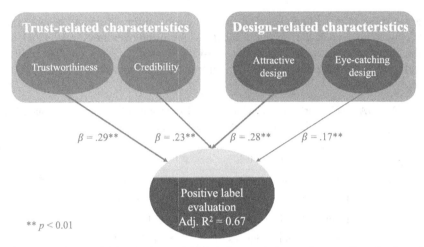

Fig. 8. Regression model for the impact of label characteristics on the overall evaluation of the "triangle" label (n = 143).

5 Discussion

In the current study, trust in a CCU label was explored and trust-building label characteristics were identified. Moreover, requirements and preferences for the specific design of a CCU label were examined. In the following, the findings from the study will be discussed. In Sect. 5.1, results for CCU label trust and impact factors on label trust will be discussed. Section 5.2 summarizes and discusses the findings on requirements for the specific label design from the label design workshop and the online survey. Based on the study results, in Sect. 5.3 practical implications for the development of the CCU label are presented. The chapter closes with the methodological limitations of the present study (Sect. 5.4).

5.1 CCU Label Trust and Trust-Relevant Label Characteristics

In the present study, a positive level of trust in the CCU label was found. A higher CCU label trust was related to a higher purchase intention for labeled CCU products, which indicates that a trusted CCU label could be a useful decision help for consumers in making an informed purchase decision for CCU products. The results mirror the relevance of trust for the willingness to buy labeled products found in past research (e.g., Feucht and Zander 2018; Schouteten et al. 2019).

Since previous research has highlighted the high importance and complex nature of trust for product labels referring to unobservable product qualities (Bleda and Valente 2009; Darnall et al. 2018; Feindt and Poortvliet 2020), it is vital to gain insights which label- and certification process-related characteristics impact trust in a CCU label. The current study revealed five factors related to (dis)trust in the CCU label: Two factors were related to the **label certification** (a transparent **certification process**, which was related to label trust, and a dependent and unfamiliar **certifying organization**, which was related to label distrust). Also, two factors were related to **information** (the **information sources** informing about the label, which was a trust factor, and the **information provided** on and about the label, which was a mixed trust/distrust factor). The last factor referred to an **unusual label design** and was related to distrust.

Respondents' self-evaluations showed that all factors except for label design were seen as important for CCU label (dis)trust. But further analysis showed that the only label factor that significantly affected both CCU label trust and purchase intention were the sources that inform the public about the CCU label, so to say that bring laypeople into first contact with the label. An explanation could be that CCU products are still in the developmental stage with only a few CCU plastic products on the market (Zimmermann and Schomäcker 2017). As laypeople are still largely unfamiliar with CCU products (e.g., Arning et al. 2019), they might have difficulties in evaluating a label for these products. In consequence, they might prefer to rely in their trust evaluations on familiar and trusted sources that provide them with reliable and credible information on the label. The importance of the search for an orientation help to develop opinions towards novel technologies was also highlighted by Feindt and Poortvliet (2020).

Although characteristics of the certification process (whether the awarding criteria and product controls are made transparent and the label is awarded by an independent organization) did not significantly impact CCU label trust, they played a role in the purchase intention for labeled CCU products. Given the relevance of a transparent certification and independent label source for label trust identified in past research (Atkinson and Rosenthal 2014; Feindt and Poortvliet 2020), future studies should examine if this factor gains in importance for CCU label trust once CCU products are more widely available and the public awareness of CCU increases. Then, it might also be that the specific label properties (related to the provided label information and label design) will rise in importance for building CCU label trust.

5.2 Integrating Laypeople's Requirements in CCU Label Design

Apart from a general examination of CCU label trust and identifying focal points for fostering trust in the CCU label, the present study also looked into the requirements and preferences of laypeople for the specific design of the label by letting laypeople create (design workshop) and evaluate (online survey) specific label concepts.

In the design workshop with laypeople, two CCU label drafts were developed by participants: one **circle-shaped** and one **triangular** label. The two label designs "circle" and "triangle" had many similarities but also some striking differences. A pivotal similarity of label concepts was the illustrated CO_2 cycle which indicated that the CCU was seen as a recycling of CO_2. Both label designs included the term "CO_2" to clarify what the label was about, i.e., that the cycle was a CO_2-cycle. At the same time both labels did not entail the abbreviation CCU because it was evaluated as too unfamiliar for laypeople. Looking at the chosen label colors, the two labels used a similar range of colors (blue/green vs. light-blue/turquoise), which were associated with nature and cleanness, and both used a color gradient to show an improvement (something bad turned into something good). In the case of the "triangle" label, the color segmentation was also used as indicator for the amount of CO_2 savings.

However, there were also some differences between the labels: First of all, a different shape was selected. While the "circle" shape is a shape already widely used for existing product labels and was chosen because it symbolized the earth and a cycle (taking up the idea of a CO_2-recycling), the "triangle" label was perceived as an unusual and eye-catching shape. Second, there were differences in the type of provided information: The "triangle" label design contained further information on the amount of CO_2 savings (given in percent) achieved by the product, whereas the "circle" label contained a reference to additional information available about the label (the label name and the URL of the label website). The design choices for the CCU label and the reasoning behind them indicated that the CCU label was closely related to the concept of organic or eco-labels for some respondents: They chose the label color and some of the displayed icons because they are already used in existing eco-labels. Also, color associations with the CCU label were linked to nature and water. This gives a first hint that the CCU product needs a notable environmental benefit to be accepted and that this benefit should be comprehensibly displayed on the CCU label. However, it is to expect that this association with eco-labels might have been also partly triggered by our instruction, in which some eco-labels (e.g., the Blue Angel and the German "Bio-Siegel" for organic production) were introduced as examples for existing product labels.

Interestingly, the developed label designs included an illustration of CO_2-emission reductions but not of the reductions in fossil resource use, although from a technical perspective the benefit of reducing fossil resource use is more relevant in the CCU context (Bruhn et al. 2016; von der Assen et al. 2014). In future studies, it should therefore be examined if fossil resource savings are a relevant label information that laypeople want to know about or if this information is not of interest for them.

The evaluation of the two label designs by the participants in the online survey revealed that the "triangle" label was preferred over the "circle" label since the evaluations of the information-, design-, and trust-related label characteristics were significantly more positive. But still, the triangle was perceived rather positive, showing that there was still potential for improving the label design. This finding highlights the high value of integrating laypeople in the development process of a CCU label to better tailor it to the needs of the public. At the same time, it underlines that a well-developed label design cannot be implemented from scratch. It needs several iterative stages, in which laypeople and experts together find adequate (= comprehensible, appealing, but also technically correct) depictions for CCU that can be displayed on the limited space.

When comparing laypeople's CCU label drafts with the current state of research on label trust and understanding, some similarities were found. But at the same time, the label drafts contained some elements that were identified as challenging in past studies and therefore need precise definition. The CCU label drafts both included cycle depictions to comprehensibly transport the idea of using CO_2 in production. Although this seems to be an important way of framing for laypeople to make sense of the CCU concept, recycling terms and logos were revealed as difficult to understand in several past studies because the recycling concept is used on manifold product labels but no uniform definition exists across these labels, which can cause misunderstandings (Taufique et al. 2019). Thus, the cycle and the information on the label need to be carefully selected and clearly defined. Another difficulty in realizing the CCU product label is the desired information about "CO_2 savings", which has also been identified by van Heek et al. (2017). Since it remained unclear what the CO_2 savings particularly referred to, future research should first clarify which specific information is most relevant for laypeople (CO_2 amount stored in the product or CO_2 savings in the production process). In a second step, it should be examined how this information can be clearly and comprehensibly transported (How do laypeople know what the given figure refers to? Do they prefer an absolute figure or a relative percentage? How can the understanding and evaluation of this figure be facilitated for laypeople?). This is especially important because past research has uncovered that, e.g., the carbon footprint of a product was difficult to grasp for laypeople (Upham et al. 2011) and it is to expect that figures referring to CCU benefits, e.g., CO_2 reductions in production, are similarly abstract.

From a design perspective, both CCU label drafts included pictures and text and thus are in line with recommendations from previous research, according to which the use of logos can attract more attention than pure text and facilitate label understanding through a higher visibility of the label (Rihn et al. 2019). Another decisive factor impacting the attention to a label is the label color (Shen et al. 2018). In the current study, laypeople's color associations with the CCU label were investigated and a turquoise or green label color were identified as preferred colors. However, the color decision for the CCU label should also consider other aspects, e.g., past research revealed that label color can have an impact on attention to the label and the decision process and insights like these are highly relevant to ensure that the label is noticed by consumers and helps them in their decision (Shen et al. 2018)

Quantifying perceptions of the two label designs "triangle" and "circle", the present research revealed the "triangle" label to be preferred over the "circle" label and to score better on information-, design-, and trust-related aspects. The overall positive perception of the "triangle" label was mostly guided by the trust- and design-related evaluations of the label: The more trustworthy, credible, attractive, and eye-catching the label was rated, the more positive it was judged. The results are in line with the importance of trust and visibility for label understanding and liking revealed in previous research (trust: Darnall et al. 2018; for an overview of the relevance of label visibility: Taufique et al. 2019). Although information-related aspects did not impact the overall positive affective evaluation of the CCU label design, it should not be concluded that the label information is negligible for a successful CCU label design because participants rated the label information (above all the information sources that inform the public about the label) as relevant for fostering their trust or distrust in the label. Also, information-related aspects such as extent, specificity, and clarity of available information have been identified in past research as crucial for a successful label adoption (Atkinson and Rosenthal 2014; Moon et al. 2017; Taufique et al. 2019). Still, it remains unclear whether information-related characteristics might have an impact on the cognitive evaluations of the CCU label. From previous research it is known that attitudes entail both cognitive and affective components (Ajzen 2001). That is why future studies should examine in further detail and across a higher number of potential CCU label designs, how affective and cognitive evaluations interplay in the acceptance of a CCU label and which label characteristics impact the two evaluation pathways. In a nutshell: The results do not underline the low relevance of CCU label information but stress the high relevance of trust and emphasize why the identified (dis)trust factors are that important for a successful CCU label.

5.3 Implications for a Successful CCU Label Design

In the following, practical implications for the development of a trust-building, informative CCU label will be derived based on the study findings.

Guidelines for the General Conception of a CCU Label. Trust-building is integral for a CCU label. Therefore, the label design and the certification process need to meet laypeople's requirements for a trusted label:

1. The introduction of the CCU label should be followed by a tailored and transparent information concept. This must include trusted information sources (in this case the media Linzenich et al. 2019) to make the public familiar with the label and transport intelligible, credible, and unambiguous information, which addresses laypeople's demands and concerns.
2. The certifying organization which awards the label is critical: An independent organization known to the public should be in charge of the label awarding. Moreover, background information must be made available about the organization.
3. The label certification process must be transparent: Information on label awarding criteria and the guidelines and timeframe of the product controls should be provided.

Guidelines for the Specific Design of a CCU Label.

1. Most recommended: Involve laypeople (the consumers) in the design of a CCU label to tailor the label to their information requirements and their levels of knowledge. This helps to avoid misunderstandings and misconceptions of the label meaning and prevents that the label ignores what laypeople care about (e.g., giving information that laypeople don't need and ignoring information people want to know).
2. A turquoise or green color should be used in the label as these were most closely associated with the CCU label by laypeople. To underline the idea of CO_2 being re-used, a color gradient from grey to green was suggested by laypeople.
3. The label design should be carefully developed because an attractive and eye-catching design (e.g., a product label in the shape of a triangle) was found to increase the positive overall evaluation of the CCU label.
4. The CCU label needs to clearly convey that it stands for the use of CO_2 in product manufacturing: the term CO_2 was thereby more well-known to laypeople than the term CCU and was proposed in both label drafts developed by laypeople.
5. One way to comprehensibly convey the concept of CCU is the depiction of a closed CO_2 cycle as this depiction was understood by laypeople as the re-use of something wasteful into something new and therefore considered suitable by them to transport the idea of CCU. As recycling depictions are widely used in product labels with different meanings, this illustration needs to be clear and unambiguously defined.
6. The CCU label should entail the amount of CO_2 reductions compared to conventional production to transparently inform consumers of the benefit that the CCU product offers and to enable them an informed purchase decision.

5.4 Limitations

Design Workshop. A shortcoming of the workshop was that the specific "drawing phase" of the label drafts was not moderated and both label drafts were developed simultaneously. Although the procedure was chosen to avoid interfering in and influencing participants' design choices, it was difficult to attribute respondents' statements and arguments to the respective label draft in the analysis. Furthermore, this procedure hampered specifying what the participants meant by some statements (e.g., how they themselves defined the displayed CO_2 savings: as CO_2 proportion stored in the CCU product or as CO_2 reduction in production?) and to understand the reasons why they chose certain design elements (e.g., why the trees were chosen as icon in the "triangle" label). In future studies, a more detailed "question round" should follow the presentation of the label drafts, where unclear label elements can be explained by the label developers and afterwards discussed by the group. This allows to better understand laypeople's mental models of the CCU concept and the CCU label and to uncover whether they have an accurate understanding of the CCU process or whether misconceptions are prevailing.

Online Survey. A methodological issue of the online survey was that color associations with the CCU label were assessed but respondents had no possibility to indicate if their association was positive or negative. Also, they were not asked why they chose this color. But this information is vital to understand how laypeople perceive and classify a CCU label (e.g., in the workshop the CCU label was sometimes linked to eco-labels in the color associations) and whether the label is a positive sign for them or maybe even a kind of product warning if it has a color with a negative connotation.

Although the obtained evaluation profiles for the CCU label designs were insightful to quantify perceptions and preferences for the CCU label drafts, the evaluations were limited to respondents' judgments how comprehensible they perceived the CCU label design. But the study lacked a check whether the intended label meaning was fully understood by laypeople or whether they misinterpreted the original intended meaning. Therefore, future studies should aim for additionally investigating laypeople's interpretations and mental models of the labels to test whether the label designs are comprehensible and unambiguous (e.g., by asking respondents to explain how they understand the label or by a multiple-choice quiz on the label meaning).

Finally, future studies should aim for a bigger, more balanced sample to assess the view of the entire population. Also, a cross-country comparison of requirements for a trusted, informative CCU label would be insightful to examine the influence of cultures and environmental policies on the acceptance of and demands for the CCU label.

6 Conclusion

The present study investigated laypeople's requirements for a trusted, informative CCU label. Trust-relevant label characteristics were examined and laypeople's perceptions and preferences for the design of the CCU label were explored. In the currently early stage of CCU implementation with first CCU products having entered the market, information sources (such as the media or one's circle of friends) were revealed as vital for building CCU label trust. Regarding design preferences for the CCU label, turquoise and green were most closely associated with the label. The overall positive evaluation of a CCU label design was guided by the perceived trustworthiness and credibility of the label and also by the attractiveness and eye-catching function of the label design. These findings should be taken into account in the development of an informative and trust-building CCU label. A CCU label could be a useful decision help for consumers whether they want to use a CCU product or a conventionally produced alternative but only if the label meets laypeople's requirements and is understood and conceptualized by label developers as transparent information to enable an informed purchase decision and not as a marketing tool to sell CCU products.

Acknowledgements. The authors thank Saskia Ziegler and Insa Menzel for research and graphics support. This work has been funded by the European Institute of Technology & Innovation (EIT) within the EnCO2re flagship program Climate-KIC and by the Deutsche Forschungsgemeinschaft (DFG, German Research Foundation) under Germany's Excellence Strategy – Cluster of Excellence 2186 "The Fuel Science Center" ID: 390919832.

Appendix

Table 3. Questionnaire items.

Constructs	Items
Self-assessed knowledge about CCU* (Cronbach's alpha = 0.92)	I feel well informed about the topic of CCU.
	I feel well informed about CO_2 capture.
	I feel well informed about the utilization of CO_2 as feedstock.
	I feel well informed about the CCU product spectrum.
CCU label trust* (Cronbach's alpha = 0.81)	I would trust the CCU product label. *(trusting intention).*
	I would use products with a CCU label without any concerns. *(trusting intention).*
	I believe that the idea of a CCU product label is well-intentioned with regard to consumer interests. *(trusting belief – benevolence).*
	I believe that the CCU product label shall inform consumers. *(trusting belief – benevolence).*
	I trust that the information displayed on the label is true. *(trusting belief – integrity).*
Purchase intention for labeled CCU products* (Cronbach's alpha = 0.87)	I would prefer products with the CCU label to conventional products.
	The CCU product label would convince me to buy novel / unfamiliar products.
	I would actively search for products with the CCU label.
	While shopping, I would purposefully look out for the CCU label.
	I would rather like to use products with the CCU label compared to conventional alternatives.

*All items were specifically formulated for CCU labels and have been validated in pre-studies. Items were derived from results of an interview pre-study and from previous research (Arning et al. 2019, Moussa and Touzani 2008).

References

Ajzen, I.: Nature and operation of attitudes. Ann. Rev. Psychol. **52**, 27–58 (2001)

Annunziata, A., Mariani, A., Vecchio, R.: Effectiveness of sustainability labels in guiding food choices: analysis of visibility and understanding among young adults. Sustain. Prod. Consumption **17**, 108–115 (2019)

Arning, K., et al.: Same or different? Insights on public perception and acceptance of carbon capture and storage or utilization in Germany. Energy Policy **125**, 235–249 (2019)

Arning, K., van Heek, J., Ziefle, M.: Risk perception and acceptance of CDU consumer products in Germany. Energy Procedia **114**, 7186–7196 (2017)

Atkinson, L., Rosenthal, S.: Signaling the green sell: the influence of eco-label source, argument specificity, and product involvement on consumer trust. J. Advertising **43**(1), 33–45 (2014)

Bleda, M., Valente, M.: Graded eco-labels: a demand-oriented approach to reduce pollution. Technol. Forecast. Soc. Change **76**(4), 512–524 (2009)

Bruhn, T., Naims, H., Olfe-Kräutlein, B.: Separating the debate on CO_2 utilisation from carbon capture and storage. Environ. Sci. Policy **60**, 38–43 (2016)

Darnall, N., Ji, H., Vázquez-Brust, D.A.: Third-party certification, sponsorship, and consumers' ecolabel use. J. Bus. Ethics **150**(4), 953–969 (2018)

D'Souza, C.: Ecolabel programmes: a stakeholder (consumer) perspective. Corp. Commun. Int. J. **9**(3), 179–188 (2004)

D'Souza, C., Taghian, M., Brouwer, A.R.: Ecolabels information and consumer self-confidence in decision making: a strategic imperative. J. Strateg. Mark. pp. 1–17 (2019)

Emberger-Klein, A., Menrad, K.: The effect of information provision on supermarket consumers' use of and preferences for carbon labels in Germany. J. Cleaner Prod. **172**, 253–263 (2018)

Feindt, P.H., Poortvliet, P.M.: Consumer reactions to unfamiliar technologies: mental and social formation of perceptions and attitudes toward nano and GM products. J. Risk Res. **23**(4), 475–489 (2020)

Feucht, Y., Zander, K.: Consumers' preferences for carbon labels and the underlying reasoning. A mixed methods approach in 6 European countries. J. Cleaner Prod. **178**, 740–748 (2018)

Field, A.: Discovering Statistics using SPSS, 3rd edn. Sage, London (2009)

Gadema, Z., Oglethorpe, D.: The use and usefulness of carbon labelling food: a policy perspective from a survey of UK supermarket shoppers. Food Policy **36**(6), 815–822 (2011)

Grunert, K.G., Hieke, S., Wills, J.: Sustainability labels on food products: consumer motivation, understanding and use. Food Policy **44**, 177–189 (2014)

Hair J.F.: Multivariate data analysis: an overview. In: Lovric, M. (ed.) International Encyclopedia of Statistical Science. Springer, Berlin, Heidelberg (2011). https://doi.org/10.1007/978-3-642-04898-2_395

Hong, W., Thong, J.Y.L., Tam, K.Y.: The effects of information format and shopping task on consumers' online shopping behavior: a cognitive fit perspective. J. Manage. Inf. Syst. **21**(3), 149–184 (2004)

Jones, C.R., Olfe-Kräutlein, B., Naims, H., Armstrong, K.: The social acceptance of carbon dioxide utilisation: a review and research agenda. Frontiers Energy Res. **5**, 11 (2017)

Kätelhön, A., Meys, R., Deutz, S., Suh, S., Bardow, A.: Climate change mitigation potential of carbon capture and utilization in the chemical industry. Proc. Natl. Acad. Sci. **116**(23), 11187–11194 (2019)

Linzenich, A., Arning, K., Ziefle, M.: Identifying the "Do's" and "Don'ts" for a trust-building CCU product label. In: Proceedings of the 8th International Conference on Smart Cities and Green ICT Systems – Volume 1: SMARTGREENS, pp. 58–69 (2019)

McKnight, D.H., Chervany, N.L.: Trust and distrust definitions: one bite at a time. In: Falcone, R., Singh, M., Tan, Y.-H. (eds.) Trust in Cyber-societies. Lecture Notes in Computer Science, vol. 2246, pp. 27–54. Springer, Berlin, Heidelberg (2001)

Moon, S.-J., Costello, J.P., Koo, D.-M.: The impact of consumer confusion from eco-labels on negative WOM, distrust, and dissatisfaction. Int. J. Advertising **36**(2), 246–271 (2017)

Moussa, S., Touzani, M.: The perceived credibility of quality labels: a scale validation with refinement. Int. J. Consum. Stud. **32**(5), 526–533 (2008)

Offermann-van Heek, J., Arning, K., Linzenich, A., Ziefle, M.: Trust and distrust in carbon capture and utilization industry as relevant factors for the acceptance of carbon-based products. Frontiers Energy Res. **6**, 73 (2018)

Osgood, C.E., Suci, G.J., Tannenbaum, P.H.: The Measurement of Meaning. University of Illinois Press, Urbana, IL (1957)

Ou, C.X., Sia, C.L.: To trust or to distrust, that is the question: investigating the trust-distrust paradox. Commun. ACM **52**(5), 135–139 (2009)

Perdan, S., Jones, C.R., Azapagic, A.: Public awareness and acceptance of carbon capture and utilisation in the UK. Sustain. Prod. Consumption **10**, 74–84 (2017)

Polonsky, M.J., Carlson, L., Prothero, A., Kapelianis, D.: A cross-cultural examination of the environmental information on packaging: implications for advertisers. In: Taylor, C.R. (Ed.) New directions in international advertising research. Advances in International Marketing (Vol. 12), pp. 153–174. Emerald Group Publishing, Bingley (2002)

Rihn, A., Wei, X., Khachatryan, H.: Text vs. logo: Does eco-label format influence consumers' visual attention and willingness-to-pay for fruit plants? an experimental auction approach. J. Behav. Exp. Econ. **82**, 101452 (2019)

Schouteten, J.J., Gellynck, X., Slabbinck, H.: Influence of organic labels on consumer's flavor perception and emotional profiling: comparison between a central location test and home-use-test. Food Res. Int. **116**, 1000–1009 (2019)

Schweizer-Ries, P.: Energy sustainable communities: environmental psychological investigations. Energy Policy **36**(11), 4126–4135 (2008)

Shen, M., Shi, L., Gao, Z.: Beyond the food label itself: how does color affect attention to information on food labels and preference for food attributes? Food Qual. Prefer. **64**, 47–55 (2018)

Taufique, K.M.R., Polonsky, M.J., Vocino, A., Siwar, C.: Measuring consumer understanding and perception of eco-labelling: item selection and scale validation. Int. J. Consum. Stud. **43**(3), 298–314 (2019)

Thøgersen, J., Haugaard, P., Olesen, A.: Consumer responses to ecolabels. Eur. J. Mark. **44**(11/12), 1787–1810 (2010)

Thonemann, N., Pizzol, M.: Consequential life cycle assessment of carbon capture and utilization technologies within the chemical industry. Energy Environ. Sci. **12**, 2253–2263 (2019)

Upham, P., Oltra, C., Boso, À.: Towards a cross-paradigmatic framework of the social acceptance of energy systems. Energy Res. Soc. Sci. **8**, 100–112 (2015)

Upham, P., Dendler, L., Bleda, M.: Carbon labelling of grocery products: public perceptions and potential emissions reductions. J. Cleaner Prod. **19**(4), 348–355 (2011)

van Heek, J., Arning, K., Ziefle, M.: Differences between laypersons and experts in perceptions and acceptance of CO_2-utilization for plastics production. Energy Procedia **114**, 7212–7223 (2017)

von der Assen, N., Bardow, A.: Life cycle assessment of polyols for polyurethane production using CO_2 as feedstock: insights from an industrial case study. Green Chem. **16**, 3272–3280 (2014)

von der Assen, N., Müller, L.J., Steingrube, A., Voll, P., Bardow, A.: Selecting CO_2 sources for CO_2 utilization by environmental-merit-order curves. Environ. Sci. Technol. **50**(3), 1093–1101 (2016)

Zimmermann, A.W., Schomäcker, R.: Assessing early-stage CO_2 utilization technologies—comparing apples and oranges? Energy Technol. **5**(6), 850–860 (2017)

Reshaping Consumption Habits by Exploiting Energy-Related Micro-moment Recommendations: A Case Study

Christos Sardianos[1](✉)(iD), Iraklis Varlamis[1](✉)(iD), Christos Chronis[1](✉)(iD),
George Dimitrakopoulos[1](✉)(iD), Abdullah Alsalemi[2](✉)(iD), Yassine Himeur[2](✉)(iD),

Faycal Bensaali[2](✉)(iD), and Abbes Amira[3](✉)(iD)

[1] Department of Informatics and Telematics, Harokopio University of Athens, Athens, Greece
{sardianos,varlamis,it21797,gdimitra}@hua.gr
[2] Department of Electrical Engineering, Qatar University, Doha, Qatar
{a.alsalemi,f.bensaali}@qu.edu.qa, him.yassine@gmail.com
[3] Institute of Artificial Intelligence, De Montfort University, Leicester, UK
abbes.amira@dmu.ac.uk

Abstract. The environmental change and its effects, caused by human influences and natural ecological processes over the last decade, prove that it is now more prudent than ever to transition to more sustainable models of energy consumption behaviors. User energy consumption is inductively derived from the time-to-time standards of living that shape the users' everyday consumption habits. This work builds on the detection of repeated usage consumption patterns from consumption logs. It presents the structure and operation of an energy consumption reduction system, which employs a set of sensors, smart-meters and actuators in an office environment and targets specific user habits. Using our previous research findings on the value of energy-related micro-moment recommendations, the implemented system is an integrated solution that avoids unnecessary energy consumption. With the use of a messaging API, the system recommends to the user the proper energy saving action at the right moment and gradually shapes user's habits. The solution has been implemented on the Home Assistant open source platform, which allows the definition of automations for controlling the office equipment. Experimental evaluation with several scenarios shows that the system manages first to reduce energy consumption, and second, to trigger users' actions that could potentially urge them to more sustainable energy consumption habits.

Keywords: Recommender systems · Energy saving recommendations · Micro-moments · Energy habits

1 Introduction

The rise of living standards in modern society over the last years has led to a surge in the daily use of technology devices and appliances [17], which in turn increased the consumption of energy resources and gave rise to new environmental and socio-economic

© Springer Nature Switzerland AG 2021
M. Helfert et al. (Eds.): SMARTGREENS 2019/VEHITS 2019, CCIS 1217, pp. 65–84, 2021.
https://doi.org/10.1007/978-3-030-68028-2_4

problems [36]. As a counterpart, technology plays an assisting role in helping users improve their energy efficiency levels. However, most of smart-home and energy related automation systems focus on increasing user's ease of access in controlling or monitoring household appliances [14, 19], but still, the choice of managing the use of these appliances solely relies on the environmental and economical awareness of the user.

Despite the fact that technology provides the means for efficient energy consumption, it is the user behavior that plays the most important role in forming the household's energy footprint [16]. Hence, it is important to motivate users —who are not committed and self-motivated— and to increase the awareness about contemporary energy issues and their dramatic repercussions. This is a key factor for increasing individual energy efficiency and consequently reducing the energy footprint of a community.

Considering the impact of motivating the user to change their everyday energy consumption, we identify the need for information technology solutions that address the problem of engaging users in adopting more sustainable energy usage tactics [13]. Everyday energy-related behavior is definitely driven by the user needs and desires. However the behavior is synthesized by many small actions, which are influenced by external factors, such as outdoor temperature and humidity (e.g. turning air-conditioning on when it is hot) and by the user's common habits (e.g. switching the water heater on after arriving home to take a bath). In tandem, user needs, user conditions and user habits shape the user's energy consumption profile.

Recommender systems aim at providing data-driven recommendations to users [27]. In the case of raising energy awareness and changing users' energy habits, these systems can be used to recommend energy-related actions to the users that could potentially affect their consumption footprint. But first, they must be able to identify users' behavior [39] in order to provide recommendations that match user profile and have a high potential of being accepted. Then, they must be capable of recommending the correct action to the user, at the right moment in order to maximize the acceptance probability. Finally, they must adjust to the user needs and gradually modify the user habits. Such personalized recommendations are also most likely to be adopted by the user in the long term and gradually transform user behavior towards energy efficiency. In order to maximise the benefit from habit change, recommendations must target frequently repeated actions and also actions that maximise the reduction of the energy footprint. They must take into account the environmental conditions (e.g. weather) and avoid inelastic user activities that have a specific appliance usage duration (e.g. cooking). As a result, any attempt to reduce energy footprint based on user habit must follow an analysis of the user habits and must be based on specific usage scenarios.

As mentioned earlier, actions that relate to energy consumption may differ among users depending on their habits, but also can be affected by external conditions (e.g. weather and season changes) or individual user needs, which both may change over time. Considering the repetitive nature of user habits and the temporal change in user needs and external conditions, it is necessary that any predictions or recommendations about user near-future actions must combine both types of information in order to improve efficiency. In this direction, we examine user's daily activities in segments, which are called user "*micro-moments*", in adoption of the term introduced by Google [26] for capturing the temporal nature of smartphone usage for covering information needs.

The proven success of micro-moments in information search and retrieval [32] can be adopted by personalized assistants that analyze contextual information from various sources (e.g. GPS data, environmental information, user status and mood, etc.), predict user needs and pro-actively recommend pieces of information or activities to the user that may be useful at that specific moment [10] or place [7].

In our previous work [29], we demonstrated how the analysis of energy consumption logs can highlight repetitive usage patterns in home appliances. These patterns correspond to the usage of specific devices at specific time-slots, every weekday or weekend and have been repeated during the whole monitoring period, thus allowing recommendations to be addressed at the right micro-moment (e.g. a few minutes before the typical usage duration ends) [5]. In this work, we build on this concept and present the system that we developed in order to take advantage of micro-moment based recommendations. The recommendations target specific usage scenarios in an office context and the whole system is implemented on a popular open source platform for home monitoring using a set of sensors and actuators and a set of automations that help reducing unnecessary energy consumption.

The main contributions of this work can be summarized as follows:

- A methodology for the analysis of energy consumption data and the extraction of habits, which has been applied on a real dataset.
- A system implementation that integrates sensors, actuators, automations and a messaging mechanism for recommending energy saving actions to the user at the right moment.
- An experimental evaluation in a real office setup of the system. The setup controls the light and monitors. Unnecessary or excessive usage is avoided by notifying the user to turn off the devices when necessary.

In sect. 2, we summarize the most important works on recommendation systems for energy efficiency and discuss the concept of micro-moments. Section 3, starts with a motivating example and then provides an overview of the proposed methodology, which has been extensively presented in a previous work [29]. In Sect. 4, we provide the details of the implemented system architecture and in Sect. 5 we present the implementation results. Finally, Sect. 6 summarizes the progress so far and the next steps of this work, which is expected to deliver a fully operational system that monitors user energy consumption habits and timely recommends action that can reduce the energy footprint.

2 Related Work

The concept of mining useful knowledge from usage logs has been discussed several times in the related literature. Although the initial focus back in 2000 was in web browsing and web usage logs [33], there are several recent works that mine user activity logs, outside of the web browsing environment, including geo-location logs [28], app usage logs [11], bio-signal logs [3], etc. The aim of geo-location log mining works is to discover hidden patterns in the user's daily behavior and either highlight interesting locations and travel sequences [12] or create recommendations for Location-Based Social

Networks [8]. Overall log mining approaches, analyze the activity logs of many users in order to detect the common context in which certain activities are preferred among users. Consequently, these patterns and the user's personal context-aware preferences are utilized in order to create personalized and context-aware recommendations [38].

The term "micro-moments" has been introduced in the literature with the 'Janus Factor' theory for determining marketing behavior [35] and describe the moments where people are positively positioned towards buying something promoted by a campaign and moments where people are skeptical and difficult to persuade. Google coined the concept of micro-moments to the spontaneous interaction with smartphones in order to learn, discover, carry out an activity, or buy a product online [26], but it soon has been expanded to more fields, introducing new types of micro-moments that span daily life and can be appropriate for the tourism industry (e.g. I want to show [21], I want to remember [9,37]).

Loviscach [23] proposed a conceptual computer-based energy efficiency recommendation system for domestic households. The solution combines the use of digital power meters, heating control systems, smartphone apps. Also, it suggests making use of deliberate decisions through adopting machine earning algorithms in order to conduct automated energy saving is also studied. The paper acts as a blueprint for future work to build upon.

In [6], a surrounding smart system that supply step-by-step recommendations at different stages such as; behavior, appliance-level and consumer-feedback is proposed. The main focus of this work is the design of a recommendation architecture for improving energy consumption behavior especially in households and dwelling areas.

In [30], energy efficiency is achieved through studying consumption profiles and preferences of the occupants. This was conducted from one side; by using a sequential pattern mining system adapted to meaningful household power usage data, and from another side by introducing a recommender system which delivers advices to consumers to decrease their power usage. Moreover, this system was tested on several households where a group of participants is selected to make rating on the influence of the recommendations on their well-being. This rating was finally deployed to adapt the system variables and turn it more precise over a second test step.

In [31], a recommender system, namely, KNOTES is proposed. It represents a social experience on a consulting recommender system for household power-saving. KNOTES attempts to generate powerful suggestions through the consumer's own preferences based on its value feeling and relevance of the guidance. Further, a recommendation reference codebook is employed, which helps avoiding duplication.

In [34], two frameworks are presented for supporting consumers making power consumption behavioral change through drawing tailored energy efficiency guidance. Both architectures employ ordinal Rasch scale which uses 79 behavioral power-efficiency rules and connect this to a consumer power efficiency aptitude for tailored guidance. Consequently, making use of Rasch-based guidance helps optimizing consumer's effort, raises choice gratification and conducts to the endorsement of more power efficiency actions.

In [2], the matrix factorization approach is deployed to develop a recommender system for advising energy-saving e-service. The authors advocated to practice database features as a contextual data which could be incorporated in the e-service based recommender system since most of related works did not consider data characteristics in developing e-service recommender systems.

In [20], a recommender system is built relying on a multi-agent system allowing the collection of power consumption patterns from sub-meters deployed in a household, gathering online electricity bills and generating advices based on usage profiles and consumer energy cost. By doing so, the recommender system suggests new moments for using the electric equipment and devices with lower price, bringing then, the cost-effectiveness for the consumers. In this sense, optimizing power usage and reducing peaks and outages is potentially attained.

In [22], the authors proposed a simple yet effective recommendation system that learns personal and collaborative consumer-preferences from archived energy usage information and then affords advices for smart home lighting controls. To this end, the smart part is accomplished through deriving a group of points for monitoring light actions when keeping a good balance between individual visual comfort and power efficiency.

In [24], a personalized recommendation system is proposed that utilizes recommendations for deducing consumer's possible concerns and requirements for power efficient devices, then recommending power efficient appliances to consumers, and accordingly engendering possibilities to preserve energy in distribution network. The recommender system is developed through carrying out a non-intrusive appliance load monitoring (NILM) scheme. It operates generalized particle filters to separate the consumer' house device usage patterns from the smart-metering records. Using NLIM outputs, a set of inference tasks was exercised to predict preferences and power usage outlines. Finally, the device profile is derived using information retrieval algorithms extracting key-words from textual device advertisements.

The current work, builds on a new type of micro-moment, which is related to the behavioral change of users towards energy efficiency. We call this the "I want to change" moment. Such moments are used to deliver the correct recommendation to the user to assist him/her to adopt a better behavior. In order to gradually achieve this habitual behavior change towards energy-efficiency, we must first detect the micro-moments by analyzing user contextual logs, associate micro-moments with specific user activities and recommend actions that can assist the user to reduce his/her energy footprint. In the following section we give a motivating example and then describe the proposed methodology.

3   Methodology

Our previous work [29] was motivated by the need to provide users with the means to improve their energy consumption profile. So it introduced a context-aware recommendation system that analyses user activities and extracts their habits. Based on these habits, the system is able to present personalized energy efficiency recommendations at the right micro-moment and place.

In order to transform users' energy habits, it is important first to detect them by processing their activity logs and then to provide the appropriate motivations that will help them change. According to the "habit loop" theory [15] a typical habitual behavior goes through three stages: i) the *cue*, a trigger that puts the brain to auto-pilot, ii) the *routine* that refers to the actual action performed by the individual following the cue and iii) the *reward*, which is the satisfaction induced from completing the routine and an indicator to the potential to repeat the behavior. Reconstructing a bad habit loop into a better one requires detecting the cue, modifying the routine and demonstrating the reward in order to strengthen the desired habitual behavior.

In order to better understand the role of micro-moment based recommendations, we may consider the case of a user, Alice, at her office at the university campus, as depicted in Fig. 1. *"Alice usually arrives at the office around 8 o'clock and starts working at the office, until she has to go to classes. During classes she is away from the office for three or more hours and she usually forgets to turn off the office lights and the computer monitors. When she returns from class, she usually has meetings with students and colleagues so she may be absent from her office for more time. In some cases, despite the outdoor conditions that may offer sufficient natural lighting, she keeps having the office lights on during the whole day. In addition, Alice tends to turn the air-conditioning system on when she arrives at the office, especially at the hot summer days, but she forgets to turn it off when leaving the office. There are also cases that she used to let the air-condition on even after returning back home at the evening in order to keep the temperature leveled until she returns the next morning."*

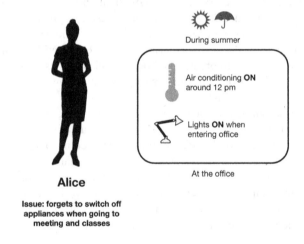

Fig. 1. Alice's use case.

The proposed recommendation framework that we have described in [29] analyzes historical information about the user's daily consumption and correspondingly extracts consumption habits. The habits result from a generalization of user activities in time and external conditions. In our example, the user habit concerning the usage of office lights and monitors will be as follows: *"The lights are switched on between 9am and 5pm during weekdays, the monitors are also on for the same periods, unless Alice switches them off. They fall into standby mode after 30 min of computer inactivity. Usually, Alice forgets to switch off the lights when she leaves the office in the afternoon, resulting raised cumulative expenses over the year"*.

In the example above, the exact times when the on and off activities happen are user-dependent (i.e. if it is at 1:00 pm or at 1:05 pm, etc.) but definitely link to Alice's schedule (e.g. before or after her weekly classes). The same holds for the exact time when she arrives and leaves the office. Similar scenarios can be applied to the usage of the air-cooling device, but they also depend on the weather conditions. Based on the actual weather and light conditions and the actual user status (e.g. user entered or exited the office) a recommendation for a repetitive action that has been properly positioned within the user daily schedule, or has been smartly shifted a few minutes earlier or later in order to save energy, will be more than welcome for the user. Such a recommendation will increase the user's trust in the recommendation system and will assist her not only to reduce expenses, but also to boost the overall sustainability footprint of the organization.

The process of creating energy efficient recommendations is based on a three-step approach as depicted in Fig. 2. The first step of the process refers to the consumption data acquisition and analysis. Based on the analysis of the user's consumption data along with environmental conditions we perform an initial step of analysis to extract meaningful insights. So we process the Consumption Logs and Weather Logs to highlight the user's consumption actions in terms of micro-moments and extract the context of user activities (i.e. when the user tends to switch on and off a specific device). Being able to identify user's energy demands on the spot, in the third step of our approach we can predict user's next energy consumption activities (e.g. 10 min after entering the office the user switches on the air-conditioning, when the natural light is above a threshold, the user does not turn on the lights etc.), which enables our recommender system to recommend energy-related actions to the user beforehand, so as to lead his energy profile in higher levels of efficiency. In the sections that follow we detail on each step of the process.

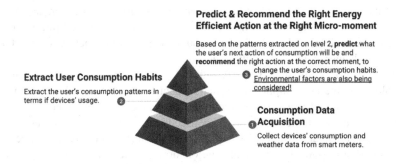

Fig. 2. Steps for data analysis and creating energy consumption-related recommendations. (Also see [29], Sect. 3).

3.1   Data Acquisition and Analysis

In order to collect the user's consumption data, we rely on WiFi-enabled smart plugs/outlets equipped in the most frequently used appliances (e.g. Sonoff Pow R2)

[18]. These smart outlets provide information about the energy consumption of each device, which we collect in a minute window. More specifically, all user's devices that consume big loads of energy are plugged in a smart plug that measures the consumption in KWh in real time. In addition, a variety of sensing modules are also installed in the place for recording contextual information (e.g. temperature, humidity, luminosity and occupancy).

3.2 Data Transformation and Preprocessing

Data collection is the first step of the process, but in order to exploit the above types of information, it is necessary to perform an initial step of analysis that will produce meaningful insights for the next steps of the pipeline. Consumption data are processed and a first level of abstraction is performed that maps on/off actions to device usage periods and characterises usage as normal, excessive, etc. In a recent work [4], we demonstrate how we characterised device usage with the help of consumption data and a classification algorithm. This analysis highlights the user's consumption actions in terms of micro-moments and then with the analysis of sensor data it is possible to extract information about the context of each user action.

As a proof of concept, in the previous work [29], we examined an online dataset provided by the University of California Irvine through its machine learning dataset repository. The dataset[1] concerns the monitoring of individual household electric power consumption. It is a multivariate time-series dataset with 2,075,259 measurements gathered in a house located in Sceaux (7km of Paris, France) between December 2006 and November 2010 (a time period of 47 months). The dataset contains information about the household global minute-averaged active power (in kilowatt), household global minute-averaged reactive power (in kilowatt) and minute-averaged voltage (in volt). The measurements concern the energy metering (in watt-hour of active energy) of three rooms of the household, the kitchen (which contains mainly a dishwasher, an oven and a microwave), the laundry room (which contains a washing-machine, a tumble-drier, a refrigerator and a light) and a set of energy consuming devices which correspond to an electric water-heater and an air-conditioner.

In the pre-processing step (see Algorithm 1), we applied a time-series analysis methodology on the consumption information data of each room. More specifically, from the actual energy consumption recorded per minute, we computed the changes between consecutive minutes and between consecutive 5-minutes periods. The first feature allowed us to isolate minutes where the power consumption increased or decreased significantly due to powering on or off one or more devices. By applying a k-Means clustering on the different power change values recorded for a room, we obtained a number of clusters of power change values that we mapped to specific actions of operating multiple devices.

The processing of the consumption log file determined when a device has been turned on or off with ample accuracy. Subsequently, it allowed the extraction of the user's actions along with the moment that they took place in terms of micro-moments (e.g. at 10:34:00 AM (GMT) the user turned on the microwave and at 11:21:00 AM

---

[1] https://archive.ics.uci.edu/ml/datasets/individual+household+electric+power+consumption.

(GMT) turned on the dishwasher). In order to map power changes to user actions we assumed that each device has a typical consumption specification. For this purpose, we adopted the values provided by the 'energy calculator' website[2] in order to get an estimation of the devices' monitored power consumption. Based on the consumption values of each device, and the devices per room, we map power changes to user actions in terms of micro-moments.

Algorithm 1. Characterize device operation action as *on* or *off*.

Require: Series of consumption data of each room recorded per minute.

  $CurrentMinute = 0$

  loop

    Detect significant power consumption changes.

    if $CurrentMinute = 5$ **then**

      Detect significant power consumption changes in 5minutes periods.

      $CurrentMinute = 0$

    end if

    $CurrentMinute \leftarrow CurrentMinute + 1$

  end loop

  Apply k-means algorithm on the power change values.

  Find clusters of power change values.

  Find the limit values between power changes.

  Map changes to actions of operating devices.

3.3 Detection of User Habits

After this process, user's micro-moment data are analyzed to extract frequent itemsets (i.e. user action and contextual conditions sets). The identification of user's frequent energy consumption habits is a key factor in the whole analysis, since this enables our system to create personalized energy saving action recommendations that shape user's consumption habits and impact the total energy consumption profile.

The habit detection task, refers to the process of identifying frequent consumption patterns (or device usage patterns) in the consumption micro-moments and associating them with weather conditions and other temporal parameters (e.g. time of day, day of the week etc.). In this step, an Association Rule Mining algorithm is employed in order to jointly process user's micro-moments data (consumption and weather conditions) and find frequent itemsets (condition sets) that are associated with an action. The Apriori association rule extraction algorithm [1] is used to uncover how items are associated to each other by locating frequently co-occurring items among the users' transactions.

The typical example for describing association rule discovery algorithms is with the analysis of user shopping carts in an online shop. Let $I = \{i_1, i_2, ..., i_n\}$ be all the possible itmes that can be found in a cart and $D = \{t_1, t_2, ..., t_n\}$ be the set of all transactions (shopping carts) in the shop's database. Each transaction in D contains a subset of the items in I. If $X, \Upsilon \subseteq I$ and $\cap = \emptyset$, then the rule $X \rightarrow \Upsilon$ implies the

---

[2] https://www.energyusecalculator.com/calculate_electrical_usage.htm.

co-occurrence of X and Υ, meaning that if item X is bought, then item Υ will also be bought together. By definition[3] *"the sets of items (for short itemsets) X and Υ are called antecedent (left-hand-side or LHS) and consequent (right-hand-side or RHS) of the rule respectively."*

In the energy recommendations scenario, the appliance, the space, the time and the other conditions are the items that can be found in the LHS part of an association rule and user actions (i.e. switch the appliance on or off) are the consequent (RHS of the rule.).

3.4 Usage Analytics, Recommendations and User Feedback

In order to demonstrate the effect of this change of energy consumption habits, the system collects and analyses user's consumption data and provides useful analytics to the user. For this purpose, the system can use a mobile app (such as the (EM)[3] Energy Tracking Application which we have developed and is shown in Fig. 3) or any other desktop application (as shown in the following section).

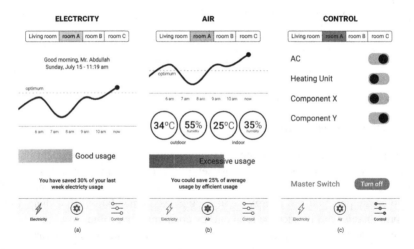

Fig. 3. (EM)[3] Energy Tracking Application. (Also see [29], Sect. 3).

4 Energy Consumption Monitoring System

4.1 Case Description

As explained in Sect. 3, the target of the demonstration scenario is a university employee, who spends a lot of time away from the office during the day, but still leaves the lights, monitor and A/C on.

The ultimate goal is to assist the user to reduce excessive usage of lights, monitors' usage and A/C power by consorting with her usage habits. For this purpose, we

---

[3] http://software.ucv.ro/~cmihaescu/ro/teaching/AIR/docs/Lab8-Apriori.pdf.

implement a monitoring system that utilizes smart meters and sensors to monitor device consumption and Alice's presence in the office, as well as the corresponding light conditions.

The first goal of the monitoring system is to identify whether there is user presence in the office or not and consequently to recommend user to switch off monitors and lights when they are not necessary (e.g. when the user is away from the office or when the natural light is sufficient). The second goal of our monitoring system is to assist the user to keep a desired room temperature based on outdoor conditions, but also taking into account the user preferences and the identified user tendencies on air-condition usage.

4.2 System Setup

In order to support the aforementioned case, a set of sensors and actuators has been deployed in two main areas, the office and the balcony in front of the office [4]. The aim was to capture not only indoor but outdoor conditions as well. For the indoor conditions, we are interested in capturing user presence, temperature, humidity and luminosity and power consumption, while the outdoor conditions monitored outside are temperature, humidity and luminosity.

For the purpose of demonstrating the efficiency of our proposed method we have deployed two types of sensor/actuator devices. The first type was commercial IoT devices from Sonoff (e.g. POW meters, Smart Switches, etc.)[5] and the second type was custom type of devices based on EPS8266 chip (NodeMCU, Wemos). The ESP8266 chip was selected based on the capability of its 2.4GHz wireless connectivity and low power consumption[6]. In both types of devices, the firmware was replaced by the TASMOTA firmware[7] using an FTDI USB programmer. The TASMOTA firmware is an open-source firmware that offers more control and better configuration on any device based on the ESP8266 chip.

In order to monitor consumption and in the same time being able to remotely control the devices, we used two Sonoff POW devices, one for the monitors and the other for the A/C unit. The Sonoff POW devices can control (turn-on/off) the devices connected to them and at the same time, record the power consumption in real-time. In addition, we have installed an RF 433 MHz wireless motion sensor to detect user presence in the office and a Sonoff Bridge device for the communication of any RF 433 MHz module with the Home Assistant dashboard. Regarding the light control of the office, we have used a Sonoff Switch as a wireless switch to control switching on or off the lights when necessary.

---

[4] An office at the Harokopio University of Athens has been used for testing.

[5] https://sonoff.itead.cc/en/.

[6] https://www.espressif.com/sites/default/files/documentation/esp8266-technical_reference_en.pdf.

[7] https://github.com/arendst/Sonoff-Tasmota/wiki.

Finally, we have installed a custom type of device using a NodeMCU chip, with a motion sensor (AM312 chip[8]) connected on it, a humidity/temperature sensor (DHT11[9]), a light sensor (analog photoresistor) and an IR transmitter. The NodeMCU unit had the role of multi-sensor and at the same time with the IR transmitter had the capability to control the air conditioning unit through the infrared signal communication.

At the balcony area, we used a custom prototype of the device (NodeMCU) connected with a humidity/temperature sensor and a light sensor. All the custom prototype devices were enclosed in custom design 3D printed boxes for the protection of the circuit, the wiring and for the smooth integration with the building rules of aesthetics. Figure 4 illustrates the top view of the area that our pilot was deployed.

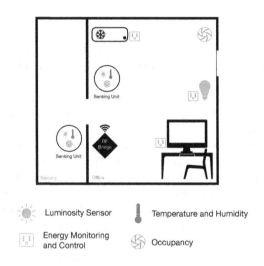

Fig. 4. The deployment of the sensors in our facilities.

4.3   Data Management and Integration

As depicted in Fig. 5 all client modules are connected through TCP/IP via Ethernet or Wi-Fi connections with a Raspberry Pi device, which also hosts the Home Assistant server. The communication between the server and the clients was based on exchanging data using MQTT communication protocol, which is also hosted as a service in the Home Assistant server. The MQTT (Message Queuing Telemetry Transport) is an ISO standard (ISO/IEC PRF 20922) publish-subscribe-based messaging protocol and it was selected based on: *i)* the requirement of minimizing network traffic, *ii)* the ability to increase the security of the connection (SSL security) and *iii)* the extra feature of different modes for Quality of Service (QoS).

Two different QoS modes have been employed depending on how crucial is the connection to a device. The switches use the QoS mode 2, in which the sender and

---

[8] http://www.image.micros.com.pl/_dane_techniczne_auto/cz%20am312.pdf.

[9] https://www.mouser.com/ds/2/758/DHT11-Technical-Data-Sheet-Translated-Version-1143054.pdf.

receiver engage in a two-level handshake to ensure only one copy of the message is received. The measurements employ the QoS mode 0, in which the message is sent only once and the client and broker take no additional steps to acknowledge delivery. For the modules controlled via infrared (IR) (e.g. Air conditioning units, TVs, etc.) on the initial configuration, an extra Arduino board (e.g. Arduino Nano) with an IR receiver connected to it has been employed.

In order to control the A/C unit from the Home Assistant platform, it is necessary to decode all the remote control signals and map them to different commands in binary format. This was done using the Arduino board and an IR receiver to collect the transmitted binary codes from the remote control. These codes were later used in the Home Assistant User Interface (UI) for creating different automations for different application scenarios. Finally, a set of motion detection sensors, which are very common in home security alarm systems, that employ the RF 433MHz wireless communication protocol have been used. The main advantages of this type of devices are their low cost and their ease of configuration and installation [25]. In addition, they are battery operated and can be readily installed in all buildings. When a motion sensor is triggered, then a unique code is published and every device with the capability to receive RF 433 MHz signals can "capture" this code and based on that may trigger predefined procedures that record an action (e.g. switch-on/off a light, enter or exit a room, etc.) For controlling all the RF 433 MHz signals, an extra receiver has been used to collect signals and transmit them to the server through the Wi-Fi connection. The messages are then used by the Home Assistant automations, as shown in Fig. 7.

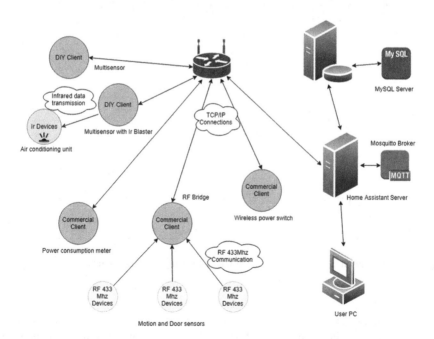

Fig. 5. Network connectivity of the components of the system.

The data storage of the system, is handled by a MySQL server, running on a PC in the same network, instead of the NoSQL option that comes as default with Home Assistant. This option allows better scalabilty of the system and moves part of the processing load from the Raspberry Pi to another device. It also allows to further expand the data analysis and processing and the monitoring system as a whole.

4.4 User Interface and Automations

In order to integrate the whole system in a user-friendly automation hub, we employed Home Assistant[10]. It is an open source automation platform that puts local control and privacy first and is powered by a worldwide community of DIY enthusiasts. In our case, the host for running Home Assistant is a Raspberry Pi 3 Model B and serves as the server part of our system architecture.

More specifically, the Home Assistant platform offers a very comfortable means to track the collected data and at the same time offers a graphical representation of the data using custom graphs. The UI is accessible through a web browser and has an easily configured layout. The user can modify the layout and monitor multiple rooms and is able to control the connected devices using virtual switches. The state of every switch gets updated automatically if the state changes through the smart device or manually. In addition, the Home Assistant UI offers the users the ability to construct custom automations following the simple flow of: "TRIGGER CONDITION ACTION".

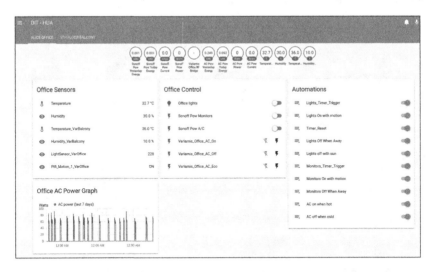

Fig. 6. The main layout of the Home Assistant UI, comprising sensors, switches, automations and analytics.

Figure 6 demonstrates the Home Assistant's main interface for the case scenario. The layout contains information about sensors' current status, switches and analytics

---

[10] https://www.home-assistant.io/.

that provides user with instant monitoring of sensor logs or consumption of the office appliances that have been integrated in the monitoring system. At the right of Fig. 6, there is the "Automations" section, which is also depicted in Fig. 7, and includes all the custom automations that control the office infrastructure (Actions) and implement energy saving and habit change scenarios (i.e. rules with **Triggers** and **Conditions**, which start the appropriate (**Action**) when met.). The actions where not directly triggered, but using the Telegram cloud-based messaging API[11] that is supported by Home Assistant, a recommendation is sent to the user. When the user accepts the recommendation, then the Action happens.

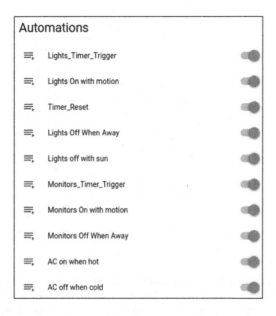

Fig. 7. The list of automations that implement the case scenario.

5   Results and Discussion

In order to control the usage of office lights, we created several triggers (Automations) that either turn on the lights, when somebody is in the office and the light levels from the sunlight are low, or turn off the lights after 15 min of inactivity in the room, based mainly on a rule-based logic. Since the experiment was performed in an office, the expected office usage times are from 8 a.m. to approximately 8 p.m., only on weekdays and with many breaks, since the office is not always occupied.

Figure 8 shows the light levels of the office for a period of 4 weeks (weeks 2 and 3 with the automations enabled and weeks 1 and 4 without automations) and the respective lights' usage time per hour (in minutes). We can see that using the automations, the office light levels (scaled between 0 for dark and 1 for maximum light) followed almost

---

[11] https://core.telegram.org/.

the same pattern, whereas the usage time of the office lights is limited during the day (when the office is occupied), with the few peaks to correspond to a continuous user presence in the office. Even in this case, the maximum usage time per hour (i.e. 60 min) was reached only a few times during weeks 2 and 3, mainly because of the plenty natural sunlight that triggered the turn off notifications. It is also obvious from the plots that the consumption during the night or the weekend is zero. From a power consumption point of view, it is worth noting that when using the automations, the average lights' usage time was 2.98 and 2.04 h (for week 2 and 3 respectively), whereas during the period that no automations were used it was 3.78 and 5.03 h per day (for weeks 1 and 4 respectively).

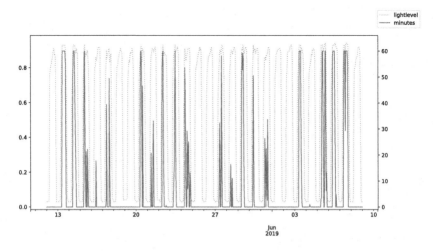

Fig. 8. Light levels of the office for a period of 4 weeks and the respective lights usage time per hour. The left vertical axis measures the light level (red line) of the office in a scale from 0 (dark) to 1 (light). The right vertical axis measures the hourly usage of lights per hour (blue line) with a maximum of 60 min.

The impact of our monitoring system is highlighted during weeks 1 and 4 when all the automations have been deactivated leading to an increase of more than 75% of the average daily usage time for weeks 2 and 3.

Evaluating the process of automatically switching off the monitors when Alice was out of the office for more than 15 min, in Fig. 9, we plot the periods during which Alice was at the office, whereas Fig. 10 contains the respective power consumption during these weeks from the two office monitors. The monitors' scenario ran for weeks 2 to 4, with automations turned on in week 2, with partial use of the automations in week 3 and without any automations in week 4.

As Fig. 9 implies, the office usage patterns were quite similar across weeks and most importantly they contain a lot of idle periods in which the office, and thus the monitors, are not used. Taking advantage of the automations that was used, Alice managed to reduce monitor consumption especially in weeks 2 and 3.

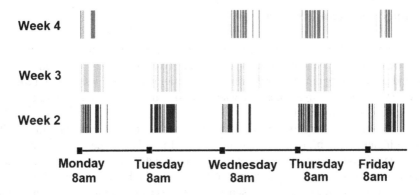

Fig. 9. The time slots during which user movement was detected at the office.

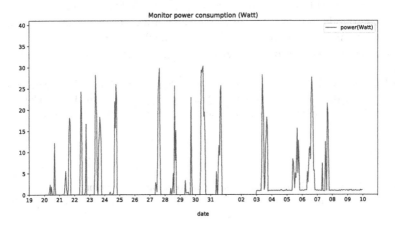

Fig. 10. Power consumption in Watts for the two office monitors for weeks 2 to 4. During week 4 no automation have been used apart from the stand by and sleep mode options of the monitors.

Based on the consumption values of the two monitors during standby (≈ 0.5 W each) and normal operation (≈ 38 W each), it is possible to draw some useful conclusions. First, the sleep/standby consumption of the two monitors adds at least 168 W to this sum (i.e. 24 h $\times$ 7 d $\times$ 0.5 W $\times$ 2 monitors), which justifies this 42% increase compared to week 2 and the 21% increase compared to week 3. Second, given that the user was at the office for 5 d, the actual monitor usage time per day for the three weeks is almost the same and ranges from 1 to 1.3 h. Although the savings for one user may not be impressive (i.e. the yearly savings will be a few dollars), projecting them to an office building or to a larger scale can be useful. It is also important to highlight that using similar automations for more devices, we shape user habits towards energy efficiency.

6   Conclusions and Next Steps

Addressing the problem of engaging users in adopting more sustainable energy usage tactics, we identify that the users' everyday energy-related behavior is driven by their needs and desires. Targeting the user's repetitive common energy consumption tasks we can create triggers that will automatically act instead of the user to lead to more efficient patterns of energy consumption.

In this work we extend our previous work on reshaping user consumption habits towards efficiency and present an implementation of a real-case scenario of our monitoring system in our facilities as a proof of concept of automating energy consumption management task. Current results show that leveraging the benefits of an open-source platform like Home Assistant and a setup of smart sensors, smart plugs and a consumption reporting mechanism we are able to facilitate the transition of the user to new consumption habits (like efficiently operating the office lights, A/C, etc.).

We are currently in the process of expanding our architecture in all of the areas of our department, that will not only allow us to efficiently use energy source in all of the department's infrastructures but will verify our system's benefits in a large-scale setup.

Acknowledgements. This paper was made possible by National Priorities Research Program (NPRP) grant No. 10–0130-170288 from the Qatar National Research Fund (a member of Qatar Foundation). The statements made herein are solely the responsibility of the authors.

References

1. Agrawal, R., Srikant, R., et al.: Fast algorithms for mining association rules. In: Proceedings of 20th International Conference Very Large Data Bases, VLDB. vol. 1215, pp. 487–499 (1994)
2. Al-zanbouri, Z., Ding, C.: Data-aware web service recommender system for energy-efficient data mining services. In: 2018 IEEE 11th Conference on Service-Oriented Computing and Applications (SOCA). pp. 57–64 (2018) https://doi.org/10.1109/SOCA.2018.00015
3. Alhamid, M.F., Rawashdeh, M., Al Osman, H., El Saddik, A.: Leveraging biosignal and collaborative filtering for context-aware recommendation. In: Proceedings of the 1st ACM International Workshop on Multimedia Indexing and Information Retrieval For Healthcare. pp. 41–48. ACM (2013)
4. Alsalemi, A., et al.: Endorsing domestic energy saving behavior using micro-moment classification. Appl. Energ. **250**, 1302–1311 (2019)
5. Alsalemi, A., Sardianos, C., Bensaali, F., Varlamis, I., Amira, A., Dimitrakopoulos, G.: The role of micro-moments: A survey of habitual behavior change and recommender systems for energy saving. IEEE Syst. J. **13**(3), 3376–3387 (2019)
6. Aritoni, O., Negru, V.: A multi-agent recommendation system for energy efficiency improvement. In: Yonazi, J.J., Sedoyeka, E., Ariwa, E., El-Qawasmeh, E. (eds.) e-Technologies and Networks for Development, pp. 156–170. Springer, Berlin Heidelberg, Berlin, Heidelberg (2011)
7. Bao, J., Zheng, Y., Mokbel, M.F.: Location-based and preference-aware recommendation using sparse geo-social networking data. In: Proceedings of the 20th International Conference on Advances in Geographic Information Systems. pp. 199–208. ACM (2012)

8. Bao, J., Zheng, Yu., Wilkie, D., Mokbel, M.: Recommendations in location-based social networks: a survey. GeoInformatica **19**(3), 525–565 (2015). https://doi.org/10.1007/s10707-014-0220-8

9. Biloš, A., Turkalj, D., Kelić, I.: Micro-moments of user experience: An approach to understanding online user intentions and begavior. Challenges of big data technology p. 67 (2016)

10. Campos, P.G., Díez, F., Cantador, I.: Time-aware recommender systems: a comprehensive survey and analysis of existing evaluation protocols. User Model. User-Adapted Int.**24**(1–2), 67–119 (2014)

11. Cao, H., Lin, M.: Mining smartphone data for app usage prediction and recommendations: a survey. Pervasive Mobile Comput. **37**, 1–22 (2017)

12. Cao, X., Cong, G., Jensen, C.S.: Mining significant semantic locations from gps data. Proc. VLDB Endowment **3**(1–2), 1009–1020 (2010)

13. Coutaz, J., et al.: Will the Last One Out, Please Turn off the Lights Promoting Energy Awareness in Public Areas of Office Buildings. In: Kameas, A., Stathis, K. (eds.) AmI 2018. LNCS, vol. 11249, pp. 20–36. Springer, Cham (2018). https://doi.org/10.1007/978-3-030-03062-9_2

14. Darby, S.J.: Smart technology in the home: time for more clarity. Build. Res. Inf. **46**(1), 140–147 (2018)

15. Duhigg, C.: The Power of Habit: Why we do what we do and how to change. Random House (2013)

16. Gram-Hanssen, K.: Efficient technologies or user behaviour, which is the more important when reducing households' energy consumption? Energ. Effi. **6**(3), 447–457 (2013)

17. Hu, S., Yan, D., Guo, S., Cui, Y., Dong, B.: A survey on energy consumption and energy usage behavior of households and residential building in urban china. Energ. Build. **148**, 366–378 (2017)

18. ITEAD Intelligent Systems: Sonoff Pow **R2**, (2016). https://sonoff.itead.cc/en/products/sonoff/sonoff-pow-r2

19. Jensen, R.H., Strengers, Y., Kjeldskov, J., Nicholls, L., Skov, M.B.: Designing the desirable smart home: A study of household experiences and energy consumption impacts. In: Proceedings of the 2018 CHI Conference on Human Factors in Computing Systems. p. 4. ACM (2018)

20. Jiménez-Bravo, D.M., Pérez-Marcos, J., la Iglesia, D.H.D., González, G.V., Paz, J.F.D.: Multi-agent recommendation system for electrical energy optimization and cost saving in smart homes. Energies **12**(7), 1–22 (2019). https://ideas.repec.org/a/gam/jeners/v12y2019i7p1317-d220432.html

21. Jørgensen, L.: I want to show-How user-centered design methods can assist when preparing for micro moments. Master's thesis, NTNU (2017)

22. Kar, P., et al.: Revicee: a recommendation based approach for personalized control, visual comfort & energy efficiency in buildings. Build. Envir. **152**, 135–144 (2019)

23. Loviscach, J.: The design space of personal energy conservation assistants. Psychnol. J. **9**(1), (2011)

24. Luo, F., et al.: Non-intrusive energy saving appliance recommender system for smart grid residential users. IET Gener. Trans. Distr. **11**(7), 1786–1793 (2017)

25. Qingyun, D., Hong, B., Yihong, L., Zexi, L., Ke, Z., Jin, W.: 433mhz wireless network technology for wireless manufacturing. In: 2008 Second International Conference on Future Generation Communication and Networking. vol. 2, pp. 393–397. IEEE (2008)

26. Ramaswamy, S.: How micro-moments are changing the rules. Think with Google (2015)

27. Ricci, F., Rokach, L., Shapira, B.: Introduction to Recommender Systems Handbook. In: Ricci, F., Rokach, L., Shapira, B., Kantor, P.B. (eds.) Recommender Systems Handbook, pp. 1–35. Springer, Boston, MA (2011). https://doi.org/10.1007/978-0-387-85820-3_1

28. Sardianos, C., Varlamis, I., Bouras, G.: Extracting user habits from google maps history logs. In: 2018 IEEE/ACM International Conference on Advances in Social Networks Analysis and Mining (ASONAM). pp. 690–697. IEEE (2018)

29. Sardianos, C., et al.:"i want to .... change" micro-moment based recommendations can change users' energy habits. In: Proceedings of the 8th International Conference on Smart Cities and Green ICT Systems (SMARTGREENS 2019). SCITEPRESS Digital Library (2019)

30. Schweizer, D., Zehnder, M., Wache, H., Witschel, H., Zanatta, D., Rodriguez, M.: Using consumer behavior data to reduce energy consumption in smart homes: applying machine learning to save energy without lowering comfort of inhabitants. In: 2015 IEEE 14th International Conference on Machine Learning and Applications (ICMLA). pp. 1123–1129 (2015). https://doi.org/10.1109/ICMLA.2015.62

31. Shigeyoshi, H., Tamano, K., Saga, R., Tsuji, H., Inoue, S., Ueno, T.: Social experiment on advisory recommender system for energy-saving. In: Yamamoto, S. (ed.) HIMI 2013. LNCS, vol. 8016, pp. 545–554. Springer, Heidelberg (2013). https://doi.org/10.1007/978-3-642-39209-2_61

32. Snegirjova, M., Tuomisto, F.: Micro-moments: new context in information system success theory. Master's thesis (2017)

33. Srivastava, J., Cooley, R., Deshpande, M., Tan, P.N.: Web usage mining: discovery and applications of usage patterns from web data. Acm Sigkdd Explorations Newsletter 1(2), 12–23 (2000)

34. Starke, A., Willemsen, M., Snijders, C.: Effective user interface designs to increase energy-efficient behavior in a rasch-based energy recommender system. In: Proceedings of the Eleventh ACM Conference on Recommender Systems. pp. 65–73. RecSys 2017, ACM, New York, USA (2017). https://doi.org/10.1145/3109859.3109902

35. Stokes, P., Harris, P.: Micro-moments, choice and responsibility in sustainable organizational change and transformation: the Janus dialectic. J. Organ. Change Manage. 25(4), 595–611 (2012)

36. Urge-Vorsatz, D., Petrichenko, K., Staniec, M., Eom, J.: Energy use in buildings in a long-term perspective. Current Opinion Envir. Sustain. 5(2), 141–151 (2013). https://doi.org/10.1016/j.cosust.2013.05.004, http://www.sciencedirect.com/science/article/pii/S1877343513000468,energysystems

37. Wang, D., Park, S., Fesenmaier, D.R.: The role of smartphones in mediating the touristic experience. J. Travel Res. 51(4), 371–387 (2012)

38. Yu, K., Zhang, B., Zhu, H., Cao, H., Tian, J.: Towards personalized context-aware recommendation by mining context logs through topic models. In: Tan, P.-N., Chawla, S., Ho, C.K., Bailey, J. (eds.) PAKDD 2012. LNCS (LNAI), vol. 7301, pp. 431–443. Springer, Heidelberg (2012). https://doi.org/10.1007/978-3-642-30217-6_36

39. Zhou, K., Yang, S.: Understanding household energy consumption behavior: the contribution of energy big data analytics. Renew. Sustain. Energy Rev. 56, 810–819 (2016)

Power Grid Capacity Extension with Conditional Loads Instead of Physical Expansions

Ramón Christen[1][(✉)], Vincent Layec[2], Gwendolin Wilke[1], and Holger Wache[2]

[1] Department of Information Technology, Lucerne University of Applied Sciences and Arts, Rotkreuz, Switzerland
{ramon.christen,gwendolin.wilke}@hslu.ch
[2] Institute of Information Systems, University of Applied Sciences and Arts Northwestern Switzerland, Olten, Switzerland
{vincent.layec,holger.wache}@fhnw.ch
http://www.hslu.ch, http://www.fhnw.ch

Abstract. A dramatic increase in network capacity demand is to be expected in the future, especially at times of high production or consumption. This is due to the electrification of the global energy system and a shift towards distributed power production from sustainable sources. Energy management solutions have been proposed that help mitigate high costs of physical grid extension by utilizing existent grid capacities more efficiently. Yet, these solutions often interfere with customer processes and/or restrict free access to the energy market. The RLS "regional load shaping" approach proposes a market-based solution that resolves this dilemma for the mid voltage grid: the RLS business model gives incentives to all stakeholders to allocate so-called "conditional loads", which are flexible loads that are not subjected to $(n-1)$ security of supply; the RLS load management solution then assigns these loads to cost-optimized time slots in the traditionally unused $N-1$ capacity band. The paper provides a validation of the technical aspects of the RLS approach: an evaluation of the day-ahead load forecasting method for industry customers is given, as well as a validation of the load optimization heuristics based on simulated capacity bottlenecks. It is shown that the prediction model provides competitive results in terms of accuracy, and that RLS method handles all provoked critical network capacity situations as expected. Particularly, $(n-1)$ security of supply is retained at all times for "unconditional" loads.

Keywords: Smart grid · Power grid · Grid capacity · Grid reinforcement load prediction · Load management

1 Introduction

The growing replacement of fossil resources by new renewables increases the electric power demand and causes a proliferation of production and consumption

© Springer Nature Switzerland AG 2021
M. Helfert et al. (Eds.): SMARTGREENS 2019/VEHITS 2019, CCIS 1217, pp. 85–109, 2021.
https://doi.org/10.1007/978-3-030-68028-2_5

concurrency. To avoid anticipated future grid congestions, higher grid capacities are needed. To mitigate the high costs of necessary future large scale physical grid expansions, IT-based energy management solutions in the Smart Grid have been proposed that help utilize existing grid capacities more efficiently [2]. However, most grid-optimizing approaches suffer from a major disadvantage: they rely on top-down regulations that may interfere with customer processes instead of providing self-regulatory market-based principles.

In [3], the authors developed a business model that provides market-based incentives for all stakeholder groups on the medium voltage grid level to use so-called "conditional" flexible loads for grid capacity optimization. In contrast to standard "unconditional" loads, conditional loads can be temporarily shedded by the utility provider whenever a grid branch is overloaded. With the introduction of conditional loads, the currently unused grid capacity dedicated to (n − 1) security of supply can be allocated for uncritical flexibilities without jeopardizing (n − 1) security of supply for unconditional loads. Conditional load usage is planned day-ahead and regionally coordinated for every grid branch by a load management software. The software is based on the "Regional Load Shaping" (RLS) approach [3,5]. It comprises a heuristic that optimizes not only grid capacity usage, but also customer-side energy prizes.

In the present paper, we test and validate technically the two major components of the RLS approach in detail: the RLS optimization heuristics and the underlying day-ahead load forecasting method. By extrapolating a real world scenario of our pilot customers to future scenarios with increased power demand and supply we simulate network congestions. The proposed load scheduling solution incoporates prize optimization heuristics and is able to handle the critical network capacity situations. For the evaluation of the day-ahead load forecasting method, we evaluate the Mean Absolute Percentage Error (MAPE) as a measure of accuracy and show that the results achieved with our pilot customers' data sets are comparable with results in the literature. Additionally, we evaluate the prediction reliability as a means for the Distribution System Operator (DSO) and end customer to assess the prediction quality from a pragmatic perspective.

2   State of the Art

2.1   Load Scheduling Approaches

Demand Response (DR) tries to shift electrical consumption to another time. Prosumers change their electric usage from its normal demand pattern in reaction to an incentive payment. [18] distinguished dispatchable and non-dispatchable programs. In dispatchable programs the systems of prosumers are controlled by the DSO. Non-dispatchable programs allow prosumers decentrally to define their own load schedule. In the latter case the tariffs vary from simple Time-Of-Use (TOU) with constant day and night prices to Real-Time Pricing (RTP), where prices are changing at each time step. The formulation of the schedulers (mathematical programming, metaheuristics or other controllers) depends on the type of tariff system, but also on the type of electrical loads, their operating constraints, the number of timesteps, the type of variables (without integer or not), as classified in [17]. The case of photovoltaic in combination with several battery types is addressed in [23]. In [6], the information about the real-time price is communicated one day in advance so prosumers do not need to predict prices. But automatic schedulers relying on the same information will plan their load in the same cheapest timestep and unfortunately create new peaks [24] (so called "load synchronization"). The issue is addressed by [15] with tariff of Inclining Block Rates (IBR) where high consumption levels are dissuasively expensive. [10] showed that the total load of a community of prosumers can be well shaped with tariffs combining RTP with IBR. But so far, no approach/tariff system targets the upper half of the transmission capacity which is usually reserved as a redundancy for the rare case of failure. That resource is mainly unused and for that purpose to expensive.

2.2 Prediction Methods for Day-Ahead Forecasting for Industry Customers

Efficient use of decentralized sustainable power production strongly relies on reliable and accurate demand prediction. The presented research relies mainly on prediction methods based on historical time series data, since the provisioning of external information, such as current production schedules, is often time consuming for customers and could not be provided by the majority of our pilot customers. A prominent example for research in time series methods for demand prediction is James W. Taylor, cf., e.g., [20–22].

It has been observed that prediction accuracy usually increases with the aggregation level of the predicted power demand, cf., e.g., [1,13,25]. [13] confirm the dependency of prediction accuracy and aggregation level, and [11] shows a similar behaviour by predicting individual residential power demand with a mean absolute percentage error (MAPE) of approx. 44%, compared to an aggregate forecast with a MAPE of approx. 8%.

Furthermore, efficiency of prediction approaches usually varies with consumption needs to be forecasted. e.g., Kong et al. [11] mention that industrial electricity consumption patterns are more regular than residential customers. Ryu [16] achieved a prediction accuracy for industrial loads with a MAPE of about 8.85%. Less accurate predictions were obtained in [7] for residential loads by means of a Kalman filter estimator. Mocanu et al. [14] presented different deep learning approaches, whereas the implementation of a Factored Conditional Restricted Bolzman Machine (FCRBM) outperformed several Machine Learning (ML) algorithms. Comparable results were achieved by Marino et al. [12] using a Long Short-Term Memory (LSTM) artificial neural network as well as by Shi [19] for household load forecasting.

3   The RLS Approach

3.1   Increasing Grid Capacity

In case of failure of a single network component (e.g. a power line or transformer unit) most grids system guarantee availability. A part of the capacity of a grid is reserved for that case, i.e. the reserved part of the grid can take over parts of the non-functional part (after isolating the failure). Usually it is called (N − 1) security of supply. As a result that percentage of the grid capacity is not used in normal operation. However, the large majority of days go without grid failure.

The RLS approach proposes to allocate the normally unused grid capacity that is reserved for (N − 1) security of supply. Conditional loads are perfect loads for using this grid reserve. In normal cases they used the former unused reserve. But in the case of a failure they can be turned off and the reserve can be used for the purpose it was originally reserved: ensuring security of supply for the *un*conditional loads. Conditional loads are by definition loads for which (1) (N − 1) security of supply is not essential (i.e. they can be turned off), (2) that are highly price-sensitive, and (3) that are flexible and may thus be used for price optimization purposes via load management. Conditional loads comprise, e.g.. the charging of stationary batteries for internal consumption or power heat coupling for fuel substitution. Unconditional loads are all other loads.

Figure 1 illustrates a simplified version of the used and unused (reserved) grid capacity. The component's maximal capacity is split in two capacity bands of 50% each. The lower band shown in blue is the capacity used in normal operation. Usually a grid is operated only in lower band. The upper band shown in grey represents the unused capacity reserved for security. We call this band the *N − 1 band* because it ensures N − 1 security to another branch. Notice that in real scenario the width of the N −1 band is determined by the component with smallest capacity. The day-ahead prediction of unconditional loads (dark blue) and the scheduling of conditional loads (green) is the subject of the rest of this paper.

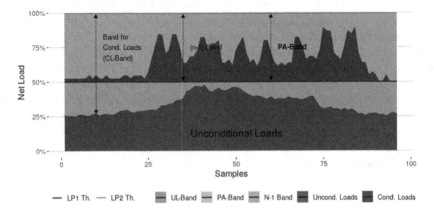

Fig. 1. Example of load schedule split in un- (blue) and conditional loads (green) [5]. (Color figure online)

In the RLS approach, the market-based *incentive for customers* to register some of their flexibilities as conditional loads is a significantly lower grid fee compared to unconditional loads. Incentives for distribution system operators (DSO) to implement the RLS approach comprise (1.) the possibility to postpone or avoid large scale physical grid expansion, (2.) achieving a small increase in income by additionally charged grid costs for the N − 1 band, and (3.) higher transparency within the grid due to customer side load measurement and DSO-registered load schedules.

3.2   Scheduling Conditional Loads

Usually customers schedule their (conditional) loads in order to minimize energy prizes. The minimization is subject to (1.) the customers' chosen prizing models, (2.) to their operating constraints (dependent on the flexible loads in use), and (3.) to given grid constraints. The risk of load synchronization is avoided with a day-ahead scheduling. The goal of the day-ahead scheduling of conditional loads is to find an overall schedule for all customers which keeps the grid in its capacity limits. Since regulations require that grid control and provision of energy supply must be operated by separate legal entities, the management software is split in two independent subsystems: the *Grid Manager (GM)* is operated by the DSO and monitors grid constraints; the *Energy Manager (EM)* implements the customer perspective and schedules for each customer its conditional loads independently. An iterative optimization heuristics implements the interaction of GM and EM in order to ensure grid and customer constraints. Each iteration comprises two steps:

1. *Local Optimization:* The EM calculates a conditional load schedule for a participating customer, which (if given) respects the grid constraints prescribed by step 2. It submits the schedule to the GM.
2. *Global Optimization:* The GM aggregates the accumulated loads from different customers and checks grid capacity constraints. In case the N-1 band capacity is exceeded, the GM curtails each customer's schedule according to their chosen prizing model and submits to the EM an adapted schedule based on load optimization on the aggregated level; they then can optimize their schedule again (step 1).

Figure 2 summarize the process. It is reiterated until a predefined time-based deadline is reached. Then the final schedules for each customers are fixed and sent to the controllers of each customer's devices.

In step one, initially each customer submits its desired schedule of conditional loads for the next day to the GM, i.e. a time series of the power of each aggregate a for each timestep t. It may be computed by solving a minimization of the daily energy costs subject to operations constraints of conditional loads, such as the energy balance for battery. Figure 3 illustrates constraints which may limit the time of operation of an aggregates: the operation is forbidden in disabled times (C. 1). The duration of each operation of aggregate must be kept

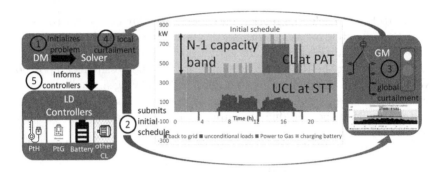

Fig. 2. Overal process of RLS with timely coordination of device manager and grid manager.

between a lower and an upper bound (C. 2–3). So does the duration of each non-operation (C. 4–5 and C. 8–9). The number of activation per day (C. 6–7) can also be constrained. Additionally, some logical constraints (like AND, OR etc.) may link the operation of several aggregates, e.g. aggregate 1 is only allowed to run if and only if aggregate 2 does not run. These kind of operation constraints allows to run an aggregate in its parameters. The scheduler needs to follow these constraints.

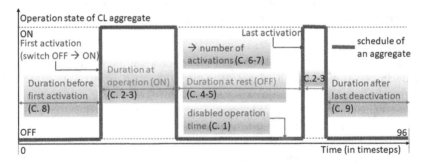

Fig. 3. Possible constraints C. 1 to C. 9 restricting the freedom of operation of each aggregate.

In step two, submitted schedules are aggregated, controlled and adjusted by the GM. If at some time steps with synchronized original loads exceeds the (reserve) capacity, the GM performs an algorithm which computes an allocation respecting them with consideration of the load asked by each customer c and their financial participation of this system of conditional loads. Once completed, a decentralized algorithm allocates loads at customer level for each of the aggregates.

3.3 Day-Ahead Load Forecasting

The second technical aspect of the RLS approach evaluated in this paper is the day-ahead prediction of the unconditional loads of industry customers. The forecasting of unconditional loads serves two purposes: (1.) It provides customers with better control of their energy usage and thereby serves as an additional incentive to participate in the program. (2.) It can be used to further optimize the usage of the currently unused grid capacity in future scenarios.

For the day-ahead load forecasting of customer load profiles, a *model selection approach (MSA)* has been applied. The MSA trains, fits and evaluates 18 different time series forecasting models based on historical load profile data. Each profile comprises 14, 28, 42, 56, 70, 140 and 210 days for every individual customer. The MSA then chooses the best model and training data length separately for each customer, evaluated by the Mean Absolute Percentage Error (MAPE performance metric. The choice is based on the best prediction performance. It is executed in regular time intervals (e.g. every month) to allow for continuous adaptations to changes in the customer load profile characteristics.

The 18 different prediction models used in the MSA are: A *benchmark model*, which reuses the load profile of the previous workday/non-working day as a forecast for the next day. A *similar days model* was included in three variants: SD1 uses the median of a set of historical days of the same weekday (e.g., the five previous Mondays) as a forecast. SD2 uses the median of a set of previous workdays or non-working days, respectively. Finally, SDEns takes the median of the forecasts of SD1 and SD2. 5 types of classical time series prediction models where included: *Exponential Smoothing (ES)*, *Random Walk Drift (RWD)*, *Hold Winters (HW)*, *Auto-Regressive Integrated Moving Average (ARIMA)* and *Generalized Autoregressive Conditional Heteroskedasticity (GARCH)*. Here, all models except HW was applied both directly to the original load profile and to the residual of the load profile after time series decomposition. The latter version is referred to with the add on *Dec* after the model name: *ES Dec, RWD Dec, ARIMA Dec*, and *GARCH Dec*. Three different types of machine learning approaches were used, namely *Support Vector Regression (SVR)*, *Feed Foreward Neural Network (FFNN)*, and deep learning with *Long Short-Term Memory (LSTM)* artificial neural networks.

We included deep learning with LSTM artificial neural networks in the MSA because LSTM have shown improved performance in several works, such as, e.g., [8] compared to simpler approaches. An LSTM neural network is an enhanced version of a Recurrent Neural Network (RNN), which, in contrast to FFNN provides the ability of a better memory of recurrent features in time series. The LSTM's 'memory cell' structure allows the network to bridge very long time lags. An LSTM network quickly learns to distinguish between two or more widely separated occurrences of a particular element in an input sequence [9]. In industrial power time series, distinct changes caused by certain loads or workflows have large time spans in between each other and can be far beyond one day, which is considered as the major sequence length. Therefore, an LSTM network with its possibility bridging long time lags often outperforms simpler methods.

Improved performance was shown particularly for deep hierarchical models of Neural Network (NN), and in cases where additional context information - such as production schedules or weather information - was provided. For our sample data, we used a LSTM network structure with two hidden layers and 128 memory cells each, and a *tanh* activation function to models list. With a learning rate of 0.003 we set an early stopping condition of 25 epoches to shorten the training sequence. The implementation of the LSTM network is build on the Keras library [4] and is abbreviated in the list of methods with *NN LSTM K* and *NN LSTM K CI* for an extended use with additional context information (CI).

4   Scheduling Verification

In order to test the scheduling approach for conditional loads, we provoke a grid congestion in a scenario based on real data of six pilot customers A, B, C, E, F and G and one ad-hoc customer X. For the verification we assumed some settings which we expect for the year 2035, because then an reasonable amount of conditional load might exist.

4.1   Energy Costs for the Verification

For all customers the loads are scheduled in order to minimize the energy costs. Costs of substituted fossil fuels and costs of electricity - via the actual power and the actual electricity price - are considered. The actual electricity is the net electricity supplied by the grid, so the sum of unconditional resp. conditional loads, corrected by the own photovoltaic (PV) production.

The electricity price is made of a spot price predicted for each hour of year 2035 plus other fees OF (grid, taxes and duties). For unconditional loads in the so-called Standard Tariff (STT), OF is assumed to grow up to $OF_{STT} = 10$ ct/kWh until 2035. For conditional loads we introduce a special tariff of electricity (noted as PAT). It differs in the costs for the middle voltage grid. The grid is already there and therefore it doesn't have extra fees; but the additional hardware needs to be funded. Also the taxes and fees are reduced because we assume that the government want to promote renewable, i.e. conditional loads. Energy spot price and use of transmission grid are unchanged. We assume for PAT an $OF_{PAT} = 4.8$ ct/kWh. An incentive is also considered in the reduced power component of the grid fee. We note $OF_{res} = 0$ ct/kWh the other fees when the electricity is fed back to the grid. Table 1 compares both tariffs.

Table 1. Electricity tariffs.

Tariff for	Component	STT 2035	PAT 2035
Energy (ct/kWh)	Spot (mean value) (A)	6.1	6.1
	Middle voltage grid (B)	3.0	0.3
	Transmission grid (C)	2.0	2.0
	Taxes and fees (D)	5.0	2.5
Energy (ct/kWh)	OF = total − A = B + C + D	10.0	4.8
Power (EUR/kW/a)	Grid	100.0	10.0

For the calculation of the costs at an time step t not only the conditional loads but also the unconditional loads and the electricity production of solar panels are needed to be considered. When both unconditional and conditional loads consume at the same time, the price is the quantity-weighted average of STT and PAT. This formulation ensures that the residuals R_t as difference between unconditional load $P_{UL,t}$ and PV production PV_t is taken into account in the scheduling of the conditional loads. Given an initial situation characterized by PV_t, $P_{UCL,t}$ and $P_{CL,t}$, any incremental increase in $P_{CL,t}$ will have lower OF in time steps with excess of photo-voltaic production than in time step with a supply from the grid. Therefore unconditional loads and PV production can not be completely left out of the target function. Figure 4 illustrates all possible cases of OF as a function of the external factors R_t on x-axis and of the conditional loads $P_{CL,t}$ on y-axis. In the lower left half of the space ($R_t + P_{CL,t} < 0$), the power is fed back to the grid and OF has the lowest value: $OF = OF_{res} = 0$. The value of OF increases successively in the three other colored areas considered in clockwise direction (blue arrow). The second area in the upper left side corresponds to import of electricity for only conditional loads at PAT and $OF = OF_{PAT} = 4.8$. In this area, $R_t < 0$ and ($R_t + P_{CL,t} > 0$). In the next area in the upper right side, electricity is imported both as CL at PAT and UCL at STT and OF takes an intermediate value between $OF_{STT} = 10.0$ and $OF_{PAT} = 4.8$. In the last area at lower right sight, electricity is imported only for UCL at STT with the highest value of OF at $OF_{STT} = 10.0$.

The effective OF for a new (positive) conditional load is not always exactly OF_{PAT}, but only in the case when it runs alone, $R_t = 0$ (arrow 2). The effective OF is the lower value 0 when it substitutes power that would else have been fed back to the grid, $R_t < 0$ (arrow 1). In analogy, a negative conditional load (discharging a battery) can in best case be counted with the OF of an unconditional load it replaces ($R_t > 0$, arrow 3). These variations in OF values (up to $OF_{STT} - OF_{res} = 10 ct/kWh$) are significant compared to daily fluctuations between minimal and maximal spot price (5.2 ct/kWh in 2035).

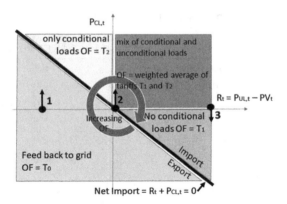

Fig. 4. Four cases of values of other fees (OF) for electricity tariff. (Color figure online)

4.2 Settings of the Experiment

Present energy usage of customers A, B, C, E, F and G are classified in Table 2 in thermal or non-thermal usage. A new customer X, representative for several new customers like freight shipping companies with new Power-To-Gas units up to 7 MW but without significant own compulsory loads nor PV, is added to simulate a congestion of the band of conditional loads. No other grid related carrier (district heating) or off grid (heating oil, pellets, etc.) is considered here.

Table 2. Energy carrier and usage of customers (lines A-C blue, E-G new).

Energy form usage	Electric cooling	Electric process	Gas process	Gas heat
A	Yes	Yes	–	Yes
B	–	Yes	–	Yes
C	Yes	Yes	Yes	Yes
E	–	Yes	Yes	Yes
F	–	Yes	Yes	Yes
G	–	Yes	–	Yes
X	–	–	–	–

For the verification we assume additional units of Table 3 are to be added. Photo-voltaic panels will be installed on their roofs. "Other" aggregates of C (a food industry) are hereby cooling machines using the frozen food as thermal storage and substituting electricity of a cooling machine of a later time step of the same day. In customer F, a reallocation of 1300 kW out of 1500 kW PtH unconditional loads of ovens into the system of conditional load is considered. There were initially two ovens of 500 kW and two ovens of 250 kW, each of them will continue to have a connection of 50 kW as unconditional load to keep the machines safe in case of an interruption of conditional loads. In customer G, three heat pumps are considered.

Table 3. Assumed new conditional loads and PV (kW) (lines A-C blue, E-G new).

	P-to-Heat	P-to-Gas	Battery	other	PV
A	500	–	–	–	1500
B	–	300	100	–	900
C	–	–	–	2 × 250	1900
E	100	100	–	–	500
F	–	1000	–	2 × (450 + 200)	1000
G	–	–	–	3 × 25	150
X	–	7000	–	–	–

4.3 Initially Submitted Schedules

Figure 5 with power on left y-axis against time on x-axis shows the initial solution (i.e. before control of grid limits) of the load scheduling problem for customers A (top row), B (middle row) and X (bottom row) for the cloudy winter day of January, 11th. Consumption respectively production are displayed separately on the left resp. right graph. Grey bands represent the split in Standard Tariff for compulsory loads in the lower part of positive power and Power Alliance Tariff in the upper part with conditional load. Negative power is fed back to the grid. For customer A, the PV unit (yellow) substitutes part of electricity import from grid (black), and is used to run the power-to-heat unit (blue) to substitute natural gas. The power-to-heat unit will also run with the cheap electricity price of PAT (black, brindled) during afternoon hours with the lowest spot price of the day. The three power-to-gas units (red) of customer X, as well as the power-to-gas unit (blue) and the charging (red) of battery of Customer B will run at the same afternoon hours as customer A due to the spot price. Discharging (green) happens here in morning hours, before charging, either for substituting import from grid (black) or for feed back to grid (purple), with a sufficient battery capacity assumed in this model.

Figure 6 displays the initial schedules of customers C, E, F and G. The cooling units of customer C are modelled like a battery but with the hygiene constraint that charging can only precede discharging, as the storage medium is frozen food. Therefore they run in the morning at a different timestep than A and B. The power-to-heat unit (electroboiler) and power-to-gas unit (electrolyser) of customer E and the power-to-gas unit (electrolyser) of customer F run as conditional loads in the afternoon hours of lowest spot price. The power-to-heat unit of F is configured to run only in moments when the oven were operational in the baseline scenario, so it excludes night and weekends. This unit has the particularity not to represent an additional consumption, but a reallocation of power from the standard tariff to the PA Tariff: when it runs at 450 kW, the total power of unconditional loads is reduced by a same amount of 450 kW. The brindled black and rose color of the lower part of the left graph represents this reduction. The rose load of the ovens in the upper part of the left graph reserved

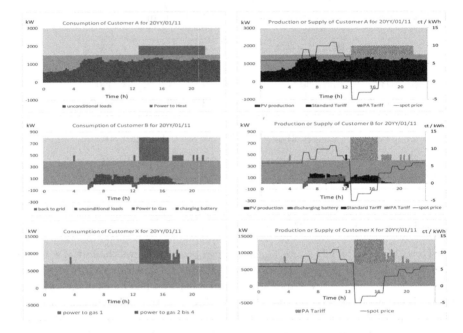

Fig. 5. First schedule solution for cust. A (top), B (mid) and X (bottom) in [5]. (Color figure online)

for conditional loads shows four possible levels of power of 450, 650, 1100 and 1300 kW depending of the number of ovens used. The values of 200 or 400 kW with only small ovens, or of 900 kW with only big ovens are not used.

The heat demand of customer G is calculated from the temperature. Thanks to the thermal inertia of the house and of the heat pumps, the heat pumps should not run exactly as the same hour as the heat demand. Load shift with a duration of up to 24 h should be possible without loss of comfort. However, to increase further the level of comfort, the maximal duration of the load shift is reduced to only 6 h. The balance between heat production and heat demand should be fulfilled in the four periods (midnight to 6 a.m.; 6 a.m. to noon; noon to 6 p.m. and 6 p.m. to midnight) of the day. In that way, the heat pumps have a limited flexibility during the day. They run as conditional load during the of lowest spot price within each of the four periods.

4.4   Curtailment in Case of Excess Load

To demonstrate grid congestion and provoke a curtailment a fictive grid configuration with four customers A, B, C and X in the same branch is assumed. The customers A, B, and C (and also the addition of customers D, E, F) would not lead to a grid congestion, but additionally customer X. Therefore we focus on the three real and one extreme customer.

Each power line (asset) has here a capacity of 12 MW and is not used over 6 MW to provide reserve capacity. In the first asset of the branch, compulsory

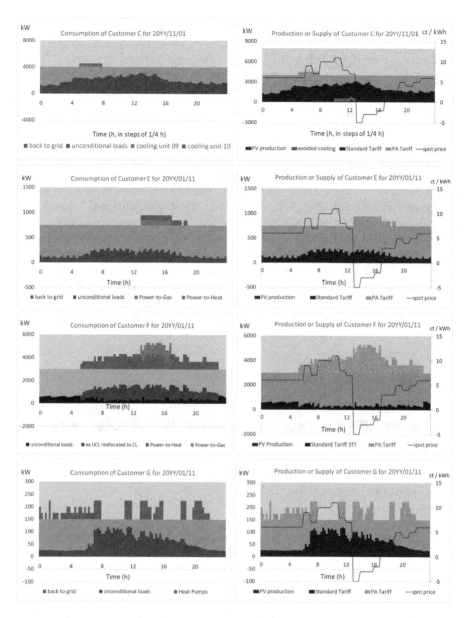

Fig. 6. Initial solution of schedule for customers C (top), E, F (middle) and G (bottom). (Color figure online)

loads reaches today 5.4 MW (no bottleneck). With the new loads, the sum grows to 13.8 MW (bottleneck). Moreover, simultaneous conditional loads can reach 8.4 MW and thus exceed the capacity of 6 MW of the N − 1 band. Within the branch E − X − C − A − B of Fig. 7, the asset E − X is the new highest used asset.

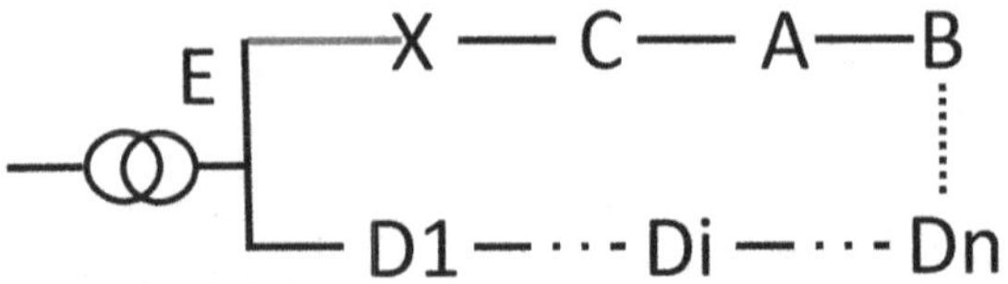

X — C — A—B

E

D1 — ⋯- Di — ⋯- Dn

Fig. 7. Assumed grid with bottleneck E – X between entrance E and customer X.

On Grid Level. GM receives the initial loads of all (four) customers including conditional an unconditional loads. As expected when the lowest electricity spot price is attained between 2 p.m. and 6 p.m., conditional loads from A, B and X get aggregated with 7.9 MW (left graph of Fig. 8). The conditional loads exceed the grid capacity limit of 6 MW of the N – 1 band. To keep the limits, they should be reduced by 1.9 MW. The needed curtailment is controlled by points which customers can buy. The curtailment is done proportionally to the number of points (allowances) of each customer. Customers with more points are less curtailed than customers with less points. The curtailed loads for all customers A, B, C and X are shown in Table 4. In case a customer asked less than its allowance (here C), the remaining non-allocated capacity is redistributed among the other customers to avoid waste of capacity.

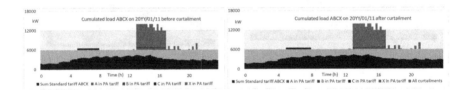

Fig. 8. Accumulated load of Customers A, B, C and X in the first asset of the grid branch: initial (left) and curtailed (right).

On Aggregate Level. After each customer receives from the GM the amount of its curtailment for each time step, it needs to determine the local curtailment on the level of each aggregate. Aggregates can consume energy in predefined stages (e.g. 0%, 25%, 50%, 75%, and 100%). The allocation with least wasted capacity over all aggregates can be solved as a subsum problem. Table 5 shows the local curtailment of time step 53 of customer B. Both units are cut in order to reach the curtailed 303 kW. In a similar way the cases of customer A (with only one unit of power-to-heat) and of customer X (with its four units of power-to-gas) are treated. The schedule of "discharging" is finally adjusted on customers with battery like B to respect the daily energy balance.

Table 4. Curtailment on grid level.

	Points	Submitted (kW)	Accepted (kW)
A	500	500	379.7
B	400	400	303.8
C	500	0	0
X	7000	7000	5316.5
Sum	8400	7900	6000

4.5 Discussion

Within this verification, where grid congestion and curtailment are provoked, two things can be noted: (1.) If the concept of conditional loads is not present, a grid reinforcement would have been needed in the first asset (even with only the new loads of customers A, B and C) because all loads together already exceed the grid limits. (2.) with the concept of conditional loads, customer X and the other customers also exceed the capacity of 6 MW of the N-1 band when the electricty costs (spot prices) are low, and a curtailment needs to be performed. But a grid reinfrocement can be prevented even such a case.

Table 5. Curtailment on aggregate level for customer B.

	Max	Levels	Original (kW)	Final (kW)
P-to-G	300	100	300	204
Charging	100	100	100	99
Sum	400	–	400	303

The RLS approach which make use of N-1 band and curtailments enables finding acceptable schedules valid for both sides. Even the curtailment of the conditional loads satisfies the grid limit without wasting of capacity in the N-1 band. In the aggregated schedule in Fig. 8, the effective use of the N-1 band drops from 26.7 % (left) to only 22.0 % (right, after curtailment) but the system is safe for all stakeholders to be operated.

5 Load Forecasting

5.1 Test Data Set

For evaluating the prediction accuracy of the Model Selection Approach (MSA) we use a data set consisting of 35 historic load profiles. For six of these profiles additional context data - regarding processing volumes and ambient temperature - was available.

The 35 historic load profiles are derived from 26 different customers, including three pilot customers. Here, all customer time series that spanned over more than one year where split into multiple fictitious end nodes of one year length each (operating under the assumption that consumer behavior did not change over the last few years). Since the research focuses on large energy consuming industrial end customers, all customers have a minimum yearly power demand of 200 kWp. After several pre-processing steps ensuring the comparability between all time series (up- or down-sampling to quarter hourly sampling intervals, replacement of missing data points, and time shifts to match summer and winter time and leap years) every end node time series comprises 35040 data points.

In addition to the historic time series data, historic context data could be obtained from the three pilot customers (A), (B) and (C) for the six end nodes A, B1, ..., B4 and C. Customer B provided recordings of processing volumes and ambient temperature. Since goods are delivered only every few days, the sampling rate of processing volumes is significantly lower than the sampling frequency of 1 per 15 min of load demand time series. The ambient temperature is measured hourly.

5.2 Evaluation of Prediction Accuracy

To evaluate the prediction accuracy of the MSA (cf. Subsect. 3.3), we compare the performance of the MSA with the performance of the single involved models in terms of the MAPE accuracy metric. When applying a single model, one fixed model is used to predict the loads of all customers. In contrast, the MSA uses for every customer the best performing model for this particular customer to perform the prediction task.

As a first step, we evaluate the MSA based on historic time series data without considering context information, because context information is available only for 6 out of 35 end nodes. In a second step, we add the available context information for LSTM artificial neural network models. This allows us to compare evaluation results with and without context data for the 6 available end nodes.

Our tests show that, without context data, the MSA performs slightly better on average than the best single model approach, achieving an average MAPE of 20.8%. Additionally, the MSA reduces the variability of accuracy results over end nodes dramatically compared to all single model approaches, thus justifying the increased computational effort of the MSA. The use of context data gives no improvement, but even worsen the prediction accuracy and is thus abandoned.

Evaluation Without Context Data. To do the comparison of the MSA with the "single model approach" based on historic time series data, we train, apply and evaluate all 18 models on all 35 historic load profiles (end nodes) in our test data set. For every end node, we randomly choose 50 days (out of 365 days) as the days to be predicted and evaluated against ground truth. To ensure comparability of the prediction performances among end nodes (which is needed for MSA model selection), the same 50 days are selected from each load profile.

The time intervals used for training lie directly before the day to be predicted. We call these time intervals *sliding windows*, since in the actual application of the day-ahead prediction, the training window is sliding forward in time, one step every day. For the evaluation on historic data, we use seven different Sliding Window Length (SWL) per customer and model, namely 14,28,42,56,70,140 and 210 days. This enables us to not only select the best model for each end node in the MSA, but also to select the best training window length for each end node and model. As a result, we arrive at 50 predictions per combination of end node, model and SWL.

To compare the different models in terms of average prediction accuracy, we calculate for every model the average MAPE over all 50 predicted days, all end nodes and all SWLs per model. On cross validation data, the MSA, achieves an average MAPE of 20.8%. This result beats the best performing single model approach by 7% and is competitive with results in literature in comparable settings [12,19].

While an accuracy improvement of 7% on average compared with the single model approach is not sufficient to justify the significantly higher computational effort of employing the MSA, tests show that the MSA reduces the variability in the accuracy significantly. Figure 9 illustrates results on cross-validation data using box plots. Here, wach colored block corresponds to one prediction model: the first 18 blocks correspond to one of the 18 instanstiations of the "single model approach", and the last block corresponds to the MSA. Every colored block comprises seven box plots, one per SWL. SWLs are ordered by increasing length, models are ordered by increasing complexity. On the y-axes, the boxplots themselves show (for each combination of model and SWL) how the average MAPE over the 50 predicted days varies with the end nodes.

It can be observed that the *model accuracy* in terms of median MAPE does *not* considerably improve by applying the MSA, and this holds for all SWLs. But it can also be observed that the *variability* of average model accuracy decreases dramatically, and it is this fact that justifies the introduction of the MSA with its considerably higher computational effort.

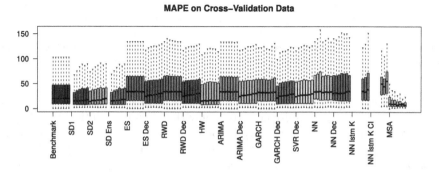

Fig. 9. Variability of the average MAPE of 18 single model approaches and the MSA. (Color figure online)

Figure 10 illustrates this fact in more detail by comparing the MSA with the single model approach for the Similar Days 1 (SD1) model with best sliding window length in terms of a histogram of average accuracy gain, i.e. $avgMAPE(SD1) - avgMAPE(MSA)$. It can be seen that the MSA provides no or little average accuracy gain for the majority of end nodes, but does improve the average prediction accuracy for some of the end nodes dramatically: for 37% of the end nodes, the average MAPE increases by more than 20%, and for one end nodes, it even increases by more than 50%. In other words, when predicting the load profiles of our industry customers day-ahead based only on historic time series, there is no one prediction method that fits all customers. Some customers simply could not be served with a "single model" approach, because the prediction would not be sufficiently accurate for practical purposes. Wrapping the model selection process in the MSA allows us to provide an integrated solution for all customers.

Another observation that can be made from Fig. 9 is that the median of the average MAPE tends to increase (i.e., the average model accuracy tends to decrease) with increasing SWL for the singel model approaches, while the opposite is the case for the MSA. To explain this effect, it is necessary to look into the single model approaches in more detail: Here we observe that the median of the average MSA. increases with increasing SWL in particular for the simple and rigid models SD1 and SD2, as well as for the decomposed time series methods and the machine learning methods. The effect is expected for the rigid models, which take averaged load profiles of nearby weekdays as prediction. Yet, the effect should be mitigated by increased model complexity/flexibility, which is not the case.

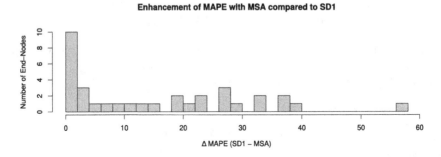

Fig. 10. Histogram of average MAPE increase compared to SD1 model with best sliding window length.

We suspect two reasons for this, which are both linked to the given project requirements: First, the requirement to deploy the intended solution at different hardware for different customers locally forces us to chose a relatively low training iteration rate (and, in case of artificial neural networks, also a relatively small network dimension) in order to save computing time. This negatively impacts more complex models stronger. Second, the requirement to provide customers and DSOs with a out-of-the-box solution that requires no or minimal adjustments per customer forces us to abstain from data specific parametrization of the models. This again impacts more complex models stronger, since higher model flexibility usually requires more data specific parametrization efforts. As a consequence, longer training times do not necessarily increase accuracy, but may even have an adverse effect. It is also consistent with the observation that the simpler models tend to perform better (over all SWLs) than the more complex models.

The MSA as a wrapper function over different models helps to overcome these obstacles by compensating the lack of adaptability, e.g. in terms of model parametrization, with a higher adaptability in terms of selecting the optimal combination of model and SWL for every specific load profile - producing the expected effect that *for the respective best model*, longer SWLs tend to be better than shorter SWLs on average. This underlines the importance of model selection for an integrated out-of-the-box solution for highly variable load profile.

Evaluation with Context Data. Load profiles from industry customers are often highly volatile, e.g., due to individual and variable production processes and schedules. This is also the case for the test data in this project. Highly volatile loads are hard to predict with high accuracy using models that rely solely on the historic time series. In these cases, additional context information that correlates with the load demand, such as production or shipment schedules, can help increase prediction accuracy. Yet, in our tests, an accuracy improvement could not be observed. On the contrary, the average MAPE deteriorated in the single model approach from 68.6% for the LSTM model without context information (NN lstm K) to 87% with context information (NN lstm K CI), resulting in worst average results over all instantiations of the single model approach. The three end nodes with best predictions results with LSTM without context data achieve a competitive average MAPE of around 14%, but results do not improve when context data ist added. In the MSA, both LSTM models are never selected.

One likely reason for the unsatisfactory outcome is the fact that not enough suitable context information was available. Table 6 shows the Pearson's correlation coefficients for ambient temperature (TAmb) and processing volumes (PVol1, PVol2) for the available years 2016 and 2017. Here it can be seen that

Table 6. Correlation of context information with power demand.

Customer	TAmb'16	PVol1'16	PVol2'16	TAmb'17	PVol1'17	PVol2'17
A	−0.0255	NA	NA	0.0068	NA	NA
B1	−0.0485	−0.2847	−0.3304	−0.0427	0.8738	0.7648
B2	−0.0391	−0.3002	−0.3345	−0.0203	0.9654	0.8949
B3	−0.0290	−0.1978	−0.2335	−0.0373	0.7224	0.6336
B4	−0.0555	−0.2722	−0.3287	−0.0006	0.9109	0.7617
C	−0.0269	NA	NA	−0.0731	NA	NA

only the correlation with processing volumes in 2017 exceeds 40%, while correlation with ambient temperature is negligible. Practically, obtaining suitable context information often proves difficult, because customers usually do not record it, or do not record it in a structured and easily accessible way. Another reason may be the fact that, again, more manual parameterisation effort is needed per end node to achieve good LSTM results. Since such efforts are in contrast to the requirement of the project to provide an out-of-the-box prediction solution for all customers, this is not an option. As a consequence, the use of context data was abandoned for the developed MSA.

5.3   Evaluation of Prediction Reliability

The MAPE as a measure of prediction *accuracy* does not provide end-customers and DSOs with a measure of prediction *reliability* (i.e., accuracy *and* precision). Yet, a reliable day-ahead prediction of load demands is pivotal for coustomers and DSOs, since it increases their ability to plan, and decreases financial risk considerably. Prediction intervals as measures of prediction reliability rely on the assumption of normally distributed errors, an assumption that is violated for most of our test data. While it is usually possible to find suitable transformations from historic data for single load profiles manually, automating this process as a part of the RLS software is not a straight forward task. And with the high variability in load profiles it is not sure that the transformation is applicable to each predicted time series. Additionally, they only provide a theoretical range comprising a certain quantity but do not quantify the reliability of the prediction. Hence, we assess the "true" reliability of prediction intervals of every single power value based on 50 predictions for each customer.

Under the assumption of normally distributed prediction errors we defined a prediction interval and determined the number of exceeding power values. The lower part of Fig. 11 shows the historic prediction reliability for our test data: for each of the 35 end nodes the percentage of observations falling in the 80%, 95%, 99% and 99.73% Prediction Interval (PI) is shown in the figure as a blue, green, yellow and grey line plot, respectively. It can be seen that the historic reliability of the 99% and 99.73% PI is greater than 95% for all end nodes. That means, a PI of 99% covers more than 95% of all predictions or the other way round, less than 5% of all predictions exceed the PI. The upper part of Fig. 11 shows the inverse percentage (i.e., the percentage of observations exceeding the upper limits of the respective PIs), together with error bars indicating the PI.

But why is the prediction error not normally distributed and what causes the higher rate of PI exceedances? It is of the nature that a prediction of a non deterministic time series always differs from ground truth. The better a time series can be described in a mathematical function i.e. with a model, the more accurate predictable it is. Time series mostly do not appear with a smoothed curve following a simple mathematical function, but show a behavior that is hard to approximate in a model. In power demand time series, especially in the industrial domain, huge load changes cause features with a high variability that are hard to predict. For estimations and decisions relying on the predictions this

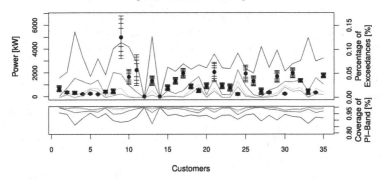

Fig. 11. Historic prediction reliability per end node. (Color figure online)

uncertainty is covered in by the PI. However, when a start or stop of a consumer with a higher power demand than the interval width of a certain point, such as a big machine, deviates from the predicted point of time, it possibly will not be covered by the PI.

While a small change in the (TS) remains as in Fig. 12 (a) within the 3σ PI-band (grey) of the prediction deviation, a large change of the real values (black) will exceed the PI-band. That means, in order to keep a large increase/decrease in the power demand within the gaussian band width of the predicted value (red), either an exact prediction of the point of time of its occurrence or a vast larger interval width is required. An amount of exceedance of the PI gets further enhanced, the smaller the variance of the prediction error of a single point is.

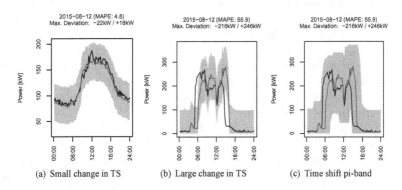

Fig. 12. Coverage limitation of the prediction interval (PI) band. Without considering a possible time shift of the measured values (b) w.r.t. the prediction, the PI-band is easily exceeded. (Color figure online)

A very pragmatic solution is the definition of a high enough maximum constant threshold over the full prediction time span. However, this reduces the flexibility of a time related load assignment and obstructs the grid capacities for flexible loads. But without a widely coverage of large time shifted changes with the PI-band there is an increased risk of a possible grid overload due to the small reliability.

For the definition of a reliable PI-band that also considers a time related uncertainty of the prediction, we enlarged the band in the time axis. A slightly shift of the upper and lower PI-band thresholds by six time steps in both directions on the time axis (1.5 h for a quarter hourly prediction interval) results in a wider and more reliable PI-band. Applying a 3σ quantile for the pi-band, it should cover 99.73% of all predictions theoretically. That allows an average number of real data outliers of 0.27%. With the extended PI-band in time, the number of customers having an average number of PI-band outliers exceeding the threshold of 0.27% could be reduced by approx. 30% from almost every second down to a ratio of 20%. Therewith, it was possible to enhance the reliability substantial.

5.4   Discussion

The high variability of the industry customer load profiles pose a challenge for accurate day-ahead load prediction in an integrated out-of-the-box solution: While relatively simple models such as 'similar days models' produce acceptable accuracy results for the majority of customers, some customer profiles can not be predicted with reasonable accuracy. We mitigate this fact by employing a model selection approach (MSA) as a wrapper function that selects for every customer the best performing model within regularly repeated learning cycles.

We show that the accuracy of the MSA with an average MAPE of 20.8% on cross validation data is comparable with results in the literature in similar settings. It achieves only a small accuracy increase on average when compared to the single model approach, but provides a drastic decrease of MAPE variability, thus increasing the prediction accuracy for some customers massively. This allows us to provide with the MSA an integrated out-of-the-box solution that achieves acceptable prediction accuracy for all customers. The additional use of customer-specific context information showed no improvement and was not included in the final implementation of the MSA.

We also show that the prediction reliability - measured as the true percentage of observations falling in the 3σ prediction interval - is satisfactory with an average of 95%. It serves to assess the practical usefulness of predictions for customers and DSOs as a day-ahead load schedule for unconditional loads within the RLS context. Here, the upper band of the prediction interval determines the margin of unused grid capacity that may be used to further optimize the scheduling of conditional loads.

To save computing effort, not all tested models are included in every learning iteration in the final implementation: A slim version of the MSA is used for regular learning/adaptation cycles that only includes those models that have been selected on cross validation data at least once. Only in every n-the learning/adaptation cycle, all the tested models are included in order to account for possible long term changes in the data.

6   Conclusions

Our enhanced RLS approach aims for a better utilization of the available grid capacity by including the N-1 band that ensures the security of supply. With simulations on the foundation of existing power grids we proved the technical feasibility. A load scheduling process for the grid in combination with a day-ahead prediction of customer specific unconditional loads enables the usage of the N-1 band. Furthermore, a continuous thresholding of the grid limits given by the DSO leading to a curtailment and rearranging of exceeding loads in advance respectively allows for a safely usage of the unused security capacity. Embedded in a real environment we have verified the approach with respect to observing all conditions.

The achievements of the project show a potential for improvements in the analysis of the fairness, efficiency and performance of the curtailment mechanism while keeping the focus on a further decrease of energy costs. With respect to the accuracy and reliability in predicting unconditional loads for the proposed RLS approach we obtained similar levels as the state of the art in the evaluation of the applied MSA.

In contrary, the auxiliary information additionally used for the prediction did not improve the prediction perceptible. Also, the extension of the applied models in the MSA with the promising LSTM network could not improve the accuracy but results in similar error values as most other models. For a further improvement with more complex models an end node specific analysis is necessary that allows a unique parametrization.

The full range of the unused grid capacity also comprises the unused part of the regular grid capacity that is integrated as part of future work. Trying to provide as much capacity as possible for mitigating future grid congestion the applied load shifting approach is to extend from the constant N-1 band to a variable band of the full remaining unused grid capacity. The limit of the full range is given by the upper threshold of the prediction interval band from the day-ahead prediction of unconditional loads.

References

1. Arora, S., Taylor, J.W.: Forecasting electricity smart meter data using conditional kernel density estimation. Omega **59**, 47–59 (2016)
2. Atzeni, I.: Distributed demand-side optimization in the smart grid. Ph.D. thesis, Universitat Politècnica de Catalunya (2014)
3. Bagemihl, J., et al.: A market-based smart grid approach to increasing power grid capacity without physical grid expansion. Comput. Sci. Res. Dev. **33**(1–2), 177–183 (2017). https://doi.org/10.1007/s00450-017-0356-5

4. Chollet, F., et al.: Keras (2015). https://keras.io
5. Christen, R., Layec, V., Wilke, G., Wache, H.: Technical validation of the RLS smart grid approach to increase power grid capacity without physical grid expansion. In: Proceedings of the 8th International Conference on Smart Cities and Green ICT Systems - Volume 1: SMARTGREENS, pp. 123–130. INSTICC, SciTePress (2019). https://doi.org/10.5220/0007717101230130
6. Doostizadeh, M., Ghasemi, H.: A day-ahead electricity pricing model based on smart metering and demand-side management. Energy **46**, 221–230 (2012)
7. Ghofrani, M., Hassanzadeh, M., Etezadi-Amoli, M., Fadali, M.S.: Smart meter based short-term load forecasting for residential customers. In: 2011 North American Power Symposium, pp. 1–5, August 2011. https://doi.org/10.1109/NAPS. 2011.6025124
8. Graves, A., Mohamed, A., Hinton, G.: Speech recognition with deep recurrent neural networks. In: 2013 IEEE International Conference on Acoustics, Speech and Signal Processing, pp. 6645–6649, May 2013. https://doi.org/10.1109/ICASSP.2013. 6638947,zSCC:0003960
9. Hochreiter, S., Schmidhuber, J.: Long short-term memory. Neural Comput. **9**(8), 1735–1780 (1997)
10. Hunziker, C., Schulz, N., Wache, H.: Shaping aggregated load profiles based on optimized local scheduling of home appliances. Comput. Sci. Res. Dev. 61–70 (2017). https://doi.org/10.1007/s00450-017-0347-6
11. Kong, W., Dong, Z.Y., Jia, Y., Hill, D.J., Xu, Y., Zhang, Y.: Short-term residential load forecasting based on LSTM recurrent neural network. IEEE Trans. Smart Grid **10**(1), 841–851 (2017)
12. Marino, D.L., Amarasinghe, K., Manic, M.: Building energy load forecasting using deep neural networks. In: IECON 2016–42nd Annual Conference of the IEEE Industrial Electronics Society, pp. 7046–7051. IEEE (2016)
13. Mirowski, P., Chen, S., Ho, T.K., Yu, C.N.: Demand forecasting in smart grids. Bell Labs Tech. J. **18**(4), 135–158 (2014)
14. Mocanu, E., Nguyen, P.H., Gibescu, M., Kling, W.L.: Deep learning for estimating building energy consumption. Sustain. Energy, Grids Netw. **6**, 91–99 (2016)
15. Mohsenian-Rad, A.H., Leon-Garcia, A.: Optimal residential load control with price prediction in real-time electricity pricing environments. IEEE Trans. Smart Grid **1**, 120–133 (2010)
16. Ryu, S., Noh, J., Kim, H.: Deep neural network based demand side short term load forecasting. Energies **10**(1), 3 (2016)
17. Shaikh, P.H., Bin Mohd Nor, N., Nallagownden, P., Elamvazuthi, I., Ibrahim, T.: A review on optimized control systems for building energy and comfort management of smart sustainable buildings. Renew. Sustain. Energy Rev. **34**, 409–429 (2014)
18. Shariatzadeh, F., Mandal, P., Srivastava, A.K.: Demand response for sustainable energy systems: a review, application and implementation strategy. Renew. Sustain. Energy Rev. **45**, 343–350 (2015)
19. Shi, H., Xu, M., Li, R.: Deep learning for household load forecasting-a novel pooling deep RNN. IEEE Trans. Smart Grid **9**(5), 5271–5280 (2018)
20. Taylor, J.W.: Triple seasonal methods for short-term electricity demand forecasting. Eur. J. Oper. Res. **204**(1), 139–152 (2010)
21. Taylor, J.W., De Menezes, L.M., McSharry, P.E.: A comparison of univariate methods for forecasting electricity demand up to a day ahead. Int. J. Forecast. **22**(1), 1–16 (2006)
22. Taylor, J.W., McSharry, P.E., et al.: Short-term load forecasting methods: an evaluation based on European data. IEEE Trans. Power Syst. **22**(4), 2213–2219 (2007)

23. Thirugnanam, K., Kerk, S.K., Yuen, C., Liu, N., Zhang, M.: Energy management for renewable microgrid in reducing diesel generators usage with multiple types of battery. IEEE Trans. Ind. Electron. **65**, 6772–6786 (2018)
24. Zhao, Z., Lee, W., Shin, Y., Song, K.: An optimal power scheduling method for demand response in home energy management system. IEEE Trans. Smart Grid **4**, 1391–1400 (2013)
25. Zufferey, T., Ulbig, A., Koch, S., Hug, G.: Forecasting of smart meter time series based on neural networks. In: Woon, W.L., Aung, Z., Kramer, O., Madnick, S. (eds.) DARE 2016. LNCS (LNAI), vol. 10097, pp. 10–21. Springer, Cham (2017). https://doi.org/10.1007/978-3-319-50947-1_2

Vehicle Technology and Intelligent Transport Systems

Neurocognitive–Inspired Approach for Visual Perception in Autonomous Driving

Alice Plebe[1]([✉])[iD] and Mauro Da Lio[2][iD]

[1] Department of Information Engineering and Computer Science,
University of Trento, Trento, Italy
alice.plebe@unitn.it
[2] Department of Industrial Engineering, University of Trento, Trento, Italy
mauro.dalio@unitn.it

Abstract. Since the last decades, deep neural models have been pushing forward the frontiers of artificial intelligence. Applications that in the recent past were considered no more than utopian dreams, now appear to be feasible. The best example is autonomous driving. Despite the growing research aimed at implementing autonomous driving, no artificial intelligence can claim to have reached or closely approached the driving performance of humans, yet. While the early forms of artificial neural networks were aimed at simulating and understanding human cognition, contemporary deep neural networks are totally indifferent to cognitive studies, they are designed with pure engineering goals in mind. Several scholars, we included, argue that it urges to reconnect artificial modeling with an updated knowledge of how complex tasks are realized by the human mind and brain. In this paper, we will first try to distill concepts within neuroscience and cognitive science relevant for the driving behavior. Then, we will identify possible algorithmic counterparts of such concepts, and finally build an artificial neural model exploiting these components for the visual perception task of an autonomous vehicle. More specifically, we will point to four neurocognitive theories: the simulation theory of cognition; the Convergence–divergence Zones hypothesis; the transformational abstraction hypothesis; the free–energy predictive theory. Our proposed model tries to combine a number of existing algorithms that most closely resonate with the assumptions of these four neurocognitive theories.

Keywords: Deep learning · Autonomous driving ·
Convergence–divergence Zones · Variational autoencoder · Free energy

1 Introduction

Artificial neural networks are responsible for the current fast resurgence of Artificial Intelligence, after several decades of slow and unsatisfactory advances, and are now at the very heart of many technology developments [7,23,54]. They have proved to be the best available approach for a variety of different problem

© Springer Nature Switzerland AG 2021
M. Helfert et al. (Eds.): SMARTGREENS 2019/VEHITS 2019, CCIS 1217, pp. 113–134, 2021.
https://doi.org/10.1007/978-3-030-68028-2_6

domains [31,40], and the design of autonomous vehicles is definitely one of the research areas to have amply benefited from this technology [2,39,55].

Actually, this success was totally unexpected because the technology development has been very little, with only relative minor improvements from a field that was stagnating at the beginning of the century. Artificial neural network found their way during the '80s, with the *Parallel Distributed Processing* (PDP) project [53]. The success of PDP was largely due to an efficient learning rule, known as *backpropagation*, which adapts the connections between units through input/output samples of the desired function. Geoffrey Hinton was one of the protagonists of the PDP project [26], who contributed specifically to the introduction of the backpropagation [52]. However, after a couple of decades, artificial neural networks exhausted their potential. Once again, Hinton gave them a new boost [27], by refining the old backpropagation method. With just relatively small advances in the learning algorithm, he made possible to train networks with more layers of neurons than before, called *deep learning* models ever since.

The most distinctive difference between the PDP generation of neural networks and current deep learning is in their scope. For the PDP project the scope was clearly indicated in the title of its main book [53]: "Explorations in the Microstructure of Cognition". On the contrary, the majority of modelers in deep learning is totally indifferent to cognition, and their scope is purely on engineering goals. In a first phase, adopting mathematical solutions alien to mental processes has been certainly a key of the success of deep learning. However, several scholar are now arguing that the segregation between the deep learning and the neurocognitive communities would be dangerous and detrimental for a further progress [22,41,60].

We agree to this position, and we deem that looking at neurocognitive facts would be especially valuable in applications such as driving. The reason is that driving is the sort of behavior for which neurocognition has changed its paradigm since the PDP era. Cognitive science of the '80s was dominated by the modular perspective [11], which divided sharply intellectual tasks such as language and categorization, from low level tasks such as vision and motor control. Since the beginning of this century cognitive science has witnessed a radical methodological revolution, often summarized as "4E cognition" [44]: embodied, embedded, enactive, and extended. One of the assumptions of 4E cognition that is most relevant to our case is that perception and action are constitutively intertwined, and not only they are contiguous to intellectual behavior, sensorimotor simulations are the basic founding of cognition as a whole. This structure of cognition is the source of the amazing human abilities of learning new forms of sensorimotor control, like driving. We believe this is a reason why none of the current available implementations of autonomous vehicles can claim to be nowhere close to the driving performance of a human being.

Such considerations lead us to reflect if it is possible to take inspiration from the mechanisms whereby the brain learns to perform such complex sensorimotor behaviors. With this paper, we propose to exploit the current most established neurocognitive theories as inspiration for designing more brain–like neural network models. In the next section we will review a number of selected neurocognitive theories relevant to our purposes. In Sect. 3 we will show that it is possible to find neural algorithms that best approximate the assumptions of such theories, and we will describe how our model put together all these algorithms. Finally, in Sect. 4 we will present the results of applying our neural model to a simulated driving environment.

This paper results from one of the research projects carried out as part of the European project Dreams4Cars, where we are developing an artificial driving agent inspired by the neurocognition of human driving, for further details refer to [46,47].

2   The Neurocognitive Point of View

Humans are able to learn an impressive range of different and very complex sensorimotor controls schemes – from playing tennis to salsa dancing. The remarkable aspect is that no motor skill is innate to humans, not even the most basic ones, like walking or grasping objects [19]. All motor controls are, in fact, *learned* through lifetime. The process of human sensorimotor learning involves sophisticated computational mechanisms, like gathering of task-relevant sensory information, selection of strategies, and predictive control [64].

The ability to drive is just one of the many highly specialized human sensorimotor behaviors. The brain learns to solve the driving task with the same kind of strategy adopted for every sort of motor planning that requires continuous and complex perceptual feedback. We deem that the sophisticated control system the human brain develops when learning to drive by commanding the ordinary car interfaces – steering wheel and pedals – may reveal precious insights on how to implement a robust autonomous driving system.

It should be noted that the human sensorimotor learning is still far from being fully understood, as there are several competing theories about which components of the brain are engaged during learning. However, a huge body of research in neuroscience and cognitive science has been produced in the past decades, which allows us to grasp some useful principles for designing an artificial driving agent capable of learning the sensorimotor controls necessary to drive.

2.1   The Simulation Theory

A well-established theory is the one proposed by Jeannerod and Hesslow, the so-called *simulation theory of cognition*, which proposes that thinking is essentially simulated interaction with the environment [24,30]. In the view of Hesslow, simulation is a general principle of cognition, explicated in at least three different components: perception, actions and anticipation. Perception can be simulated by internal activation of sensory cortex in a way that resembles its normal activation during perception of external stimuli. Simulation of actions can be performed when activating motor structures, as during a normal behavior, but suppressing its actual execution. Moreover, Hesslow argues that actions can trigger perceptual simulation of their most probable consequences.

The most simple case of simulation is mental imagery, especially in visual modality. This is the case, for example, when a person tries to picture an object or a situation. During this phenomenon, the primary visual cortex (V1) is activated with a simplified representation of the object of interest, but the visual stimulus is not actually perceived [35,43].

2.2 Convergence-Divergence Zones

Any neural theory claiming to explain the simulation process is required in the first place to simultaneously:

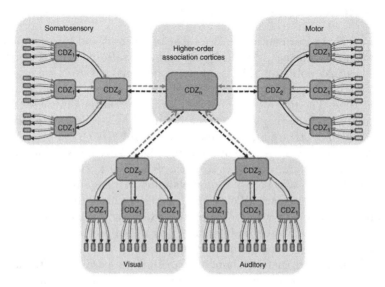

Fig. 1. Schematic representation of Damasio's CDZ framework [42, Fig. 1]. Neuron ensembles in early sensorimotor cortices of different modalities send converging forward projections (red arrows) to higher-order association cortices, which, in turn, project back divergently (black arrows) to the early cortical sites, via several intermediate steps. (Color figure online)

1. identify the neural mechanisms able to extract information relevant to the action, from a large amount of sensory data;
2. recall related concepts from memory during imagery.

A prominent proposal in this direction is the formulation of the convergence-divergence zones (CDZs) [42]. They derive from an earlier model [8] which highlighted the "convergent" aspect of certain neuron ensembles, located downstream from primary sensory and motor cortices. Such convergent structure consists in the projection of neural signals on multiple cortical regions in a many-to-one fashion. The primary purpose of convergence is to record, by means of synaptic plasticity, which patterns of features – coded as knowledge fragments in the early cortices – occur in relation with a specific concept. Such records are built through experience, by interacting with objects. On the other hand, a requirement for convergence zones (already found in the first proposal of Damasio) is the ability to reciprocate feedforward projections with feedback projections in a one-to-many fashion. This feature is now made explicit in the CDZ formulation.

The convergent flow is dominant during perceptual recognition, while the divergent flow dominates imagery. Damasio postulates that switching between one of the two modes may depend on time-locking. If activation in a CDZ is synchronous with activity in separate feeding cortical sites, than perceptual recognition takes place. Conversely, imagery is driven by synchronization with backprojecting cortical areas.

Convergent-divergent connectivity patterns can be identified for specific sensory modalities, but also in higher order association cortices, as shown in the hierarchical structure in Fig. 1. It should be stressed that CDZs are rather different from a conventional processing hierarchy, where processed patterns are transferred from earlier to higher cortical areas. In CDZs, part of the knowledge about perceptual objects is retained in the synaptic connections of the convergent-divergent ensemble. This allows to reinstate an approximation of the original multi-site pattern of a recalled object or scene.

2.3   Transformational Abstraction

One of the major challenge in cognitive science is explaining the mental mechanisms by which we build conceptual abstractions. The conceptual space is the mental scaffolding the brain gradually learns through experience, as internal representation of the world [56]. As highlighted by [45] CDZs are a valid systemic candidate for how the formation of concepts takes place at brain level. However, the idea of CDZ is just sketched and cannot provide a detailed mechanism for conceptual abstractions.

According to the historical empiricist tradition, conceptual abstractions is derived from experience, mostly perceptual experience. This direction fits perfectly with the approach implemented by artificial neural networks. Still, a difficulty with acquiring even moderately abstract categories lies in the mutually inconsistent manifestations of the characteristic features of a category, in each of its real exemplars. In visual data, for example, object translation, rotation, motion in depth, deformation and lighting changes can drastically entangle features of objects belonging to the same category. Conversely, the perceptual appearance of two unrelated objects, like a close flying insect and a far distant vulture, can be very similar. A suggested solution to this difficult issue is in the transformational abstraction [5,22] performed by a hierarchy of cortical operations, as in the ventral visual cortex [49]. The essence of transformational abstraction, from a mathematical point of view, should lie in the combination of two operations: linear convolutional filtering and nonlinear downsampling. Operations of this sort have been identified in the primary visual cortex [17,28,29], and the staking of this process in hierarchy is well recognized in the primate ventral visual path [10,12,61].

Note that transformational abstraction is one of the possible interpretation of the convergent zone in the CDZ theory, even if it lacks a specification of the divergent counterpart, which can lead from the abstraction of a concept to its use during mental imagination. Transformational abstraction is conceived as a general road to conceptual abstractions, nevertheless, it is highly relevant in the case of driving. As will be discussed in Sect. 3.4, during the drive, the sensori-motor control relies heavily on a small number of known concepts, abstracted from visual space.

2.4   The Predictive Theory

The reason why cognition is mainly explicated as simulation, according to Hess-low or Jeannerod, is because the brain through simulation can achieve the most precious information of an organism: a prediction of the state of affairs in the environment in the future. The need of predicting, and how it mold the entire cognition, has become the core of a different, but related, theory which has gained large attention in the last decade, made popular under the term "Bayesian brain", "predictive brain", or "free-energy principle for the brain". The leading figure of this theory is Karl Friston [13,14]. According to Friston the behavior of the brain – and of an organism as a whole – can be conceived as minimization of free-energy, a quantity that can be expressed in several ways depending on the kind of behavior and the brain systems involved.

Free-energy is a concept originated in thermodynamics, as a measure of the amount of work that can be extracted from a system. What is borrowed by Fris-ton is not the thermodynamic meaning of the free-energy, but its mathematical form only. This mathematical form is derived from the framework of variational Bayesian methods in statistical physics, where the intractable problem of infer-ring the posterior distribution over a random variable is approximated by a different, and more tractable, auxiliary distribution [63]. We will see in Sect. 3.3 how the same probabilistic framework will be used in the derivation of a deep neural model. The basic form of the free-energy under the variational Bayesian framework is borrowed by Friston for abstract entities of cognitive value. For example, this is his free-energy formulation in the case of perception [15, p.427]:

$$F_P = \Delta_{\mathrm{KL}}\Big(\breve{p}(c|z)\|p(c|x,a)\Big) - \log p(x|a) \tag{1}$$

where x is the sensorial input of the organism, c is the collection of the environmental causes producing x, a are actions that act on the environment to change sensory samples, and z are inner representations of the brain. The quantity $\breve{p}(c|z)$ is the encoding in the brain of the estimate of causes of sensorial stimuli. The quantity $p(c|x,a)$ is the conditional probability of sensorial input conditioned by the actual environmental causes c. The discrepancy between the estimated probability and the actual probability is given by the Kullback-Leibler divergence Δ_{KL}. The minimization of F_P in Eq. (1) optimizes z. In the case of action the free energy formulation by Friston becomes [15, p.428]:

$$F_A = \Delta_{KL}\Big(\breve{p}(c)\|p(c)\Big) - \log p(x|c, a) \tag{2}$$

and optimizes a.

All formalization in Eqs. (1) and (2) are just abstract, without details on how the variables can be explicitate, and how the equations can be solved.

3   Artificial Mental Imagery

Over the years the CDZ hypothesis has found support of a large body of neurocognitive and neurophysiological evidence. However, it is a purely descriptive model and does not address the crucial issue of how the same neural assembly, which builds connections by experiences in the convergent direction, can computationally work in the divergent direction as well. At the moment, there are no computational models that faithfully replicate the behavior of CDZs, however, we found a number of independent notions, introduced in the field of artificial intelligence for different purposes, which bear significant similarities with the CDZ scheme. Here we will first introduce these notions independently, then we will describe our model which, by taking together these pieces, builds up a neural architecture inspired by CDZs.

3.1   Convergence–Divergence in the Autoencoder

In the realm of artificial neural networks, the computational idea that most closely resonate with CDZ is the *autoencoder*. It is an idea that has been around for a long time [25], but more recently has been the cornerstone of the evolution from shallow to deep neural architectures [27,62]. The crucial issue of training neural architectures with multiple internal layers was initially solved associating each internal layer with a Restricted Boltzmann Machine [27], so that they can be pre-trained individually in unsupervised manner. The adoption of autoencoders overcame the training cost of Boltzmann Machines: each internal layer is trained in unsupervised manner, as an ordinary fully connected layer. The key idea is to use the same input tensor as target of the output, and therefore to train the layer to optimize the reconstruction of the input [38]. In the first layer the inputs are that of the entire neural model, and for all subsequent layers the hidden units' outputs of the previous layer are now used as input. The overall result is a regularization of the entire model similar to the one obtained with Boltzmann Machine [1], or even a better one [62].

Soon after, the refinement of algorithms for initialization [18] and optimization [33] of weights, made any type of unsupervised pre-training method superfluous. However, autoencoders continue to play their basic role for capturing compact information from high dimensional data, and their use within this scope has been expanded. In this kind of models the task to be solved by the network is to simulate as output the same data fed as input. The advantage is that while learning to reconstruct the input information, the model develops a very compact internal representation of the input space. The basic structure of an autoencoder, independently of the details of the various implementations, is composed of two neural models:

$$f_\Theta : \mathcal{Z} \to \mathcal{X} \tag{3}$$

$$g_\Phi : \mathcal{X} \to \mathcal{Z} \tag{4}$$

The first one is the *decoder*, often called the *generative* model, which reconstructs high dimensional data $x \in \mathcal{X}$ taking as input low dimensional compact representations $z \in \mathcal{Z}$. The model is fully fixed by the set of parameters Θ. The model in Eq. (4) is called *encoder* and computes the compact representations $z \in \mathcal{Z}$ of a high dimensional input $x \in \mathcal{X}$. This model is determined by its set of parameters Φ. In the autoencoder's architecture the parameters Θ and Φ are learned by minimizing the error between input samples x_i and the outputs $f(g(x_i))$. There is a clear correspondence between the encoder and the convergence zone in the CDZ neurocognitive concept, and similarity between the decoder and the divergence zone.

3.2 Convergence–Divergence as Convolution–Deconvolution

Let us now dive into detail of how convergence can be achieved inside autoencoders. The most common way is stacking feed-forward layers with decreasing number of units. There is, however, an interesting alternative closely related to the transformational abstraction hypothesis described in Sect. 2.3: the *deep convolutional neural networks* (DCNNs). One again, this architecture was introduced by Hinton [36], by adapting an old model of the PDP era, called *Neocognitron* [16], into a deep architecture. The DCNN implements the hierarchy of convolutional filtering alternated with nonlinear downsampling, and it is considered the essence of transformational abstraction. The old Neocognitron of Fukushima alternates layers of *S-cell* type units with *C-cell* type units, which naming are evocative of the classification in simple and complex cells by Hubel and Wiesel [28,29]. The S-units act as convolution kernels, while the C-units downsample the images resulting from the convolution, by spatial averaging. The crucial difference from conventional convolutions in image processing [4,51] is that now the kernels are learned. The DCNNs of Hinton and co-workers are "deep" versions of Neocognitron, using several layers of convolutions, each with a large number of different kernels, typically tens of millions.

DCNNs do not only resonate with the theoretical proposal of transformational abstraction, there is a growing evidence of striking analogies between patterns in DCNN models and patterns of voxels in the brain visual system. One of the first attempt to relate results of deep learning with the visual system was based on the idea of adding at a given level of an artificial network model a layer predicting in the space of voxel response, and to train this level on sets of images and corresponding fMRI responses [20]. Using this method, a DCNN model [6] was compared with fMRI data [21]. Initially, subjects were presented with 1750 natural images and voxel responses in progressively downstream areas – from V1 up to LO (*Lateral Occipital Complex*) – were recorded. The same images were presented to the model, and the output of the convolutional layers were trained – with a simple linear predictor – to predict voxel patterns. As a result, DCNN model responses were predictive of the voxels in the visual cortex above chance, with good prediction accuracy especially in the lower visual areas. This first unexpected result was immediately followed by several other studies, using variants of the same technique [9,32,58], finding reasonable agreement between features computed by DCNN models and fMRI data.

DCNNs are therefore a highly biologically plausible implementation for the convergence zone in CDZs, at least in the case of visual information. Convolutional neural models do not include a divergence counterpart, typically the outputs of the last convolutions are fed into ordinary feed forward layers to produce a classification. This gap was filled with the *deconvolutional* neural networks [65–67], performing alternation of unpooling and linear filtering. Each step of these two operations reconstruct a higher level of spatial dimension of the data, up to the full high dimension of the original image. Note that the nonlinear downsampling done in DCNNs is a non invertible operation, therefore it is not possible to reconstruct faithfully the upsized representations by unpooling. Zeiler and co-workers circumvented the problem by saving additional information during the poolings done in the convolution stages for exploitation during unpooling, but this strategy is clearly non biological plausible. However, the stacked combination of deconvolution and unpooling is the current neural implementation more close to the idea of divergence zone of CDZs.

3.3   Variational Bayes and Autoencoders

In the last few years there has been renewed interest in the area of Bayesian probabilistic inference in learning models of high dimensional data. The Bayesian framework, variational inference in particular, has found a fertile ground in combination with neural models. Two concurrent and unrelated developments [34,48] have made this theoretical advance possible, connecting autoencoders and variational inference. This new approach became quickly popular under the term *variational autoencoder*, and a variety of neural models including such idea have been proposed over the years, see [59] for a review.

We will show in a while that the adoption of variational inference lead to a mathematical formulation impressively similar to the concept of free energy in Friston. This close analogy went unnoticed by all the main developers of variational autoencoder. It is not so surprising because mainstream deep learning is driven by engineering goals without any interest in connections with cognition. Within the philosophy of the Dreams4Car project, illustrated in the Introduction Sect. 1, the strong connection between a well established cognitive theory and a computational solution, greatly argues in favor of adopting such solution.

The variational inference framework takes up the issue of approximating the probability distribution $p(\boldsymbol{x})$ of a high dimensional random variable $\boldsymbol{x} \in \mathcal{X}$, such as the visual scene that hits the retina of a living agent, or the camera of an artificial agent. A candidate in approximating the real unknown probability distribution is a neural network such as that in Eq. (3). The neural network by itself is deterministic, but its output distribution can be easily computed as follows:

$$p_\Theta(x|z) = \mathcal{N}\left(x|f_\Theta(z), \sigma^2 I\right) \tag{5}$$

where $\mathcal{N}(x|\mu, \sigma)$ is the Gaussian function in x, with mean μ and standard deviation σ. Using Eq. (5) it is now possible to express $p_\Theta(x)$, which is the desired approximation of $p(x)$:

$$p_\Theta(x) = \int p_\Theta(x, z)dz = \int p_\Theta(x|z)p(z)dz \tag{6}$$

It is immediate to recognize that the kind of neural network performing the function $f_\Theta(\cdot)$ is exactly the decoder part in the autoencoder, corresponding to the divergence zone in the CDZ neurocognitive concept. In the case when $\mathcal{X}$ is the domain of images, $f_\Theta(\cdot)$ comprises a first layer that rearranges the low-dimension variable x in a two dimensional geometry, followed by a stack of deconvolutions, up to the final geometry of the x images.

In Eq. (6) there is clearly no clue on what the distribution $p(z)$ might be, but the idea behind variational autoencoder is to introduce an auxiliary distribution q from which to sample z, and it is made by an additional neural network. Ideally this model should provide the posterior probability $p_\Theta(z|x)$, which is unknown. This second neural model is of the kind in Eq. (4), and as done in Eq. (5), its probability distribution is:

$$q_\Phi(z|x) = \mathcal{N}\left(z|g_\Phi(x), \sigma^2 I\right) \tag{7}$$

The model $f_\Theta(\cdot)$ functions as decoder, and $g_\Phi(\cdot)$ is the encoder part in the autoencoder, projecting the high dimensional variable x into the low dimensional space $\mathcal{Z}$. It continues to play the role of the convergence zone in the CDZ idea.

The measure of how well $p_\Theta(x)$ approximates $p(x)$ for a set of $x_i \in \mathcal{D}$ sampled in a dataset $\mathcal{D}$ is given by the log-likelihood:

$$\ell(\Theta|\mathcal{D}) = \sum_{x_i \in \mathcal{D}} \log \int p_\Theta(x_i|z)p(z)dz \tag{8}$$

This equation cannot be solved because of the unknown $p(z)$, and here comes the help of the auxiliary probability $q_\Phi(z|x)$. Each term of the summation in Eq. (8) can be rewritten as follows:

$$\ell(\Theta|x) = \log \int p_\Theta(x, z)dz$$
$$= \log \int \frac{p_\Theta(x, z)q_\Phi(z|x)}{q_\Phi(z|x)}dz$$
$$= \log \mathbb{E}_{z \sim q_\Phi(z|x)}\left[\frac{p_\Theta(x, z)}{q_\Phi(z|x)}\right] \tag{9}$$

where in the last passage we used the expectation operator $\mathbb{E}[\cdot]$. Being the log function concave, we can now apply Jensen's inequality:

$$\ell(\Theta, \Phi|\boldsymbol{x}) = \log \mathbb{E}_{z \sim q_\Phi(z|x)} \left[\frac{p_\Theta(\boldsymbol{x}, \boldsymbol{z})}{q_\Phi(\boldsymbol{z}|\boldsymbol{x})} \right]$$

$$\geq \mathbb{E}_{z \sim q_\Phi(z|x)} \left[\log p_\Theta(\boldsymbol{x}, \boldsymbol{z}) \right] - \mathbb{E}_{z \sim q_\Phi(z|x)} \left[\log q_\Phi(\boldsymbol{z}|\boldsymbol{x}) \right] \qquad (10)$$

Since the derivation in (10) is smaller or at least equal to $\ell(\Theta|\boldsymbol{x})$, it is called the *variational lower bound*, or *evidence lower bound* (ELBO). Note that now in $\ell(\Theta, \Phi|\boldsymbol{x})$ there is also the dependency from the parameters Φ of the second neural network defined in (7).

It is possible to rearrange further $\ell(\Theta, \Phi|\boldsymbol{x})$ in order to have $p_\Theta(\boldsymbol{x}|\boldsymbol{z})$ instead of $p_\Theta(\boldsymbol{x}, \boldsymbol{z})$ in Eq. (10), moreover, we can now introduce the *loss function* $\mathcal{L}(\Theta, \Phi|\boldsymbol{x})$ as the value to be minimized in order to maximize ELBO:

$$\mathcal{L}(\Theta, \Phi|\boldsymbol{x}) = -\ell(\Theta, \Phi|\boldsymbol{x})$$

$$= -\int q_\Phi(\boldsymbol{z}|\boldsymbol{x}) \log \frac{p_\Theta(\boldsymbol{x}, \boldsymbol{z})}{q_\Phi(\boldsymbol{z}|\boldsymbol{x})} d\boldsymbol{z}$$

$$= -\int q_\Phi(\boldsymbol{z}|\boldsymbol{x}) \log \frac{p_\Theta(\boldsymbol{x}|\boldsymbol{z}) p_\Theta(\boldsymbol{z})}{q_\Phi(\boldsymbol{z}|\boldsymbol{x})} d\boldsymbol{z}$$

$$= \Delta_{\mathrm{KL}}\big(q_\Phi(\boldsymbol{z}|\boldsymbol{x}) \| p_\Theta(\boldsymbol{z})\big) - \mathbb{E}_{z \sim q_\Phi(z|x)} \left[\log p_\Theta(\boldsymbol{x}|\boldsymbol{z}) \right] \qquad (11)$$

where the last step uses the Kullback-Leibler divergence Δ_{KL}. By comparing Eq. (11) with the formulation of the free-energy principle by Friston (1) their coincidence appears immediately.

The formulation in (11) seems to be still intractable, because contains the term $p_\Theta(\boldsymbol{z})$, but there is a simple analytical formulation of the Kullback-Leibler divergence in the Gaussian case (see appendix B in [34]):

$$\Delta_{\mathrm{KL}}\left(q_\Phi(\boldsymbol{z}|\boldsymbol{x}) \| p(\boldsymbol{z})\right) = -\frac{1}{2} \sum_{i=1}^{Z} \left(1 + \log\left(\sigma_i^2\right)\right) - \mu_j^2 - \sigma_i^2) \qquad (12)$$

where μ_i and σ_i are the i-th components of the mean and variance of $\boldsymbol{z}$ given by $q_\Phi(\boldsymbol{z}|\boldsymbol{x})$.

3.4   A CDZ-like Model for Driving

We have reviewed several components that match quite closely the relevant neurocognitive theories identified in Sect. 2. The model we propose attempts to weave together these components, finalized at visual perception in autonomous driving agents. There is a range of different levels at which we can design such models. Similarly to the hierarchical arrangement of CDZs in the brain, as described by Meyer and Damasio (again, Fig. 1), variational autoencoder models embedding convolution and deconvolution operations can be placed at a level depending on the relevant representational space.

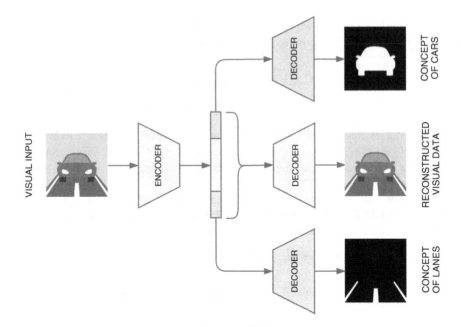

Fig. 2. The architecture of our model. The variational autoencoder has an encoder compressing an RGB image to a compact high-feature representation. Then 3 decoders map different part of the latent space back to separated output spaces: the decoder on the center outputs into the same visual space of the input; the other two decoders project into conceptual space, producing binary images containing, respectively, `car` entities and `lane marking` entities.

In the context of Dreams4Cars, we considered as a fundamental level of model design the processes that start from the raw image data and converge up to a low-dimension representation of visual features. Consequently, the divergent path outputs in the same format as the input image. At an intermediate level, the convergent processing path leads to representations that are no more in terms of visual features, rather in terms of concepts. As discussed in Sect. 2.3, our brain naturally projects sensorial information, especially visual, into conceptual space, where the local perceptual features are pruned, and neural activation code the nature of entities present in the environment that produced the stimuli. In the driving context it is not necessary to infer categories for every entity present in the scene, it is useful to project in conceptual space only the objects relevant to the driving task. In the model here presented we choose to consider the two main concepts of `cars` and `lane markings`.

As depicted in Fig. 2, the model is composed by one shared encoder and three independent decoders:

$$f_{\Theta_V} : \mathcal{Z} \to \mathcal{X} \tag{13}$$

$$f_{\Theta_C} : \mathcal{Z}_C \to \mathcal{X}_C \tag{14}$$

$$f_{\Theta_L} : \mathcal{Z}_L \to \mathcal{X}_L \tag{15}$$

$$g_\Phi : \mathcal{X} \to \mathcal{Z} \tag{16}$$

where the subscript V denotes visual space, the subscripts C and L are for the cars and lane markings concepts, respectively. For a vector in the latent space it holds:

$$z \in \mathcal{Z} = [z_C, \tilde{z}, z_L] \tag{17}$$

$$\mathcal{Z} = \mathbb{R}^{N_V}$$

$$\mathcal{Z}_C = \mathbb{R}^{N_C}$$

$$\mathcal{Z}_L = \mathbb{R}^{N_L}$$

$$N_C = N_L < \frac{N_V}{2} \tag{18}$$

In the first expression $z_{\{C,\mathcal{L}\}}$ are the two segments inside the latent vector z representing the car and lane concepts, respectively. The segment in between, $\tilde{z}$, encodes generic visual features, and the entire latent vector z represents in visual space. The rationale for this choice is that in mental imagery there is no clear cut distinction between low–level features and semantic features, the entire scene is mentally reproduced, but including the awareness of the salient concepts present in the scene. There is no reason for using different latent space size for the concepts car and lane, as expressed in Eq. (18), where the inequality reflects the partitioning of z according to Eq. (17).

Note that the idea of partitioning the entire latent vector into meaningful components is not new. In the context of processing human heads the vector has been forced to encode separate representations for viewpoints, lighting conditions, shape variations [37]. In [68] the latent vector is partitioned in one segment for the semantic content and a second segment for the position of the object. Our approach is different. While we keep disjointed the two segments for the car and lane concepts, we full overlap these two representations within the entire visual space. This way, we adhere entirely to the CDZ principle, and try to achieve the full scene by divergence, but at the same time including awareness for the car and lane concepts.

By calling $\Theta = [\Theta_V, \Theta_C, \Theta_L]$ the vector of all parameters in the three decoders, the loss functions of the model is derived from the basic Eq. (11). At each iteration t a random batch $\mathcal{B} \subset \mathcal{D}$ is presented, and the following loss is computed:

$$\mathcal{L}(\Theta, \Phi | \mathcal{B}) = \left(1 - (1 - k_0)\kappa^t\right) \sum_x^{\mathcal{B}} \Delta_{\mathrm{KL}}\big(q_\Phi(z|x) \| p_{\Theta_{\mathrm{V}}}(z)\big)$$

$$- \sum_x^{\mathcal{B}} \lambda_{\mathrm{V}} \mathbb{E}_{z \sim q_\Phi(z|x)} \left[\log p_{\Theta_{\mathrm{V}}}(x|z)\right]$$

$$- \sum_x^{\mathcal{B}} \lambda_{\mathrm{C}} \mathbb{E}_{z_{\mathrm{C}} \sim \Pi_{\mathrm{C}}(q_\Phi(z|x))} \left[\log \widetilde{p}_{\Theta_{\mathrm{C}}}(x|z_{\mathrm{C}})\right]$$

$$- \sum_x^{\mathcal{B}} \lambda_{\mathrm{L}} \mathbb{E}_{z_{\mathrm{L}} \sim \Pi_{\mathrm{L}}(q_\Phi(z|x))} \left[\log \widetilde{p}_{\Theta_{\mathrm{L}}}(x|z_{\mathrm{L}})\right] \qquad (19)$$

Few observations are due for the differences between this equation and the basic loss equation (11). First of all, there is a delay in including the contribution of the Kullback-Leibler divergence, because initially the encoder is unlikely to provide any meaningful probability distribution $q_\Phi(z|x)$. There is a cost factor for the Kullback-Leibler component, set initially at a small value k_0 and gradually increased up to 1.0, with time constant κ. This strategy was first introduced in the context of variational autoencoders for language modeling [3].

All the components next to the Kullback-Leibler divergence are errors in the reconstruction of the imagined scene or the imagined concepts, and their relative contributions are weighted by the parameters $\lambda_{\{\mathrm{V,C,L}\}}$. Their purpose is mainly to normalize the range of the errors, which is quite different from visual to conceptual spaces. For this reason, typically $\lambda_{\mathrm{V}} \neq \lambda_{\mathrm{C}} = \lambda_{\mathrm{L}}$.

The second component of the loss in Eq. (19) computes the error in visual space, using the entire latent vector z, and corresponds precisely to the second component in the basic loss (11). The last two components compute the error in the conceptual space, and are slightly different. Only the relevant portion of the latent vector z is used, by the projection operators $\Pi_{\{\mathrm{C,L}\}}$, where the subscripts C and L are for the car and lane concepts, as usual. In addition, a variant of the standard cross entropy is used, with the symbols $\widetilde{p}_{\Theta_{\{\mathrm{C,L}\}}}$, in order to account for the large unbalance between the number of pixel belonging to a concept, and all the other pixels, typical of ordinary driving scenes. For each concept, we precompute a coefficient to be applied to the true value class:

$$P = \left(\frac{1}{NM} \sum_i^N \sum_j^M y_{i,j}\right)^{\frac{1}{k}} \qquad (20)$$

where N is the number of pixels in an image, M is the number of images in the training dataset, and P is the ratio of true value pixels over all the pixels in the dataset. The parameter k is used to smooth the effect of weighting by the probability of ground truth, a value evaluated empirically as valid is 4. This strategy has been first introduced in the context of medical image processing [57].

4   Results

We present here a selection of results achieved with an instance of the model described in the previous section. This architecture is described by the parameters shown in Table 1. In our experiments for training and testing the presented model, we adopted the SYNTHIA dataset [50], a large collection of synthetic images representing various urban scenarios. The dataset is realized using the game engine Unity, and it is composed of ∼100k frames of driving sequences recorded from a simulated camera on the windshield of the ego car. We found this dataset to be well suited for our experiment because, despite being generated in 3D computer graphics, it offers a wide variety of illumination and weather conditions, resulting occasionally in very adverse driving conditions. Each driving sequence is replicated on a set of different environment conditions which includes seasons, weather and time of the day. Figure 3 gives an example of the variety of data coming from the same frame of a driving sequence. Moreover the urban environment is very diverse as well, ranging from driving on freeways, through tunnels, congestion, "NewYork-like" city and "European" town – as they describe. Overall, this dataset appears to be a nice challenge for our variational autoencoder.

Fig. 3. Samples from the SYNTHIA dataset. All images show the same frame of a driving sequence, but under different environmental and lighting conditions. The two left columns show variations of sunny environments, while the two right columns depict settings with low illumination and adverse weather conditions.

Figure 4 shows the results of our artificial CDZ model for a set of driving sequences. The images produced by the model are processed to better show at the same time the results on conceptual space and visual space. The colored overlays highlight the concepts computed by the network, the cyan regions are the output of the **car** divergent path, and the yellow overlays are the output of the **lane markers** divergent path. These results nicely show how the projection of the sensorial input (original frames) into conceptual representation is very

City driving sequence   Freeway driving sequence
Input frame   Model output   Input frame   Model output

Fig. 4. Results of our model for two driving sequence of the SYNTHIA dataset: city centre and freeway driving, each in sunny environments (top) and adverse conditions (bottom). In the table, odd columns show the input frames, even columns show the outputs of our neural network. In the output images, the background is the result of the visual-space decoder, the output of the `car` conceptual-space decoder is highlighted in cyan, in pink the output of the `lane markings` conceptual-space decoder.

Table 1. Parameters of the architecture used to produce the final results. Note that the size of the latent space is 128, of which 16 neurons represent the `cars` concept and other 16 neurons represent the `lane markings` concept.

Encoder	Convolution	$7 \times 7 \times 16$
	Convolution	$7 \times 7 \times 32$
	Convolution	$5 \times 5 \times 32$
	Convolution	$5 \times 5 \times 32$
	Dense	2048
	Dense	512
Latent		128 $[16, 96, 16]$
Decoders	Dense	2048
	Dense	4096
	Deconvolution	$5 \times 5 \times 32$
	Deconvolution	$5 \times 5 \times 32$
	Deconvolution	$7 \times 7 \times 16$
	Deconvolution	$7 \times 7 \times 3$

effective in identifying and preserving the sensible features of `cars` and `lane markings`, despite the large variations in lighting and environmental conditions.

Table 2 display the IoU *(Intersection over Unit)* scores obtained by the network over the SYNTHIA dataset. The table shows how the task of recognizing the "car concept" generally ends up in better scores, with respect to the "lane marking concept". An explanation of why the latter task is more difficult can be the very low ratio of pixel belonging to the class of lane markings, over the entire image size. However, the performance of the model are satisfying, exhibiting the best accuracy in the driving sequences on highways, and in the sunniest lighting conditions (spring and summer sequences).

To demonstrate the generative capabilities of our model, we verified the result of interpolating two latent space representations. The images on the left and right of Fig. 5 are the two input images, while in the middle there are the images generated from the interpolation of the compact latent spaces of the inputs. Even in the case of very different input images, the interpolation generates novel and plausible scenarios, proving the robustness of the learned latent representation.

Lastly, we would like to stress again that the purpose of our network is not mere segmentation of visual input. The segmentation task is to be considered as a support task, used to enforce the network to learn a more robust latent space representation, which now is explicitly taking into consideration two of the concepts that are fundamental to the driving tasks.

Table 2. IoU scores over the SYNTHIA dataset, grouped into the 5 different driving sequences of the dataset (table on top) and into 9 different environmental and lighting conditions (bottom). The results are given for the two "concepts" of cars and lane markings, and their joint mean.

	all	Highway 1	NewYork 1	European	NewYork 2	Highway 2
Car	0.8566	0.9245	0.9084	0.9037	0.9123	**0.9251**
Lane	0.6627	**0.8161**	0.6900	0.7522	0.6709	0.7493
mIoU	0.7597	**0.8703**	0.7992	0.8280	0.7916	0.8373

	dawn	fall	fog	night	rain	spring	summer	sunset	winter
Car	0.8896	0.8852	0.8872	0.9009	0.9002	0.9201	**0.9264**	0.8978	0.9101
Lane	0.6399	0.7319	0.6509	0.6897	0.7096	**0.7696**	0.7532	0.7247	0.7502
mIoU	0.7648	0.8086	0.7691	0.7953	0.8049	**0.8449**	0.8398	0.8113	0.8302

Fig. 5. Two examples of interpolation between latent space representations. For each sequence, images on the top left and bottom right are the inputs, the other images are obtained by interpolating the two latent spaces of the input images.

5   Conclusions

We presented a neural model for visual perception in the context of autonomous driving, grounded in a number of concepts from neuroscience and cognitive science. The main guiding principle is the CDZs proposed by Meyer and Damasio that in our context represent the neural correlate of mental imagery as simulation, following Jeannerod and Hesslow. CDZs find their best artificial cousin in the neural autoencoder architecture. For the choice of how to realize the convergence zone in the encoder, the guiding cognitive theory is that of transformational abstraction, suggesting the adoption of convolutional networks. One more theoretical contribution, the free-energy principle of Friston, further suggests to refine the autoencoder architecture as variational autoencoder. Based on these premises, our model aims at gaining an internal low–level representation of two spaces: the visual one and the conceptual one. The latter is limited to the two most crucial concepts during driving: `cars` and `lane markings`. We succeeded in achieving an internal representation as compact as with 128 units only, of which 16 units are enough to recognize the `car` concepts in any location of the visual space, and similarly for the `lane` concept. Our future plans involve the finalization of the higher level model of the architecture which computes motor commands from the conceptual representation of the environment presented in this work.

Acknowledgements. This work was developed inside the EU Horizon 2020 Dreams4Cars Research and Innovation Action project, supported by the European Commission under Grant 731593. The Authors want also to thank the Deep Learning Lab at the ProM Facility in Rovereto (TN) for supporting this research with computational resources funded by Fondazione CARITRO.

References

1. Bengio, Y.: Learning deep architectures for AI. Found. Trends Mach. Learn. **2**, 1–127 (2009)
2. Bojarski, M., et al.: Explaining how a deep neural network trained with end-to-end learning steers a car. CoRR abs/1704.07911 (2017)
3. Bowman, S.R., Vilnis, L., Vinyals, O., Dai, A.M., Jozefowicz, R., Bengio, S.: Generating sentences from a continuous space. CoRR abs/1511.06349 (2015)
4. Bracewell, R.: Fourier Analysis and Imaging. Springer, Heidelberg (2003). https:// doi.org/10.1007/978-1-4419-8963-5
5. Buckner, C.: Empiricism without magic: transformational abstraction in deep convolutional neural networks. Synthese **195**, 5339–5372 (2018)
6. Chatfield, K., Simonyan, K., Vedaldi, A., Zisserman, A.: Return of the devil in the details: delving deep into convolutional nets. CoRR abs/1405.3531 (2014)
7. Chui, M., et al.: Notes from the AI frontier: insights from hundreds of use cases. Technical report, April, McKinsey Global Institute (2018)
8. Damasio, A.: Time-locked multiregional retroactivation: a systems-level proposal for the neural substrates of recall and recognition. Cognition **33**, 25–62 (1989)
9. Eickenberg, M., Gramfort, A., Varoquaux, G., Thirion, B.: Seeing it all: convolutional network layers map the function of the human visual system. NeuroImage **152**, 184–194 (2017)
10. Felleman, D.J., Van Essen, D.C.: Distributed hierarchical processing in the primate cerebral cortex. Cerebr. Cortex **1**, 1–47 (1991)
11. Fodor, J.: Modularity of Mind: and Essay on Faculty Psychology. MIT Press, Cambridge (1983)
12. Freedman, D.J., Riesenhuber, M., Poggio, T., Miller, E.K.: Categorical representation of visual stimuli in the primate prefrontal cortex. Science **291**, 312–316 (2001)
13. Friston, K.: The free-energy principle: a unified brain theory? Nat. Rev. Neurosci. **11**, 127–138 (2010)

14. Friston, K., Fitzgerald, T., Rigoli, F., Schwartenbeck, P., Pezzulo, G.: Active inference: a process theory. Neural Comput. **29**, 1–49 (2017)
15. Friston, K., Stephan, K.E.: Free-energy and the brain. Synthese **159**, 417–458 (2007)
16. Fukushima, K.: Neocognitron: a self-organizing neural network model for a mechanism of pattern recognition unaffected by shift in position. Biol. Cybern. **36**, 193–202 (1980)
17. Gilbert, C.D., Wiesel, T.N.: Morphology and intracortical projections of functionally characterised neurones in the cat visual cortex. Nature **280**, 120–125 (1979)
18. Glorot, X., Bengio, Y.: Understanding the difficulty of training deep feedforward neural networks. In: International Conference on Artificial Intelligence and Statistics, pp. 249–256 (2010)
19. Grillner, S., Wallén, P.: Innate versus learned movements - a false dichotomy. Progress Brain Res. **143**, 1–12 (2004)
20. Güçlü, U., van Gerven, M.A.J.: Unsupervised feature learning improves prediction of human brain activity in response to natural images. PLoS Comput. Biol. **10**, 1–16 (2014)
21. Güçlü, U., van Gerven, M.A.J.: Deep neural networks reveal a gradient in the complexity of neural representations across the ventral stream. J. Neurosci. **35**, 10005–10014 (2015)
22. Hassabis, D., Kumaran, D., Summerfield, C., Botvinick, M.: Neuroscience-inspired artificial intelligence. Neuron **95**, 245–258 (2017)
23. Hazelwood, K., et al.: Applied machine learning at Facebook: a datacenter infrastructure perspective. In: IEEE International Symposium on High Performance Computer Architecture (HPCA), pp. 620–629 (2018)
24. Hesslow, G.: The current status of the simulation theory of cognition. Brain **1428**, 71–79 (2012)
25. Hinton, G., Zemel, R.S.: Autoencoders, minimum description length and Helmholtz free energy. In: Advances in Neural Information Processing Systems, pp. 3–10 (1994)
26. Hinton, G.E., McClelland, J.L., Rumelhart, D.E.: Distributed representations. In: Rumelhart and McClelland [53], pp. 77–109
27. Hinton, G.E., Salakhutdinov, R.R.: Reducing the dimensionality of data with neural networks. Science **28**, 504–507 (2006)
28. Hubel, D., Wiesel, T.: Receptive fields, binocular interaction, and functional architecture in the cat's visual cortex. J. Physiol. **160**, 106–154 (1962)
29. Hubel, D., Wiesel, T.: Receptive fields and functional architecture of mokey striate cortex. J. Physiol. **195**, 215–243 (1968)
30. Jeannerod, M.: Neural simulation of action: a unifying mechanism for motor cognition. NeuroImage **14**, S103–S109 (2001)
31. Jones, W., Alasoo, K., Fishman, D., Parts, L.: Computational biology: deep learning. Emerg. Top. Life Sci. **1**, 136–161 (2017)
32. Khan, S., Tripp, B.P.: One model to learn them all. CoRR abs/1706.05137 (2017)
33. Kingma, D.P., Ba, J.: Adam: a method for stochastic optimization. In: Proceedings of International Conference on Learning Representations (2014)
34. Kingma, D.P., Welling, M.: Auto-encoding variational bayes. In: Proceedings of International Conference on Learning Representations (2014)
35. Kosslyn, S.M.: Image and Brain: the Resolution of the Imagery Debate. MIT Press, Cambridge (1994)

36. Krizhevsky, A., Sutskever, I., Hinton, G.E.: ImageNet classification with deep convolutional neural networks. In: Advances in Neural Information Processing Systems, pp. 1090–1098 (2012)
37. Kulkarni, T.D., Whitney, W.F., Kohli, P., Tenenbaum, J.B.: Deep convolutional inverse graphics network. In: Advances in Neural Information Processing Systems, pp. 2539–2547 (2015)
38. Larochelle, H., Bengio, Y., Louradour, J., Lamblin, P.: Exploring strategies for training deep neural networks. J. Mach. Learn. Res. **1**, 1–40 (2009)
39. Li, J., Cheng, H., Guo, H., Qiu, S.: Survey on artificial intelligence for vehicles. Autom. Innov. **1**, 2–14 (2018)
40. Liu, W., Wang, Z., Liu, X., Zeng, N., Liu, Y., Alsaadi, F.E.: A survey of deep neural network architectures and their applications. Neurocomputing **234**, 11–26 (2017)
41. Marblestone, A.H., Wayne, G., Kording, K.P.: Toward an integration of deep learning and neuroscience. Front. Comput. Neurosci. **10** (2016). Article 94
42. Meyer, K., Damasio, A.: Convergence and divergence in a neural architecture for recognition and memory. Trends Neurosci. **32**, 376–382 (2009)
43. Moulton, S.T., Kosslyn, S.M.: Imagining predictions: mental imagery as mental emulation. Philos. Trans. Roy. Soc. B **364**, 1273–1280 (2009)
44. Newen, A., Bruin, L.D., Gallagher, S. (eds.): The Oxford Handbook of 4E Cognition. Oxford University Press, Oxford (2018)
45. Olier, J.S., Barakova, E., Regazzoni, C., Rauterberg, M.: Re-framing the characteristics of concepts and their relation to learning and cognition in artificial agents. Cogn. Syst. Res. **44**, 50–68 (2017)
46. Plebe, A., Da Lio, M., Bortoluzzi, D.: On reliable neural network sensorimotor control in autonomous vehicles. IEEE Trans. Intell. Transp. Syst. **21**, 711–722 (2019)
47. Plebe, A., Donà, R., Rosati Papini, G.P., Da Lio, M.: Mental imagery for intelligent vehicles. In: Proceedings of the 5th International Conference on Vehicle Technology and Intelligent Transport Systems, pp. 43–51. INSTICC, SciTePress (2019)
48. Rezende, D.J., Mohamed, S., Wierstra, D.: Stochastic backpropagation and approximate inference in deep generative models. In: Xing, E.P., Jebara, T. (eds.) Proceedings of Machine Learning Research, pp. 1278–1286 (2014)
49. Rolls, E., Deco, G.: Computational Neuroscience of Vision. Oxford University Press, Oxford (2002)
50. Ros, G., Vazquez, L.S.J.M.D., Lopez, A.M.: The SYNTHIA dataset: a large collection of synthetic images for semantic segmentation of urban scenes. In: Proceedings of IEEE International Conference on Computer Vision and Pattern Recognition, pp. 3234–3243 (2016)
51. Rosenfeld, A., Kak, A.C.: Digital Picture Processing, 2nd edn. Academic Press, New York (1982)
52. Rumelhart, D.E., Durbin, R., Golden, R., Chauvin, Y.: Backpropagation: The basic theory. In: Chauvin, Y., Rumelhart, D.E. (eds.) Backpropagation: Theory, Architectures and Applications, pp. 1–34. Lawrence Erlbaum Associates, Mahwah (1995)
53. Rumelhart, D.E., McClelland, J.L. (eds.): Parallel Distributed Processing: Explorations in the Microstructure of Cognition. MIT Press, Cambridge (1986)
54. Schmidhuber, J.: Deep learning in neural networks: an overview. Neural Netw. **61**, 85–117 (2015)
55. Schwarting, W., Alonso-Mora, J., Rus, D.: Planning and decision-making for autonomous vehicles. Ann. Rev. Control Robot. Auton. Syst. **1**, 8.1–8.24 (2018)

56. Seger, C.A., Miller, E.K.: Category learning in the brain. Ann. Rev. Neurosci. **33**, 203–219 (2010)
57. Sudre, C.H., Li, W., Vercauteren, T., Ourselin, S., Cardoso, M.J.: Generalised dice overlap as a deep learning loss function for highly unbalanced segmentations. In: Cardoso, J., et al. (eds.) Deep Learning in Medical Image Analysis and Multimodal Learning for Clinical Decision Support, pp. 240–248 (2017)
58. Tripp, B.P.: Similarities and differences between stimulus tuning in the inferotemporal visual cortex and convolutional networks. In: International Joint Conference on Neural Networks, pp. 3551–3560 (2017)
59. Tschannen, M., Lucic, M., Bachem, O.: Recent advances in autoencoder-based representation learning. In: NIPS Workshop on Bayesian Deep Learning (2018)
60. Ullman, S.: Using neuroscience to develop artificial intelligence. Science **363**, 692–693 (2019)
61. Van Essen, D.C.: Organization of visual areas in macaque and human cerebral cortex. In: Chalupa, L., Werner, J. (eds.) The Visual Neurosciences. MIT Press, Cambridge (2003)
62. Vincent, P., Larochelle, H., Lajoie, I., Bengio, Y., Manzagol, P.A.: Stacked denoising autoencoders: learning useful representations in a deep network with a local denoising criterion. J. Mach. Learn. Res. **11**, 3371–3408 (2010)
63. Šmídl, V., Quinn, A.: The Variational Bayes Method in Signal Processing. Springer, Heidelberg (2005). https://doi.org/10.1007/3-540-28820-1
64. Wolpert, D.M., Diedrichsen, J., Flanagan, R.: Principles of sensorimotor learning. Nat. Rev. Neurosci. **12**, 739–751 (2011)
65. Zeiler, M.D., Fergus, R.: Visualizing and understanding convolutional networks. In: Fleet, D., Pajdla, T., Schiele, B., Tuytelaars, T. (eds.) ECCV 2014. LNCS, vol. 8689, pp. 818–833. Springer, Cham (2014). https://doi.org/10.1007/978-3-319-10590-1_53
66. Zeiler, M.D., Krishnan, D., Taylor, G.W., Fergus, R.: Deconvolutional networks. In: Proceedings of IEEE International Conference on Computer Vision and Pattern Recognition, pp. 7–15 (2010)
67. Zeiler, M.D., Taylor, G.W., Fergus, R.: Adaptive deconvolutional networks for mid and high level feature learning. In: International Conference on Computer Vision, pp. 6–14 (2011)
68. Zhao, J., Mathieu, M., Goroshin, R., LeCun, Y.: Stacked what-where autoencoders. In: International Conference on Learning Representations, pp. 1–12 (2016)

Dynamic Vehicle Routing Under Uncertain Energy Consumption and Energy Gain Opportunities

Giorgos Polychronis$^{(\boxtimes)}$ and Spyros Lalis

Department of Electrical and Computer Engineering,
University of Thessaly, Volos, Greece
{gpolychronis,lalis}@uth.gr

Abstract. The amount of energy that needs to be spent by a vehicle to travel between different locations, and the amount of energy that can be regained at certain locations, may not always be known in advance with certainty. In this case, the path that needs to be followed by the vehicle in order to visit some points of interest without exhausting its energy reserves, has to be determined in a dynamic way, via an online algorithm. To this end, we propose a heuristic which takes dynamic routing decisions based on the actually remaining energy of the vehicle and the estimated energy costs/gains of different path options. We evaluate the algorithm via simulations, showing that it always achieves better results than the statically optimal path-planning algorithm and close to optimal results as long as the energy storage capacity of the vehicle is not marginally sufficient to travel between locations where the vehicle can gain some energy. In addition, we investigate different variants of the algorithm that trade-off the achieved coverage for less runtime complexity.

Keywords: Traveling Salesman Problem · Vehicle Routing Problem · Uncertainty · Dynamic route planning

1 Introduction

The Vehicle Routing Problem (VRP), which is an extension of the Traveling Salesman Problem (TSP), consists in finding a travel path/plan to be followed by a vehicle in order to visit a set of target locations. While the VRP has been traditionally studied for vehicles that are driven/controlled by a human, this problem becomes even more important in the context of unmanned vehicles (UVs), which will play a major role in a wide range of next-generation applications. For instance, aerial drones are already employed in agriculture and surveillance. A typical scenario is for a UV to visit specific locations or scan an entire area by passing through specific waypoints in order to take measurements or to detect objects/phenomena of interest. To take an example, a drone can be used to scan a crop field in order to detect spots that are infected with pests. Similarly, in search and rescue missions, a drone scan an area to find a missing

© Springer Nature Switzerland AG 2021
M. Helfert et al. (Eds.): SMARTGREENS 2019/VEHITS 2019, CCIS 1217, pp. 135–155, 2021.
https://doi.org/10.1007/978-3-030-68028-2_7

person. It is clearly desirable for UVs to perform such missions in an efficient way. In particular, they should not have to return all the way back to the home base in order to refuel or to recharge/change their batteries as this may lead to significant delays.

The VRP has been studied in several variants and for different types of constraints regarding the paths that can be followed by the vehicle, the locations to be visited, or the time window where certain locations have to be visited. Also, in some formulations, the vehicle is assumed to have finite fuel/energy reserves or serving capacity, which can be replenished by visiting special (depot) nodes. In this article, we investigate a different variant of the VRP, where there is some *uncertainty* regarding both the energy consumption of the vehicle during travel and the opportunities for the vehicle to regain some energy en route. Due to this uncertainty, a plan that is computed in an offline manner may turn out to be infeasible during the mission, in which case the vehicle will deplete its energy reserves without having visited all locations of interest. A more dynamic approach is required, allowing routing decisions to be taken and modified at runtime, based on the situation that is actually experienced during the mission.

The work presented here is a continuation of [28], where the problem was defined and a first heuristic was proposed for it. The main contributions are: (i) we present an extended version of the MaxBudget heuristic [28], which includes some optimizations that increase the robustness of the proposed paths against the uncertainty of energy consumption and energy gains; (ii) we evaluate the proposed heuristic via simulations where we vary key configuration parameters in order to explore trade-offs between the degree to which the mission is achieved and the runtime complexity of the algorithm.

The rest of the article is structured as follows. Section 2 captures the problem in a formal way. Section 3 describes the proposed heuristic. Section 4 presents the results of the simulation experiments that we have conducted to evaluate the algorithm. Section 5 gives an overview of related work, pointing out the main differences with our work. Finally, Sect. 6 concludes the paper.

2   System Model

This section presents the system model and defines the problem we study in a more formal way. The model is intentionally kept abstract so that it can be used to capture different real-world scenarios. A similar description can be found in [28], we repeat this here for the sake of completeness.

2.1   Terrain

We model the terrain where the mission takes place as a directed graph $(\mathcal{N}, \mathcal{E})$, where $\mathcal{N}$ is the set of nodes and $\mathcal{E}$ is the set of edges between nodes. Each node $n_i \in \mathcal{N}$ represents a location that can be visited by the vehicle. Each edge $e_{i,j} \in \mathcal{E}$ represents a possible movement of the vehicle from node n_i to node n_j without going via some intermediate node(s). Edges are directed and there can be at most one edge between two nodes per direction. Note that $e_{i,j} \in \mathcal{E} \nRightarrow e_{j,i} \in \mathcal{E}$, i.e., it may be possible for the vehicle to move directly from n_i to n_j but not the other way around.

The vehicle can move between nodes by traveling across the edges. We encode a travel path as the sequence of nodes that are visited by the vehicle, including the start and end node of the path. Specifically, $p_{k_1,k_2,k_3,..,k_{m-1},k_m}$ denotes the path that starts from node n_{k_1}, goes through n_{k_2}, n_{k_3} etc., and ends at node n_{k_m}. Equivalently, $p_{k_1,k_2,k_3,..,k_{m-1},k_m}$ corresponds to the sequence of edges $(e_{k_1,k_2}, e_{k_2,k_3}, ..., e_{k_{m-1},k_m})$. Finally, let $len(p)$ be the number of edges (hops) in path p, and let $nodes(p)$ be the set of nodes in p.

2.2 Energy Reserves, Energy Costs, Energy Gains

To be realistic, we assume that the vehicle has limited energy storage capacity B_{max}. This can be thought of as the capacity of a fuel tank or the capacity of a battery, depending on whether the vehicle is equipped with an internal combustion engine or an electrical motor. Let $b \leq B_{max}$ denote the current energy budget (reserves) of the vehicle at a given point in time.

When the vehicle moves, it consumes some of its energy in order to drive its motors. Let $c_{i,j}$ denote the energy cost incurred when the vehicle moves from n_i to n_j over $e_{i,j}$, also referred to as edge cost. If the vehicle has an energy budget b and moves from n_i to n_j over $e_{i,j}$, the remaining energy budget will be $b' = b - c_{i,j}$. If $b' \leq 0$, the vehicle will exhaust its energy and it will stop (abort the mission) before reaching n_j. The edge cost is *not known* in advance with certainty. More specifically, we let the edge cost $c_{i,j}$ be a random variable over the range $[c_{i,j}^{min}..c_{i,j}^{max}]$ with an expected/mean value of $c_{i,j}^{mean}$.

The vehicle may also increase its energy budget during its journey, by gaining some energy at so-called *depot* nodes. One can think of depot nodes as refueling or recharging stations. Similarly to the edge costs, the amount of energy that can be gained at a depot node n_i is a random variable g_i over the range $[g_i^{min}..g_i^{max}]$ with an expected/mean value of g_i^{mean}. Without loss of generality, we assume that depot nodes are known in advance. Let $\mathcal{D} = \{n_i | g_i^{min} > 0\}$ be the set of all depot nodes, i.e., all nodes with a non-zero probability of energy gain.

2.3 Path Feasibility

Based on the definitions that were given above, it is straightforward to calculate the remaining available energy of the vehicle when starting with an initial budget b and after following a multi-hop path p from n_i to n_j, as follows:

$$rem(b, p_{i,k_1,k_2,...,k_m,j}) = \begin{cases} min(B_{max}, b + g_i) - c_{i,j}, & \text{if } m = 0 \\ rem(rem(b, p_{i,k_1}), p_{k_2,...,k_m,j}), & \text{if } m > 0 \end{cases} \quad (1)$$

On the one hand, if $m = 0$ then p includes a single, direct hop from n_i to n_j, in which case the gain of n_i is added to the initial budget b (up to the maximum energy storage capacity B_{max}) and then the cost of $e_{i,j}$ is subtracted in order for the vehicle to move from n_i to n_j. Note that the gain at the destination node n_j (if any) is not taken into account, because this cannot be exploited in order to cross the edge $e_{i,j}$.

On the other hand, if $m > 0$ then p includes at least two hops. Then, the budget that remains after taking p is equal to the remaining budget for the path without the first hop, starting with a budget that is equal to the remaining budget after taking the first hop. As in the 1-hop path, the remaining budget of a multi-hop path does not include the gain at the destination node n_j.

We can then define the feasibility of a planned path p, assuming the vehicle has a current remaining budget b, as follows. We say that $p_{k_1,k_2,...,k_m}$ is feasible if for all prefix paths $p_{k_1,k_2,...,k_x}, 1 < x \leq m$ (including the full path itself) it holds that $rem(b, p_{k_1,k_2,...,k_x}) > 0$. In words, p is feasible if the vehicle will not exhaust its budget at any point along p.

2.4   Problem Statement

The set $V \subseteq N$ includes the nodes that correspond to the target locations that have to be visited by the vehicle. We are interested in algorithms that guide the movement of the vehicle so that it ideally manages to visit all nodes in V without exhausting its budget while en route. In other words, starting with an initial budget b, the algorithm needs to find a feasible path $p_{k_1,k_2,,...,k_m}$ so that $V \subseteq nodes(p)$. Note that in the general case the vehicle may start its journey from node $n_s \notin V$. Also, the path that will be followed by the vehicle may include nodes that do not belong in V.

3   MaxBudget2 Algorithm

To solve the problem, we propose a heuristic algorithm, called MaxBudget2. This is an extension of the MaxBudget algorithm that is described in [28]. We present the algorithm in a top-down fashion, starting from the high-level logic and then discussing the more detailed aspects of path planning.

3.1   Basic Operation

The input to the algorithm is the node n_s from where the mission starts, the initial energy reserves *budget* of the vehicle (without the gains of the start node n_s) and the set V of the nodes to visit. The algorithm returns the set of target nodes which the vehicle did not manage to visit. In the ideal case where the vehicle visits all nodes of interest, the returned set is empty.

The basic operation principle includes two steps, which can be repeated a number of times. In a first step, a path is planned from the current node (initially, this is the start node) to some node of interest. In a second step, the vehicle follows that path. After each hop, a reality-check is performed by comparing the remaining budget of the vehicle to the corresponding estimation that was made during planning. If things are more or less according to plan, the vehicle continues its journey along the planned path. Else, a new path is planned from the current node to some node of interest (not necessarily the same one as before). Replanning also takes place when a target node is reached, so that the vehicle can visit the remaining nodes of interest.

The planned paths are chosen based on estimations for the edge costs and node gains (recall that these are not known beforehand and are discovered only when the vehicle actually crosses an edge or visits a node, respectively). This is done in two different estimation modes. In the *normal* mode, the cost/gain estimates correspond to the *expected/mean* of the respective random distributions. In the *optimistic* mode, the estimated edge costs correspond to the *minimum* of the respective distributions, while the estimates for the node gains correspond to the *maximum* of the respective distributions. The algorithm by default tries to find a feasible path using the normal path planning mode, and only if this fails it uses the optimistic mode. If no feasible path is found in the optimistic planning mode, the vehicle has reached a dead end and the algorithm terminates (without having visited all target nodes). A dead end is also reached when the vehicle exhausts its budget while trying to follow a planned path.

Unlike the MaxBudget algorithm [28], which may remain in the optimistic path planning mode for several consecutive hops, MaxBudget2 immediately reverts to the normal mode after performing a successful hop that was planned in the optimistic mode. It is still possible to perform consecutive hops in the optimistic planning mode, however this is done only after trying to find a path in the normal planning mode. This increases the chances of finding paths that will turn out to be feasible in practice.

The high-level algorithmic skeleton is shown in Algorithm 1. The path-planning logic is in the *PlanPath2()* function, which takes as parameters the start node, the currently available budget, the set of nodes to be visited and the estimation mode, and returns the path to be followed. The returned path p is a complex data structure, where (among other information) $p.len$ is the length of the path, $p.hops[k], 0 \leq k \leq p.len$ are the individual hops of the path, $p.hops[k].n$ is the node at the kth hop of the path and $p.hops[k].b$ is the estimated remaining budget at this point (without the potential energy gain of node $p.hops[k].n$). Note that $p.hops[0].n$ is the start node and $p.hops[0].b$ the initial budget of the vehicle, while $p.hops[p.len].n$ is the end node and $p.hops[p.len].b$ the estimated remaining budget at the end of the path (without the potential gain of the end node).

Next, we discuss in more detail the core path planning logic in *PlanPath2()*, and the additional information that is stored in the path structure, which is internally produced/used by this function.

Algorithm 1. High-level operation of the MaxBudget2 algorithm.

---

function MaxBudget2($n_s, budget, \mathcal{V}$)
    $n_{cur}, b, \mathcal{V}' \leftarrow n_s, budget, \mathcal{V} - n_s$ ▷ current node, current budget, nodes to visit
    $p \leftarrow null$ ▷ planned path to next target node
    while $\mathcal{V}' \neq \emptyset$ **do**
        if $p = null$ **then**
            $mode \leftarrow$ MODE_NORMAL
            $p \leftarrow$ PlanPath2($n_{cur}, b, \mathcal{V}', mode$)
            if $p = null$ **then**
                $mode \leftarrow$ MODE_OPTIMISTIC
                $p \leftarrow$ PlanPath2($n_{cur}, b, \mathcal{V}', mode$)
                if $p = null$ **then**   ▷ no feasible path found, dead end
                    return $\mathcal{V}'$
                end if
            end if
            $k \leftarrow 1$ ▷ init hop counter
        end if
        $b \leftarrow \min(b + g_{cur}, B)$ ▷ enjoy node gain
        $n_{nxt} \leftarrow p.hops[k].n$ ▷ take next hop
        $b \leftarrow b - c_{cur,nxt}$ ▷ pay travel cost
        if $b < 0$ **then**   ▷ budget exhausted, dead end
            return $\mathcal{V}'$
        end if
        $n_{cur}, \mathcal{V}' \leftarrow n_{nxt}, \mathcal{V}' - n_{nxt}$
        if $(k < p.len) \wedge (mode = NORMAL) \wedge (\frac{|p.hops[k].b-b|}{p.hops[k].b} \leq Threshold)$ **then**
            $k \leftarrow k + 1$ ▷ proceed with the next hop of the planned path
        else
            $p \leftarrow null$ ▷ plan new path
        end if
    end while
    return $\mathcal{V}'$
end function

3.2 Path Planning Logic

The path planning logic is described in Algorithm 2. The basic idea of the heuristic is to pick paths that lead to nodes of interest while maximizing the remaining budget of the vehicle. The intuition behind this is that the budget that remains available after visiting a node of interest can be exploited in the future to visit the remaining nodes of interest.

Function *PlanPath2()* finds the budget-wise most beneficial feasible paths from the current start node to *every* node of interest. The core path planning logic is in function *MaxBudgetPaths2()*, which is discussed in the sequel. Then, the next destination node is chosen so that the corresponding path leads to the maximum remaining budget. To increase the robustness against the uncertainty of the energy costs and gains during travel, ties are broken based on the path-wide low watermark for the estimated budget of the vehicle, which indicates how

Algorithm 2. Path planning logic of the MaxBudget2 algorithm.

---

function PLANPATH2(n_s, $budget$, $\mathcal{V}$, $mode$)
    $p[|\mathcal{N}|] \leftarrow$ MAXBUDGETPATHS2(n_s, $budget$, $mode$)   ▷ max budget paths to all nodes
    $n_d \leftarrow null$ ▷ preferred destination node/path
    for each $n_i \in \mathcal{V}$ **do**
        if ($n_d = null$) $\vee$ BETTER($p[n_i], p[n_d]$) **then**
            $n_d \leftarrow n_i$
        end if
    end for
    if $n_d = null$ **then**
        return $null$
    else
        return $p[n_d]$
    end if
end function

function MAXBUDGETPATHS2(n_s, $budget$, $mode$)
    $p[|\mathcal{N}|]$ ▷ path from n_s to every n_i
    $p_0[|\mathcal{N}|]$ ▷ path from n_s to every n_i without cycles at n_i
    for each $n_i \in \mathcal{N} | n_i \neq n_s$ **do**
        $p[n_i] \leftarrow (null, -\infty, -\infty)$
        $p_0[n_i] \leftarrow (null, -\infty, -\infty)$
    end for
    $p[n_s] \leftarrow (n_s, budget, budget)$
    $p_0[n_s] \leftarrow (n_s, budget, budget)$
    repeat
        $update \leftarrow false$
        for each $n_i, n_j | e_{ij} \in \mathcal{E}$ **do**
            $b \leftarrow \min(p[n_i].b + g_i^{mode}, B_{max}) - c_{ij}^{mode}$
            $lowb \leftarrow \min(p[n_i].lowb, b)$
            if ($b > 0$) **then**   ▷ hop from n_i to n_j expected to be feasible
                $p' \leftarrow p[n_i] + (n_j, b, lowb)$
                $p'_0 \leftarrow$ **pathToFirstOccurrence**(p', n_j)
                if BETTER($p'_0, p_0[n_j]$) $\vee$ (EQ($p'_0, p_0[n_j]$) $\wedge$ BETTER($p', p[n_j]$)) **then**
                    $p[n_j] \leftarrow p'$
                    $p_0[n_j] \leftarrow p'_0$
                    $update \leftarrow true$
                end if
            end if
        end for
    until $update = false$
    return $p_0[]$
end function

function BETTER(p', p)
    return (($p'.b > p.b$) $\vee$ ($p'.b = p.b \wedge p'.lowb > p.lowb$)$\vee$
            ($p'.b = p.b \wedge p'.lowb = p.lowb \wedge p'.len < p.len$))
end function

function EQ(p', p)
    return ($p'.b = p.b \wedge p'.lowb = p.lowb \wedge p'.len = p.len$)
end function

close the vehicle is expected to come to exhausting its budget if it follows that path. The rationale is that paths with a larger value for the low watermark are less likely to turn out to be infeasible when the vehicle actually tries to follow them. If there are still several options to choose from, preference is given to the shortest path. This is because the inaccuracy of the budget estimation increases with every hop, thus shorter paths are more likely to turn out as planned. We note that the MaxBudget algorithm [28] breaks ties only based on the path length (it does not use the low watermark criterion).

The path selection logic is given in the *Better()* function. As mentioned above, $p.hops[k].b$ stores the estimated remaining budget of the vehicle after performing the kth hop without taking into account any potential gain at node $p.hops[k].n$. During the core path planning process, additional information is generated and stored into the path data structure. More specifically, $p.hops[k].lowb$ stores the estimated path-wide budget low watermark until the kth hop. For convenience, we let $p.b = p.hops[p.len].b$ and $p.lowb = p.hops[p.len].lowb$ store the estimated available budget and the estimated path-wide low watermark at the end of the path, respectively.

The heart of the path planning heuristic lies in the *MaxBudgetPaths2()* function, which is invoked from within *PlanPath2()* to get a proposed path from the current node to every other node in the graph. It is based on the principle of the Bellman-Ford (BF) algorithm [4,12], with some extensions that we have introduced to support our heuristic.

More specifically, instead of finding the shortest paths from a given node to all other nodes, we adapt BF to find the budget-wise most beneficial feasible paths between a given source node and all other nodes in the graph, i.e., the paths from the source node to every other node that maximize the remaining budget without exhausting in at any point along the path. One of the key features of the heuristic is that it considers paths that may have so-called beneficial cycles, which increase the estimated remaining budget of the vehicle (in order for this to be possible, a beneficial cycle has to include at least one depot node). This allows the vehicle to gain some energy even this means that it has to deviate from the shortest path that leads to a node of interest. Note that, due to the budget constraint, a beneficial cycle cannot lead to an infinite loop. Once the budget of the vehicle reaches the upper bound B_{max} during a beneficial cycle, any additional cycles are superfluous as they merely lead to the same expected budget at the destination node n_j and are not included in the proposed plan. A detailed description of these extensions is given in [28].

Again, unlike MaxBudget, a newly discovered path p' from the source node n_s to a destination node n_i is preferred to an existing path p from n_s to n_i, based not only on the estimated budget but also on the estimated path-wide low watermark, leaving the path length only as a last-level tie-break. Furthermore, the comparison is made for the sub-paths p'_0 and p_0 without taking into account beneficial cycles (if any) that involve the destination node n_i, and only if these turn out to be equivalent (in terms of budget, low watermark and length) are the full paths p' and p compared with each other. When no more path updates take place, the *MaxBudgetPaths2()* function returns a path from n_s to each other node n_i that includes only the first occurrence of n_i.

3.3 Complexity

The time complexity of the algorithm depends on the *PlanPath2()* function. In turn, the complexity of *PlanPath2()* is dominated by that of the *MaxBudgetPaths2()* function, since the logic that follows after the invocation of *MaxBudgetPaths2()* is merely linear to the number of nodes.

Let $N = |\mathcal{N}|$ be the number of nodes and $E = |\mathcal{E}|$ be the number of edges in the terrain graph. Also, let C be the average number of beneficial cycles that can be exploited to increase the budget of the vehicle for each examined path, and let M be the average length of such cycles. Then, the complexity of the *MaxBudgetPaths2()* function is $O(E \times (N + C \times M))$. This is because each execution of the *for-each-edge* loop in function *MaxBudgetPaths2()* includes E steps (one for each edge of the graph), while the number of times this loop is repeated, i.e., the number of *repeat-until* loop iterations in *MaxBudgetPaths2()*, depends on the maximum path length between any two nodes, which is equal to $O(N + C \times M)$. As a reference, the complexity of the original BF algorithm is $O(E \times N)$ (in this case, cycles are not allowed hence $C = 0$ and the maximum path length becomes $O(N)$).

Note that *PlanPath2()* and *MaxBudgetPaths2()* are invoked at most twice per hop. If the current plan was devised in normal mode and the budget check that is performed after taking the last hop is successful, the next hop is taken along the planned path. Else, a new path is planned in the normal mode. If this attempt fails, one more planning attempt is performed in the optimistic mode. Of course, the number of path planning attempts that will be performed during a mission can be much smaller, and each invocation may involve a different number of iterations of the *repeat-until* loop in the *MaxBudgetPaths2()* function.

4 Evaluation

This section gives an evaluation of the MaxBudget2 heuristic via simulation experiments. We start by presenting the system setup used for our experiments and the performance evaluation metrics. Then, we investigate the performance of the algorithm for different configuration parameters that trade-off time complexity with the success of the mission. Finally, we compare our heuristic with indicative reference algorithms, including the previous version of the MaxBudget algorithm described in [28].

4.1 System Setup

The graph topology used in our experiments is a 10×10 grid. Each node is connected via symmetrical bi-directional edges to its horizontal and vertical neighbors. The diameter d of the graph is 18 hops. We introduce 2 depot nodes, chosen randomly at positions $(2,5)$ and $(8,6)$ in the grid. The depot nodes remain the same in all experiments. Also, in all experiments, the vehicle starts its journey from the node with position $(0,0)$.

With no loss of generality, we set the maximum budget limit $B_{max} = 1000$ and the initial budget of the vehicle equal to B_{max}. The edge costs follow a symmetrical double-truncated normal distribution with $c^{min} = c^{mean} - \frac{c^{mean}}{2}$ and $c^{max} = c^{mean} + \frac{c^{mean}}{2}$. We perform experiments for different $c^{mean} = \frac{B_{max}}{a}$, where a is the so-called *autonomy* of the vehicle and is equal to the average number of hops that can be performed with the maximum budget without gaining any energy at a depot node. We investigate different degrees of autonomy as a function of the graph diameter: *high* autonomy d, *medium-high* $\frac{5}{6} \times d$, *low-medium* $\frac{2}{3} \times d$ and *low* autonomy $\frac{1}{2} \times d$. Obviously, higher degrees of autonomy enable the vehicle to travel further and hopefully visit more target nodes without having to visit a depot node in order to regain some energy.

For the gain of depot nodes we adopt a symmetrical double-truncated normal distribution with $g^{mean} = \frac{3}{4} \times B_{max}$. The rationale is that even if the vehicle reaches a depot node with a marginally exhausted budget, it will still be able to restore its budget to a significant degree, on average to 75% of B_{max}. The lower and upper bounds of the gain distribution are set to $g^{min} = g^{mean} - \frac{g^{mean}}{3}$ and $g^{max} = g^{mean} + \frac{g^{mean}}{3}$, respectively.

For each autonomy degree (different edge cost distribution) we test 100 different scenarios. In each scenario, 100 different values are randomly produced offline for the cost of each edge and the gain of each depot node, according to the respective distributions. The values for each edge and depot node are stored in separate files, from where they are retrieved at runtime each time the vehicle actually crosses that particular edge and visits that particular depot node, respectively (we have confirmed that in our experiments no edge/node is crossed/visited for more than 100 times). This way it is possible to repeat a scenario for exactly the same edge cost and node gain conditions.

Finally, we vary the set of nodes to be visited by the vehicle $\mathcal{V}_x \subset \mathcal{N}$, where $x = \frac{|\mathcal{V}_x|}{|\mathcal{N}|}$. We consider four cases: $x = 5\%, 10\%, 20\%$ and 30%. For each $\mathcal{V}_x$ case, we test the algorithms on three different set of target nodes, $\mathcal{V}_{x_k}, 1 \leq k \leq 3$. These are constructed in a random way, however we make sure that $\mathcal{V}_{5_k} \subset \mathcal{V}_{10_k} \subset \mathcal{V}_{20_k} \subset \mathcal{V}_{30_k}$ in order to have continuity across the different experiments. For brevity, in most cases, we report the average result achieved over all $\mathcal{V}_{x_k}$ rather than showing results for each $\mathcal{V}_x$ separately.

4.2   Metrics

To evaluate the degree to which the mission is accomplished, we use as a metric the so-called *coverage* of the path that was followed by the vehicle. Assuming the vehicle travelled along path p, the coverage is equal to the ratio between the number of the nodes of interest in p and the total number of nodes of interest: $\frac{|nodes(p) \cap \mathcal{V}|}{|\mathcal{V}|}$. The ideal case is for the algorithm to find a path p with coverage

1. Note that for some problem settings, with lower autonomy degrees, it may be impossible to achieve this.

As a practical metric for the time complexity (overhead) of the heuristic, we report the average number of *repeat-until* loop iterations in the *MaxBudget-Paths2()* function for each hop that is performed by the vehicle during travel. This is equal to $\frac{R}{len(p)}$, where the R is total number of the *repeat-until* loop iterations executed in the entire mission and p is the path that was followed by the vehicle.

4.3 Budget Check Threshold

Recall that after each hop that is performed by the vehicle, it is checked whether the current plan is still realistic or a replanning is needed (see Algorithm 1). This check is done by comparing the actual remaining budget to the one that was estimated during planning. If the difference is above a certain threshold, another path is planned. Also, when an optimistically planned hop is performed successfully, the mode changes back to normal.

In a first series of experiments, we investigate the impact of this threshold on the performance of the algorithm. More specifically, we test three different threshold values: 5%, 10% and 20%. As a reference, we use a simpler version of the algorithm where the path is replanned after every hop, irrespectively of how close the current budget situation is to what was estimated when the path was planned.

The results are shown in Fig. 1. Due to space limitations, we report the average coverage and complexity (number of iterations per hop) over all experiments for the different sets of target nodes $V_x, x = 5, 10, 20, 30$. As can be seen, increasing the threshold leads to a reduction of the runtime complexity but also reduces the coverage of the algorithm. This is expected given that larger thresholds translate to greater tolerance for the deviation of the actual vs. the estimated remaining budget, which, in turn, reduces the number of path replannings. However, this comes at an increased risk of following paths that will not turn-out as planned. Note that the impact in complexity becomes less significant for larger threshold values, whereas the coverage drops steadily, in particular for marginal degrees of autonomy.

As a reasonable trade-off between the coverage and the runtime complexity of the algorithm, in the rest of the experiments we set the budget check threshold to 5%. As can be seen in Fig. 1, the coverage is close to that achieved when replanning after every single hop, with less than half the complexity.

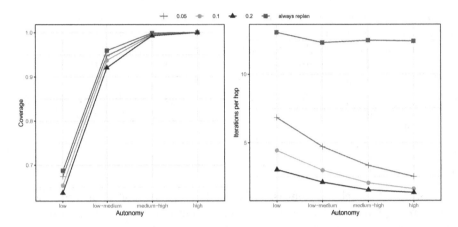

Fig. 1. Performance for different budget check threshold values (average over all $\mathcal{V}_x$).

4.4 Disallowing Cycles

We have conducted a second series of experiments to investigate the impact of allowing the planned paths to contain (beneficial) cycles. In this case, we compare the proposed algorithm with a modified variant that prohibits the exploration of cycles during path planning in the *MaxBudgetPaths2()* function.

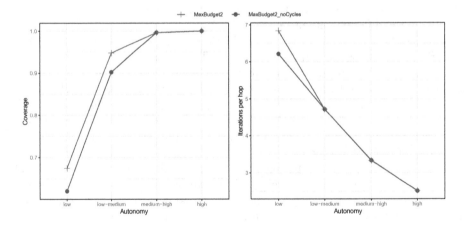

Fig. 2. Performance when disallowing cycles (average over all $\mathcal{V}_x$).

Figure 2 shows the performance of the no-cycles variant vs. the unrestricted algorithm. It can be seen that the ability of the path planning logic to exploit beneficial cycles has a positive impact on the coverage for the lower degrees of autonomy (low and low-medium). This is reasonable as the ability to regain energy through beneficial cycles becomes more crucial when the vehicle can only perform a small number of hops without gaining some energy at a depot node in order to be able to continue its journey.

It is interesting to note that the no-cycles variant has a reduced complexity only for the low degree of autonomy, whereas for higher autonomy degrees the complexity is practically identical to that of the unrestricted algorithm. We provide some brief insight as to why this is so. On the one hand, the average number of per hop path plannings (invocations of the *MaxBudgetPaths2()* function) is practically the same in both variants of the algorithm; in both cases, more replannings take place as the autonomy drops and the estimated remaining budget deviates from the actual one – the width/variance of the edge cost distribution increases with the mean edge cost, thus the estimations for lower degrees of autonomy are more likely to be inaccurate. On the other hand, the no-cycles variant consistently performs fewer loop iterations per planning attempt. This difference becomes larger when the autonomy is low, because without the ability to increase the budget via beneficial cycles the path planning logic finds a larger number of paths to be infeasible and does not further pursue them. As a consequence, the search space is reduced compared to the unrestricted variant.

Overall, allowing planned paths to contain beneficial cycles increases the coverage of the algorithm without a large penalty in complexity. For this reason, in the following experiments, we use the unrestricted version of the MaxBudget2 algorithm.

4.5   Path Length Reduction

As one more option to decrease the runtime complexity, we investigate the performance of the algorithm when restricting the length of the paths that are planned in the *MaxBudgetPaths2()* function. We experiment with three upper bounds as a function on the diameter d of the graph, limiting the path length to $\frac{2}{3} \times d = 12$, $\frac{5}{6} \times d = 15$ and $d = 18$ hops. The results are shown in Fig. 3.

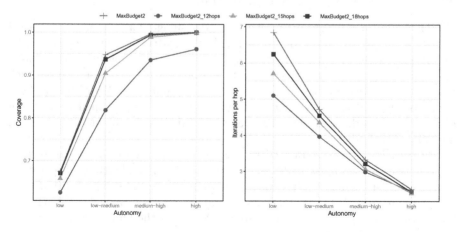

Fig. 3. Performance for different path length limits (average over all $s\mathcal{V}_x$).

A first observation is that, as expected, limiting the length of the planned paths decreases the complexity but also leads to a decreased coverage. The reason is twofold. By decreasing the maximum number of allowed hops, the path planning logic in the *MaxBudgetPaths2()* function cannot always find paths to all target nodes. In addition, the paths that are found to some of the target nodes may still miss opportunities to visit nearby depot nodes and/or to perform beneficial cycles.

A second observation is that the relatively moderate path length limit of 18 hops can be afforded for all degrees of autonomy. The limit of 15 hops also results in good coverage, similar to that of the unrestricted path search, except for low-medium autonomy. This is because the increased reduction of the path search space is more critical in the cases where the vehicle marginally misses some opportunities for energy gains. When the autonomy of the vehicle is low, there are less such missed opportunities hence the difference vs. the less restricted or unrestricted path search becomes smaller. Limiting the length of the path search even further, to 12 hops, does not pay-off as it leads to clearly worse coverage even for high degrees of autonomy.

Limiting the length of the planned paths leads to a notable reduction of the complexity only for the lower degrees of autonomy. As the autonomy degree increases, the complexity converges to that of the unrestricted path search. The reason is that even though the hop-limited variants perform slightly more per hop plannings than the unrestricted variant, they perform consistently fewer iterations per planning attempt. This difference steadily increases as the autonomy becomes smaller for reasons similar to those explained above (in the discussion of the no-cycles variant), thereby leading to significantly reduced runtime complexity; the stricter the path length limit, the lower the runtime complexity. However, in all variants, the number of replannings decreases for higher degrees of autonomy hence this difference gradually becomes less relevant. Ultimately, for high autonomy, all variants have practically the same complexity.

4.6   Comparison with Other Algorithms

In a last series of experiments, we compare MaxBudget2 and its more restricted variant with a 18-hop limit during path planning with the older version of the MaxBudget algorithm. As a reference, we use an *oracle* algorithm that has a priori knowledge of the actual edge costs and node gains that would apply each time the vehicle were to cross an edge or visit a depot node. We also consider a *static* variant that uses fixed edge costs and depot node gains, equal to the mean of the respective distributions. A more detailed description of these algorithms, including MaxBudget, is given in [28].

Figure 4 shows the coverage that is achieved by the algorithms, separately for the different sets of target nodes $\mathcal{V}_x$. It can be seen that MaxBudget2 performs close to the Oracle for the three higher autonomy degrees (high, medium-high, low-medium) and all $\mathcal{V}_x$. When the autonomy is low, MaxBudget2 still achieves an average coverage of 67.5% compared to 86.4% of the Oracle (a difference of

18.9%). This can be considered satisfactory given that in this case the autonomy is insufficient to achieve full coverage.

Note that MaxBudget2 achieves better coverage than the old MaxBudget algorithm, in all cases. The difference becomes more significant as the autonomy decreases, namely MaxBudget2 has 4.9% and 6.8% better coverage for low-medium and low autonomy, respectively (on average over all V_x). This is because the robustness of the paths that are planned in MaxBudget2 becomes more crucial in stricter system configurations. Also, the difference is bigger for the larger sets of target nodes V_{20} and V_{30}. For instance, when the vehicle autonomy is low, MaxBudget2 achieves 8.3% and 10.6% better coverage than MaxBudget for V_{20} and V_{30}, respectively. The reason is that the robustness of path planning has a greater impact when the vehicle has to travel over longer distances in order to visit more nodes of interest.

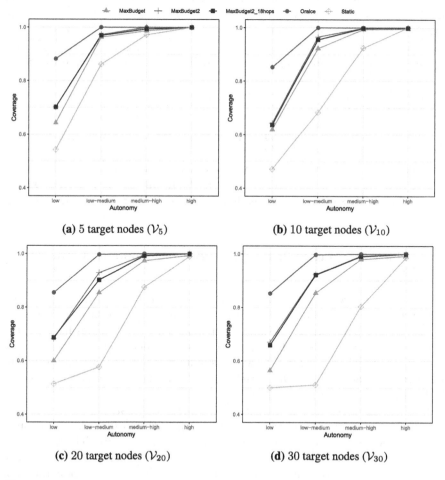

Fig. 4. Performance vs. other algorithms for the different sets of target nodes V_x.

Like the unrestricted MaxBudget2 algorithm, the restricted variant where a 18-hop limit is applied in the path planning step, consistently outperforms MaxBudget. Despite the reduction of the search space, the algorithm still manages to find robust paths to some of the target nodes, leading to a good coverage. A rather surprising result is that for V_{20} and low autonomy the hop-limited variant achieves (slightly) better coverage than the unrestricted variant. Since the planned paths have fewer hops than in the unrestricted variant, the estimations for the remaining budget at the end of the path are more accurate/more likely to be close to the actual values that will be experienced in reality. This trade-off between estimation accuracy (due to the shorter path length) and budget maximization (the primary selection criterion in the unrestricted variant) seems to play in favor of the former. One could explore this trade-off by following a hybrid heuristic that combines the budget maximization principle with the budget estimation accuracy/certainty, but this is beyond the scope of this work.

Finally, the Static algorithm achieves a much worse coverage than all other algorithms, except for high autonomy. Its coverage drops sharply for lower autonomy degrees (medium-high, low-medium, low) and this effect becomes even stronger for larger sets of target nodes (V_{10}, V_{20} and V_{30}). This clearly shows the importance of dynamic replanning in challenging system configurations.

5   Related Work

The Vehicle Routing Problem (VRP) has a long history and has been extensively studied in the literature. Over time, many variants have been proposed and investigated, with different goals, constraints and assumptions motivated from various real-world scenarios (surveys can be found in [29] and [27]). Next, we discuss the variants of the problem that are closer to our work, and point out the differences.

5.1   Vehicle Routing with Fuel/Energy Constraints and Periodic Visits

In the so-called *periodic vehicle routing problem* and *multi-depot periodic vehicle routing problem* [1,2,8,11,13,30,37], the objective is to periodically visit a set of destinations (target nodes) using one or more vehicles. Vehicles have limited energy reserves and may recharge/refuel at special depot stations. There are more variations where the targets have different priorities, vehicles have different capabilities/capacities, and the targets must be visited within a time interval. We briefly discuss indicative work below.

Work in [21] investigates the problems of *persistent visitation with fuel constraints*. In this case, the vehicle perpetually visits the target nodes (customer nodes), while each customer must be visited at a specific rate. The fuel of the vehicle is limited, so it is necessary to visit nodes with refueling properties. The objective is to satisfy the rate of visit for each destination while keeping the total cost of fuel consumption to a minimum.

The problem of *continuous monitoring* is studied in [25], where the mission is performed by several heterogeneous vehicles that use different types of batteries. The objective is to periodically visit a set of target nodes with different priorities, which determine the rate at which each node needs to be visited. The vehicles can change their batteries at specific depot nodes, but each depot node has a limited supply of batteries for each type. In this case, the objective is to minimize the penalty that is incurred when failing to visit a target node at the desired rate.

The main difference with the work presented here is that in our case the cost of travel between nodes as well as the amount of energy/fuel that can be gained at depot nodes, is not known a priori with full certainty. Also, we do not deal with periodic visits.

5.2   Vehicle Routing with Stochastic Elements

The objective of *vehicle routing problem with stochastic demands* is to use a fleet of one or more vehicles with finite serving capacity and possibly some fuel constraints in order to visit and serve a set of target nodes (customers). The target nodes are fixed, but the exact demand of each customer is not a priori known. As a consequence, when a vehicle visits a customer, it may find out that the demand exceeds its remaining servicing capacity. Failure to service the customer comes at a penalty. Alternatively, the vehicle may restore its capacity at a depot node and then return to the customer to provide the required service. This problem is researched in many works [6, 7, 16, 20, 22, 23, 31, 33]. Furthermore, [10] and [24] investigate the problem for the more general case where the goal is to minimize the travel time, which also needs to be kept below a given bound.

In the *vehicle routing problem with stochastic travel times*, a fleet of one or more vehicles, which may have capacity and/or fuel constraints, visit a set of known targets. In this case, the travel time is a random variable. Also, each target has a time window during which it is available for visits by a vehicle. If the target is not visited/served within that time window, there is a penalty. The objective is to route the vehicles so as to minimize the total penalty. Algorithms tackling this problem are described in [9, 17, 19, 26, 34–36].

The *vehicle routing problem with stochastic customers* consists in using a fleet of vehicles, which may have capacity and/or fuel constraints, to visit a set of target customers. However, these targets require a visit only with some probability, thus a vehicle may end-up visiting a node that does not need to be serviced. Indicative approaches can be found in [5, 14, 15]. In [14, 15] the objective is to minimize the expected total cost, while [5] tries to maximize the number of serviced customers. Moreover, in [5], the problem is investigated for a partially dynamic environment where some customers are priori known and others appear with randomness. In addition, each customer needs to be visited within certain time windows.

One more variation is the *same day delivery* problem, where delivery requests to customers arrive stochastically during the day and must be completed within a time window. Such algorithms have been proposed in [18] and [38]. The objective in [18] is to find the best routes for the day that maximize the number of served customers, while [38] studies the trade-off between service maximization and travel cost minimization. The main difference vs. the VRP with stochastic customers is that once the vehicle has chosen to visit a customer it cannot change its route to service a newly issued delivery request, instead it must first return to the depot.

Our work is more similar to the VRP with stochastic travel times. However, the main constraint is the travel time, whereas in our work it is the energy of the vehicle, which can be replenished by visiting depot nodes. In the VRP with stochastic demands, the vehicle is always allowed to go to a depot node to restore its capacity. This is a major difference compared to our work, where the vehicle stops (the mission terminates) when the energy resources/budget is exhausted. As a consequence, it is not always possible to visit all nodes, in contrast to most other problem formulations where this is always feasible and the problem consists in minimizing the travel cost and/or time violation penalty. In this sense, our work is closer to [10] and [24], which have a similar constraint for the travel cost. But in our case the stochasticity concerns the travel cost and energy gains, not the customer demands, and the objective is to maximize the number of target nodes that are visited by the vehicle.

5.3 Energy-Efficient Path Planning

Several algorithms have been designed to compute an energy-efficient route between two nodes, based on an abstract graph where the weights at edges represent the energy consumption or the energy restoration. The difference to a typical shortest-path algorithm is that the computed routes minimize the sum of edge costs, not the number of edges. For instance, [32] deals with the problem as a special case of the constrained shortest path problem, while in [3] the problem of energy-efficient path planning is viewed as a cost minimization problem. In both cases, the ability of the vehicle to gain energy/recharge is modeled by introducing edges with negative weights.

Our work is related to the problem of finding a cost-effective path between two nodes. However, the minimization of the travel cost per se is not as central as in the above algorithms, because it can be counter-balanced by gaining energy at depot nodes. What is ultimately important is for the vehicle to follow a path that turns out to be feasible, while visiting as many target nodes as possible. To this end, the MaxBudget2 heuristic employs a suitably adapted version of the Bellman-Ford algorithm [4, 12], which finds the path between two nodes that maximizes the energy reserves of the vehicle (as opposed to minimizing travel cost). Also, our version can exploit beneficial cycles, which is not allowed in the original algorithm as the travel cost could then be reduced infinitely. The main difference with the old MaxBudget algorithm [28] is the increased robustness of the planned paths, by giving preference to paths that do not involve cycles and breaking ties based on the path-wide budget low watermark.

6 Conclusion

We propose a path planning heuristic for a variant of the vehicle routing problem, where both the travel cost and the energy gain opportunities at depot nodes are stochastic and the vehicle is not allowed to exhaust its energy during travel. Paths to the target nodes are planned by estimating the remaining budget after each hop, giving preference to paths that maximize the remaining budget without performing any cycles and breaking ties based on the path-wide low budget watermark; cycles are exploited if they can increase the expected budget. We experiment with different variants of the heuristic that trade-off coverage with runtime complexity. We also compare our approach with other algorithms, showing that it achieves good results, especially for system configurations where it is indeed infeasible to visit all nodes of interest.

Based on the results of our experiments, a promising direction for future work is to explore a hybrid approach where the primary path selection criterion is a combination of the estimated remaining budget and the accuracy/certainty of the estimate. We also plan to experiment with different graph topologies in combination with more informed values for the edge costs, the node gains and the budget constraint, based on concrete application scenarios. Further, we wish to evaluate the memory footprint and real-time performance of the algorithm on embedded platforms, such as the companion boards that can be used together with the autopilot infrastructure of unmanned vehicles.

Acknowledgements. This research has been co-financed by the European Union and Greek national funds through the Operational Program Competitiveness, Entrepreneurship and Innovation, under the call RESEARCH - CREATE - INNOVATE, project PV-Auto-Scout, code T1EDK-02435.

References

1. Alonso, F., Alvarez, M.J., Beasley, J.E.: A tabu search algorithm for the periodic vehicle routing problem with multiple vehicle trips and accessibility restrictions. J. Oper. Res. Soc. **59**(7), 963–976 (2008)
2. Angelelli, E., Speranza, M.G.: The periodic vehicle routing problem with intermediate facilities. Eur. J. Oper. Res. **137**(2), 233–247 (2002)
3. Artmeier, A., Haselmayr, J., Leucker, M., Sachenbacher, M.: The optimal routing problem in the context of battery-powered electric vehicles. In: CPAIOR Workshop on Constraint Reasoning and Optimization for Computational Sustainability (CROCS) (2010)
4. Bellman, R.: On a routing problem. Q. Appl. Math. **16**(1), 87–90 (1958)
5. Bent, R.W., Van Hentenryck, P.: Scenario-based planning for partially dynamic vehicle routing with stochastic customers. Oper. Res. **52**(6), 977–987 (2004)
6. Bertsimas, D.J.: A vehicle routing problem with stochastic demand. Oper. Res. **40**(3), 574–585 (1992)
7. Chepuri, K., Homem-De-Mello, T.: Solving the vehicle routing problem with stochastic demands using the cross-entropy method. Ann. Oper. Res. **134**(1), 153–181 (2005)

8. Cordeau, J.F., Gendreau, M., Laporte, G.: A tabu search heuristic for periodic and multi-depot vehicle routing problems. Netw. Int. J. **30**(2), 105–119 (1997)

9. Ehmke, J.F., Campbell, A.M., Urban, T.L.: Ensuring service levels in routing problems with time windows and stochastic travel times. Eur. J. Oper. Res. **240**(2), 539–550 (2015)

10. Erera, A.L., Morales, J.C., Savelsbergh, M.: The vehicle routing problem with stochastic demand and duration constraints. Transp. Sci. **44**(4), 474–492 (2010)

11. Escobar, J.W., Linfati, R., Toth, P., Baldoquin, M.G.: A hybrid granular tabu search algorithm for the multi-depot vehicle routing problem. J. Heuristics **20**(5), 483–509 (2014)

12. Ford Jr., L.R.: Network flow theory. Technical report, Rand Corp Santa Monica Ca (1956)

13. Gaudioso, M., Paletta, G.: A heuristic for the periodic vehicle routing problem. Transp. Sci. **26**(2), 86–92 (1992)

14. Gendreau, M., Laporte, G., Séguin, R.: An exact algorithm for the vehicle routing problem with stochastic demands and customers. Transp. Sci. **29**(2), 143–155 (1995)

15. Gendreau, M., Laporte, G., Séguin, R.: A tabu search heuristic for the vehicle routing problem with stochastic demands and customers. Oper. Res. **44**(3), 469–477 (1996)

16. Juan, A., Faulin, J., Grasman, S., Riera, D., Marull, J., Mendez, C.: Using safety stocks and simulation to solve the vehicle routing problem with stochastic demands. Transp. Res. Part C Emerg. Technol. **19**(5), 751–765 (2011)

17. Kenyon, A.S., Morton, D.P.: Stochastic vehicle routing with random travel times. Transp. Sci. **37**(1), 69–82 (2003)

18. Klapp, M.A., Erera, A.L., Toriello, A.: The dynamic dispatch waves problem for same-day delivery. Eur. J. Oper. Res. **271**(2), 519–534 (2018)

19. Laporte, G., Louveaux, F., Mercure, H.: The vehicle routing problem with stochastic travel times. Transp. Sci. **26**(3), 161–170 (1992)

20. Laporte, G., Louveaux, F.V., Van Hamme, L.: An integer L-shaped algorithm for the capacitated vehicle routing problem with stochastic demands. Oper. Res. **50**(3), 415–423 (2002)

21. Las Fargeas, J., Hyun, B., Kabamba, P., Girard, A.: Persistent visitation with fuel constraints. Proc.-Soc. Behav. Sci. **54**, 1037–1046 (2012)

22. Marinaki, M., Marinakis, Y.: A glowworm swarm optimization algorithm for the vehicle routing problem with stochastic demands. Expert Syst. Appl. **46**, 145–163 (2016)

23. Marinakis, Y., Iordanidou, G.R., Marinaki, M.: Particle swarm optimization for the vehicle routing problem with stochastic demands. Appl. Soft Comput. **13**(4), 1693–1704 (2013)

24. Mendoza, J.E., Rousseau, L.M., Villegas, J.G.: A hybrid metaheuristic for the vehicle routing problem with stochastic demand and duration constraints. J. Heuristics **22**(4), 539–566 (2016)

25. Mersheeva, V.: UAV routing problem for area monitoring in a disaster situation. Ph.D. thesis Alpen-Adria-Universität Klagenfurt Austria (2015)

26. Miranda, D.M., Conceição, S.V.: The vehicle routing problem with hard time windows and stochastic travel and service time. Expert Syst. Appl. **64**, 104–116 (2016)

27. Mor, A., Speranza, M.: Vehicle routing problems over time: a survey (2018)

28. Polychronis, G., Lalis, S.: Dynamic vehicle routing under uncertain travel costs and refueling opportunities. In: 5th International Conference on Vehicle Technology and Intelligent Transport Systems, pp. 52–63 (2019)

29. Psaraftis, H.N., Wen, M., Kontovas, C.A.: Dynamic vehicle routing problems: three decades and counting. Networks **67**(1), 3–31 (2016)
30. Rahimi-Vahed, A., Crainic, T.G., Gendreau, M., Rei, W.: A path relinking algorithm for a multi-depot periodic vehicle routing problem. J. Heuristics **19**(3), 497–524 (2013)
31. Rei, W., Gendreau, M., Soriano, P.: A hybrid Monte Carlo local branching algorithm for the single vehicle routing problem with stochastic demands. Transp. Sci. **44**(1), 136–146 (2010)
32. Sachenbacher, M., Leucker, M., Artmeier, A., Haselmayr, J.: Efficient energy-optimal routing for electric vehicles. In: AAAI, pp. 1402–1407 (2011)
33. Secomandi, N.: A rollout policy for the vehicle routing problem with stochastic demands. Oper. Res. **49**(5), 796–802 (2001)
34. Taş, D., Gendreau, M., Dellaert, N., Van Woensel, T., De Kok, A.: Vehicle routing with soft time windows and stochastic travel times: a column generation and branch-and-price solution approach. Eur. J. Oper. Res. **236**(3), 789–799 (2014)
35. Taş, D., Dellaert, N., Van Woensel, T., De Kok, T.: Vehicle routing problem with stochastic travel times including soft time windows and service costs. Comput. Oper. Res. **40**(1), 214–224 (2013)
36. Van Woensel, T., Kerbache, L., Peremans, H., Vandaele, N.: A vehicle routing problem with stochastic travel times. In: 4th Aegean International Conference on Analysis of Manufacturing Systems Location, Samos, Greece (2003)
37. Vidal, T., Crainic, T.G., Gendreau, M., Lahrichi, N., Rei, W.: A hybrid genetic algorithm for multidepot and periodic vehicle routing problems. Oper. Res. **60**(3), 611–624 (2012)
38. Voccia, S.A., Campbell, A.M., Thomas, B.W.: The same-day delivery problem for online purchases. Transp. Sci. **53**(1), 167–184 (2017)

Frontal Vehicle Body Damage Assessment in Surveillance Camera Images Using Deep Learning Techniques

Burak Balcı[✉] and Yusuf Artan[✉]

Video Analysis Group, Havelsan Incorporation, Ankara, Turkey
{bbalci,yartan}@havelsan.com.tr

Abstract. Vehicle body damage detection from still images has received a considerable interest in traffic safety and insurance industries for the past few years. Existing vehicle body damage detection studies are typically proposed towards solving the claim leakage problem that is commonly encountered in the auto insurance claims. However, these studies use images taken from a short proximity (<3 m) to the vehicle or to the damaged region of vehicle in their decision making process. In this study, we investigate the vehicle frontal body damage detection problem in images captured from roadway surveillance cameras that are installed on fixed platforms. Proposed method utilizes ubiquitously used deep learning based object detection, feature representation and image classification methods to determine damage status for a given vehicle image. In particular, vehicle frontal region symmetry property and deep feature representations are utilized in the decision making stage as explained in the methodology section. Experimental results show that proposed method achieves 91% accuracy on a test dataset that includes a broad variety of damage types.

Keywords: Traffic enforcement · Damage detection · Symmetry · Deep learning · Single shot Multi-box detector (SSD)

1 Introduction

Recently, we have seen a surge in the applications of computer vision and deep learning towards intelligent transportation systems (ITS) solutions such as traffic enforcement, driving assistive systems and autonomous driving [1–10]. By leveraging the existing camera infrastructure installed on highways and roads, transportation authorities were able to reduce their service and staffing costs while boosting operational efficiency. These technological developments have also impacted traffic safety industry as well. With the proliferation of video surveillance systems, manual police effort has been reduced significantly in many traffic enforcement tasks such as front seat occupancy detection, seat belt enforcement, and distracted driver detection tasks [3, 5, 6]. In recent years, traffic authorities are interested in automated damaged vehicle detection from roadway camera images, sample images are illustrated in Fig. 1, to quickly identify vehicles that are involved in hit and run accidents. Moreover, they desire this detection

© Springer Nature Switzerland AG 2021
M. Helfert et al. (Eds.): SMARTGREENS 2019/VEHITS 2019, CCIS 1217, pp. 156–172, 2021.
https://doi.org/10.1007/978-3-030-68028-2_8

system to utilize existing camera infrastructure that is already installed on fixed platforms on roads. Over the past few years, various studies proposed methods towards vehicle body damage detection using camera images. However, these vehicle damage detection and recognition solutions have typically been proposed towards auto insurance industry to reduce the claim leakage problem [11, 14, 15, 18]. These earlier studies on damage detection and categorization tasks typically proposed view agnostic methods using close–up pictures of the damaged region. Most of these earlier approaches have used machine learning and deep learning techniques in their analysis. For instance, in a recent study, [14] developed a 3D computer aided design (CAD) model based approach in which a CAD model and RGB image were analyzed together to determine damaged regions of a vehicle using machine learning techniques. However, the need for a 3D model for every vehicle model prohibits wide-spread usage of this method. In another study, Patil et al. [11] introduced a deep learning based vehicle body damage classification method to classify an image into one of 8 classes (bumper dent, door dent, glass shatter, headlamp broken, scratch, smash, tail-lamp broken, non-damaged). The success of this method depends strongly on the localization of the damaged area. In that study, the authors utilized a close-up image of the damaged region which did not pose a challenge in their analysis. In another study [17] recently proposed a Mask R-CNN based approach to localize damaged regions of vehicles. Similar to others, this method works well for close up images and is not tested on distant images. In general, convolutional neural networks (CNNs) [7, 19] have been applied to structural damage assessment in these studies [16–18]. Another recent study by Li et al. [15] proposed an object detector based approach to detect the damaged regions and a CNN based classification of damage regions. As mentioned earlier, these methods are designed for insurance company claims and they are not directly applicable to fixed platform cameras since roadway cameras are designed for monitoring a large area in the roadways. In the case of vehicle body damage detection problem using roadway cameras, the existence of left/right symmetry is an important indicator in differentiating between damaged and non-damaged vehicles. Human cognition may easily perform symmetry analysis on front view vehicle images to assess damage status of the vehicle. For instance, Fig. 2 presents visual examples in which symmetry information allow us to recognize damage status even for vehicle models that may be unknown to us. Symmetry detection in images has been important concept in computer vision, and earlier studies proposed various machine learning based approaches to this problem [24, 25].

In this study, we propose a novel method towards damage status detection using the symmetry information by computing the similarity of the left and right halves of a tightly cropped region of the front side of the vehicle in roadway camera images. As shown in our experiments, adding symmetry information substantially improves prediction performance in this task. Proposed method utilizes a popular deep learning based object detection technique, single shot multi box (SSD) [8, 9] object detector, to extract a tight region of the front side of the vehicle that would be used for symmetry analysis. This is similar to an earlier vehicle parts based object detection study by He et al., [23] which utilizes deformable part based object detector to localize front hood, headlight and license plate regions, and classify features from these regions using ensemble of neural networks. Once the vehicle's front region is localized, *InceptionV3* convolutional neural

Fig. 1. Roadway surveillance system portrayal and sample vehicle images captured by it. Roadway camera images may be near infrared (NIR) or color (RGB) images.

Fig. 2. Damaged vehicle images captured by a roadway surveillance camera. Red rectangles encapsulate the damaged regions.

network (CNN) [19] based feature extraction approach is used to derive symmetry feature vectors, which are used by a linear support vector machine (SVM) classifier to determine damaged/non-damaged class status of the vehicle. With this study, we enriched the paper [27] by expanding it with new pre-processing and alternative feature extractor methods. With the expanding methodology, new datasets have been formed, new experiments and comparative analyses have been added. Also, we have significantly increased the size of the existing test dataset and renew previously performed experiments with this larger dataset in order obtain more reliable test results. In addition, we have improved the analysis of previous work by including a more detailed review of literature compared to the conference paper [27].

Figure 3 shows the general outline of the method proposed in this study. Upon the capture of a vehicle image, we detect the frontal vehicle region within the incoming vehicle image. Next, we determine the exact location and symmetrical center of the front region of the vehicle using SSD based vehicle parts detector model. Finally, using the symmetry derived deep feature representation, we determine vehicle body damage status. In Sect. 2, we summarize the steps of the proposed methods in more details. In Sect. 3, we first describe our experimental setup, data collection and we present a comparison of the performances of the proposed methods. Finally, we present our conclusions in Sect. 4.

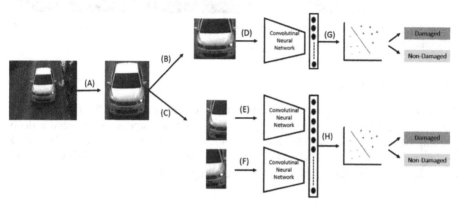

Fig. 3. Overview of the proposed vehicle damage assessment method. Vehicle detection is performed on the raw image (A). Next, we tightly crop the front region (B) and determine halves (C) of the detected vehicle. In part (D) we extract features with a CNN model using the cropped front vehicle region image. In part (E) and (F), we extract features from the halves of the vehicle separately and combine them. Finally, in part (G) and (H) we classify extracted features using SVMs.

2   Methodology

In this section, we describe the stages presented in Fig. 3 in more details. As the first step in our methodology, we detect the vehicle within the raw image using a pre-trained *VGG16* based SSD model available in the literature [8] as described in Sect. 2.1. This allows us to ignore the rest of the image since it is irrelevant to vehicle body damage detection task. However, this detection result typically includes the roof of the vehicle as shown in Fig. 3. (A). Therefore, we developed a model to tightly crop the front region of the detected vehicle image as described in Sect. 2.2. Using the tightly cropped frontal region image, we generate deep feature representations of vehicle as explained in Sect. 2.3. Finally, by applying a classification operation on these derived feature vectors, we determine the damage status of the vehicle.

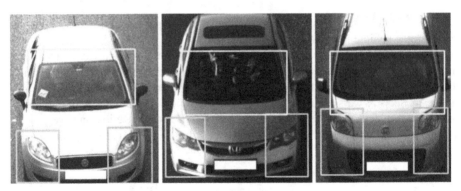

Fig. 4. Detected regions (3 parts; windshield, left headlight and right headlight) of a vehicle with SSD vehicle parts detector.

2.1 Vehicle Detection

As the first step in vehicle damage detection task, we need to localize the vehicle within the image captured by the surveillance camera. For this purpose, we utilized a deep learning based SSD model to localize the vehicle. Prior studies have shown that SSD model trained with *PASCAL VOC* [7, 21] is one of the most successful detectors in the literature for objects belonging 20 classes including *cars* [8].

2.2 Vehicle Frontal Parts Detection

Once the vehicle is detected in the raw image, we tightly crop the vehicle image to get rid of the roof region and the other possible non-vehicle regions. To this end, we localize parts of the vehicle (front windshield, right headlight and left headlight) in the

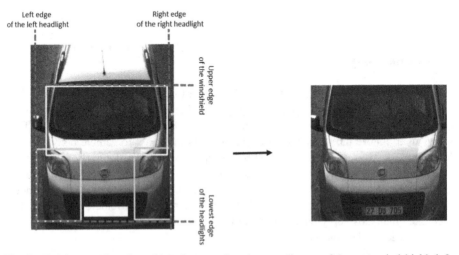

Fig. 5. Tightly cropping the vehicle image using the coordinates of 3 parts; windshield, left headlight and right headlight.

image and utilize the coordinates of these regions to tightly capture the vehicles' frontal region. For the frontal parts detection, we have fine-tuned a pre-trained *VGG16* based SSD model with our frontal parts detection dataset. The details of the training dataset and fine-tuning process are explained in Sect. 3.2. Figure 4 shows detected vehicle parts drawn over input images. After detection of frontal parts, we crop the front region of the vehicle using windshield, left/right headlight region coordinates as shown in Fig. 5.

2.3 Feature Extraction

Once the frontal region of the vehicle is detected as outlined in Sect. 2.2, we extract features to perform damage analysis. Unlike earlier approaches that utilize color and edge based features (such as SIFT and HOG), our proposed method is a deep feature representation based approach. In terms of the deep feature extraction, we utilized *InceptionV3* model [19] trained on *ImageNet* image classification dataset [20] due to its computational efficiency and success in vehicle re-identification problem as described in [12]. In this study, we have designed and analyzed 4 distinct deep learning feature representation approaches as explained in next subsections.

2.3.1 Transfer Learning

In our first approach, we utilized *InceptionV3* model trained on *ImageNet* dataset without any further training or fine-tuning using our existing dataset. Deep CNN models trained with *ImageNet* dataset are strong candidates to derive meaningful feature vectors in our case since *car* class is included as one of the learned 1000 classes in *ImageNet* dataset. In this approach, we use a pre-trained *InceptionV3* model as a feature extractor by getting a *2048*-d vector output of global average pooling layer as shown in Fig. 6. Figure 7 illustrates transfer learning approach for feature representation of the vehicle image. For the remainder of this study, we refer this feature as F_{TL}.

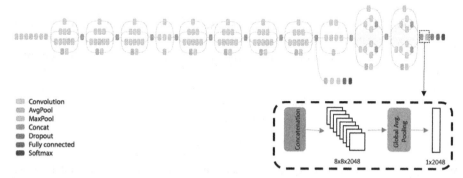

Fig. 6. InceptionV3 model architecture diagram [19]. Utilized feature extraction layers and their outputs are shown in dashed rectangle.

In our approaches, feature representation of the input images is one of the key points for the success of the proposed damage detection methods. To this end, we investigate the

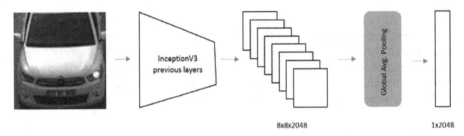

8x8x2048   1x2048

Fig. 7. Transfer learning based feature extraction method.

effect of CNN model fine-tuned specifically for vehicle images. The motivation behind the idea is the potential improvement in the damage detection accuracy that could be provided by improving the vehicle specific feature representation capability of the CNN model. It has been shown that *InceptionV3* model is very successful at image classification task when there is enough training data [12, 19]. Instead of utilizing *InceptionV3* model trained as a general purpose object classifier with *ImageNet* dataset stated as in previous paragraph, we also utilize InceptionV3 model fine-tuned for vehicle make-model recognition as feature extractor. We have fine-tuned the pre-trained *InceptionV3* model with our vehicle make-model recognition (VMMR) dataset containing day-time vehicle images. The details of the training dataset and training process are explained in Sect. 3.3.

2.3.2 Early Symmetrical Analysis

Second approach directly utilizes the visual symmetry property of non-damaged vehicles, in which if we divide the frontal region of the vehicle in 2 parts, left and right part should have high similarity score. Therefore, we partitioned the frontal region of the vehicle image into left and right parts, and mirror the left part image. Then, we derive a feature vector for each of these parts using the *InceptionV3* CNN model as specified in Sect. 2.3.1.

Assuming that the symmetrical parts have also similar representations in the feature space, we may combine the deep feature vectors of both parts using Eq. (1) or Eq. (2) as employed in previous Natural Language Processing studies [13] to represent semantic similarity.

$$X_{diff} = abs\left(X_{Left} - X_{Right}\right) \tag{1}$$

$$X_{prod} = X_{Left} \odot X_{Right} \tag{2}$$

where X_{Left} is the deep feature vector representation corresponding to the left half image and X_{Right} denotes the deep feature vector representation corresponding to the right half image. Note that $\odot$ operation shown in Eq. (2) is the element-wise product (a.k.a hadamard product) of X_{Left} and X_{Right} feature representations. While Eq. (1) is attenuating similar features, Eq. (2) stimulates the features of similar regions. Finally we obtain a *2048*-d feature vector representing the vehicle. Figure 8 visually illustrates the feature extraction process. For the remaining part of this study, we refer this feature as $F_{ESA\text{-}DIFF}$ or $F_{ESA\text{-}MUL}$ with respect to Eq. (1) and Eq. (2), respectively.

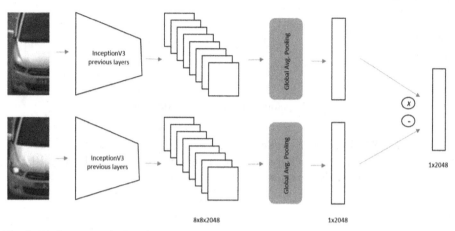

Fig. 8. Early symmetrical analysis feature extraction method. One branch for each of the right side and mirrored lefts side images.

2.3.3 Late Symmetrical Analysis

Similar to the Early Symmetrical Analysis, Late Symmetrical Analysis also utilizes the visual symmetry property of vehicles. However, unlike the Early Symmetrical Analysis approach, we considered to utilize symmetry information in the produced deep feature representation map instead of the input image. Throughout the convolutional blocks, CNNs transform the input image into feature maps by preserving spatial distribution of learned features. Thus, feature map of a non-damaged vehicle that is more compact representations of input image carries the symmetry property of the input image. This approach introduces more efficient way to utilize the symmetry property because it needs one forward pass in feature extractor network unlike the method described in Sect. 2.3.2. We utilize a pre-trained *InceptionV3* model by getting $8 \times 8 \times 2048$ shaped feature map output of its last concatenation layer shown in Fig. 6. Behaving to this feature map as symmetrical representation of original image, we divide it into $8 \times 4 \times 2048$ shaped left/right parts and mirror the left side. Then, we combine halves using operations shown in Eq. (1) and Eq. (2) alternatively. Finally, we apply global average filtering operation as in original InceptionV3 architecture onto resulting feature map to obtain *2048*-d feature vector representation of vehicle. A visual illustration of this approach can be found in Fig. 9. For the remaining part of this study, we refer this feature as $F_{LSA\text{-}DIFF}$ or $F_{LSA\text{-}MUL}$ with respect to the employed equation type.

2.3.4 Combined Feature Representation

In this approach, we utilize both symmetrical analysis features obtained in Sect. 2.3.3 and features of original image obtained in Sect. 2.3.1 to enrich the representation of

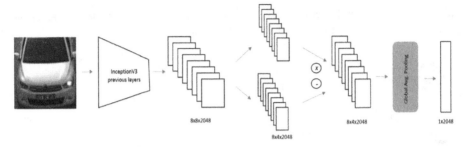

Fig. 9. Late symmetrical analysis feature extraction method.

vehicle image. We concatenate two feature vectors to combine the information and get *4096*-d feature vector. A visual illustration of this approach can be found in Fig. 10. For the remainder of this study, we refer this feature as F$_{\text{COMB}}$.

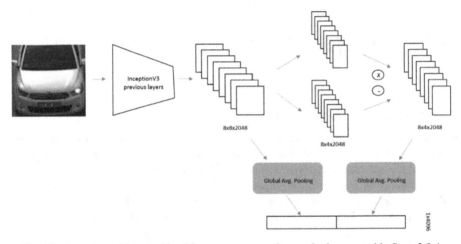

Fig. 10. Overview of the combined feature representation method presented in Sect. 2.3.4.

2.4 Classification

Upon the completion of feature extraction for damaged and non-damaged vehicle images, next, we build a separate binary classifier model for each type of feature representation approach mentioned in Sect. 2.3. Similar to [22], we utilized a linear support vector machine (SVM) to perform the classification using these feature vectors.

3 Experiments

3.1 Damage Classification Dataset and SVM Training

In this study, we utilized RGB camera images containing the frontal view of vehicles. Figure 11 shows several sample images used in our study. In contrast to the abundance of vehicle images, damaged vehicles could be rarely seen in real life images. Thus, firstly we collected damaged vehicle images from the Internet and then we added same number of non-damaged vehicle images to prevent uneven distribution of training dataset classes. Apart from the training dataset, we formed a completely distinct test dataset. In order to test the models, we collected 2000 non-damaged vehicle images and 300 damaged vehicle images. Table 1 shows the distribution of the number of images in our training, validation and test datasets.

Fig. 11. Sample detected vehicle images from the dataset. The first row shows non-damaged vehicles, the second row shows damaged vehicles.

Table 1. Number of images used in this study.

No. images	Training dataset	Validation dataset	Test dataset
Damaged	300	50	300
Non-damaged	300	50	2000

In the training stage of linear SVM model, we utilized 700 feature vectors (350/350 images for damaged and non-damaged classes) computed from images in training and validation dataset. We utilized 600 images for training and 100 images for validation purposes. In our training process, parameter selection is performed using validation performances.

3.2 Vehicle Frontal Parts Detection Dataset and Training

In the training process of the vehicle parts detection model, we utilized non-damaged dataset (training & validation data) for model training purposes. Vehicle parts, namely, windshield, right headlight and left headlight regions of the vehicles in these datasets are manually annotated for each image. Fine tuning operation is performed by freezing the weights of the first three convolutional blocks of the *VGG16* based SSD model. The rationale behind this strategy is based on 2 facts. First, three convolutional blocks trained with a large dataset (*ImageNet*) behave as a feature extractor. Thus, there is no need to update these weights with our relatively small dataset. Secondly, since the first feature map to be analyzed to detect objects fall into 4th convolutional block, it is logical to update weights starting from there. In our fine tuning operations, we set the batch size as 16. As learning hyper parameters, Adam optimizer [26], with a relatively small learning rate 0.0003 is utilized. We finalize the fine tuning process with respect to the validation performance of the model.

3.3   VMMR Dataset and Training

For the purposes of developing a vehicle make model recognition (VMMR) model, we utilized RGB surveillance camera and internet search-engines to collect vehicle images to train our vehicle make-model recognition model. In the training process of the vehicle make and model recognition model, we utilized a dataset consisting of 125,794 images belonging to 41 different vehicle makes as well as 857 different models. Out of 125,794 total images, 104,791 images have been collected from the Internet, and 21,003 day-time images have been collected from the roadway surveillance cameras. During the training process, 80% of them are utilized to train the model and remaining (20%) part is used for validation purposes.

In the training process of vehicle make-model recognition model, we apply consecutive transfer learning and fine tuning approaches because our training dataset contains 147 images per class on average. To this end, first we transfer the weights of the *InceptionV3* model trained with *ImageNet* classification dataset. And then its *1000*-d output layer is replaced with *857*-d output layer with soft-max activation. Finally fine tuning operation is performed by freezing the weights of the first 172 layers of the pre-trained model. The number of layers to be re-trained is determined experimentally. In our fine tuning process, batch size is set as 4 and stochastic gradient descent (SGD) with momentum optimizer with learning rate 0.0005 and momentum rate 0.9 is employed. Also, learning rate decay of 0.000001 is applied at each epoch. We finalize the fine tuning process with respect to the validation performance of the model. Validation accuracy of the trained VMMR model is 95%. Figure 12 shows the graphs of the change in accuracy and loss throughout the epochs of training process.

3.4   Result

In this section, we present and discuss the performance of the proposed 4 distinct vehicle body damage detection methods. Although evaluation of these methods consist of the analysis of three sub-stages of the overall pipeline, effect of first 2 stage (vehicle detection and vehicle frontal parts detection) on the performance results is negligible thanks to their successful detection rates. For the first stage, detailed performance analysis of the utilized model for vehicle detection could be seen in the paper [8].

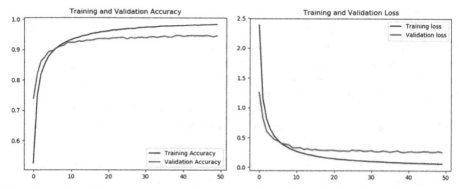

Fig. 12. Changes in accuracy rates and losses throughout the VMMR model training process. VMMR model obtained in 44th epoch is utilized in our experiments.

For the second stage, we performed vehicle parts detection on the 2300 test images described in Sect. 3.1 to tightly crop the vehicle images. Vehicle parts detector model successfully cropped % 97 of these images by detecting all of the 3 parts needed for tight crop operation. Analysis of the results shows that excessive amount of damage on the vehicle parts may cause the model not recognize them. This observation could be used to decide if a vehicle is damaged in this stage and may make feature extraction and SVM classification stages redundant. Figure 13 shows vehicle parts detection results that reflect our observation. We have manually cropped the remaining 3% of the test images in order use all of them in the performance analysis of SVM classifiers.

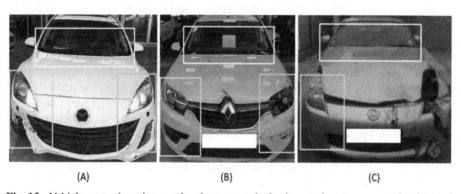

(A)   (B)   (C)

Fig. 13. Vehicle parts detection results show excessively damaged parts may not be detected. In image (A), all parts are non-damaged and successfully detected. In image (B), although right headlight is broken, right headlight region is successfully detected. In image (C), right headlight is absent and hereby right headlight region could not be detected.

We evaluated the performance of the SVM classifiers trained using reported feature representations on test images. We utilize accuracy metric to compare the performances. In our results, we report damaged and non-damaged class accuracies as well as the average accuracy values so that class imbalance would not mislead overall performance results. Table 2 presents the performance results of 4 different feature representation techniques using absolute difference and hadamard product in their feature generation process. Among the methods using one kind of feature representations (F_{TL}, F_{ESA}, F_{LSA}), the one utilizing F_{TL} yields the highest accuracy rate of 88.1%. Although it seems classification without utilizing symmetrical analysis is more successful, in order to observe the effect of symmetrical analysis more clearly we need to take into account the performances of combined feature representations noting that the performances of the F_{TL}, F_{LSA}, and F_{ESA} methods are close to each other.

Table 2. Accuracy rates of feature representations obtained using ImageNet classifier InceptionV3 model as base model. (F_{TL} approach is independent of the absolute difference and hadamard product operations).

	Absolute difference (DIFF)			Hadamard product (MUL)		
	Damaged class accuracy	Nondamaged class accuracy	Average accuracy	Damaged class accuracy	Nondamaged class accuracy	Average accuracy
F_{TL}	0.920	0.842	0.881	0.920	0.842	0.881
F_{ESA}	0.912	0.716	0.814	0.945	0.775	0.860
F_{LSA}	0.920	0.825	0.873	0.886	0.854	0.870
F_{COMB}	0.930	0.888	**0.909**	0.935	0.842	**0.889**

Among the symmetrical analysis techniques, late symmetrical analysis approach gives higher overall accuracies than the early symmetrical analysis technique in both cases ($F_{LSA-DIFF}$ or $F_{LSA-MUL}$). Despite the similar theoretical background, F_{LSA} methods outperform the F_{ESA} methods in terms of both computational efficiency (as stated in Sect. 2.3.3) and overall accuracy. Thus, we ignored F_{ESA} features and combined two feature representations, F_{LSA} and F_{TL}, as described in Sect. 2.3.4 to boost the performance of similarity analysis. When comparing the average accuracy performances of the other classifiers with F_{COMB}, F_{COMB} yields the highest accuracy rate in terms of both absolute difference (90.9%) and hadamard product (88.9%) cases. These results demonstrate that proposed symmetrical analysis approach boosts the performance of damage assessment classifier. However, there is no apparent superiority between using absolute difference or hadamard product functions in symmetrical analysis process according to Table 2.

We also investigate the effect of feature extractor on damage detection performance. Thus, we repeat the same experiments with the same methods utilizing the weights of the model trained for vehicle make model classification instead of the weights of the model trained for *ImageNet* object classification in their feature extraction stage. Table 3 presents the performance results of 4 different feature representation techniques using absolute difference and hadamard product functions in their feature generation process. In contrast to our intuition, using the vehicle make model recognition model decreased the performance results in almost all cases, except for F_{ESA} with absolute difference function. However, our inference in Table 2 related to performance boost obtained with combined feature representation, coincides with the results shown in Table 3. Again, damage classifier utilizing combined feature representation of vehicle image yields the highest accuracy rates in terms of both absolute difference (84.8%) and hadamard product (73.9%) cases. Absolute difference function seems preferable by performing 11% better than hadamard product. Our prediction related to the performance drop caused by VMMR model is that fine-tuning the CNN model for vehicle make-model classification task shifts the attention of the model to more specific and distinctive structures of vehicles and it makes CNN model tend to produce more superficial representation of many vehicle regions that could be damaged. In order to be able to explain the reasons behind the performance drop in a more definite way, further studies are needed.

Table 3. Accuracy rates of feature representations obtained VMMR classifier InceptionV3 model as base model. (F_{TL} approach is independent of the absolute difference and hadamard product operations).

	Absolute difference (DIFF)			Hadamard product (MUL)		
	Damaged class accuracy	Nondamaged class accuracy	Average accuracy	Damaged class accuracy	Nondamaged class accuracy	Average accuracy
F_{TL}	0.750	0.719	0.735	0.750	0.719	0.735
F_{ESA}	0.925	0.745	0.835	0.666	0.808	0.737
F_{LSA}	0.899	0.769	0.834	0.635	0.802	0.719
F_{COMB}	0.817	0.878	**0.848**	0.675	0.802	**0.739**

Overall results of experiments introduce 3 main outcomes related to proposed vehicle damage assessment methods:

- For deep feature extraction, general purpose object classifier model is preferable to vehicle make model (VMMR) classifier model.
- Transfer learning and similarity analysis together boosts the performance of the vehicle damage classifier and produce the highest accuracies.
- For symmetrical analysis approach, absolute difference operation performs better than hadamard product operation.

Visual analysis of classification results produced by F_{COMB} presents the performance of the model in a more intuitive way. The first row in Fig. 14 presents accurately classified vehicles with varying damages. The second row in Fig. 14 presents incorrectly classified vehicles with some minor or evenly distributed damages. These results show that F_{COMB} is able to represent vehicles with non-symmetrical and noticeable damages successfully in its feature space.

The computation time of proposed methods are analyzed using a computer with Nvidia GeForce GTX 780 Ti GPU card, 16 GB RAM, Intel Core i7 processor. SSD based vehicle and vehicle parts detection, InceptionV3 based feature extraction and SVM

Fig. 14. Sample damaged vehicle images in the test set collected from the Internet [28] with red ellipses enclosing the ground truth damaged areas. The first row shows samples successfully classified as damaged. The second row shows incorrectly classified damaged vehicle samples.

classification tasks are analyzed on GPU. SSD model performs vehicle detection and vehicle parts detection tasks at approximately 60 ms. Inference time of the *InceptionV3* model is approximately 40 ms and SVM classification takes 10 ms on average. Table 4 shows the overall run-times of the proposed pipelines utilizing each feature extraction methods. The operations specific to each feature extraction method have minor costs and they are negligible.

Table 4. Run time analysis of proposed methods.

	Run time (msec)
F_{TL}	170
F_{ESA}	170
F_{LSA}	170
F_{COMB}	170

4 Conclusion

This study proposes various deep learning based approaches towards the vehicle damage detection task using roadway camera images. In our analysis, we have investigated the ways of utilizing pre-trained CNN models for the case of a limited dataset. Furthermore, we have also put effort to utilize symmetry property of frontal designs of the vehicles in order to cope up with the dataset limitations. We used a semantic similarity analysis based approach in utilizing the symmetry property of vehicles' frontal views. Moreover, symmetry property is also utilized in the deep feature extraction process. Our experimental analysis shows that the ensemble model (F_{COMB}) that combines the symmetrical analysis feature representation (F_{LSA}) and transfer learning feature representation (F_{TL}) yields the most accurate result with the accuracy rates of 90.9% and 88.9%. These results indicates that image classifier model pre-trained with *Imagenet* dataset could be utilized as a baseline feature extractor for vehicle damage assessment task and semantic similarity analysis boosts the performance by improving the damage specific representation capability of feature space. In future work, we plan to train and test the proposed methods on a larger dataset including night-time images. Also, we plan to focus on image completion approaches emerged with Generative Adversarial Network (GAN) literature for vehicle damage detection task.

References

1. Loce, R.P., Bernal, E.A., Wu, W., Bala, R.: Computer vision in roadway transportation systems: a survey. J. Electron. Imaging **22**(4), 041121 (2013)
2. Janai, J., Guney, F., Behl, A., Geiger, A.: Computer vision in autonomous vehicles: problems, datasets and state-of-the-art. https://arxiv.org/abs/1704.05519 (2017)
3. Artan, Y., Bulan, O., Loce, R.P., Paul, P.: Passenger compartment violation detection in HOV/HOT lanes. IEEE Trans. Intell. Transp. Syst. **17**(2), 395–405 (2016)
4. Seshadri, K., Juefei-Xu, F., Pal, D. K., Savvides, M., Thor, C.: Driver cell phone usage detection on Strategic Highway Research Program (shrp2) face view videos. In: Proceedings of the IEEE Conference on Computer Vision and Pattern Recognition Workshops, pp. 35–43 (2015)
5. Elihos, A., Alkan, B., Balci, B., Artan, Y.: Comparison of image classification and object detection for passenger seat belt violation detection using NIR & RGB surveillance camera images. In: 15th IEEE International Conference on Advanced Video and Signal Based Surveillance (AVSS), pp. 1–6 (2018)
6. Balci, B., Alkan, B., Elihos, A., Artan, Y.: Front seat child occupancy detection in roadway surveillance images. In: ICIP'2018, IEEE Conference on Image Processing (2018)
7. Simonyan, K., Zisserman, A.: Very deep convolutional networks for large-scale image recognition, arXiv:1409.1556 (2014)
8. Liu, W., et al.: SSD: single shot multibox detector. In: Leibe, B., Matas, J., Sebe, N., Welling, M. (eds.) ECCV 2016. LNCS, vol. 9905, pp. 21–37. Springer, Cham (2016). https://doi.org/10.1007/978-3-319-46448-0_2
9. Huang, J., et al.: Speed/accuracy trade-offs for modern convolutional object detectors. arXiv: 1611.10012v3 (2017)
10. IBM. IBM Smarter Cities Public Safety, Law Enforcement Report (2012)
11. Patil, K., Kulkarn, M., Sriraman, A., Karande, S.: Deep learning based car damage classification. In: 16th IEEE International Conference on Machine Learning and Applications (ICMLA), pp. 50–54. IEEE (2017)
12. Kanacı, A., Zhu, X., Gong, S.: Vehicle re-identification by Fine grained cross-level deep learning. In: British Machine Vision Conference (BMVC), pp. 772–788 (2017)
13. Blacoe, W., Lapata, M.: A comparison of vector-based representations for semantic composition. In: Proceedings of 2012 Joint Conference on Emprical Methods in natural Language Processing and Computational Natural Language Learning, pp. 546–556 (2012)

14. Jayawardena, S.: Image based automatic vehicle damage detection. Ph.D. Dissertation, Australian National University (2013)
15. Li, P., Shen, B.Y., Dong, W.: An anti-fraud system for car insurance claim based on visual evidence, arXiv:1804.11207v1 (2018)
16. Cha, Y.J., Choi, W., Buyukozturk, O.: Deep learning based crack damage detection using convolutional neural networks. Comput. Aided Civ. Infrastruct. Eng. 32(5), 361–378 (2017)
17. MaskRCNN.:https://www.analyticsvidhya.com/blog/2018/07/building-mask-r-cnn-model-detecting-damage-cars-python (2018)
18. Tractable: https://www.tractable.io (2018)
19. Szegedy, C., Vanhoucke, V., Ioffe, S., Shlens J., Wojna, Z.: Rethinking the inception architecture in computer vision, arXiv:1512.00567v3 (2015)
20. Deng, J., Dong, W., et al.: ImageNet: a large scale hierarchical image database. In: CVPR'2009 IEEE Conference on Computer Vision and Pattern Recognition (CVPR), pp. 248–255. IEEE (2009)
21. Everingham, M., Gool, L.V., Williams, W.K.I., Winn, J., Zisserman, A.: The PASCAL visual object classes (VOC) challenge. Int. J. Comput. Vis. 88, 303–338 (2010). https://doi.org/10.1007/s11263-009-0275-4
22. Razavian, A.S., et al.: CNN features off the shelf: an astounding baseline for recognition. arXiv:1403.6382v3, pp. 1–8 (2014)
23. He, H., Shao, Z., Tan, J.: Recognition of car makes and models from a single traffic-camera image. IEEE Trans. Intell. Transp. Syst. 16(6), 3182–3192 (2015)
24. Loy, G., Eklundh, J.-O.: Detecting symmetry and symmetric constellations of features. In: Leonardis, A., Bischof, H., Pinz, A. (eds.) ECCV 2006. LNCS, vol. 3952, pp. 508–521. Springer, Heidelberg (2006). https://doi.org/10.1007/11744047_39
25. Shechtman, E., Irani, M.: Matching local self-similarities across images and videos. In: IEEE Conference on Computer Vision and Pattern Recognition, pp. 1–8. IEEE (2007)
26. Kingma, D., Ba, J.: Adam: a method for stochastic optimization. arXiv:1412.6980 (2014)
27. Balci, B., Artan, Y., Alkan, B., Elihos, A.: Front-view vehicle damage detection using roadway surveillance camera images. In: VEHITS'2019, International Conference on Vehicle Technology and Intelligent Transport Systems, pp. 193–198 (2019)
28. Sahibinden: https://www.sahibinden.com (2019)

Efficient Symbolic Routing Encoding for In-vehicle Network Optimization

Fedor Smirnov[1]([✉]) [iD], Behnaz Pourmohseni[1] [iD], Michael Glaß[2] [iD],
and Jürgen Teich[1] [iD]

[1] Friedrich-Alexander-Universität Erlangen-Nürnberg (FAU),
Cauerstr. 11, 91058 Erlangen, Germany
`{fedor.smirnov,behnaz.pourmohseni,juergen.teich}@fau.de`
[2] Universität Ulm, Albert-Einstein-Allee 11, 89081 Ulm, Germany
`michael.glass@uni-ulm.de`

Abstract. As a consequence of the steadily increasing complexity of modern automotive applications, the efficient and optimal design of in-vehicle communication networks necessitates techniques for automated network optimization and, in particular, message routing. Hereby, the major portion of symbolic routing optimization techniques found in literature are either constraint- or enumeration-based. While the former encode the inclusion of each individual network component into the message route, the latter require a computationally expensive enumeration of all possible transmission routes. This work presents a novel routing optimization technique that combines the advantages of these two approaches. There, a lightweight preprocessing step identifies network areas where each pair of resources can be connected by exactly one route. Any message route through such an area is directly dictated by the source and the destination of the message, so that these areas do not offer any potential for routing optimization. In this work, we provide an in-depth discussion of preprocessing techniques required to identify so-called *proxy areas* around end nodes which do not offer any routing variety. Moreover, we propose an extension of the preprocessing which—in contrast to existing preprocessing techniques—is capable of finding so-called *express areas*, i.e., internal regions of the network offering no routing variety. We demonstrate how variety awareness can be introduced into existing constraint-based approaches to improve both the run time of the optimization and the quality of the optimization results. Experimental results for three different topologies of in-vehicle networks give evidence that, compared to s.o.t.a. approaches for routing optimization, the proposed approaches deliver optimization results of equal or higher quality, offer an optimization speedup of up to ×186, and can, therefore, be used for the optimization of significantly larger automotive networks.

Keywords: DSE · Network optimization · Automotive networks

© Springer Nature Switzerland AG 2021
M. Helfert et al. (Eds.): SMARTGREENS 2019/VEHITS 2019, CCIS 1217, pp. 173–199, 2021.
https://doi.org/10.1007/978-3-030-68028-2_9

1 Introduction

Throughout the last decade, the large number of innovative applications has made the design of automotive communication networks significantly more complex. The quickly growing demand for computation and communication power is met by an increasing number of electronic control units (ECUs) integrated in a vehicle, so that automotive communication networks keep growing in both size and complexity. Novel communication protocols make the design process even more complex, as they introduce additional constraints which must be considered during message routing. Modern automotive wiring harnesses significantly contribute to the overall weight and monetary cost of vehicles[1]. Moreover, automotive networks are used to transmit the messages of distributed safety-critical applications such as airbag control or driver assistance and must, therefore, be regarded as safety-critical components and optimized w.r.t. transmission reliability. This ongoing increase in (a) the size of communication networks and (b) the number and complexity of design objectives render the manual design of automotive communication networks impractical, if at all feasible, since the design space features an extensive number of possible network designs and each considered design has to be evaluated w.r.t. many—oftentimes conflicting and non-linear—design objectives such as monetary cost, weight, transmission timing, and transmission reliability.

Approaches for design automation offer an interesting opportunity to overcome the shortcomings of manual design, as they reduce design errors and offer design solutions of higher quality [23]. Consequently, this research area receives great attention from the scientific community. As finding the optimal network design is an NP-hard problem [2], an enumeration of all possible combinations of design decisions is computationally infeasible, except for very small problem sizes. Moreover, especially for complex communication networks, a large portion of possible combinations of design decisions result in infeasible solutions, e.g., network designs lacking transmission routes between senders and receivers. As a remedy, most design automation approaches rely on constraint sets that describe conditions that must be satisfied for a network design to be valid, e.g., constraints to enforce that a valid network contains a transmission path between the sender and the receiver(s) of each message. The resolution of the constraint set, i.e., finding an assignment of the design decision variables that satisfies all constraints, is then either used as a repair mechanism (to *repair* infeasible designs into valid ones) as part of a dedicated optimizer, e.g., an evolutionary algorithm [12], or even as the main optimization mechanism [18].

In the embedded domain, the so-called *system synthesis*, i.e., the implementation of an application on a given network architecture, is typically decomposed into a set of *allocation*, *binding*, and *routing* decisions [2]. In this context, *symbolic DSE* is used for system synthesis. There, individual design decisions are encoded using Boolean variables (hence the term *symbolic*) and the search space

---

[1] Nowadays, a wiring harness features roughly 23 kg in weight and 1.2 km in length [8].

of valid design solutions is defined by a set of (Pseudo-)Boolean constraints. These so-called *synthesis constraints* encode a valid binding of the application's tasks onto the network's resources, a valid allocation of the required resources, and a valid routing of messages that are transmitted between resources executing data-dependent tasks. The computational effort for the generation and resolution of these constraints, which has an immense impact on the efficiency and even the feasibility of the overall optimization [22], typically scales exponentially with the number of encoded decision variables. An efficient encoding of feasible routings is particularly important since routing constraints—except for the most trivial network topologies—constitute the most complex part of the synthesis constraint set and introduce the largest share of encoded decision variables.

The majority of s.o.t.a. routing encoding approaches fall into one of the following two classes: (a) so-called *route preprocessing (RP)* approaches which rely on a preprocessing phase to find all possible routes connecting each pair of nodes [6,10]. During the optimization, one of the preprocessed routes that connect the message's source to its destination is selected for each message. Alternatively, (b) so-called *componential assembly (CA)* approaches are based on a symbolic routing encoding, i.e. the introduction of binary activation variables that represent the inclusion of each network component—e.g., a link or a node—into the route of each message and the formulation of constraints to ensure the assembly of valid routes [1,16,17,24]. The resolution of these constraints provides an assignment of the activation variables based on which a valid route is constructed by assembling the activated components.

As shown in [7], the strengths and weaknesses of RP and CA approaches are somewhat complimentary. CA approaches encode the usage of each network component per message, regardless of the network topology. This not only introduces a high number of encoding variables—especially in case of complex routing behaviors like multicasts [14] or redundant transmissions [29]—but also results in an unnecessarily complex description of the routing optimization search space. RP approaches, on the other hand, use the preprocessing phase to acquire total knowledge on the network topology and provide the optimizer with a compact description of the actual search space. However, their need for an enumeration of all routing possibilities limits the applicability of RP approaches to *sparsely-connected* network topologies where the number of possible routes is small, even for large networks. For *densely-connected* network topologies, the encoding overhead of CA approaches is more than compensated by their superior scalability. Furthermore, the fine-grained encoding of routing decisions in CA approaches not only enables the formulation of additional constraints, e.g., to respect link capacity or the mutual exclusion of components, but also provides optimization results of significantly higher quality when optimizing objectives such as monetary cost or reliability, which are strongly influenced by individual components of the routes [29].

Contribution. Real-life communication networks rarely completely fall into one of the two extreme connectivity categories listed above (dense or sparse), but

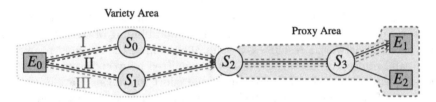

Fig. 1. Resource network consisting of a variety area (yellow/left) and a proxy area (green/right). All differences between the routes connecting ECU E_0 to ECU E_1 (I, II, and III) occur within the variety area [27]. (Color figure online)

rather constitute a connection of several subnetworks, each being either sparse or dense. This holds particularly true for automotive networks: On the one hand, safety-critical ADAS applications make a certain degree of transmission redundancy mandatory. On the other hand, the high cost pressure and the necessity to reuse network designs from previous car generations prohibit the free practice of redundancy at every possible point. Rather than that, it seems more likely that redundancy is considered only for the most critical components, e.g., links which are especially vulnerable or important. This redundancy scheme results in network topologies in which several sparsely-connected subnetworks are connected with each other via densely-connected network regions.

CA and RP approaches excel for routing optimization in either densely- or sparsely-connected networks, respectively. They, however, suffer in efficiency or practicability when applied to the compound network topologies described above. In [27], we have introduced an optimization approach that combines the strengths of these two strategies and proves effective for such networks. In this approach, the given network is partitioned into network areas of one of the two following types: (a) *proxy areas* which offer exactly one routing possibility between each pair of nodes contained within them and (b) areas with a *variety* of different routing possibilities between each node pair, the so-called *variety areas*. The proposed approach alleviates the optimization's computational overhead by exploiting the fact that—since any potential for routing optimization is based on a variety of different routing options—excluding proxy areas from the optimization does not limit the search space, as any valid route can be unambiguously described by specifying its route segments within the variety areas.

This idea is exemplified for the simple network in Fig. 1. The figure depicts a communication network consisting of one variety area (yellow, left) and one proxy area (green, right). For a communication between ECU E_0 and ECU E_1, the architecture offers three distinct routes (I, II, and III) which differ from each other only in their respective segment in the variety area and are identical within the proxy area. Each and every route between E_0 and E_1 can, therefore, be uniquely specified by its route segment in the variety area (the segment between E_0 and S_2).

The main idea from [27] is to enable a more efficient routing encoding by exploiting the knowledge that certain subregions of the given network do not offer routing variety. In addition to a more in-depth explanation of the techniques proposed in [27], the work at hand extends this approach by introducing the concept of so-called *express areas*. Similarly to proxy areas, express areas constitute network regions without routing variety. However, while proxy areas are built around communication end nodes, express areas are situated in network regions further away from the end nodes.

As part of our contribution, we (a) present lightweight algorithms that identify proxy and express areas of the given network and (b) propose two approaches to exploit the knowledge about routing variety within any existing CA routing optimization approach. The hereby obtained encoding of the routing search space is tailored to the given network topology, combines the efficiency of RP route optimization approaches with the scalability and extensibility of CA approaches, and can be applied to any application and any network. Experimental results for three topologies of in-vehicle networks give evidence that an optimization based on the concept of routing variety is faster by up to two orders of magnitude, yields optimization results of equal or higher quality compared to s.o.t.a. routing optimization approaches, and, consequently, enables an automated design optimization of systems which are significantly larger than what existing approaches can practicably optimize.

2   Related Work

A large amount of work on the topic of routing optimization during the design of embedded systems can be found in literature. The authors of [30] provide an introduction to the general problem and to various existing routing algorithms. A detailed performance comparison between RP and CA approaches is given in [7]. There, the authors show that RP approaches can outperform CA approaches in sufficiently sparse networks. In general, RP approaches are not considered to be a good practice, as enumerating all routing possibilities is an NP-hard problem. To overcome the scalability problem, RP approaches, therefore, often limit the search space. The authors of [10], for instance, consider only the K shortest routes, while the RP heuristic presented in [6] is targeted at reusing the already allocated links.

The majority of existing routing optimization approaches can be viewed as CA approaches. An encoding describing the activation of links in AFDX networks is presented in [1]. The authors of [15] present a constraint set that can be used for a simultaneous optimization of the routing, the allocation, and the task mapping of an embedded system. Indeed, the easy modification to certain design goals is an additional advantage of CA approaches. For example, several works present constraint sets for a joint optimization of routing and transmission schedule [16,17,24,25] or even the optimization of the VLAN partitioning of an automotive network [28]. Yet, to the best of our knowledge, existing CA approaches formulate the constraints regardless of the topology. In a previous work [27], we have shown that information about the proxy regions of the given network can be exploited to increase the efficiency of routing encoding approaches. In the work at hand, we provide a more detailed description of the ideas presented in [27] and show how these ideas can be extended by the concept of so-called express areas to further improve the encoding efficiency and the quality of the optimization results.

3   System Model

The strategies presented in this paper can be applied to any routing optimization approach relying on a CA routing encoding. Without loss of generality, we use the graph-based system model presented in [14] for the explanations throughout the paper. There, the entire search space of the design problem at hand is modeled by the so-called *specification*. Each valid problem solution—referred to as an *implementation*—is generated based on the specification by resolving the synthesis constraints.

3.1   Specification

The specification comprises the *architecture graph*, the *application graph*, and the *mapping edges* which connect the two graphs.

The architecture graph $\mathcal{G}_R(\mathcal{N}_R, \mathcal{E}_l)$ consists of resource nodes $\mathcal{N}_R = \mathcal{N}_E \cup \mathcal{N}_S$, which are connected by bidirectional link edges $l \in \mathcal{E}_l$. In the context of automotive communication networks, each resource is either an ECU $E \in \mathcal{N}_E$ or a switch $S \in \mathcal{N}_S$.

The application graph $\mathcal{G}_A(\mathcal{N}_T, \mathcal{E}_d)$ contains task nodes $\mathcal{N}_T = \mathcal{N}_P \cup \mathcal{N}_C$ and data dependencies $\mathcal{E}_d$. Each task is either a process $P \in \mathcal{N}_P$ or a message $C \in \mathcal{N}_C$, while each data dependency is a directed edge between a message and a process. We refer to the predecessor and the successor tasks of a message as the *source* and *destination tasks* of the message.

Each mapping edge $m = (P, E) \in \mathcal{E}_m$ between a process $P \in \mathcal{N}_P$ and an ECU $E \in \mathcal{N}_E$ indicates that the process P can be implemented on ECU E.

3.2   Implementation

An implementation represents a valid solution of the system synthesis problem and is derived from the specification through the resolution of a set of *allocation, binding*, and *routing* constraints:

- **Allocation:** A subset of the architecture graph $\mathcal{G}_R$ is chosen to form the allocated architecture graph. In a valid design, a resource is allocated only if it is used to execute at least one processes or to transmit at least one message.
- **Binding:** Processes are bound to ECUs by choosing exactly one mapping edge for each process. This edge then identifies the ECU where the process is executed in the implementation, the so-called *binding target* of the process.

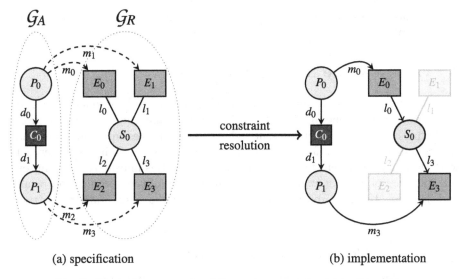

(a) specification   (b) implementation

Fig. 2. Illustrative example of the system model used in this work.

- **Routing:** In the implementation, the route of each message $C \in \mathcal{N}_C$ is represented by a *routing graph* $\vec{\mathcal{G}}_R(C)$, a directed acyclic subgraph of $\mathcal{G}_R$. A routing graph starts at the binding target of the source task of its message and has the binding target(s) of the destination task(s) as leaf(/ves), fulfilling the data dependencies.

3.3   Illustrative Example

An illustrative example of the system model used in this work is given in Fig. 2. Figure 2a shows an example specification, while Fig. 2b depicts an implementation that can be generated based on this specification.

The specification in Fig. 2a consists of the application graph $\mathcal{G}_A$ on the left, the architecture graph $\mathcal{G}_R$ of the right, and the mapping edges between the two graphs. The application graph contains the two process tasks P_0 and P_1. The data dependency between P_0 is P_1 is represented by the communication task C_0 and the dependency edges d_0 and d_1. The architecture graph represents an automotive Ethernet network where the four ECUs E_0–E_3 are connected by the Ethernet switch S_0 and the links l_0–l_3. The mapping edges m_0 and m_1 (m_2 and m_3) indicate that the process task P_0 (P_1) can be implemented on the ECUs E_0 and E_1 (E_2 and E_3).

Figure 2b illustrates an implementation that can be generated based on the specification from Fig. 2a. The process tasks P_0 and P_1 are bound onto the ECUs E_0 and E_3 by activating the mapping edges m_0 and m_3, respectively. The data dependency between P_0 and P_1 is satisfied by routing message C_0 over the route consisting of the resources E_0, S_0, and E_3 and the links l_0 and l_3. Resources E_1

and E_2 and the links l_1 and l_2 are not allocated, since they are used neither for the execution of processes nor for the transmission of messages.

4   Variety-Aware Routing Encoding

This section contains the main contributions of the work at hand. We start by explaining the general idea of routing variety and the concepts of proxy and express areas. We then present lightweight preprocessing algorithms that gather routing-variety information by identifying these areas in any given network. Finally, we present two approaches to exploit this information to improve the efficiency of routing exploration and the quality of the optimization results and show how these approaches can be integrated into a given routing constraint set.

4.1   General Idea: Proxy and Express Areas

In CA routing optimization approaches, the inclusion of a link in the route of a message is reflected by a binary decision variable. Such a variable is encoded for each link and each message. While this strategy ensures that no route is excluded from the search space, it introduces unnecessary encoding variables for most networks.

Proxy Areas. Consider, e.g., l_0 in Fig. 3a. This link connects ECU E_0 to the rest of the network via switch S_0. Since E_0 is accessible solely through l_0, one can conclude that l_0 is necessarily used in **each and every** route to/from E_0. Thus, encoding a decision variable for the inclusion of l_0 in routes to/from E_0 provides no added optimization value, as each route starting/ending at E_0 (referred to as a *proxy slave*) can be uniquely specified using a corresponding route starting/ending at S_0 (referred to as the *proxy master* of E_0).

Extending the concept of proxy (master/slave) relations to larger network areas provides an even more compact routing encoding. Consider, e.g., ECUs E_5–E_8 and the switches S_6 and S_7 in Fig. 3. In the terminology used in this paper, we summarize these resources and the links between them as a so-called *proxy area* with S_6 as the proxy master of the entire area. Between each pair of resources within a proxy area, there exists exactly one possible route. In particular, there is exactly one possible route between any of these resources and S_6, the proxy master of the area. Consequently, any connection between a resource outside the proxy area and a resource within the area consists of an *external* route that connects the outside resource to the proxy master and an *internal* route connecting the proxy master to the proxy slave inside the proxy area. Only the external route can be established in multiple different ways (using different sets of links) and is, therefore, relevant for routing optimization. Contrary to that, there is only one possible way to create the internal route. Links within proxy areas, thus, provide no benefit for routing optimization and can be excluded from the routing encoding.

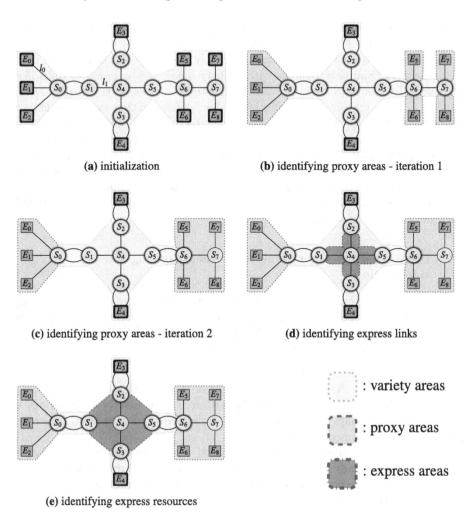

(a) initialization

(b) identifying proxy areas - iteration 1

(c) identifying proxy areas - iteration 2

(d) identifying express links

(e) identifying express resources

: variety areas

: proxy areas

: express areas

Fig. 3. Iterative identification of proxy and express areas. The proxy areas (green, dashed) are identified by iteratively establishing transitive proxy relations between resource pairs. Next, the express areas (violet, dashed and dotted) are identified by searching for the express links which connect two otherwise disconnected parts of the network. The variety areas (yellow, dotted) encompass all proxy masters (blue glow) and are reduced in each iteration. (Color figure online)

Express Areas. Proxy areas are built around communication end nodes and, consequently, are situated at the boundaries of a network. An additional observation about certain network links makes it possible to identify so-called *express areas*, i.e., internal network regions which do not offer routing variety. Consider, e.g., link l_1 in Fig. 3a. This link connects two otherwise disconnected regions of the network, separating the network into a left (ECUs E_0–E_2 and switches S_0 and S_1) and a right (ECUs E_3–E_8 and switches S_2–S_7) part. Consequently, link

l_1 is (a) **always** included in the route of any message which is transmitted from the left to the right part of the network or vice versa and (b) **never** included in the route of a message which is transmitted only within the left or the right part of the network. Similarly to links within proxy areas, the inclusion of links like l_1—referred to as *express links*—into the route of a message is directly determined by the source and the destination of the message, so that express links can be excluded from routing optimization without losing any optimization potential. Analogously to proxy areas, express links connected to the same resources and resources which are connected exclusively to express links can be summarized to express areas. During the optimization of message routings, only the route segments to and from proxy masters at the border of express areas can be optimized, while the resources and links within express areas can be excluded from the routing encoding.

4.2   Preprocessing Algorithms to Gather Routing-Variety Information

The proxy and the express areas in a given network are identified by gathering information about the routing variety offered by the links of the network. In this section, we present two lightweight algorithms that can be used to find the proxy and the express areas of a network, respectively.

Identifying Proxy Areas. The proxy areas of the network are identified using the iterative algorithm described by Algorithm 1. This algorithm generates a dictionary which maps resources to their respective proxy masters (where a proxy master is mapped to itself).

Initially, every resource is mapped to itself and registered into $\mathcal{L}$, a list of potential masters (lines 5–7 in Algorithm 1). Over the course of several iterations (lines 9–19), the algorithm (I) examines every resource in the list (line 11), (II) identifies proxy slaves (resources with only one neighbor denoted as master—line 12), (III) updates their map entry with their sole neighbor as their proxy master (line 13), and (IV) eliminates them from the list of masters (line 15). Proxy relations are transitive. Thus, if R_m is identified as master of R, R_m automatically becomes the master of each resource $\widetilde{R}$ that was hitherto considered as a slave of R (lines 17–19). The algorithm terminates when no new proxy slaves are found during an iteration.

The functionality of the algorithm for the identification of proxy areas is illustrated in Figs. 3d and e. Each subsequent iteration identifies new proxy slaves, expands the proxy areas and shrinks the variety areas. The algorithm terminates when no new proxy slaves are found in iteration 2 (Fig. 3c). Except the proxy masters E_3–E_4 and S_0–S_6, which form the variety area of the network, all resources are then located inside proxy areas.

Algorithm 1. Identifying Proxy Areas.

Input: Architecture graph $\mathcal{G}_R$
Output: Dictionary $\mathcal{M}$ mapping each resource $R \in \mathcal{N}_R$ to its proxy master

1: **procedure** IDENTIFYPROXYAREAS($\mathcal{G}_R$)
2:     $\mathcal{M} = \{\}$ ▷ Dictionary mapping a resource to its proxy master
3:     $\mathcal{S} = \{\}$ ▷ Dictionary mapping a resource to a list of its proxy slaves
4:     $\mathcal{L} = [\,]$ ▷ List of resources considered proxy masters
5:     **for all** $R \in \mathcal{N}_R$ **do**
6:         $\mathcal{M}(R) = R$
7:         $\mathcal{L}.add(R)$
8:     $foundProxySlaves = True$
9:     **while** $foundProxySlaves$ **do**
10:         $foundProxySlaves = False$
11:         **for all** R in $\mathcal{L}$ **do:**
12:             **if** $numberOfMasterNeighbors(R) == 1$ **then**
13:                 $\mathcal{M}(R) = masterNeighbor(R)$
14:                 $\mathcal{S}(\mathcal{M}(R)).add(R)$
15:                 $\mathcal{L}.remove(R)$
16:                 $foundProxySlaves = True$
17:                 **for all** $\widetilde{R} \in \mathcal{S}(R)$ **do**
18:                     $\mathcal{M}(\widetilde{R}) = \mathcal{M}(R)$
19:                     $\mathcal{S}(\mathcal{M}(R)).add(\widetilde{R})$
20:     **return** $\mathcal{M}$

Identifying Express Areas. After the proxy areas of the given network have been identified by Algorithm 1, the preprocessing is completed by applying Algorithm 2. For each link within the variety area, this algorithm checks whether this link is an express link (lines 4–11 in Algorithm 2). A link is considered an express link if by removing it from the architecture graph, the graph is separated into two disconnected subgraphs. To identify an express link, the algorithm, therefore, creates a copy of the architecture graph (line 7), removes the link in question from the graph copy (line 8), and checks—using a graph traversal technique, e.g., depth-first search—whether the end points of the link are still connected in the graph copy after the link has been removed (line 9). After all express links have been identified, all resources that have only express links as adjacent edges are designated as express resources (lines 12–14).

The identification of express areas is illustrated in Figs. 3d–e. Identifying four links as express links and the switch S_4 as an express resource establishes an express area and further reduces the variety area.

It should be noted that, following the definition given in Sect. 4.1, proxy links can be considered as a special type of express links. Consequently, it is in principle sufficient to use Algorithm 2 to identify all links offering no routing variety. However, due to the fact that it does not require graph traversal operations, Algorithm 1 offers a better scalability than Algorithm 2 and can significantly reduce the variety area after a short computation time. Overall, using Algo-

---

Algorithm 2. Identifying Express Areas.

Input: Architecture graph $\mathcal{G}_R$, list of links outside of proxy areas $\mathcal{E}_l^v$
Output: List of express links $\mathcal{E}_l^e$; list of express resources $\mathcal{N}_R^e$

1: **procedure** IDENTIFYEXPRESSAREAS($\mathcal{G}_R$, $\mathcal{E}_l^v$)
2:     $\mathcal{E}_l^e = [\,]$
3:     $\mathcal{N}_R^e = [\,]$
4:     **for all** $l \in \mathcal{E}_l^v$ **do**
5:         $R_s = endPointOne(\mathcal{G}_R, l)$
6:         $R_d = endPointTwo(\mathcal{G}_R, l)$
7:         $\mathcal{G}_R' = \mathcal{G}_R$
8:         $\mathcal{G}_R'.remove(l)$
9:         $isExpress = \neg isDestinationReachableFromSource(\mathcal{G}_R', R_d, R_s)$
10:        **if** $isExpress$ **then**
11:            $\mathcal{E}_l^e.add(l)$
12:    **for all** $R \in \mathcal{N}_R$ **do**
13:        **if** $\mathcal{E}_l^e.containsAll(getIncidentEdges(\mathcal{G}_R, R))$ **then**
14:            $\mathcal{N}_R^e.add(R)$
15:    **return** $\mathcal{E}_l^e$, $\mathcal{N}_R^e$

---

rithm 1 and Algorithm 2 in combination, thus, results in a short preprocessing which identifies all network elements offering no routing variety.

4.3   Adaptation of Existing Constraint Systems

By exploiting the knowledge about routing variety, network regions which do not offer any benefit for routing optimization can be excluded from the routing encoding, significantly reducing the number of encoding variables and improving the optimization efficiency. Following the steps presented in this subsection, this technique can be used with any routing optimization approach based on the encoding of individual network components. We first detail how existing constraint sets can be adapted to only encode route segments within variety areas and then propose two approaches to create the internal routes within proxy/express areas.

Routing Encoding in Variety Areas. CA encodings built on the assumption of fix source and destination resources that are known prior to the constraint formulation, e.g., [1] or [16], do not require any adaptation of the constraints. The impact area of these encodings can be limited by using the proxy masters over which the message enters/leaves the variety area—instead of the proxy slaves actually sending/receiving the message—as the start/end points of the encoded route, while allowing resources on the border of express areas (resources S_1, S_2, S_3, and S_4 in Fig. 3) to behave like end nodes, i.e., have activated in-edges without activated out-edges or vice versa.

Approaches where the source and the destination of the message transmission are not known during the constraint formulation—such as [14] or [29], in which routing and task mapping are optimized jointly—require an adaptation of the constraints. Such approaches implicitly encode the transmission end points of a message as the binding targets of the source/destination tasks of that message. For these cases, we propose to encode variables that indicate the start and the end points of the encoded route within variety areas as follows.

We introduce variables[2] C_R^S and C_R^D to encode the end points of a route within the variety area. Variable C_R^S reflects that resource R is the route start point of message C in the variety area. Similarly, variable C_R^D reflects that resource R is the route end point of message C in the variety area. We introduce new constraints to encode the activation of C_R^S and C_R^D according to the binding of the source/destination tasks of C and the proxy relations determined by Algorithm 1 presented in Sect. 4.2. The constraints state that a proxy master R is the route start point for message C (thus, $C_R^S = 1$) if the source task of C is bound either onto R or onto one of its proxy slaves and is not the start point (thus, $C_R^S = 0$) otherwise, encoded by constraints (1) and (2), respectively. The constraints that encode the activation of C_R^D are generated analogously. Given these variables, existing routing encodings can be adapted by inserting these end-point variables into any routing constraint that relates to the start or the end point of the message route.

$$\forall C \in \mathcal{N}_C, \widetilde{P} \in \mathcal{N}^-(C), \widetilde{R} \in \mathcal{N}_R, \widetilde{m} = (\widetilde{P}, \widetilde{R}) \in \mathcal{E}_m, R = \mathcal{M}(\widetilde{R}) \in \mathcal{N}_R^V:$$

$$\widetilde{m} - C_R^S \leq 0 \tag{1}$$

$$C_R^S - (\sum_{\widetilde{m}} \widetilde{m}) \leq 0 \tag{2}$$

In the formulation above, $\mathcal{N}^-(C)$ and $\mathcal{N}^+(C)$ denote predecessor and successor tasks of message C, respectively. $\mathcal{N}_R^V$ designates all proxy masters. Function $\mathcal{M} : \mathcal{N}_R \rightarrow \mathcal{N}_R^V$ returns the proxy master of a resource, as determined by Algorithm 1 from Sect. 4.2.

Route Creation in Proxy/Express Areas. We propose two different approaches to create the routes within network areas offering no routing variety.

Exclusive Approach. In the first approach, referred to as the *exclusive* approach, proxy and express areas are not considered in the encoding of routing constraints. Therefore, the resolution of the routing constraints—adapted as detailed above— yields only the route segments within the variety areas of the network. Then, in a post-processing step, we extend the yielded route segments with the unique internal routes (within the proxy and the express areas) that connect proxy masters to the actual source and destination resources and create the connections leading through the express areas to construct the complete message route, which

---

[2] Throughout this paper, all encoding variables are differentiated from the components of the system model (detailed in Sect. 3) by a bold font. For example, m denotes the encoding variable that is set to 1 iff mapping m is activated.

is used for the evaluation of the resulting design solutions w.r.t. design objectives such as cost, timing, or reliability.

Compact Approach. The exclusive approach offers the largest reduction of encoding variables and the maximal optimization speedup. For certain problems, however, ignoring the network areas offering no routing variety may reduce the optimization effectiveness, as it limits the ability to formulate additional constraints regarding, e.g., the capacity of the links within these parts of the network. We address these cases with a second approach for the creation of route segments within proxy/express areas. In this so-called *compact* approach, the activation of internal links is encoded with a constraint set tailored to the conditions found within proxy/express areas. By exploiting the fact that neither routing cycles nor redundant route segments are possible within areas without routing variety, the compact approach requires only a small number of constraints that are formulated based on—already existing—variables that describe task mapping and component activation.

The compact approach is implemented by formulating constraints (3)–(6) for each resource within a proxy or an express area. They ensure that the source process of a message may only be mapped onto a resource inside a proxy/express area if the resource is the binding target of a destination process or has at least one activated out-link (3). An in-link of a resource may only be active if the resource is the binding target of a destination process or has at least one activated out-link (5). Analogous constraints apply to the binding of destination processes (4) and the activation of out-links (6). Note that these constraints are formulated with the assumption of routing optimizations like [14] or [29], where the end points of the routes are not fixed[3].

$$\forall C \in \mathcal{N}_C, P \in \mathcal{N}^+(C), \tilde{P} \in \mathcal{N}^-(C), m = (P, R) \in \mathcal{E}_m, \tilde{m} = (\tilde{P}, R) \in \mathcal{E}_m,$$
$$l = (R, \tilde{R}) \in \mathcal{E}_l:$$

$$\tilde{m} - \left(\left(\sum_m m\right) + \left(\sum_l C_{l=(R,\tilde{R})}\right)\right) \leq 0 \qquad (3)$$

$$\forall C \in \mathcal{N}_C, P \in \mathcal{N}^+(C), \tilde{P} \in \mathcal{N}^-(C), m = (P, R) \in \mathcal{E}_m, \tilde{m} = (\tilde{P}, R) \in \mathcal{E}_m, \tilde{l} = (\tilde{R}, R) \in \mathcal{E}_l:$$

$$m - \left(\left(\sum_{\tilde{m}} \tilde{m}\right) + \left(\sum_{\tilde{l}} C_{\tilde{l}=(\tilde{R},R)}\right)\right) \leq 0 \qquad (4)$$

$$\forall C \in \mathcal{N}_C, P \in \mathcal{N}^+(C), m = (P, R) \in \mathcal{E}_m, \tilde{l} = (\tilde{R}, R) \in \mathcal{E}_l, l = (R, \tilde{R}) \in \mathcal{E}_l:$$

$$C_{\tilde{l}=(\tilde{R},R)} - \left(\left(\sum_m m\right) + \left(\sum_l C_{l=(R,\tilde{R})}\right)\right) \leq 0 \qquad (5)$$

---

[3] The constraint adaptation for the simpler case with known route end points ([1], [16]) is trivial and, therefore, not discussed here.

$\forall C \in \mathcal{N}_C, \widetilde{P} \in \mathcal{N}^-(C), \widetilde{m} = (\widetilde{P}, R) \in \mathcal{E}_m, \widetilde{l} = (\widetilde{R}, R) \in \mathcal{E}_l, l = (R, \widetilde{R}) \in \mathcal{E}_l$:

$$C_{l=(R,\widetilde{R})} - ((\sum_{\widetilde{m}} \widetilde{m}) + (\sum_{\widetilde{l}} C_{\widetilde{l}=(\widetilde{R},R)})) \leq 0 \tag{6}$$

5 Experiments

We perform several experiments to evaluate the impact of routing-variety awareness on the scalability and the result quality of multi-objective routing optimization approaches for three common classes of in-vehicle networks, namely, *double-star*, *many-core*, and *backbone*. In the double-star and the many-core experiments, we investigate how the scalability and the result quality of an approach based on a variety-unaware *baseline* routing encoding improves when it is extended with the *exclusive* or the *compact* implementations of the proxy concept presented in Sect. 4.3, while the backbone experiments evaluate the impact of considering express areas during routing encoding.

To evaluate the overall quality of the Pareto-optimal system design solutions found during the optimization process under each investigated encoding approach, we use the well-established *ε-dominance indicator* [9] from the multiobjective optimization domain. Broadly speaking, this scalar measure reflects the distance in the multi-dimensional objective space between a reference set of high-quality solutions and the set of Pareto-optimal solutions found by the evaluated approach. For two solution sets, obtained using two different optimization approaches, the one with a **lower** ε-dominance exhibits a smaller distance from the reference set and a **higher quality** of obtained solutions w.r.t. the design objectives. For all experiments presented in this section, the reference set is a collection of the best solutions found throughout the optimization processes of all approaches. We plot the ε-dominance of each investigated approach versus the optimization run time. This enables a compact representation and comparison of optimization speed, optimization convergence, preprocessing time overhead, and the time required for the constraint resolution throughout the optimization process.

We use the OPENDSE [21] system design optimization framework in all experiments. It employs the SAT-Decoding system synthesis approach [12] which uses the SAT4J [11] constraint solver and implements the broadly-used NSGA-II [3] multi-objective genetic algorithm to control the solution strategy used by SAT4J. Both SAT4J and NSGA-II are integrated into the OPT4J [13] optimization framework which is used by OPENDSE. Each optimization run comprises 1,000 generations. In each generation, 25 new solutions are generated using genetic operators on the previously found solutions, and the population of solutions found so far is updated accordingly. We consider a population size of 100 solutions.

5.1   Double-Star Topology

In our first case study, we consider a safety-critical application and double-star network topologies, where the links between the two stars offer the possibility for redundant routing. The message routing is optimized w.r.t. two design objectives, namely *transmission reliability* and *number of allocated links*[4]. The application processes exchange a total of 64 safety-critical messages, which are transmitted in both uni- and multicast fashions. Figure 4 illustrates an exemplary 24-ECU double-star network topology composed of two 12-ECU stars. The two stars are connected over two communication hops, with the possibility for redundant transmission between the two stars. Within each star, the connection between each ECU and its immediate switch offers no possibility for redundancy, so that each star constitutes a proxy area.

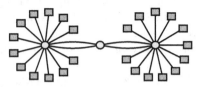

Fig. 4. Exemplary double-star network topology with 24 ECUs connected by 3 switches.

For this experiment, we implemented the routing encoding from [29]. This encoding is used as the *baseline* routing optimization approach. To implement the proposed approaches, we refine the baseline encoding by identifying proxy areas of the network and implementing the *compact* and the *exclusive* encoding approaches detailed in Sect. 4. For each optimization approach, we perform 40 optimization runs. The experimental results presented in the following are an average among the 40 optimization runs for each approach. Figure 5 illustrates the ε-dominance of the investigated routing optimization approaches (baseline, compact, and exclusive) versus their optimization run time for four double-star networks composed of different numbers of ECUs (8, 24, 40, and 56), equally distributed between the two stars.

In terms of result quality, all approaches perform similarly well, indicated by their ε-dominance indices at the end of the optimization. Here, the exclusive approach offers an average final ε-dominance of 0.03, and thereby, slightly outperforms the baseline and compact approaches which offer an average final ε-dominance value of 0.052 and 0.053, respectively.

In terms of optimization run time, however, the variety-aware approaches, i.e., compact and exclusive, offer a significant optimization speedup which scales with the complexity of the problem. Recall that for each message, the baseline approach encodes the activation of every individual link in the network, even

---

[4] This case study is inspired by a similar case study investigated in [29].

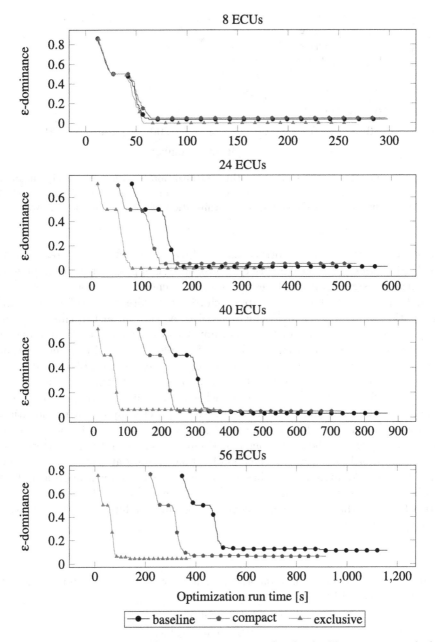

Fig. 5. Average ε-dominance of 40 optimization runs for the double-star case study for networks with 8, 24, 40, and 56 ECUs. Exploiting proxy areas results in an optimization speedup that scales with the network size.

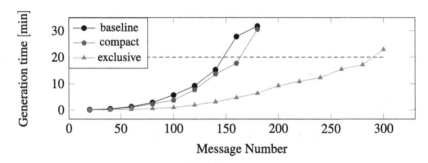

Fig. 6. Excluding proxy areas from the optimization decision space significantly reduces the constraint generation time. For a fixed time budget, e.g., 20 min (dashed line), the exclusive approach enables the optimization of considerably larger systems.

though a big part of the network is contained within the two proxy areas (stars) which do not offer any routing variety. The exclusion of proxy areas from the routing encoding significantly reduces the number of encoded decision variables, see Table 1. As a result, the baseline approach requires more time (a) for constraint formulation and preprocessing which is visible as the initial run time offset in the plots in Fig. 5 and (b) for the constraint resolution which results in a higher overall run time. A comparison among the four plots in Fig. 5 also reveals that these time overheads—just like the number of the encoded variables—scale with the problem complexity. Note that the time required for the identification of proxy areas for the variety-aware approaches is negligible in comparison to the time taken for constraint formulation, which is reflected by the nearly identical run time of all approaches for the smallest network. All in all, the proposed variety-aware approaches, compact and exclusive, significantly outperform the baseline approach, as they offer results of similar quality at a smaller optimization run time. Compared to the baseline approach, the compact approach offers an optimization speedup of up to ×1.26 with an average of ×1.14 over the four networks, while the exclusive approach achieves an speedup of up to ×3.06 with an average of ×2.04.

Table 1. Number of encoding variables for 64 messages in double-star topologies with different numbers of ECUs.

#ECUs	#variables	
	Baseline	Exclusive
8	2,988	2,453
24	8,088	3,658
40	14,831	4,092
56	24,199	4,526

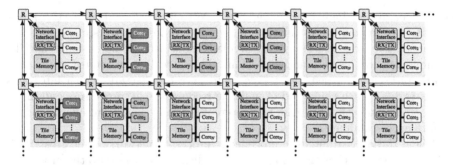

Fig. 7. A heterogeneous tiled many-core architecture.

To further investigate the scalability of the proposed approaches, we measured the time required for the generation of the routing constraints for an exemplary 24-ECU double-star topology for different numbers of messages. The results are illustrated in Fig. 6. Since routing constraints are generated at design time, the time required for their generation is not subject to any hard restrictions. However, the constraint generation time scales exponentially with the number of variables and may quickly render an approach impractical. Indeed, with the ongoing growth in the size of automotive networks and the number of transmitted messages, the time required for the generation of routing constraints is progressively becoming the limiting factor for the applicability of existing routing optimization approaches. The baseline and the compact approaches are based on the same set of variables and display similar generation times, which quickly grow with the number of messages in the system. While the exclusive approach also displays an exponentially growing generation time, the required constraints are generated within significantly shorter time intervals. With a time budget of 20 min (dashed horizontal line in Fig. 6), the exclusive approach, e.g., is able to generate constraints for systems with twice as many messages as the other two approaches. The exclusive approach, therefore, enables the automatic optimization of considerably larger systems.

5.2 Many-core Topology

Many-core architectures represent an emerging class of architectures in the embedded computing domain which offer the scalable computation and communication power required by modern embedded applications. A many-core architecture integrates an extensive number of—oftentimes heterogeneous—processors onto a single chip where the processors are interconnected by a communication network, referred to as a *Network-on-Chip* (NoC). The NoC interconnects the so-called processor tiles of the many-core in a grid fashion. Each tile consists of multiple resources, including processors and memories, interconnected via a bus. A part of such an architecture is illustrated in Fig. 7.

Over the past decade, many-core architectures have been increasingly viewed as promising candidates for emerging automotive applications, as they offer an order of magnitude higher processing power cost-efficiently and enable the implementation of the mixed-ASIL isolation, required for ISO 26262, see, e.g., [5]. The authors of [19] propose a many-core architecture which is tailored to the specific requirements in the automotive domain. This so-called *integrated automotive architecture* closely resembles a *tiled many-core architecture*, which integrates *processor tiles* (each composed of multiple resources, e.g., processors and memories) on a chip with a 2D grid NoC interconnection scheme and offers superior performance scalability.

While these distributed heterogeneous processor networks offer great flexibility, finding the optimal mapping of an application's tasks onto the processors of a tiled chip is a considerable challenge. Moreover, recent research [31] shows that a deterministic routing approach—such as XY-routing, which is commonly used in the many-core domain—may render numerous system design solutions infeasible due to the violation of link capacities, thus, limiting the number and the quality of feasible solutions. Exploring the space of routing possibilities may, therefore, significantly increase the quality of found solutions.

In our next case study, we investigate the impact of the proposed approaches on the efficiency and scalability of routing optimization in many-core automotive systems. In order to optimize the non-redundant message routes, we have implemented the approach presented in [14] which we consider as the *baseline* routing optimization approach. We extend the baseline with the proposed *compact* and *exclusive* variety-aware strategies which are then compared against the baseline approach.

The goal of our system synthesis optimization is to find implementations of an automotive application with 21 messages provided by the Embedded System Synthesis Benchmarks Suite (E3S) [4] on 3×3- and 4×4-tiled many-core architectures with 4 processor cores on each tile. The platform is optimized w.r.t. two design objectives, namely *energy dissipation* and *makespan*[5]. For both architecture sizes (3×3 and 4×4), the bandwidth of each inter-tile link is quantized into 5 (hard) or 10 (relaxed) equal budgets, hereafter referred to as *link capacity*, that can be utilized by the routed messages. We use additional constraints to ensure that the bandwidth capacity of each link is strictly respected. Since the exclusive approach disregards links within proxy areas, we use an additional evaluator—namely, link capacity evaluator—to check the feasibility of found design solutions in terms of respecting link capacities inside proxy areas.

Figure 8 illustrates the ε-dominance of the investigated routing optimization approaches (baseline, compact, and exclusive) versus their optimization run time, averaged over 5 optimization runs. The proposed variety-aware routing optimization approaches (compact and exclusive) outperform the baseline approach in both (a) the quality of obtained solutions (indicated by lower ε-dominance indices at the end of the optimization) and (b) optimization run time.

Since each processor tile can be regarded as a proxy area, a large portion of the networks is excluded from the routing constraints of the proposed

---

[5] During the experiments, the energy dissipation is calculated using the energy model from [32], while the makespan is calculated using the timing analysis from [20].

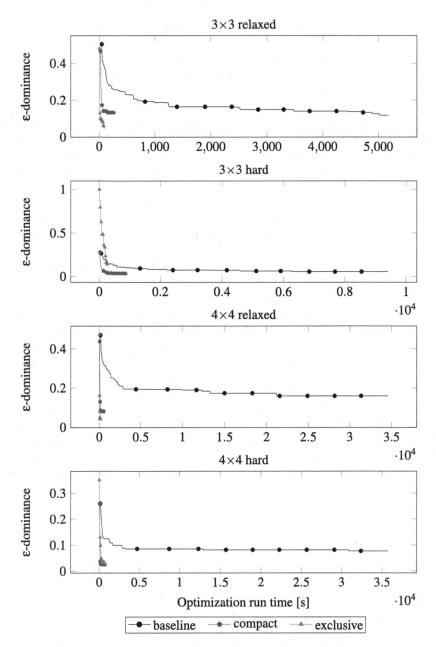

Fig. 8. Average ε-dominance of 5 optimization runs for the many-core case study. Variety-aware approaches yield design solutions of higher quality and offer an optimization speedup that scales with the complexity of the optimization problem.

approaches. This significantly reduces the number of encoding variables (see Table 2) and the time required for constraint generation (see Fig. 9). Nonetheless, due to the complex nature of tiled many-core architectures, the complexity of the routing constraint set has a higher impact (compared to the sheer number of variables) on the run time of routing optimization and the quality of the final solutions. Here, both the exclusive approach, which completely ignores the numerous proxy areas, and the compact approach, which uses a much simpler constraint set for the routing encoding within proxy areas (compared to baseline), require a considerably shorter time for the constraint resolution. Consequently, since the constraint set has to be resolved per network design generated throughout the exploration, the rapid constraint resolution of the variety-aware approaches results in a reduction of up to two orders of magnitude in the total optimization run time, compared to the baseline approach. Moreover, their simpler constraint sets make it easier for the optimizer to learn correlations between individual design decisions and the design objectives, so that both the compact and the exclusive approaches yield solutions of significantly higher quality compared to the baseline, especially for the more complex 4 × 4 architecture.

On average, the baseline approach offers a final ε-dominance of 0.102 and is outperformed by both the compact and the exclusive approaches, which exhibit an average final ε-dominance of 0.067 and 0.065, respectively. Compared to the baseline, the compact approach offers an average optimization speedup of ×33. The exclusive approach offers a speedup of ×81 on average and a maximum speedup of ×186 in case of the 4 × 4 relaxed architecture.

A comparison between the exclusive and the compact approach offers another interesting insight. With a link capacity of 10 (relaxed), finding routes without link capacity violation is relatively easy, so that the exclusive approach can create a sufficiently big population of feasible solutions and outperform the other two approaches in both run time and result quality. However, with a link capacity of 5 (hard), creating feasible solutions becomes more difficult. The constraints used in the exclusive approach cannot prevent capacity violations within

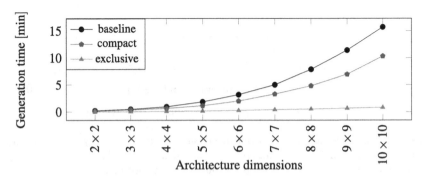

Fig. 9. Excluding proxy areas from the formulation of routing constraints reduces the time required for constraint generation and enables the automatic optimization of considerably larger systems.

proxy areas, because the links within these areas are not considered during constraint formulation. Consequently, the exclusive approach wastes a large share of the optimization time creating solutions with capacity violations on links in proxy areas, which are rejected by the capacity evaluator. Contrary to that, the compact approach is aware of every link in the architecture and offers the possibility to encode constraints that prevent link capacity violations in the first place. The compact approach, thus, explores a search space devoid of infeasible solutions and yields optimization results of higher quality compared to the exclusive approach.

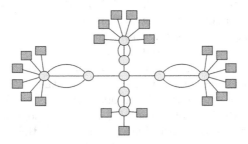

Fig. 10. Backbone topology where a central network consisting of five switches is connected to four domains.

5.3 Backbone Topology

In our third experiment series, we consider a backbone network topology. As opposed to automotive networks where the ECUs are organized in isolated domains such as engine control, entertainment, or powertrain, this emerging topology features a central network area—the so-called *backbone*—connecting all domains of the automotive network. Figure 10 illustrates the network

Table 2. Number of encoding variables for 21 messages in different many-core architectures.

Architecture dimension	#variables	
	Baseline	Exclusive
2×2	4,629	984
6×6	42,397	9,888
10×10	119,135	28,040

architecture used for the experiments of the backbone topology series. There, the backbone in the central region of the network consists of five switches. Each of the four domains—modeled as a gateway switch connected to several ECUs—can be connected to the backbone using one (non-redundant), two (redundant), or three (double-redundant) links.

Similarly to the first case study described in Sect. 5.1, the goal of the experiment is a concurrent optimization of the transmission reliability—quantified by the MTTF—and the monetary cost—quantified by the number of allocated links—of the communication network. Note that the backbone experiment series differs from the experiments in Sects. 5.1 and 5.2 in both the used optimizer and the compared optimization approaches. Compared to the networks considered in the previous experiments, the network used for the backbone experiments is more complex and offers a significantly larger design space. To compensate for the higher complexity of the optimization problem, we use the optimizer from [26], which has been shown to be more effective than the original SAT-Decoding, for the backbone experiments. Moreover, the backbone network contains an express area (the central backbone region). This network can, thus, be used to evaluate the gain of considering express regions when applying the variety-awareness mechanisms introduced in Sect. 4. To this end, we investigate how the run time of the optimization experiment and the quality of the optimization results change when the variety-unaware routing encoding approach from [29] (baseline) is extended by (a) an express-area-unaware exclusive implementation of the proxy concept (exclusive) and (b) by an exclusive implementation which—additionally to the proxy areas—considers the express area of the network (exclusiveExpress).

The results of the backbone experiment series are visualized in Fig. 11. The presented results are an average over 10 optimization runs for each approach. The four plots illustrate the ε-dominance indicator versus the optimization run time for the architecture illustrated in Fig. 10 and safety-critical automotive applications where the processes exchange 30, 64, 90, and 120 messages, respectively.

Overall, the baseline, the exclusive, and the exclusiveExpress approaches exhibit an average final ε-dominance of 0.597, 0.289, and 0.125, respectively. Furthermore, compared to the baseline approach, the exclusive and the exclusiveExpress approaches offer an average speedup of ×2.78 and ×2.98, respectively. These results indicate that (a) considering routing variety provides a significant speedup and a higher quality of the optimization results and that (b) the quality of the optimization results can be further improved by considering express areas during routing encoding.

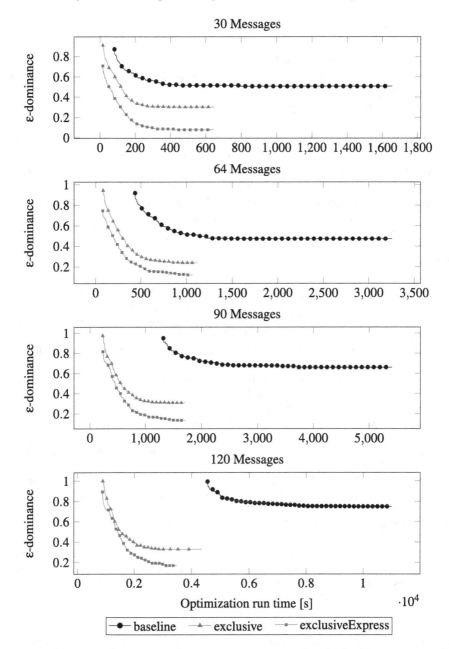

Fig. 11. Average ε-dominance of 10 optimization runs for the backbone case study for applications with 30, 64, 90, and 120 messages. Exploiting proxy areas results in a significant speedup and a higher result quality, which is further increased by considering express areas.

6 Conclusions

In this work, we propose a novel strategy for an automated routing optimization of in-vehicle networks. The proposed approach exploits knowledge about so-called proxy and express areas in the network, i.e., regions that do not offer any routing variety. We have presented lightweight preprocessing algorithms that identify proxy and express areas in a network, proposed two approaches to exploit this knowledge during routing optimization, and shown how the presented strategy can be integrated into existing symbolic routing encodings. Experimental results for three types of automotive networks give evidence that variety-aware approaches for routing encoding provide design solutions of equal or higher quality, are up to 186 times faster, and enable the automatic optimization of considerably larger systems than variety-unaware approaches.

References

1. Al Sheikh, A., Brun, O., Chéramy, M., Hladik, P.E.: Optimal design of virtual links in AFDX networks. Real-Time Syst. **49**(3), 308–336 (2013)
2. Blickle, T., Teich, J., Thiele, L.: System-level synthesis using evolutionary algorithms. Des. Autom. Embed. Syst. **3**, 23–58 (1998)
3. Deb, K., Pratap, A., Agarwal, S., Meyarivan, T.: A fast and elitist multiobjective genetic algorithm: NSGA-II. IEEE Trans. Evol. Comput. **6**, 182–197 (2002)
4. Dick, R.: Embedded system synthesis benchmarks suite (E3S) (2010). http://ziyang.eecs.umich.edu/dickrp/e3sdd/
5. Fuhrman, T., Wang, S., Jersak, M., Richter, K.: On designing software architectures for next-generation multi-core ECUs. SAE Int. J. Passeng. Cars Electron. Electr. Syst. **8**(2015-01-0177), 115–123 (2015)
6. Gavrilut, V., Zarrin, B., Pop, P., Samii, S.: Fault-tolerant topology and routing synthesis for IEEE time-sensitive networking. In: Proceedings of RTNS (2017)
7. Graf, S., Reimann, F., Glaß, M., Teich, J.: Towards scalable symbolic routing for multi-objective networked embedded system design and optimization. In: Proceedings of CODES+ISSS (2014)
8. International Cablemakers Federation: ICF News. International Cablemakers Federation (2015)
9. Laumanns, M., Thiele, L., Deb, K., Zitzler, E.: Combining convergence and diversity in evolutionary multiobjective optimization. Evol. Comput. **10**, 263–282 (2002)
10. Laursen, S.M., Pop, P., Steiner, W.: Routing optimization of AVB streams in TSN networks. ACM SIGBED Rev. **13**(4), 43–48 (2016)
11. Le Berre, D., Parrain, A.: The SAT4J library, release 2.2, system description. J. Satis. Boolean Model. Comput. **7**, 59–64 (2010)
12. Lukasiewycz, M., Glaß, M., Haubelt, C., Teich, J.: SAT-decoding in evolutionary algorithms for discrete constrained optimization problems. In: IEEE Congress on Evolutionary Computation (2007)
13. Lukasiewycz, M., Glaß, M., Reimann, F., Teich, J.: Opt4J - a modular framework for meta-heuristic optimization. In: Proceedings of GECCO (2011)
14. Lukasiewycz, M., Shreejith, S., Fahmy, S.A.: System simulation and optimization using reconfigurable hardware. In: Proceedings of ISIC (2014)

15. Lukasiewycz, M., Streubühr, M., Glaß, M., Haubelt, C., Teich, J.: Combined system synthesis and communication architecture exploration for MPSoCs. In: Proceedings of DATE (2009)
16. Mahfouzi, R., Aminifar, A., Samii, S., Rezine, A., Eles, P., Peng, Z.: Stability-aware integrated routing and scheduling for control applications in ethernet networks. In: Proceedings of DATE (2018)
17. Nayak, N.G., Dürr, F., Rothermel, K.: Time-sensitive software-defined network (TSSDN) for real-time applications. In: Proceedings of RTNS (2016)
18. Neubauer, K., Wanko, P., Schaub, T., Haubelt, C.: Exact multi-objective design space exploration using ASPmT. In: Proceedings of DATE (2018)
19. Obermaisser, R., El Salloum, C., Huber, B., Kopetz, H.: From a federated to an integrated automotive architecture. IEEE Trans. Comput.-Aid. Des. Integr. Circ. Syst. 28(7), 956–965 (2009)
20. Pourmohseni, B., Smirnov, F., Wildermann, S., Teich, J.: Isolation-aware timing analysis and design space exploration for predictable and composable many-core systems. In: Proceedings of ECRTS (2019)
21. Reimann, F., Lukasiewycz, M., Glaß, M., Smirnov, F.: OpenDSE - open design space exploration framework (2018). http://opendse.sourceforge.net/
22. Richthammer, V., Glaß, M.: On search-space restriction for design space exploration of multi-/many-core systems. In: Proceedings of MBMV (2018)
23. Sangiovanni-Vincentelli, A., Di Natale, M.: Embedded system design for automotive applications. Computer 40(10), 42–51 (2007)
24. Schweissguth, E., Danielis, P., Timmermann, D., Parzyjegla, H., Mühl, G.: ILP-based joint routing and scheduling for time-triggered networks. In: Proceedings of RTNS (2017)
25. Smirnov, F., Glaß, M., Reimann, F., Teich, J.: Optimizing message routing and scheduling in automotive mixed-criticality time-triggered networks. In: Proceedings of DAC (2017)
26. Smirnov, F., Pourmohseni, B., Glaß, M., Teich, J.: IGOR, get me the Optimum! Prioritizing important design decisions during the DSE of embedded systems. In: Proceedings of CODES+ISSS (2019)
27. Smirnov, F., Pourmohseni, B., Glaß, M., Teich, J.: Variety-aware routing encoding for efficient design space exploration of automotive communication networks. In: Proceedings of VEHITS (2019)
28. Smirnov, F., Reimann, F., Teich, J., Glaß, M.: Automatic optimization of the VLAN partitioning in automotive communication networks. ACM Trans. Des. Autom. Electron. Syst. (TODAES) 24(1), 9 (2018)
29. Smirnov, F., Reimann, F., Teich, J., Han, Z., Glaß, M.: Automatic optimization of redundant message routings in automotive networks. In: Proceedings of SCOPES (2018)
30. Wang, B., Hou, J.C.: Multicast routing and its QoS extension: problems, algorithms, and protocols. IEEE Netw. 14(1), 22–36 (2000)
31. Weichslgartner, A., Gangadharan, D., Wildermann, S., Glaß, M., Teich, J.: DAARM: design-time application analysis and run-time mapping for predictable execution in many-core systems. In: Proceedings of CODES+ISSS (2014)
32. Wolkotte, P.T., Smit, G.J., Kavaldjiev, N., Becker, J.E., Becker, J.: Energy model of networks-on-chip and a bus. In: International Symposium on System-on-Chip (SoC) (2005)

Comparison of Cargo Securing Methods During Transport on Different Quality Roads

Martin Vlkovský[1]([✉]) [iD] and Hana Vlachová[2] [iD]

[1] Department of Logistics, University of Defence, Kounicova 65, Brno, Czech Republic
martin.vlkovsky@unob.cz
[2] Study Office, University of Defence, Kounicova 65, Brno, Czech Republic
hana.vlachova@unob.cz

Abstract. The chapter compares the values of shocks (acceleration coefficients and securing forces) generated by the Tatra T-810 on high-quality road (highway) and lower-quality road (road paved with granite blocks). To obtain primary data, a transport experiment was performed to measure shocks (acceleration coefficients) during transportation on given types of roads using a three-axis accelerometer with a datalogger and a calibration certificate – OM-CP-ULTRASHOCK-5-CERT. For each (transport) route two datasets were obtained, which were analysed using suitable statistical tools – characteristics. The mean values and variations of measured acceleration coefficients on the roads are compared. The graphical comparison of the roads studied is covered in a separate section. Furthermore, the required securing forces in the x and y axes are calculated according to EN 12195-1:2010 and are compared not only for individual datasets, but also with the theoretical securing force based on normative values of acceleration coefficients. It also includes the determination of the probability of exceeding, respectively double exceeding of the "normatively determined" limits of securing forces. The results of the transport experiment show that the magnitude of generated shocks is even higher at a lower average transport speeds on a low-quality roads. The distribution of acceleration coefficient values also differs for both roads.

Keywords: Transport experiment · Road safety · Cargo securing · Acceleration coefficients · Securing forces · Statistical analysis

1 Introduction

Within the European Union (EU), over 76% of cargo is transported using road transport [6]. Over the last ten years (2008–2017), a total of 147,047,868,000 tons of freight was transported across the EU, an annual average of 14,704,787,000 tons of transported cargo [5].

Due to these large volumes of cargo transported by road, a high number of roads are overloaded. According to the Road Transport Services Center, established by the Ministry of Transport of the Czech Republic, over a half of all vehicles are overloaded during weight checks, which amount to over 2,000 per year in the Czech Republic [2].

© Springer Nature Switzerland AG 2021
M. Helfert et al. (Eds.): SMARTGREENS 2019/VEHITS 2019, CCIS 1217, pp. 200–219, 2021.
https://doi.org/10.1007/978-3-030-68028-2_10

According to the Regional Road Administration and Road Maintenance statistics, a single truck will damage a road more than 10,000 passenger cars [1]. Cargo transport makes high demands on road infrastructure that is more quickly worn out (damaged). Annual maintenance is not always able to ensure its required quality.

Quality of roadways directly affects the magnitude of the inertial forces that affect cargo during transport. Generally, on a damaged road, characterized by a large amount of unevennesses (holes, seals, etc.), higher values of acceleration coefficients (shocks) that directly affect the magnitude of inertial forces are assumed. On the basis of the assumed size of inertial forces acting on transport, it is necessary to choose appropriate methods of securing (fastening) cargo and evaluating the lashing capacity of the respective fastening means.

Determining the magnitude of the inertia in the actual transport is possible by using a suitable measuring device (accelerometer) and the appropriate calculation, mainly by using the formulas from the norms, e.g. EN 12195-1:2010 [4]. Selected cargo shippers and carriers use accelerometers to detect undesirable shocks (acceleration) during shipment of particularly fragile or otherwise sensitive goods (dangerous goods etc.). These are, for example, multinational companies DHL [3], GEIS [7] or TNT [15].

Exceptions do not even apply in an advanced army, such as the United States Army, which complements its transport and transport means (mainly containers) with a set of measuring devices that monitor (among others) the cargo space [14]. The temperature, relative humidity, acceleration in individual axes, etc. are determined in the respective transport means.

From the point of view of inertial forces influencing cargo, the key values of acceleration coefficients in individual axes are primarily influenced by the following three basic factors:

– vehicle,
– driver,
– road [11, 18].

In the case of a vehicle, it is also important whether it is moving with or without cargo. The key technical factors of the vehicle are its tires, chassis, structure of the vehicle hull and its connection with the chassis, including the age of the vehicle and its individual components, etc. The driver's driving style is a significant factor, especially the speed of the vehicle as well as driver's skills, experience and mental condition [17, 24].

The purpose of this chapter is to prevent problems associated with incorrect or insufficient cargo securing through knowledge of the transport parameters – the roads before it starts – and thus increase transport safety. The risks associated with inertia forces on cargo are generally higher for specific shipments that are carried by the military or components of the Integrated Rescue System [19].

2 Transport Experiment

The transport experiment was carried out on two types of roads using a Tatra T-810 6x6 (T-810) with mileage less than 45,000 km. The first type of highway was the D1 highway, measured from Brno to Vyškov and back. The second type was a lower quality transport road (third class road); a paved road measured from the Vyškov to Dědice and back [25].

The transport experiment was undertaken by one professional driver and a 3-axis accelerometer with a datalogger and a calibration certificate – OMEGA-OM-CP-ULTRASHOCK-5 (see the Fig. 1).

A measuring range of ±5 g was used to obtain the values of the acceleration coefficients. A sampling rate of 512 Hz was used with a record for every second of the highest (or possibly) lowest value of the respective acceleration coefficient in the given axis (x, y and z) [8]. The axes are designated according the Fig. 2: x – longitudinal, y – transverse and z – vertical.

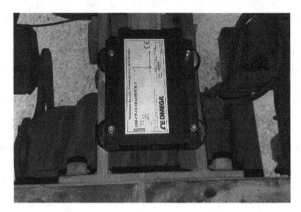

Fig. 1. Mounting of the measuring device [25].

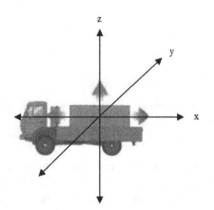

Fig. 2. Axes designation [13].

The accelerometer was mounted on the steel center frame of the vehicle body in the front of the T-810 load compartment and the transport experiment was carried out without any load and in optimal climatic conditions included dry roads, excellent visibility, absence of congestion and rainfall. Outdoor temperature was in the range of 7–11 °C.

2.1   Methods

To accomplish a comparison of the above described roads, as specified in Sect. 2.2, descriptive statistics were used and basic descriptive characteristics were found (mean values – arithmetic mean, modus and median, variance, coefficients of skewness and kurtosis). Comparison also includes the detection of extreme values in individual axes (both positive and negative). The selected values are compared with the use of one and two-choice tests of statistical hypotheses on the equivalence of mean values (arithmetic mean of absolute values of acceleration coefficients) and variance (part 2.3). The significance level $\alpha = 0.05$ is used for all tests.

In a separate Sect. 2.4 a graphical comparison of the distribution of measured values of acceleration coefficients on the examined roads is shown.

In a separate section, the securing forces needed to properly secure the load are calculated, statistically compared for individual datasets, as well as compared with theoretical securing forces based on normative values of acceleration coefficients. Statistical equality tests are used for comparison. The section also includes the determination of the probability of exceeding; respectively double exceeding of theoretical securing forces according to EN 12195-1:2010.

The basic parameters for carrying out statistical equality tests are used in the same way as were used for the comparison of experimentally determined data (acceleration coefficients).

The probability of exceeding, respectively double exceeding of the "normatively determined" values of the securing forces in the x and y axes. The z-axis (F_z) is not calculated in accordance with EN 12195-1:2010 because it is assumed that F_z is always less than (or equal to) at least one of the other forces (F_x or F_y).

Lower Bound (LB), Upper Bound (UB) and Parameter Estimate (PE) are calculated for each parameter. The existence and non-existence of a statistically significant difference at the required level of significance can be deduced from the above mentioned boundaries and PE.

2.2   Basic Descriptive Characteristics of Measured Data Files

The first data file (dataset 1) was obtained on the Brno-Vyškov (highway) route (see the Fig. 3). In a stretch of 27.0 km long, a total of 3,804 values of acceleration coefficients were recorded and the average vehicle speed was 76.66 km·h^{-1} [25].

The basic descriptive characteristics of dataset 1 as well as the extremes in the individual axes, in both positive and negative directions are illustrated in Tables 1 and 2.

According to Table 1, a higher value of kurtosis coefficient in z-axis can be identified which is slightly elevated (positive), while in the other two axes, the values are less than 0. This is due, among other things, to the displacement of the coordinate axis due to gravity acceleration.

Z-axis variance is also more than 13 times smaller than the y-axis, respectively almost 10× in the x-axis. Extremes – the highest and lowest values of the acceleration coefficients in the individual axes are given in Table 2. The highest value of the acceleration coefficient was in the y-axis where the measured value $c_y = 2.51$, corresponding to 2.5 times the gravity acceleration g [25].

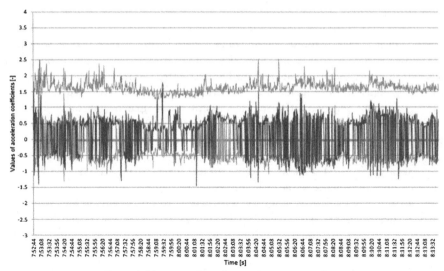

Legend: blue – x axis, red – y axis, grey – z axis.

Fig. 3. Dataset 1 – raw data [25]. (Color figure online)

Table 1. Dataset 1 – basic descriptive characteristics.

Characteristics	x	y	z
Arithmetic mean	−0.2953	0.2284	1.6381
Modus	−0.6100	0.5100	1.6000
Median	−0.5400	0.5000	1.6200
Variance	0.2923	0.4059	0.0304
Skewness coef.	1.0464	−0.5862	1.0127
Kurtosis coef.	−0.5327	−0.7773	2.2971

Source: [25].

Table 2. Dataset 1 – extremes of measured acceleration coefficient values.

Extremes	x	y	z
Positive	1.4400	2.5100	1.5300
Negative	−1.3200	−1.4700	–

Source: [25].

The second data file (formally identified with Dataset 2) was obtained on the route Vyškov–Brno (highway). In a 27.0 km long section, a total of 4,059 values of acceleration coefficients were recorded and the average speed of the vehicle was

71.84 km·h^{-1}. The basic descriptive characteristics of Dataset 2 and the extremes in the individual axes, in the positive and negative directions, are presented in Tables 3 and 4.

Table 3. Dataset 2 – basic descriptive characteristics.

Characteristics	x	y	z
Arithmetic mean	−0.2530	0.2226	1.7075
Modus	−0.6500	0.6900	1.6700
Median	−0.5900	0.5700	1.6900
Variance	0.4330	0.5169	0.0291
Skewness coef.	0.7439	−0.5277	1.1093
Kurtosis coef.	−1.1524	−1.2530	5.5130

Source: [25].

Table 4. Dataset 2 – extremes of measured acceleration coefficient values.

Extremes	x	y	z
Positive	1.6700	2.3100	1.9600
Negative	−1.3600	−1.2900	–

Source: [25].

Table 3 shows a higher coefficient of kurtosis in the z-axis. The highest measured value within Dataset 2 (Table 4) was in the y-axis ($c_y = 2.31$), roughly equivalent to 2.3 times the gravity acceleration g.

A third data set (formally marked with Dataset 3) was obtained on the route Vyškov–Dědice (the road paved with granite blocks). Over a 4.3 km long section, a total of 1,182 acceleration coefficient values were recorded and the average vehicle speed was 39.29 km·h^{-1}. The basic descriptive characteristics of Dataset 3 and the extremes in the individual axes, in the positive and negative directions, are presented in Tables 5 and 6.

Table 5 identified higher kurtosis in the z-axis. The highest measured value within Dataset 2 (Table 6) was in the z axis ($c_z = 3.11$), roughly equivalent to more than 3.1 times the gravity acceleration g.

A fourth data set (formally marked with Dataset 4) was obtained on the route Dědice–Vyškov (road paved with granite blocks). Along a 4.3 km long section, a total of 1,203 acceleration coefficient values were recorded and the average speed of the vehicle was 38.60 km·h^{-1}. The basic descriptive characteristics of Dataset 4 and extremes in individual axes, positive and negative, are given in Tables 7 and 8.

Table 7 shows the difference in variance of the z-axis, which is significantly lower than that of the other two axes. The highest measured is in the y-axis ($c_z = 2.70$), which corresponds to 2.7 times the gravitational acceleration g.

Table 5. Dataset 3 – basic descriptive characteristics.

Characteristics	x	y	z
Arithmetic mean	−0.1904	0.0730	1.9924
Modus	0.4500	0.4100	1.6000
Median	−0.5150	0.4500	1.9500
Variance	0.7927	1.0016	0.1784
Skewness coef.	0.1441	−0.2296	0.9992
Kurtosis coef.	−1.1163	−1.0862	1.9430

Source: [25].

Table 6. Dataset 3 – extremes of measured acceleration coefficient values.

Extremes	x	y	z
Positive	1.8300	2.2800	3.1100
Negative	−3.0800	−2.4400	–

Source: [25].

Table 7. Dataset 4 – basic descriptive characteristics.

Characteristics	x	y	z
Arithmetic mean	−0.4425	0.0562	2.0047
Modus	−0.8000	0.8300	2.0000
Median	−0.7300	0.4500	1.9500
Variance	0.7532	1.1867	0.1742
Skewness coef.	0.9505	0.0755	0.8825
Kurtosis coef.	−0.1423	−1.1141	0.7597

Source: [25].

Table 8. Dataset 4 – extremes of measured acceleration coefficient values.

Extremes	x	y	z
Positive	1.9700	2.7000	2.6300
Negative	−2.3000	−2.4200	–

Source: [25].

2.3   Comparison of Acceleration Coefficients

For the purpose of comparing a high-quality road (highway) with a poor quality road (paved with granite blocks), partial zero and alternative hypotheses were formulated to compare the individual datasets (d_1–d_4) in pairs. Two single-choice tests of partial statistical hypotheses were used for testing:

- mean values compliance test,
- variances compliance test.

The zero hypothesis is assumed to be valid (resp. partial zero hypotheses for the respective dataset pairs) concerning the parity of the relevant dataset parameters, for the mean values $\mu = \mu_0$, resp. variances $\sigma^2 = \sigma_0^2$. For an alternative hypothesis in the double – side test applies $\mu \neq \mu_0$, resp. $\sigma^2 \neq \sigma_0^2$. Subsequently, one-sided tests are performed to determine whether $\mu > \mu_0$ or $\mu < \mu_0$, resp. $\sigma^2 > \sigma_0^2$ or $\sigma^2 < \sigma_0^2$.

For test purposes, a critical value range was constructed and a test criterion value calculated.

To test the hypothesis an appropriate statistic $T = T(x_1, x_2,..., x_n)$ is used, the so-called test criterion that has, when the zero hypothesis is valid, known probability distribution (Student's or t-distribution).

The area of these values of statistics is divided into two disjoint fields:

- $W_{1-\alpha}$ is the domain of accepting a zero hypothesis – a set of values that testify in favor of a zero hypothesis,
- W_α is a critical domain (domain of zero hypothesis rejection) – that testify in favor of an alternative hypothesis.

For example, for the hypothesis test of the mean value μ of the normal distribution zero hypothesis: $\mu = \mu_0 \rightarrow$ alternative hypothesis: $\mu > \mu_0$ will be critical domain W_α = $\{t, t \geq t_{1-\alpha}(\nu)\}$, where μ_0 is the expected value of the parameter μ, t is the value of the test criterion and $t_{1-\alpha}(\nu)$ is quantile of Student's distribution – so-called critical value [12]. Tests for variances are performed analogously. For all tests, the chosen level of significance was $\alpha = 0.05$.

On the basis of these tests, the individual partial zero hypotheses were verified, from which the relevant conclusions are subsequently formulated.

A normality test was performed prior to statistical analysis. Normality was verified graphically using Q-Q plots [10], including the determination of skewness and kurtosis coefficients. Minor deviations from normality were found, especially when testing the kurtosis of distribution. However, the graphical analysis did not show significant deviations from normality, theoretical quantile and the corresponding empirical quantiles were approximately on a straight line [21].

The Stat1 software tool was used to perform statistical hypothesis tests [12].

In individual partial tests (Table 9), the hypotheses on equivalence of the mean values are always tested (arithmetic means in absolute value) $\mu_{i(abs)}$ for given values of acceleration coefficients in individual axes (c_x, c_y and c_z). Analogously, variances in acceleration coefficients in individual axes are tested. The aim of the tests is to find out whether the individual data sets (d_1–d_4) significantly statistically differ at the $\alpha = 0.05$ level of significance.

Table 9 shows that, using a mean value (arithmetic averages in absolute values), there is a statistically significant difference between individual datasets with the exception of d_3–d_4, where it shows the similarities of both files found on the same road in the opposite direction. A statistically significant difference between d_3 and d_4 was shown only in the axes x and y.

Table 9. Comparison of mean values (in absolute values) of acceleration coefficients in all three axes.

Characteristics	$\mu_{i(abs)}$		
Coef. \ Dataset	c_x	c_y	c_z
d_1–d_2	$\mu_1 < \mu_2$	$\mu_1 < \mu_2$	$\mu_1 < \mu_2$
d_1–d_3	$\mu_1 < \mu_3$	$\mu_1 < \mu_3$	$\mu_1 < \mu_3$
d_1–d_4	$\mu_1 < \mu_4$	$\mu_1 < \mu_4$	$\mu_1 < \mu_4$
d_2–d_3	$\mu_2 < \mu_3$	$\mu_2 < \mu_3$	$\mu_2 < \mu_3$
d_2–d_4	$\mu_2 < \mu_4$	$\mu_2 < \mu_4$	$\mu_2 < \mu_4$
d_3–d_4	$\mu_3 < \mu_4$	$\mu_3 < \mu_4$	NO

Note: *NO indicates the non-demonstration of a statistically significant difference between the monitored data files at the level of significance $\alpha = 0.05$. Statistically significant differences demonstrated for all three axes are marked green.*

Source: [25].

From partial hypothesis tests it follows that, from the point of view of the mean values (arithmetic averages in absolute values), there is a statistically significant difference at the level of significance $\alpha = 0.05$ between a high-quality road (highway) and a lower quality road (paved with granite blocks). The conclusion is valid in both directions. Because it is valid, it means that values are statistically significantly lower (in all three axes) for datasets 1 and 2 compared to datasets 3 and 4.

Table 10 shows that, by using variances, there is a statistically significant difference between individual datasets with the exception of d_1 and d_2, respectively d_3 and d_4. Where the similarity can be seen in both pairs of files found on the same traffic path in the opposite direction. Statistically significant difference d_1–d_2 is only shown in the axes x and y. Between the d_3–d_4 datasets a statistically significant difference was not demonstrated in either of the axes.

Partial hypothesis tests show that, from the point of view of the variances, there is a statistically significant difference in the level of significance $\alpha = 0.05$ between a high-quality transport road (highway) and a lower quality road (paved with granite blocks). The conclusion is valid in both directions, because the results show that variances are statistically significantly lower (in all three axes) for dataset 1 and 2 compared to dataset 3 and 4. For some axes, it can be assumed that a statistically significant difference between the pairs of the dataset with a higher test strength (at the level of significance $\alpha = 0.01$) would be demonstrated.

Table 10. Comparison of variances acceleration coefficients across all three axes.

Characteristics	σ_i^2		
Coef. Dataset	c_x	c_y	c_z
d_1–d_2	$\sigma_1^2<\sigma_2^2$	$\sigma_1^2<\sigma_2^2$	NO
d_1–d_3	$\sigma_1^2<\sigma_3^2$	$\sigma_1^2<\sigma_3^2$	$\sigma_1^2<\sigma_3^2$
d_1–d_4	$\sigma_1^2<\sigma_4^2$	$\sigma_1^2<\sigma_4^2$	$\sigma_1^2<\sigma_4^2$
d_2–d_3	$\sigma_2^2<\sigma_3^2$	$\sigma_2^2<\sigma_3^2$	$\sigma_2^2<\sigma_3^2$
d_2–d_4	$\sigma_2^2<\sigma_4^2$	$\sigma_2^2<\sigma_4^2$	$\sigma_2^2<\sigma_4^2$
d_3–d_4	NO	NO	NO

Note: *NO indicates the non-demonstration of a statistically significant difference between the monitored data files at the level of significance α = 0.05. Statistically significant differences demonstrated for all three axes are marked green.*

Source: [25].

2.4 Graphical Comparison of Roads

The individual datasets (d_1–d_4) can be viewed in terms of the number of values of the acceleration coefficients in the individual axes that fall within the respective intervals. Figures 4, 5, 6 and 7 show the frequencies of acceleration coefficients in individual axes, divided into intervals of multiples of gravitational acceleration (0.5 g).

It can be seen from Figs. 4, 5, 6, and 7 that the character of the distribution of values at individual intervals differs significantly between the tested roads. Although the

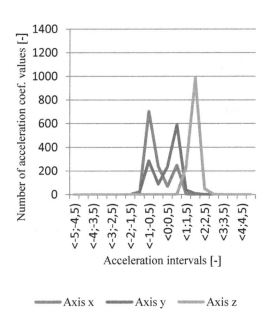

Fig. 4. Dataset 1 – frequency of acceleration coefficients [25].

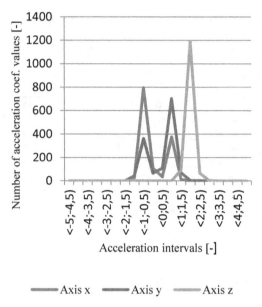

Fig. 5. Dataset 2 – frequency of acceleration coefficients [25].

frequencies of the acceleration coefficients differ, it is possible to illustrate the different character of the high-quality road (highway) and the lower quality road (road paved with granite blocks).

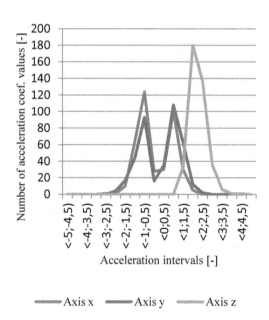

Fig. 6. Dataset 3 – frequency of acceleration coefficients [25].

This conclusion can be demonstrated by the number of intervals in which the values of the coefficients of acceleration in the individual axes fall. While for dataset 1 it is 6 in the x-axis, 8 in the y-axis and 4 in the z-axis, respectively 7, 8 and 4 for dataset 2, on lower quality road it is for the dataset 3 in the x-axis 10, in the y-axis 10 and in the z-axis 7, respectively 9, 11 and 6 for dataset 4.

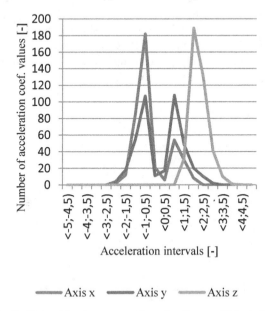

Fig. 7. Dataset 4 – frequency of acceleration coefficients [25].

2.5   Comparison of Securing Forces

Using the measured data – values of acceleration coefficients, the inertia forces acting on the fastening system (fastening straps) were calculated. The calculated inertia forces represent either a theoretical (based on normatively determined acceleration coefficients) or a practical requirement for a fastening system (in this case lashing capacity of the fastening strap). Based on the measured data and the basic objective is the practical application of the evaluation of the transport experiment, the calculated values of the inertia forces for each axis and every second of transport shall correspond to the required securing forces developed by the fastening system. For the fastening strap it is its lashing capacity (LC).

In order to calculate the magnitude of the inertia forces and the corresponding securing forces, a securing cargo that is standard on the vehicle type (T-810) is selected. Commercially available textile fastening straps without information about lashing capacity are used for securing. In practical application of the results, the lashing capacity would be determined from the required locking force as: nLC, where n is the number of fastening straps used.

The securing has been constructed based on the following assumptions:

- the securing calculation is based on the placement of two pallet units of 1,200 × 800 × 1,600 mm each and weight 1,000 kg (total weight of the model load is m = 2,000 kg),
- the pallet units are placed side by side (no gap), transversely to the direction of travel of the vehicle,
- the specific model attachment also corresponds to the angle between the strap and the plane of the loading area of the vehicle β = 88.75°, which is based on the loading width of the vehicle (see Fig. 8),
- standard textile fastening strap with Top-Over Lashing method is used for fastening; the number of straps (n) of given LC is left as a parameter,
- the friction coefficient for wood-plywood is used as μ = 0.3 and the safety coefficient for the x-axis: $f_{s(x)} = 1.1$ and for the y-axis: $f_{s(y)} = 1.25$.

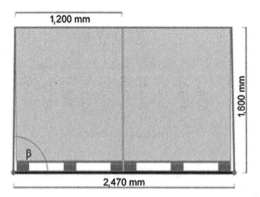

Fig. 8. Model of securing on T-810, own.

Statistical equality tests are used to compare datasets with each other and the calculated securing force based on normative values of acceleration coefficients for two basic:

- mean values compliance test,
- variance compliance test,

and two additional parameters:

- probability of exceeding the "normative" limit,
- the probability of double exceeding the "normative" limit.

Statistical equality tests are performed analogously to the previous tests on two parameters. It includes determination of upper bound, lower bound and parameter estimation. From these limits it is possible to determine not only whether the monitored datasets differ statistically significantly, but also the differences between the "magnitude of deviations".

Statistical equality tests are again performed at significance level α = 0.05.

In accordance with EN 12195-1:2010, the securing forces (F_x, F_y) are calculated, which at the same time correspond to the expected magnitude of inertia forces acting on the load, resp. fastening strap [20]:

$$F_x = \frac{(c_x - \mu \cdot c_z) \cdot m \cdot g}{2n \cdot \mu \cdot \sin \alpha} \cdot f_s \quad [N] \tag{1}$$

$$F_y = \frac{(c_y - \mu \cdot c_z) \cdot m \cdot g}{2n \cdot \mu \cdot \sin \alpha} \cdot f_s \quad [N] \tag{2}$$

With respect to model parameters that are the same in all four cases (for all datasets), the values of the "normatively determined" securing forces are as follows: $F_x = 17{,}989$ N and $F_y = 12{,}265$ N. In general, isolated exceedances are not considered to be a major problem. Frequent exceedances of these values have an impact on the service life of the fastening means, in this case the fastening straps. However, if this is a very common phenomenon in a given transport and the mean value (usually using the arithmetic mean or median) exceeds the "normatively determined" values of the securing forces, the impact on the strap's service life is essential and there is a risk of damage to the fastening strap, resp. partial components (e.g. ratchets, end components). If the mean value exceeds the double of "normatively determined" values of the securing forces, this is already a risky method of securing. If exceeding is triple, there is a risk of breaking the strap and the situation can be considered potentially dangerous in relation to cargo securing.

The values of the securing forces are given in Table 11 for an overview, including the securing forces based on the normatively determined acceleration coefficients (formally designated F_{xn}, F_{yn}) according to EN 12195-1:2010.

Table 11. Values of securing forces.

Characteristics	μ_i			
Dataset	Forces			
	F_{xi}	F_y	F_{xn}	F_{yn}
Dataset 1	30,363	19,820	17,989	12,265
Dataset 2	31,623	23,794	17,989	12,265
Dataset 3	34,606	35,944	17,989	12,265
Dataset 4	43,441	40,455	17,989	12,265

Source: Modified [25].

It is apparent from Table 11 that, due to the existence of a large number of extreme values in the set, the arithmetic means values are high and in all cases exceed the values of the securing forces resulting from the normatively set acceleration coefficients. The worst situation is in the last dataset (d_4), when the vehicle generated the greatest shocks compared to other datasets and the mean value exceeded the "normatively determined" values of the securing forces 2.4 times in the x-axis and resp. 3.3 times in the y-axis. Especially in the y-axis, the values of inertia forces (shocks) can be considered extreme and the requirements for the magnitude of the securing forces are also high, which is also related to the probability of exceeding (π_i) resp. double exceedance (γ_i) of the "normatively determined" values of the securing forces (see Table 12).

Table 12 shows that for all datasets there are a large number of securing force values that exceed the limit foreseen in EN 12195-1:2010. From the given measurement result it is possible to easily deduce the probabilities of exceeding, respectively double exceeding of the "normatively determined" securing forces on the respective surface and in the respective direction on the tested route. The high probability of double exceeding the assumed magnitude of the securing forces in the respective axes is, in particular, alarming. The worst results are, according to the assumptions, in dataset 4, where the probabilities of exceeding the "normatively determined" securing forces in both axes are greater than 75% and in case of double exceeding of more than 61%.

Table 12. Probability of exceeding, respectively double exceeding of the standard.

Characteristics	π_i		γ_i	
Dataset	Forces			
	F_x	F_y	F_x	F_y
Dataset 1	0.7484	0.4203	0.5237	0.3273
Dataset 2	0.6888	0.5299	0.5950	0.3673
Dataset 3	0.6117	0.7107	0.4898	0.5305
Dataset 4	0.8005	0.7581	0.6683	0.6110

Source: Own.

In terms of the interpretation of the results, it can be stated that such a number of exceedances will have a significant impact on the choice of the method of fastening, resp. lashing capacity of the strap. If the lashing capacity corresponding to EN 12195-1:2010 were chosen, there is a high probability that the fastening straps would be minimally damaged during transport if they would not break at the moment of extreme values (for dataset 4, the maximum determined values are $F_x = 117,830$ N and $F_y = 133,407$ N). Although these are isolated extreme values (the highest calculated values using experimentally measured acceleration coefficients), the model 2 tonne load at this time "behaves" as 5.89 t, resp. 6.67 t heavy load.

Furthermore, by means of statistical equality tests, a comparison of individual datasets is performed using arithmetic mean and variance. As an additional parameter the probability of exceeding, resp. double exceeding the assumed values of the securing forces is used (see Table 13). This is demonstrated on the one hand by using primary data (values of acceleration coefficients) and on the other hand by using calculated securing forces which correspond to real acting magnitudes of inertia forces.

For the additional parameters (probabilities of exceeding or double exceeding the assumed values of the securing forces), these are only valid for d_1–d_4 and d_2–d_4. Also in the other comparisons resulting from Table 13, it can be observed that there is a large

Table 13. Statistical equality tests – securing forces.

Confidence interval for	Inertial force values							
	F_x				F_y			
$d_1?d_2$	σ_1/σ_2	$\mu_1-\mu_2$	$\pi_1-\pi_2$	$\gamma_1-\gamma_2$	σ_1/σ_2	$\mu_1-\mu_2$	$\pi_1-\pi_2$	$\gamma_1-\gamma_2$
LB	0.850	−2,557	0.025	−0.109	0.909	−5,562	−0.148	−0.076
UB	0.947	39	0.094	−0.033	1.013	−2,386	−0.072	−0.004
PE	0.897	−1,259	0.060	−0.071	0.960	−3,974	−0.110	−0.040
$d_1?d_3$	σ_1/σ_3	$\mu_1-\mu_3$	$\pi_1-\pi_3$	$\gamma_1-\gamma_3$	σ_1/σ_3	$\mu_1-\mu_3$	$\pi_1-\pi_3$	$\gamma_1-\gamma_3$
LB	0.553	−7,025	0.083	−0.023	0.616	−19,325	−0.348	−0.259
UB	0.649	−1,460	0.191	0.090	0.723	−12,923	−0.243	−0.147
PE	0.600	−4,243	0.137	0.034	0.669	−16,124	−0.295	−0.203
$d_1<d_4$	σ_1/σ_4	$\mu_1-\mu_4$	$\pi_1-\pi_4$	$\gamma_1-\gamma_4$	σ_1/σ_4	$\mu_1-\mu_4$	$\pi_1-\pi_4$	$\gamma_1-\gamma_4$
LB	0.650	−15,474	−0.098	−0.198	0.631	−23,750	−0.388	−0.338
UB	0.762	−10,682	−0.006	−0.091	0.739	−17,520	−0.288	−0.229
PE	0.705	−13,078	−0.052	−0.145	0.684	−20,635	−0.338	−0.284
$d_2?d_3$	σ_2/σ_3	$\mu_2-\mu_3$	$\pi_2-\pi_3$	$\gamma_2-\gamma_3$	σ_2/σ_3	$\mu_2-\mu_3$	$\pi_2-\pi_3$	$\gamma_2-\gamma_3$
LB	0.617	−5,788	0.023	0.049	0.642	−15,354	−0.238	−0.219
UB	0.723	−178	0.131	0.161	0.753	−8,946	−0.134	−0.108
PE	0.669	−2,983	0.077	0.105	0.697	−12,150	−0.186	−0.163
$d_2<d_4$	σ_2/σ_4	$\mu_2-\mu_4$	$\pi_2-\pi_4$	$\gamma_2-\gamma_4$	σ_2/σ_4	$\mu_2-\mu_4$	$\pi_2-\pi_4$	$\gamma_2-\gamma_4$
LB	0.725	−14,241	−0.158	−0.126	0.657	−19,779	−0.278	−0.298
UB	0.849	−9,396	−0.065	−0.020	0.770	−13,542	−0.178	−0.189
PE	0.786	−11,819	−0.112	−0.073	0.712	−16,661	−0.228	−0.244
$d_3?d_4$	σ_3/σ_4	$\mu_3-\mu_4$	$\pi_3-\pi_4$	$\gamma_3-\gamma_4$	σ_3/σ_4	$\mu_3-\mu_4$	$\pi_3-\pi_4$	$\gamma_3-\gamma_4$
LB	1.064	−12,291	−0.251	−0.246	0.927	−8,692	−0.104	−0.149
UB	1.296	−5,380	−0.127	−0.111	1.129	−330	0.019	−0.012
PE	1.174	−8,836	−0.189	−0.178	1.023	−4,511	−0.042	−0.081

PE – parameter estimation
LB – Lower 95% confidence interval
UB – Upper 95% confidence interval
green – statistically significant difference (α = 0.05)
white – no statistically significant difference was found
orange – opposite inequality has been found
Source: Own.

number of extreme values in the dataset 4, partly also when compared to measurements on the same route (surface) in the opposite direction.

The results of statistical equality tests show that at the significance level $\alpha = 0.05$ there was a difference between the monitored surfaces for the two basic parameters, i.e. there is a statistically significant differences between the datasets d_1–d_3, d_1–d_4, d_2–d_3 a d_2–d_4. It can be stated that the investigated vehicle T-810 generates on road paved with granite blocks in average more shocks even at about half the speed.

The speed of the vehicle has not been determined, but corresponds to the normal speed corresponding to the surface and other conditions (e.g. weather), while observing the general principles of driving safety.

Assuming the creation of a model that compares transport on the surfaces surveyed at the same speed, the results would be different, but would not correspond to the reality and common principles of cargo transport.

The main aim of the chapter is to present practical recommendations for securing and transporting cargo, e.g. in military conditions or for the needs of the Integrated Rescue System and emergency supplies.

3 Results and Discussion

On the basis of these comparisons, it is obvious that even at a lower average speed (about half) there is a statistically significant difference between the tested roads at the significance level $\alpha = 0.05$. This conclusion applies to both tested basic descriptive characteristics (mean values in absolute values as well as variance of values of acceleration coefficients in all three axes). The same conclusion applies to the two basic parameters when comparing the respective securing forces.

It can be concluded that the T-810 vehicle generates on lower quality road (third class road) in average greater shocks (higher values of acceleration coefficients) even at about half the average transport speed. At higher speeds on a lower quality road, even greater differences in shocks can be expected. Generated shocks can be quantified as inertial forces that act not only on the cargo but also on the vehicle and the driver.

The graphical comparisons show a different distribution of values for each type of road. Primarily the graphical view of their variance in single intervals of 0.5 g differs significantly. Whereas for dataset 1 and 2 there is an average variance at 6 intervals, for datasets 3 and 4 it is almost at 9 intervals.

The results of comparing the datasets with the primary data are also confirmed by the calculated requirements for the magnitude of the securing forces and their comparison between individual datasets. Obviously, the T-810 vehicle generates generally higher inertia values than predicted, which increases the requirement for the securing forces of the respective fastening system (in this case the lashing capacity of the fastening straps used).

4 Conclusions

Shocks during transport affect the vehicle, the load and the driver. Chapter analyzed their influence on the freight, resp. on the load securing system. Based on the results, it can be stated that in real conditions the expected values of acceleration coefficients, resp. sizes of securing forces according to EN 12195-1:2010, are often exceeded. This happens not only on lower-quality roads, but also on high-quality roads, where higher speed is expected. According to the above mentioned norm, a suitable method of securing the load is chosen and if the assumptions in it do not correspond to reality in some cases, the securing system may be insufficient in terms of the required securing forces or completely unsuitable. Insufficiently or improperly secured cargo is not only a risk for the cargo itself, but also represents secondary risks such as damage to the vehicle, other technical means on the vehicle, cause a traffic accident involving injury, damage to the environment or other property damage [22].

The results of the analysis presented by the chapter can be mainly used to optimize the fastening of cargo by choosing a more suitable fastening system or fasteners with the corresponding lashing capacity. Lashing capacity must correspond to actual shocks (the magnitude of the acceleration coefficients, respectively resulting inertial forces), rather than simply theoretical assumptions of the standards.

The results show that, although conclusions can be drawn from the statistical evaluation of primary data (values of acceleration coefficients in individual axes), the real values of the inertia forces acting on the load (vehicle, driver) may exceed the "normatively" determined magnitude of securing forces even more. While the extremes in the x and y axes (the highest values in the absolute value) were measured "only" $c_x = 2.3$, resp. $c_y = 2.7$, which is 2.9 times, respectively 4.5 times the normative limit, for the securing forces it is even almost 6.6 times, resp. 10.9 times the expected magnitude of inertia forces.

A specific area of transport is the shipping of dangerous items, especially those that are directly affected by the shocks. These primarily include various types of explosives [23], that are transported by the army using their own or contracted vehicles.

In further research, the spectral analysis enables to transform the data (signal) of the time series into a frequency domain, which allows examination of other aspects of transport – cargo securing [9].

Acknowledgements. The paper was written with the support of the project of long-term strategy of organization development: ROZVOLOG: Development of Capabilities and Sustainability of Logistics Support (DZRO ROZVOLOG 2016–2020), funded by the Ministry of Defense of the Czech Republic.

References

1. Aktulane – Auto: Aktualne.cz. One Overloaded Truck Destroys the Road More than 10,000 Cars (2018). https://zpravy.aktualne.cz/ekonomika/auto/jeden-pretizeny-kamion-znici-sil nici-vic-nez-10tisic-osobnic/r~ed413f3a900011e89f80ac1f6220ee8/?redirected=153597 8107. Accessed 25 Sept 2018
2. Center of Road Transport Services. Cspsd.cz. Mobile Expert Units (2014). http://www.cspsd. cz/mobilni-expertni-jednotky. Accessed 10 Nov 2018
3. DHL: Dhl.com. Transportation Managements. (2018). http://www.dhl.com/en/logistics/ industry_sector_solutions/consumer_logistics/transportation_management.html#.WtiCQt Rua70. Accessed 05 Nov 2018

4. EN 12195-1: Load restraining on road vehicles – safety – part 1: calculation of securing forces. UNMZ (2010)

5. European Commision: Eurostat. Ec.europa.eu. Goods Transport by Road (2018). http://ec.europa.eu/eurostat/tgm/table.do?tab=table&init=1&language=en&pcode=ttr00005&plugin=1. Accessed 12 Nov 2018

6. Fenollar Solvay, A., Haberstroh, M., Thelen, S., Schilberg, D., Jeschke, S.: New intermodal loading units in the European transport market. In: Jeschke, S., Isenhardt, I., Hees, F., Henning, K. (eds.) Automation, Communication and Cybernetics in Science and Engineering 2015/2016, pp. 687–697. Springer, Cham (2016). https://doi.org/10.1007/978-3-319-42620-4_52

7. GEIS: Geis-group.com. Global Logistics (2018). https://www.geis-group.com/en/ltl-and-ftl. Accessed 06 Nov 2018

8. Grzesica, D., et al.: Measurement and analysis of truck vibrations during off-road transportation. In: VETOMAC XIV – The 14th International Conference on Vibration Engineering and Technology of Machinery. MATEC Web of Conferences (2018)

9. Grzesica, D., Wiecek, P.: Advanced forecasting methods based on spectral analysis. In: WMCAUS 2016 (2016). Procedia Engineering. Elsevier. ISSN 1877-7058

10. Johnson, R.A., Wichern, D.W.: Applied Multivariate Statistical Analysis. Prentice-Hall International (2007). ISBN 0130418072

11. Lerher, T.: Cargo Securing in Road Transport Using Restraining Method with Top-Over Lashing. Nova, New York (2015). ISBN 978-1-61122-002-5

12. Neubauer, J., et al.: Principles of Statistics: Applications in Technical and Economic Disciplines, 1st edn. Grada, Prague (2016). ISBN 978-80-247-5786-5

13. Proridice. Proridice.eu. Cargo Securing – Basic Information (2019). http://soubory.proridice.eu/naklady/upevneni_nakladuCZ.pdf. Accessed 10 Jan 2019

14. Savi Technology. Savi.com. Get Better Asset Data Using Proven Sensor and Reader Hardware (2018). http://www.savi.com/wp-content/uploads/Hardware_Overview_Final.pdf. Accessed 01 Nov 2018

15. TNT. Analysis.tu-auto.com. Express and Fleet Tlematics (2018). http://analysis.tu-auto.com/fleet-and-asset-management/tnt-express-and-fleet-telematics. Accessed 06 Nov 2018

16. Vlkovský, M., Veselík, P.: Cargo securing – comparison of different quality roads. Acta Universitatis Agriculturae et Silviculturae Mendelianae Brunensis **67**(4), 1015–1023 (2019). ISSN 1211-8516

17. Vlkovský, M., et al.: The cargo securing based on European standards and its applicability in off-road transport conditions. In: ICTTE Belgrade 2016 – Proceedings of the Third International Conference on Traffic and Transport Engineering. Transport Means 2018 – Proceedings of the 22nd International Scientific Conference Part I. City Net Scientific Research Center Ltd. (2016). ISBN 978-86-916153-3-8

18. Vlkovský, M., et al.: Cargo securing and its economic consequences. In: Transport Means 2018 – Proceedings of the 22nd International Scientific Conference Part I. Kaunas University of Technology (2018)

19. Vlkovský, M., et al.: Wavelet based analysis of truck vibrations during off-road transportation. In: VETOMAC XIV – The 14th International Conference on Vibration Engineering and Technology of Machinery. MATEC Web of Conferences (2018)

20. Vlkovský, M., et al.: Impact of shocks on cargo securing during the road transport. In: WMCAUS 2019 IOP Conference Series: Materials Science and Engineering. IOP Science (2019)

21. Vlkovský, M., et al.: Cargo securing during transport depending on the type of a road. In: WMCAUS 2017 IOP Conference Series: Materials Science and Engineering. IOP Publishing Ltd. (2017). ISSN 1757-8981

22. Vlkovský, M., et al.: Cargo securing during transportation – using extreme values. In: Applied Technical Sciences and Advanced Military Technologies. Nicolae Balcescu Land Forces Academy (2017). ISSN 1843-682X
23. Vlkovský, M., Rak, L.: Cargo securing in selected vehicles and transport of explosives. Perner's Contacts **XII**(3), 101–110 (2017). ISSN 1801-674X
24. Vlkovský, M., Šmerek, M.: Statistical analysis of driving style and its effect on cargo securing. In: ICTTE Belgrade 2018 – Proceedings of the Fourth International Conference on Traffic and Transport Engineering. City Net Scientific Research Center Ltd. (2018)
25. Vlkovský, M., Vlachová, H.: Securing cargo during transport on roads of different quality. In: VEHITS 2019 – Proceedings of the 5th International Conference on Vehicle Technology and Intelligent Transport Systems. Scitepress (2019)

Analysis of Motorcycle Crashes in Chile Using Spatial Statistics

Carola Blazquez[1](✉) ⓘ and María José Fuentes[2]

[1] Department of Engineering Sciences, Universidad Andres Bello, Viña del Mar, Chile
cblazquez@unab.cl
[2] Universidad Andres Bello, Viña del Mar, Chile

Abstract. In this study, spatial statistical methods were used to perform a global and local spatial autocorrelation of motorcycle crashes at the commune level, and to determine whether crash clusters with high crash-related variable values tend to persist during the 2011–2015 period. High global spatial patterns of motorcycle crashes are perceived during the spring at signalised intersections and resulting in fatality outcomes throughout the five-year study period. Recurrent high local spatial clustering of motorcycle collisions arose in the morning on weekdays and on sunny days due to the loss of control of the vehicle, or the imprudence of the driver or pedestrian, and involving male young adults. Communes located in the city of Santiago and the surrounding areas present high spatial clustering for most crash attributes. The results of this study should guide authorities to target efforts towards policy measures, in order to improve motorcycle safety in Chile.

Keywords: Motorcycle crashes · Spatial autocorrelation · Spatial clusters

1 Introduction

According to the World Health Organization, traffic crashes cause 1.2 million fatalities every year and are the main cause of death of young adults between 15 and 29 years of age worldwide. Approximately 23% of these deaths are motorcyclists, 22% are pedestrians, and 4% are cyclists [1]. In Chile, 2,178 people were killed as a result of traffic crashes in 2016, presenting an increase of 4.9% with respect to 2010. This high mortality rate is partly due to the exponential increase of vehicles in the last few years. Additionally, Chile is the OECD member country with the worst fatality rate with 11.9 deaths per 100,000 inhabitants and with 4.5 deaths per 10,000 motorised vehicles [2].

In Chile, almost 19,000 crashes occurred between 2011 and 2015 that involved motorcycles. The national statistics indicate that deaths caused by such crashes are ranked third and that the total number of injuries are placed fourth with respect to other types of crashes [3]. Being vulnerable road users, motorcyclists are 27 times more frequently killed in crashes per travelled vehicle mile than motor vehicle passengers [4].

The motorcycle market increases every year in many countries worldwide, and it is expected to continue increasing in Chile as well [5, 6]. On average, the total number of motorcycles increased in 16.7% between 2017 and 2018 [7]. In 2018, motorcycles

M. Helfert et al. (Eds.): SMARTGREENS 2019/VEHITS 2019, CCIS 1217, pp. 220–244, 2021.
https://doi.org/10.1007/978-3-030-68028-2_11

constituted 3.5% (189, 588) of all registered vehicles in the country with approximately 10.1 motorcycles per 1,000 inhabitants [8]. Motorcycles are deemed as an economical and convenient transport mode with respect to congestion, fuel consumption, ease of parking, etc. Therefore, it may be anticipated that the number of motorcycle crashes will grow in time. Thus, there is a need for a spatial and temporal analysis of these crashes in Chile.

Recent studies have analysed motorcycle crashes employing different approaches. A multiple correspondence analysis was performed by Jalayer and Zhou [9] to conclude that light conditions, time of day, driver condition, and weather conditions are the key factors contributing to the frequency and severity of at-fault motorcycle-involved crashes in the state of Alabama. Flask et al. [10] employed Bayesian multi-level mixed effects models to analyse motorcycle crashes at the road segment level. The authors concluded that among different characteristics of the road segments, smaller lanes and shoulder widths, larger horizontal degree of curvature and larger maximum vertical grades will increase the prediction of crashes. In another study, a deep learning framework was developed to predict motorcycle crash severities, which were related to rider ejection, two-way roads, curved roads, and weekends [11]. Lee et al. [12] employed a flexible mixed multinomial logit fractional split model to analyse the proportions of crashes by vehicle type (including motorcycles). This study concluded that the total employment density has the most significant and negative influence on the motorcycle crash proportion, and that the proportions of households with no vehicle negatively impact the proportion of motorcycle crashes. Chung and Song [13] employed multivariable statistical methods to identify the critical factors associated to age, motorcycle speed, curved sections, among others that impact motorcycle crash severity in Korea. Ding et al. [14] developed multivariate injury risk models for motorcyclists in Germany. The authors concluded that a strong relation exists between relative speed and injury risk for motorcyclists. The potential temporal instability in the factors (e.g., motorcyclists' attributes, rider behaviour, and roadway conditions) affecting motorcycle crash-injury severities in the state of Florida was assessed by Alnawmasi and Mannering [15] using random parameters multinomial logit models. Finally, by employing ordered probit models, Zhou and Chin [16] studied the high injury severity of motorised vehicles and motorised two-wheelers (motorcycles) involved in loss-of-control of single vehicle crashes in Singapore. The findings of this study reveal that race, at-fault status, road traffic type, lighting and colliding with stationary object are factors that impact particularly the high severity of motorcyclists.

Other researchers have studied the spatial problem using statistical methods such as spatial autocorrelation to identify spatial clusters of road crashes. For example, Dezman et al. [17] analysed hotspots of traffic crashes at the census tract level in Baltimore using spatial autocorrelation techniques. Spatial autocorrelation was used to examine hotspots of time of occurrence, severity, and location of traffic crashes aggregated to the traffic analysis zonal level in Shiraz, Iran [18]. In another study, Pour et al. [19] applied spatial autocorrelation to detect any dependency between time and location of vehicle-pedestrian crashes in Melbourne. Blazquez et al. [20] performed a spatial autocorrelation analysis of cargo trucks on Chilean highways at the global and local level. Yet another study was performed by Aghajani et al. [21] to identify spatial and temporal patterns of traffic crashes, and to determine hotspots of fatal and injury outcomes in Iran. Saadat et al.

[22] employed spatial autocorrelation to identify spatial patterns of fatality outcomes in motorcycle crashes at the district level in Tehran. Ghandour et al. [23] used spatial autocorrelation with the Lebanese crash dataset to study the spatial clustering behaviour and hazard vulnerability of vehicle crashes. Recently, Blazquez and Fuentes [24] studied motorcycle crash attributes in Chile using spatial autocorrelation analysis. This study advances the work of [24] by determining global and local significant patterns of different motorcycle crash-related variables (e.g., type of crash, relative location, contributing factors, and road safety measures) at the commune level in Chile, and assessing whether a spatial dependence of such patterns persisted during the 2011–2015 period. The results of this macroscopic crash study provides a decision-making tool for helping authorities and safety professionals allocate resources and apply policy based countermeasures.

2 Methodology

The spatial statistical methods were applied to determine the spatial association of the value of a certain variable at a given location with values of that variable at neighbouring locations at the global and local level [25]. First, the global Moran's I index was employed to test the general spatial autocorrelation of the main crash attributes and road safety indicators for each year of the studied period. Second, a local Moran's I statistic was employed to detect statistically significant clusters with respect to each of the crash-related variables.

The global Moran's I indicator is used to identify statistically significant spatial patterns of crashes by quantifying the magnitude of clustering or dispersion of these crashes with Eq. 1.

$$I = \frac{n \sum_{i=1}^{n} \sum_{j=1}^{n} w_{ij}(x_i - \bar{x})(x_j - \bar{x})}{S_o \sum_{i=1}^{n}(x_i - \bar{x})^2} \forall i, j \qquad (1)$$

where x_i is the variable value at a particular location i, $\bar{x}$ is the mean of the variable, w_{ij} are the elements of a spatial matrix with weights representing proximity relationships between location i and neighbouring location j, S_O is the summation of all elements w_{ij}, and n is the total number of locations.

The values of Moran's I may range between -1 (representing perfect dispersion with a strong negative autocorrelation) and 1 (indicating perfect clusterisation with a strong positive autocorrelation). A random spatial pattern exists when the value of Moran's I is near zero. The results of the spatial autocorrelation are interpreted within the context of its null hypothesis, which denotes that an attribute is randomly distributed among features in the study area. The Z score method is employed to compute the statistical significance of the Moran's I index. A positive Z score for a feature indicates that the neighbouring features have similar values, whereas a negative Z score denotes that the feature is surrounded by dissimilar values.

While the global Moran's I provides a single value to measure the overall spatial pattern of a certain attribute throughout a complete study area, Anselin´s local Moran's I examines the existence of local spatial clusters of similar high, low, or atypical values (e.g., high value surrounded by low attribute value location, and low values with high attribute value neighbouring features) at certain locations, as described in Anselin [26]. Thus, the results of this statistic shows the value similarity of a location to its neighbours, and in addition, tests the significance of this similarity [27]. The local Moran's I index is expressed by Eq. 2.

$$I_i = \frac{x_i - \overline{X}}{S_i^2} \sum_{j=1, j \neq 1}^{n} w_{ij}(x_i - \overline{X}) \tag{2}$$

where x_i is the variable value at location i, $\overline{x}$ is the mean of the variable, w_{ij} is the spatial weight between locations i and j, S_i is the sum of the weights, and n is the total number of locations.

Similarly to the global indicator, the spatial patterns are associated to Z score values to determine the statistical significance of the results. Positive Z score values imply that neighbouring values are similar and negative values indicate that near values are dissimilar [28]. This study will focus on identifying locations of clusters of high motorcycle crash attribute values.

3 Data Description

The National Commission of Traffic Safety (CONASET, acronym in Spanish) provided the 2011–2015 crash database employed in this study. A total of 18,826 motorcycle crashes were successfully aggregated into 343 communes, as shown in Fig. 1. This figure shows that five communes (Arica, Antofagasta, Copiapó, La Serena, and Coquimbo) present a high number of such crashes in the north zone of Chile, many crashes prevailed in several communes of the centre zone of the country, and the communes of Coyhaique and Punta Arenas in the south zone have the largest number of motorcycle crashes.

The main variables of the motorcycle crashes were classified into eight groups (road safety measures, temporal attributes, personal characteristics, type of crash, relative location, contributing factors, type of zone, and weather conditions), as shown in Table 1. This table shows an increase in the total number of motorcycle crashes over time and that this number almost doubled in 2015 with respect to previous years. Similarly, an evident increase is perceived in 2015 in the road safety measures related to crasher per 100,000 population and 10,000 registered vehicles. On average, approximately 74% of the crashes occurred on a weekday and 26% during the weekend. For every year of the study period, motorcycle crashes occurred during night between 6 pm and 6 am with an average of 40.9%, followed by the afternoon between 12 pm and 6 pm with an average of 32.8%, and the morning between 6 am and 12 pm with an average of 24%. Regarding the season of the year, most motorcycle crashes arose during the summer (30.7%), followed by crashes during the fall (29%), spring (20.3%), and winter (20%). Additionally, most crashes occurred in urban areas (85%) and on sunny days (86%).

The imprudence of the driver was the main contributing cause of these crashes, representing 40% of the total number of crashes. On average, collision between two or more moving vehicles (56.8%) was the most frequent type of crash, followed by impacts with static vehicles or objects (19.9%), pedestrian crashes (10.3%), and rollovers (8.9%). With respect to the relative location of motorcycle crashes, 38.0% of these crashes

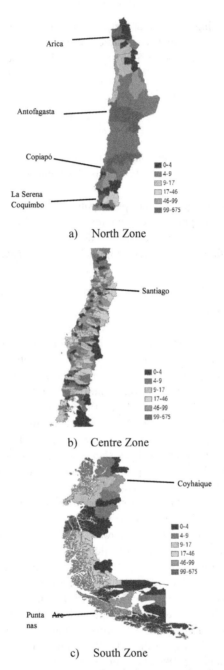

Fig. 1. Motorcycle crashes for the 2011–2015 period aggregated at the commune level for the a) North Zone, b) Centre Zone, and c) South Zone [24].

Table 1. Descriptive statistics for each analysed variable per year (adapted from [24]).

Variable	2011	2012	2013	2014	2015	Total
Road safety measures						
Number of crashes	2315	2786	3463	3445	6819	18828
Crashes per 100,000 population	13.5	14.0	23.9	16.1	32.8	20.1
Crashes per 10,000 registered vehicles	10.8	6.7	8.3	6.3	11.9	8.8
Type of injury						
Fatalities	29	78	72	75	151	405
Seriously injured	146	285	349	334	1336	2450
Slightly injured	2127	2647	2588	6569	5339	19270
Temporal attributes						
Day of week						
Weekday	1651	2063	2543	2580	5017	13854
Weekend	664	723	920	865	1802	4974
Time of day						
Morning	618	724	878	820	1585	4625
Afternoon	808	970	1211	1148	2183	6320
Night	889	1092	1374	1477	3051	7883
Season						
Spring	466	745	765	947	1842	3818
Summer	581	699	922	1699	1874	5775
Fall	710	712	969	1386	1690	5467
Winter	558	630	807	360	1413	3768
Personal characteristics						
Age group						
<18 years old	195	234	272	255	365	1321
19–33 years old	756	913	1141	1130	4075	8015
34–64 years old	1117	1365	1603	1565	1848	7498
>65 years old	113	166	200	212	114	805
Gender						
Female	571	786	878	907	901	4043
Male	1744	2000	2585	2538	5918	14785
Type of crash						
Collision	1150	1393	1811	1826	4508	10684

(continued)

Table 1. (*continued*)

Variable	2011	2012	2013	2014	2015	Total
Impact	579	649	854	899	779	3763
Pedestrian crash	318	410	431	407	370	603
Rollover	156	170	217	175	950	1668
Relative location						
Straight section	1250	1513	1850	1783	3660	10056
Curved section	138	162	242	265	461	1268
Intersection with signage	654	822	967	1019	1877	4282
Intersection without signage	111	123	147	148	324	837
Contributing factors						
Imprudence of driver	866	1079	1756	1433	2428	7562
Imprudence of pedestrian	242	296	312	357	467	1674
Loss of control	225	282	272	309	1900	2988
Driving under influence alcohol	197	213	237	244	748	1639
Other causes	420	533	639	732	944	3268
Type of zone						
Urban	1962	2341	2903	2928	5868	16002
Rural	353	445	560	517	949	2824
Weather conditions						
Sunny	2154	2323	2907	2799	5939	16122
Drizzly	8	41	28	38	34	149
Foggy	5	15	23	19	16	1619
Rainy	55	133	150	180	332	850
Cloudy	93	272	351	408	495	1619

occurred on straight road segments and 6.7% on curved road sections, whereas 22.7% and 4.4% of motorcycle crashes arose at intersections with traffic signals and without signage, respectively.

Regarding the type of injury, 405 victims were killed and 2,450 people suffered serious injuries as a result of motorcycle crashes during the studied period. Male victims were more involved in motorcycle crashes than females with 78.5%. In addition, young adults between 19 and 33 years old and adults between 34 and 64 years old represent the largest age groups of victims involved in motorcycle crashes with 45.4% and 42.5%, respectively, during the study period.

4 Results

An incremental spatial autocorrelation analysis was first performed to obtain a distance threshold or bandwidth value for each analysed crash variable and year. This parameter value maximizes the spatial autocorrelation (Z score), meaning that a cluster exists up to this calculated distance with a statistical significance of 0.01. These distance thresholds were employed in both global and local spatial autocorrelation analyses. Z score values greater than 1.96 with a 95% confidence were utilised to determine the statistical significance for each value of the motorcycle crash variables in such analyses.

Table 2 shows the global spatial autocorrelation results. The average and standard deviation values of the global Moran's I index were computed only for those crash variables that presented a recurrent clustering of at least three years during the studied period. Different strength measures of persistent global spatial patterns are observed among the different crash variables. For example, motorcycle crashes that occurred at signalised intersections present a stronger positive spatial pattern with an average global Moran's I value of 0.088 during the five years of the study period than any other analysed variable in the table.

Among all road safety measures, crashes per 100,000 population presents the highest positive clustering of 0.51. With respect with the type of injury, crash-caused fatalities clustered during all five years of the 2011–2015 period with a high average clustering intensity of 0.073, followed by slight injury outcomes with an average global positive autocorrelation of 0.050, and victims that were seriously injured with a value of 0.021. Although a large percentage of crashes occurred during weekdays, similar global spatial clustering of motorcycle crashes is observed during weekdays and weekends with 0.048 and 0.042, respectively. Similarly, approximately 1.4 and 1.7 times more crashes occurred in the afternoon and night, respectively, than during the morning. However, the highest overall clustering of crashes occurred during the morning with 0.048. While most motorcycle crashes occurred in the summer, a large average global clustering is observed in the spring (0.087). The largest percentage of motorcycle crashes involve young adults and adults, nevertheless, the largest global spatial clustering is perceived in the age group of victims over 65 years old during the five years of the study period. Female and male victims are positively clustered with values of 0.055 and 0.059, respectively.

Regarding the type of crash, collisions between moving vehicles present a global positive autocorrelation of 0.053 and are clustered during the whole study period, followed by impacts with static vehicles (0.036) and pedestrian crashes (0.034). Whereas, rollovers of motorcycle crashes were insignificant during the study period. The relative locations of motorcycle crashes show positive global spatial dependences of arising along straight (0.053) and curved (0.066) road sections, and at intersections with and without traffic signals for all studied years. Insignificant results were obtained for crashes that occurred on rural zones, and thus, these are not listed in Table 2. Whilst motorcycle crashes that arose in urban zones tend to cluster during four years of the study period with an average clustering intensity of 0.051.

The contributing cause related to driving under the influence of alcohol shows the largest clustering intensity (0.064) among all contributing factors, as in the results of [29]. However, the loss of control of the vehicle, the imprudence of pedestrians, and the imprudence of drivers are other causes with high average Moran's I values of 0.059,

Table 2. Results of recurrent global spatial autocorrelation of motorcycle crashes (adapted from [24]).

Variable	Average Moran's I	Standard deviation Moran's I	Number of clustering years
Road safety measures			
Number of crashes	0.049	0.009	5
Crashes per 100,000 population	0.051	0.026	5
Crashes per 10,000 registered vehicles	0.024	0.022	5
Type of injury			
Fatalities	0.073	0.029	5
Seriously injured	0.021	0.019	3
Slightly injured	0.050	0.041	5
Temporal attributes			
Day of week			
Weekday	0.048	0.009	5
Weekend	0.042	0.017	5
Time of day			
Morning	0.048	0.025	5
Afternoon	0.037	0.016	5
Night	0.030	0.012	5
Season			
Spring	0.087	0.102	5
Summer	0.035	0.018	5
Fall	0.043	0.018	5
Winter	0.042	0.018	5
Personal characteristics			
Age group			
<18 years old	0.043	0.031	4
19–33 years old	0.041	0.027	4
34–64 years old	0.046	0.018	5
>65 years old	0.065	0.040	5
Gender			
Female	0.055	0.036	4

(*continued*)

Table 2. (*continued*)

Variable	Average Moran's I	Standard deviation Moran's I	Number of clustering years
Male	0.059	0.033	5
Type of crash			
Collision	0.053	0.027	5
Impact	0.036	0.015	5
Pedestrian crash	0.034	0.036	3
Relative location			
Straight section	0.053	0.027	5
Curved section	0.066	0.031	5
Intersection with signage	0.088	0.017	5
Intersection without signage	0.053	0.028	5
Contributing factors			
Imprudence of driver	0.051	0.041	4
Imprudence of pedestrian	0.055	0.041	3
Loss of control	0.059	0.036	5
Driving under influence alcohol	0.064	0.039	4
Other causes	0.037	0.023	5
Type of zone			
Urban	0.051	0.035	4
Weather conditions			
Sunny	0.064	0.023	5
Drizzly	0.085	0.023	4
Foggy	0.044	0.023	4

0.055, and 0.051, respectively, which persisted for three or more years. Finally, the weather conditions of motorcycle crashes tend to cluster during all five years of the study period for sunny days with an average statistic value of 0.064, and during four years for drizzly and foggy days with an average global Moran's I value of 0.085 and 0.044, respectively. No significant results were observed for motorcycle crashes that occurred on rainy or cloudy days.

This study focuses on the location of motorcycle crash clusters with high crash-related variable values surrounded by high crash-related variable values (High-High local spatial pattern, HH). The number of HH spatial clusters for each analysed motor-cycle crash variable per year are shown in Table 3. This table indicates that the largest total number of HH crashes (287) during the studied period are related to motorcycle crashes that occurred on road with straight sections, followed by roads with curved sec-tions (253) and fatality outcomes (253). In addition, morning crashes present the largest average clustering intensity of 72.6, followed by those crashes that occurred at signalised intersections with a value of 71.7.

Note that although approximately 7% of all reported crashes occurred on curved road segments, these tend to locally cluster with high values over time. Similarly, very few motorcycle crashes occurred on drizzly days compared to the other weather conditions. However, 226 HH clusters of such crashes arise on drizzly days during the 2011–2015 period. Although approximately 5% of the crashes involve the elderly, this age group presents 181 HH clusters. Additionally, 42.5% of the victims are adults (34–64 years old) and 182 HH clusters are observed for this age group.

Over the study period, most crashes clustered locally during the morning with 163 HH and presented the highest clustering intensity, but the largest number of crashes occurred at night, as indicated in Table 1. Interestingly, among all seasons, the winter season has the highest number of HH with 168, but the strongest clustering intensity is observed in crashes that occurred in the spring (68.2). Similar number of HH clusters is identified in crashes that arose in the weekdays and weekends, concurring with the global spatial autocorrelation analysis results.

Note that motorcycle crashes that resulted in rollovers on rainy or cloudy days along rural areas present a low existence or lack of clustering over time. Additionally, notice that the total number of HH clusters for all contributing causes of motorcycle crashes is greater than 200, which highlights the importance of these factors among the generation of these crashes. On average, there are several large numbers of HH clusters of motorcycle collisions that occurred on sunny days along straight or curved road segments caused by the loss of control of the vehicle or the imprudence of the driver or the pedestrian generating fatality outcomes.

Figure 2–11 present spatial clusters at the commune level for each analysed motor-cycle crash variable that persisted for three, four, or five years of the studied period using the local Moran's I statistic. These figures depict that the communes belonging to four out of 16 regions of the country (Metropolitan Region, and regions of Valparaiso, O´Higgins, and Maule) represent statistically significant HH spatial patterns. This result may be explained by the high population and the substantial increase in the usage of motorcycles as a transport mode in these four regions between 2011 and 2015.

The HH clustering of road safety indicators are presented in Fig. 2. The communes of Viña del Mar, Valparaiso, and Quilpue in the Region of Valparaiso, several communes in the Metropolitan Region, Rancagua in the Region of O´Higgins, and Curico in the Region of Maule presented recurrent HH crash clusters for all years of the study period. Whereas, crashes per 100,000 population clustered for 3 years in the communes of San José de Maipo, Providencia, and Vitacura in the Metropolitan Region, and Curico in the Region of Maule. Crashes per 10,000 vehicles clustered spatially for less than three years, and thus, a figure is not presented for this variable. Figure 3 depicts the recurrent HH clusters of fatality outcomes that persisted for the whole studied period in

Table 3. Number of HH spatial clusters of motorcycle crash attributes that arose during the 2011–2015 period (adapted from [24]).

Variable	Year					$\sum$ HH
	2011	2012	2013	2014	2015	
Road safety measures						
Number of crashes	28 (62.6)	36 (56.4)	37 (60.2)	39 (58.9)	31 (92.5)	171 (66.1)
Crashes per 100,000 population	7 (38.5)	30 (25.7)	1 (3.9)	64 (57.1)	18 (27.9)	120 (30.6)
Crashes per 10,000 registered vehicles	2 (42.9)	16 (27.6)	3 (69.4)	48 (29.7)	32 (24.2)	101 (38.7)
Type of injury						
Fatalities	54 (46.4)	46 (44.9)	52 (48.4)	51 (58.4)	50 (61.5)	253 (51.9)
Seriously injured	46 (31.5)	0	23 (33.0)	31 (38.4)	49 (44.7)	149 (36.9)
Slightly injured	55 (44.7)	39 (20.8)	20 (12.8)	48 (45.7)	61 (56.4)	223 (36.1)
Temporal attributes						
Day of week						
Weekday	31 (62.1)	34 (57.9)	40 (59.2)	35 (80.2)	33 (86.5)	173 (69.2)
Weekend	27 (48.8)	37 (53.5)	32 (59.4)	40 (60.7)	35 (75.2)	171 (59.5)
Time of day						
Morning	25 (62.6)	32 (59.5)	33 (50.5)	36 (95.4)	37 (94.8)	163 (72.6)
Afternoon	28 (57.9)	27 (53.9)	23 (50.6)	33 (77.4)	31 (82.9)	142 (64.5)
Night	28 (47.5)	29 (49.7)	23 (44.9)	35 (66.9)	37 (77.0)	152 (57.2)
Season						
Spring	23 (59.8)	31 (52.9)	38 (72.5)	33 (72.0)	31 (83.6)	156 (68.2)
Summer	25 (41.6)	25 (56.0)	33 (48.6)	40 (80.0)	34 (72.8)	157 (59.8)
Fall	31 (75.6)	26 (53.1)	32 (61.1)	37 (68.0)	34 (82.5)	160 (68.1)
Winter	35 (49.9)	34 (59.6)	35 (57.5)	26 (67.4)	38 (85.9)	168 (64.1)
Personal characteristics						
Age group						
<18 years old	24 (44.3)	18 (37.1)	34 (46.6)	35 (75.9)	35 (45.9)	146 (50.0)
19–33 years old	21 (50.9)	38 (66.7)	34 (58.9)	39 (87.8)	28 (77.7)	160 (68.4)
34–64 years old	35 (63.8)	30 (52.8)	40 (57.8)	37 (63.5)	40 (87.5)	182 (65.1)
>65 years old	35 (41.9)	45 (53.1)	30 (50.4)	32 (68.1)	39 (56.9)	181 (54.1)
Gender						
Female	23 (42.8)	31 (71.3)	36 (52.9)	38 (76.4)	29 (65.6)	157 (61.8)

(continued)

Table 3. (*continued*)

Variable	Year					$\sum$ HH
	2011	2012	2013	2014	2015	
Male	31 (59.5)	36 (53.0)	38 (60.3)	38 (72.6)	34 (85.3)	177 (66.1)
Type of crash						
Collision	57 (41.6)	45 (31.3)	53 (33.6)	24 (59.8)	45 (42.5)	224 (41.8)
Impact	61 (32.6)	30 (70.3)	31 (80.7)	38 (52.2)	4 (72.3)	164 (61.6)
Pedestrian crash	62 (28.4)	12 (4.4)	7 (11.6)	54 (45.4)	49 (45.3)	184 (27.0)
Rollover	10 (23.4)	0	7 (16.3)	14 (5.9)	25 (39.6)	56 (16.8)
Relative location						
Straight section	61 (34.7)	50 (38.2)	58 (37.1)	68 (35.9)	50 (53.7)	287 (39.9)
Curved section	35 (41.2)	50 (39.4)	60 (37.4)	51 (53.2)	57 (55.0)	253 (45.3)
Intersection with signage	30 (83.3)	34 (63.8)	39 (52.2)	39 (75.1)	34 (84.1)	176 (71.7)
Intersection without signage	34 (42.5)	35 (37.5)	39 (54.8)	40 (52.1)	35 (77.6)	183 (52.9)
Contributing factors						
Imprudence of driver	51 (44.5)	44 (17.1)	43 (37.5)	55 (58.9)	47 (20.2)	240 (35.6)
Imprudence of pedestrian	30 (24.3)	48 (39.7)	53 (43.1)	56 (53.5)	53 (58.3)	240 (43.8)
Loss of control	27 (13.3)	50 (61.2)	56 (36.9)	53 (49.1)	59 (53.7)	245 (42.8)
Driving under influence alcohol	25 (12.1)	55 (31.3)	45 (15.1)	54 (56.2)	53 (54.6)	232 (33.9)
Other causes	48 (62.9)	38 (38.4)	42 (21.3)	49 (63.9)	29 (44.3)	206 (46.2)
Type of zone						
Urban	56 (46.9)	4 (13.3)	24 (11.3)	51 (5.9)	60 (20.8)	195 (18.5)
Rural	0	8 (9.8)	5 (5.1)	49 (39.1)	61 (20.4)	123 (14.9)
Weather conditions						
Sunny	50 (49.6)	41 (42.5)	47 (36.2)	48 (52.4)	54 (53.1)	240 (46.8)
Drizzly	0	57 (48.1)	62 (50.7)	52 (59.5)	55 (57.2)	226 (53.9)
Foggy	0	30 (26.4)	17 (41.9)	48 (44.2)	55 (35.2)	150 (29.5)
Rainy	19 (43.2)	0	0	21 (52.5)	16 (61.4)	56 (52.4)
Cloudy	40 (72.8)	0	0	0	36 (59.9)	76 (26.5)

Note: Average local Moran´s I values of HH crashes are shown in parenthesis.

the communes situated in the Metropolitan Region, and the regions of Valparaiso and O´Higgins. Whereas HH clusters of seriously or slightly injured victims are recurrent

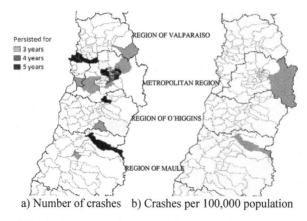

a) Number of crashes   b) Crashes per 100,000 population

Fig. 2. HH spatial clusters for each road safety measure.

for a smaller number of years and only in some communes of these regions. Although Fig. 4a) and 4b) present communes with similar HH clusters, slightly more communes are perceived as recurrent HH clusters during the weekday. Regarding the time of day, 32 communes are perceived as HH clusters of morning and night crashes, whereas 25 communes are observed as HH clusters of afternoon crashes over three or more years (See Fig. 5). The communes of Ñuñoa, Puente Alto, and Santiago in the Metropolitan Region, Quilpue and Valparaiso in the Region of Valparaiso, and Rancagua in the Region of O'Higgins persisted as HH crash clusters during the complete study period for all seasons of the year, as shown in Fig. 6.

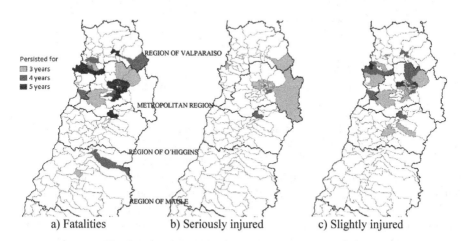

a) Fatalities   b) Seriously injured   c) Slightly injured

Fig. 3. HH spatial clusters for each type of injury [24].

As the results presented in Table 3, Fig. 7 shows that collisions represent the largest number of HH spatial clusters among all types of crashes. These clusters are mostly located in communes of the Region of Valparaiso and Metropolitan Region. Notice that

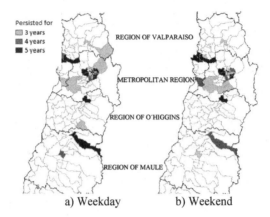

a) Weekday   b) Weekend

Fig. 4. HH spatial clusters for days of the week.

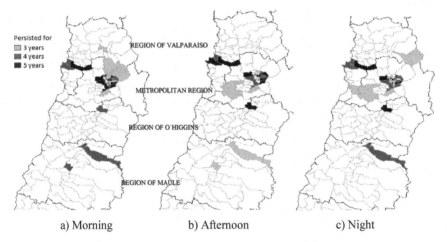

a) Morning   b) Afternoon   c) Night

Fig. 5. HH spatial clusters for each time of the day.

rollover-related crash HH clusters are not shown since such clusters in all communes were positive and significant for less than three years.

Figure 8 presents the recurrent HH clusters of motorcycle crashes with respect to their relative location at the commune level. For all types of relative locations, this figure shows that HH clusters in some communes in the Region of Valparaiso and in the Metropolitan Region, and in the commune of Rancagua in the Region of O'Higgins persisted for the five years of the studied period. Conversely, recurrent HH clusters appeared along straight and curved road sections in many communes in the centre of the Metropolitan Region (particularly in the city of Santiago).

Communes in the four regions shown in Fig. 9 present persistent HH clusters due to the imprudence of the pedestrian, whereas clustering of crashes due to imprudence of the driver that persisted for all five years of the 2011–2015 are concentrated in the city of Santiago, a couple of communes in the Region of Valparaiso, and Rancagua in

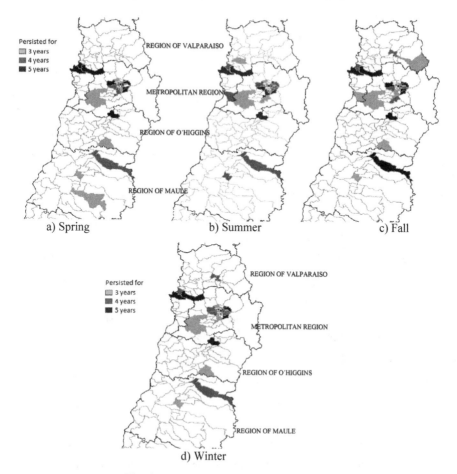

Fig. 6. HH spatial clusters for each season.

the Region of O'Higgins. This figure also suggests that motorcycle crashes due to the loss of control and driving under the influence of alcohol are highly clustered during the five years of the studied period in few communes in the city of Santiago and Region of Valparaiso. HH clusters appear in a lesser degree as a result of other causes.

Recurrent spatial clustering of crashes that occurred in urban areas are recurrent for 3 or 4 years during the studied period in communes of the regions of O'Higgins and Maule, as shown in Fig. 10. No HH clustering of crashes in rural zones was perceived in any commune for three or more years.

Regarding the weather conditions, Fig. 11 depicts HH spatial clusters of crashes that arose on sunny and drizzly days that persisted for three or more years. Concurring with the results in Table 3, this figure shows that communes with clustering of crashes on sunny days persisted for three to five years, whilst more communes are displayed with crash clusters during drizzly days for three and four years of the studied period.

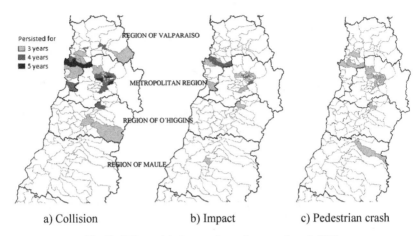

a) Collision   b) Impact   c) Pedestrian crash

Fig. 7. HH spatial clusters for each type of crash [24].

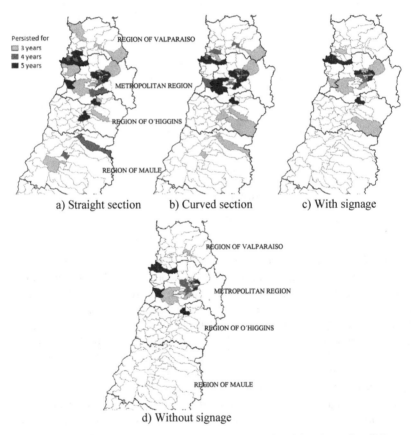

a) Straight section   b) Curved section   c) With signage

d) Without signage

Fig. 8. HH spatial clusters for the relative location of motorcycle crashes [24].

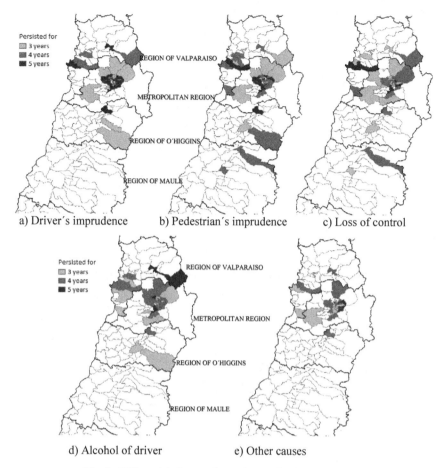

Fig. 9. HH spatial clusters for each contributing factor [24].

The top five Chilean communes with the largest number of HH for the 41 analysed crash-related variables in the five-year period are shown in Fig. 12. This figure shows that four out of these five communes with the most number of HH crash attributes are located in the Metropolitan Region.

Table 4 presents the average values of the local Moran's I index and the Z score in parenthesis for recurrent crash attributes for the five communes depicted in Fig. 12. Those communes with no values indicate that that particular variable was significant for less than three years. Overall, Santiago has the highest intensity of HH clusters in 27 of the crash-related variables when compared to the rest of the communes, similarly to the findings in Blazquez and Celis [30] and Blazquez et al. [31]. In particular, significantly higher clustering of morning crashes at intersections with traffic signs on weekdays generating fatality outcomes are perceived in this commune.

a) Urban zone

Fig. 10. HH spatial clusters of crashes in urban zones [24].

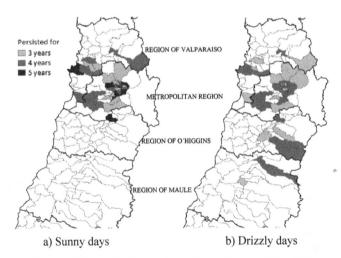

a) Sunny days   b) Drizzly days

Fig. 11. HH spatial clusters for each weather condition [24].

Fig. 12. Communes with the largest number of HH attribute clusters during the 2011–2015 period (adapted from [24]).

Table 4. Local autocorrelation results of motorcycle crash attributes for the top five communes with most HH crash clusters (adapted from [24]).

Variable	Commune				
	Las Condes	Ñuñoa	Puente Alto	Rancagua	Santiago
Road safety measures					
Crashes	106.5 (11.8)	113.9 (12.6)	154.2 (17.0)	121.3 (13.3)	199.1 (22.1)
Crashes per 100,000 population	45.5 (5.0)	38.8 (4.4)	–	40.5 (4.5)	33.9 (3.8)
Crashes per 10,000 registered vehicles	–	28.9 (3.4)	–	18.4 (2.2)	28.0 (3.3)
Type of injury					
Fatalities	107.2 (4.2)	118.1 (4.2)	162.5 (4.2)	120.0 (4.0)	207.1 (4.2)
Seriously injured	42.3 (2.7)	41.3 (2.8)	80.4 (2.5)	50.2 (2.7)	48.7 (2.7)
Slightly injured	71.5 (3.4)	138.3 (3.8)	147.5 (3.8)	85.8 (3.7)	113.7 (3.3)
Temporal attributes					
Day of week					
Weekday	111.4 (12.3)	129.9 (14.3)	144.3 (15.9)	116.7 (12.8)	201.4 (22.2)
Weekend	87.1 (9.6)	53.3 (5.9)	156.2 (17.2)	86.5 (9.6)	151.8 (16.8)
Time of day					
Morning	158.3 (17.4)	147.3 (16.3)	150.7 (16.6)	88.2 (9.7)	207.5 (22.9)

(continued)

Table 4. (*continued*)

Variable	Commune				
	Las Condes	Ñuñoa	Puente Alto	Rancagua	Santiago
Afternoon	92.7 (10.3)	95.2 (10.6)	137.0 (15.2)	113.6 (12.5)	169.6 (18.8)
Night	92.8 (10.3)	86.4 (9.6)	134.6 (14.8)	102.0 (11.2)	135.9 (15.0)
Season					
Spring	104.2 (11.5)	104.9 (11.6)	116.8 (12.8)	66.7 (7.3)	176.8 (19.5)
Summer	89.5 (9.9)	80.6 (8.1)	141.9 (15.6)	106.2 (11.7)	141.9 (15.1)
Fall	106.5 (11.8)	106.5 (11.8)	150.7 (16.6)	110.2 (12.1)	181.8 (20.0)
Winter	91.6 (10.2)	112.7 (12.5)	112. (12.5)	112.7 (12.4)	162.8 (18.1)
Personal characteristics					
Age group					
<18 years old	56.8 (6.6)	54.4 (6.3)	106.5 (12.2)	88.1 (10.1)	118.6 (13.5)
19–33 years old	107.2 (12.3)	124.5 (14.2)	146.7 (16.8)	112.3 (12.8)	179.8 (20.5)
34–64 years old	118.8 (13.1)	109.3 (12.0)	147.4 (16.2)	108.7 (11.9)	191.3 (21.0)
>65 years old	63.0 (7.1)	79.4 (8.9)	92.7 (10.3)	118.9 (13.3)	110.8 (12.5)
Gender					
Female	78.5 (8.8)	61.1 (6.9)	131.1 (14.7)	109.8 (12.3)	175.4 (19.7)
Male	108.4 (11.9)	121.6 (13.4)	147.9 (16.2)	106.8 (11.7)	188.5 (20.7)
Type of crash					
Collision	58.6 (3.6)	96.2 (3.7)	124.7 (3.6)	84.7 (3.0)	141.1 (3.5)
Impact	82.1 (3.4)	72.9 (2.7)	71.1 (3.7)	73.0 (3.2)	180.4 (3.6)
Pedestrian crash	105.8 (3.5)	40.3 (3.6)	117.4 (3.5)	62.8 (3.5)	149.6 (3.5)
Relative location					
Straight section	74.4 (3.7)	108.6 (3.8)	163.2 (3.7)	95.5 (3.6)	134.4 (3.6)
Curved section	86.1 (4.0)	87.9 (3.9)	129.1 (3.8)	84.1 (3.5)	176.0 (3.8)
Intersection with signage	132.5 (15.6)	122.3 (14.3)	169.9 (19.8)	136.7 (16.0)	216.5 (25.2)
Intersection without signage	53.3 (6.3)	151.2 (17.6)	88.8 (10.4)	84.6 (9.9)	117.3 (13.6)
Contributing factors					
Imprudence of driver	64.2 (3.6)	58.2 (3.3)	68.5 (3.4)	97.5 (3.2)	153.7 (3.1)
Imprudence of pedestrian	98.0 (3.8)	104.1 (4.0)	142.1 (4.1)	86.3 (3.5)	187.1 (4.1)

(*continued*)

Table 4. (*continued*)

Variable	Commune				
	Las Condes	Ñuñoa	Puente Alto	Rancagua	Santiago
Loss of control	124.0 (4.2)	111.7 (3.8)	174.8(4.2)	70.8 (4.0)	194.6 (4.2)
Driving under influence alcohol	105.3 (3.7)	103.9 (3.6)	111.3 (3.7)	95.7 (3.5)	149.3 (3.5)
Other causes	59.9 (3.4)	122.3 (3.3)	93.4 (3.2)	67.2 (3.3)	62.8 (2.9)
Type of zone					
Urban	–	–	–	57.0 (2.6)	–
Weather conditions					
Sunny	98.1 (4.1)	71.9 (4.0)	161.8 (3.9)	94.7 (3.9)	133.5 (3.9)
Drizzly	122.5 (4.5)	136.0 (4.7)	171.5 (4.5)	129.0 (4.2)	235.8 (4.5)
Rainy	–	–	–	–	62.3 (2.3)

5 Discussion

The vast majority of the crash-related variables have their highest value in the year 2015 (See Table 1). For example, the age group of young adults (particularly, male drivers) presented a dramatic increase of 360.6% in crash involvement as the number of crashes increased. The share of collisions almost tripled between 2014 and 2015, resulting in double the number of deaths and four times the number of seriously injured victims. These results suggest the urgency of further research using the Chilean crash dataset of recent years, in order to provide prioritise interventions of safety measures in those communes with high motorcycle crash risk.

The global spatial autocorrelation results reveal that certain crash-related variables tend to cluster although these present low values. Approximately 2% of the victims are killed as a results of motorcycle crashes, but this variable presents the highest global Moran's I value of 0.073 when compared to the other types of injuries. Analogously, 61.2% of the crashes occur along straight road segments. However, crashes at signalised intersections resulted in the largest positive global spatial clustering among all relative locations. Additionally, crashes that occur during drizzly days in the spring are more incline to globally cluster than other weather conditions and seasons, respectively.

Both global and local spatial autocorrelation analyses obtained similar results for some variables. For example, over 250 out of 343 communes were identified as HH clusters of fatalities with the strongest clustering intensity among other injury types. In addition, motorcycle crashes have a tendency to cluster locally particularly in the morning and weekdays during drizzly days.

Overall, a large number of HH clusters of collisions due to the loss of control are present on sunny days in the Metropolitan Region and regions of Valparaiso, O'Higgins, and Maule. Regarding the personal characteristics of the victims, more HH crash clusters are obtained that involve adults between 34 and 64 years of age, but crashes that involve young adults present a higher clustering intensity. More male drivers participate in motor-cycle crashes than female drivers (78.5% vs 21.5%) perhaps because approximately 94% of motorcycle riders are males [5].

A large number of motorcycle crashes tend to cluster spatially along straight and curved road segments. Drivers have a tendency to increase their travel speeds as straight road sections are encountered, which may increase the likelihood of causing crashes with serious outcomes. Motorcyclists are more prone to crashes at curves, which may generate a significant impact on crash severity or fatality, as shown in [13]. The highest intensity of local crash clusters appear at signalised intersections, possibly due to the imprudence of the driver and pedestrians. Motorcyclists are particularly vulnerable at signalised intersections since they are over exposed as they gather near the stop line [32].

With respect to the zone type, crashes that occurred in urban zones are globally and locally clustered. According to the ANIM database [5], 90% of the motorcycles are employed in urban areas for commuting trips to work. Thus, a low number of crashes (15%) occur in rural areas. However, although no positive spatial pattern of rural crashes are observed from a global perspective, a considerable increase in the number of HH spatial crash clusters that arose in rural areas are detected in the last couple of years. This increase should be further investigated using crash data from more recent years to identify any additional trend.

The analysis results indicate that over 40% of the motorcycle crashes occurred in the Metropolitan Region during the studied period. The large number of HH clusters of crashes in this area is due to the fact that over 50% of Chile´s population resides in the Metropolitan Region and the surrounding areas, and approximately 55.5% of the total number of motorcycles nationwide are registered in these regions, which are more prone to be exposed to traffic crashes.

Amid the top five communes with most number of HH clusters, the commune of Santiago presents the strongest intensity of such clusters for most of the analysed variables. This result may be attributed to that this commune has the largest number of registered motorcycles in Chile with a total of 5.571 motorcycles in 2015, and an increase of 23.6% in the number of registered motorcycles between 2011 and 2015. Additionally, Santiago is a commune that has a daily floating population of approximately 2 million people due to its strong political, economic, and commercial activities in an area of only 23.2 km^2, and a residential population of 404,495 inhabitants [33]. Authorities and CONASET should prioritize the promotion and education of the community about road safety in this commune.

6 Conclusions

This study employed spatial statistics to identify global and local spatial autocorrelation of motorcycle crashes in Chile at the commune level. Recurrent statistically significant crash clusters were also obtained during the 2011–2015 period. Eight groups of motorcycle crash variables were analysed in the autocorrelation analysis. Global autocorrelation results indicate that variables associated with collisions occurring at signalised intersections on drizzly days during the spring, and resulting in fatality outcomes are spatially autocorrelated for the whole study period.

The local spatial autocorrelation results suggest the presence and persistence of HH spatial clusters of crash-related variables in the communes located in the Region of Valparaiso, Metropolitan Region, Region of O'Higgins, and Region of Maule. The commune of Santiago located in the Metropolitan Region presents the highest clustering intensity of motorcycle crashes. Local authorities should prioritize this commune to implement specific interventions that may help improve traffic safety.

References

1. World Health Organization, WHO. Global status report on road safety (2015). https://www.who.int/violence_injury_prevention/road_safety_status/2015/GSRRS2015_Summary_EN_final2.pdf. Accessed 30 Sep 2018
2. International Traffic Safety Data and Analysis Group, IRTAD, Road Safety Annual Report (2017). https://www.oecd-ilibrary.org/transport/road-safety-annual-report-2017_irtad-2017-en. Accessed 31 Jul 2018
3. Comisión Nacional de la Seguridad del Tránsito, CONASET, Siniestros de Tránsito de ocupantes de motocicletas y consecuencias (2016). https://www.conaset.cl/programa/observatorio-datos-estadistica/biblioteca-observatorio/informes-tematicos/#motocicletas. Accessed 13 Apr 2018
4. National Highway Traffic Safety Administration, NHTSA, Traffic Safety Facts (2012). https://crashstats.nhtsa.dot.gov/Api/Public/ViewPublication/812016. Accessed 10 Nov 2018
5. Asociación Nacional de Importadores de Motocicletas, ANIM. Actualidad del mercado en Mundo Motos 2016 (2015). http://www.anim.cl/anim-clp1820/. Accessed 22 Sep 2018
6. MT Motores, Espacial Mercado de motos en Chile. Diario La Tercera (2016). https://www.pressreader.com/chile/la-tercera-mt-motores/20160930/281505045711190. Accessed 02 Oct 2018
7. Smotos, Mercado chileno: Venta de motos 2018 sube un 16.7 y ¡vamos por la calle! (2018). https://smotos.cl/mercado-chileno-venta-de-motos-2018-sube-un-16-7-y-vamos-por-la-calle/. Accessed 08 Aug 2019
8. Instituto Nacional de Estadística, INE, Anuario Estadísticas Vitales (2018). http://www.ine.cl/estadisticas/demograficas-y-vitales. Accessed 31 Jul 2019
9. Jalayer, M., Zhou, H.: A multiple correspondence analysis of at-fault motorcycle-involved crashes in Alabama. J. Adv. Transp. **50**, 2089–2099 (2016)
10. Flask, T., Schneider, W., Lord, D.: A segment level analysis of multi-vehicle motorcycle crashes in Ohio using Bayesian multi-level mixed effects models. Saf. Sci. **66**, 47–53 (2014)
11. Das, S., Dutta, A., Dixon, K., Minjares-Kyle, L., Gillette, G.: Using deep learning in severity analysis of at-fault motorcycle rider crashes. J. Transp. Res. Board **2672**(34), 122–134 (2018)
12. Lee, J., Yasmin, S., Eluru, N., Abdel-Aty, M., Cai, Q.: Analysis of crash proportion by vehicle type at traffic analysis zone level: A mixed fractional split multinomial logit modeling approach with spatial effect. Accid. Anal. Prev. **111**, 12–22 (2018)
13. Chung, Y., Song, T.-J.: Safety analysis of motorcycle crashes in Seoul metropolitan area, South Korea: an application of nonlinear optimal scaling methods. Int. J. Environ. Res. Public Health **15**(12), 2702 (2018)
14. Ding, C., Rizzi, M., Strandroth, J., Sander, U., Lubbe, N.: Motorcyclist injury risk as a function of real-life crash speed and other contributing factors. Accid. Anal. Prev. **123**, 374–386 (2019)
15. Alnawmasi, N., Mannering, F.: A statistical assessment of temporal instability in the factors determining motorcyclist injury severities. Anal. Methods Accid. Res. **22**, 100090 (2019)
16. Zhou, M., Chin, H.C.: Factors affecting the injury severity of out-of-control single-vehicle crashes in Singapore. Accid. Anal. Prev. **124**, 104–112 (2019)

17. Dezman, Z., et al.: Hotspots and causes of motor vehicle crashes in Baltimore, Maryland: a geospatial analysis of five years of police crash and census data. Injury **47**(11), 2450–2458 (2016)
18. Soltani, A., Askari, S.: Exploring spatial autocorrelation of traffic crashes based on severity. Injury **48**(3), 637–647 (2017)
19. Pour, A., Moridpour, S., Tay, R., Rajabifard, A.: Influence of pedestrian age and gender on spatial and temporal distribution of pedestrian crashes. Traffic Inj. Prev. **19**(1), 81–87 (2018)
20. Blazquez, C., Picarte, B., Calderon, J.F., Losada, F.: Spatial autocorrelation analysis of cargo trucks on highway crashes in Chile. Accid. Anal. Prev. **120**, 195–210 (2018)
21. Aghajani, M., Dezfoulian, R., Arjroody, A., Rezaei, M.: Applying GIS to identify the spatial and temporal patterns of road accidents using spatial statistics (case study: Ilam Province, Iran). Transp. Res. Procedia **25**, 2126–2138 (2017)
22. Saadat, S., Rahmani, K., Moradi, A., Zaini, S., Darabi, F.: Spatial analysis of driving accidents leading to deaths related to motorcyclists in Tehran. Chin. J. Traumatol. **22**, 148–154 (2019)
23. Ghandour, A., Hammoud, H., Telesca, L.: Transportation hazard spatial analysis using crowd-sourced social network data. Phys. A: Stat. Mech. Appl. **520**, 309–316 (2019)
24. Blazquez, C., Fuentes, M.J.: Global and local spatial autocorrelation of motorcycle crashes in Chile. In: Proceedings of the 5th International Conference on Vehicle Technology and Intelligent Transport Systems, pp. 159–170. SciTePress, Heraklion, Crete (2019)
25. Mitra, S.: Spatial autocorrelation and bayesian spatial statistical method for analysing intersections prone to injury crashes. J. Transp. Res. Board **2136**, 92–100 (2009)
26. Anselin, L.: Local indicators of spatial association-LISA. Geog. Anal. **27**, 93–115 (1995)
27. Meng, Q.: The spatiotemporal characteristics of environmental hazards caused by offshore oil and gas operations in the Gulf of Mexico. Sci. Total Environ. **565**, 663–671 (2016)
28. Manepalli, U., Bham, G., Kandada, S.: Evaluation of hot spots identification using Kernel Density Estimation (K) and Getis-Ord (Gi*) on I-630. In: Proceedings 3rd International Conference on Road Safety and Simulation 17, Transportation Research Board, Indianapolis, Indiana (2011)
29. Blazquez, C., Puelma, I., Khan, G.: Spatial analysis of bicycle crashes in Chile. In: Proceedings 18th IEEE International Conference on Intelligent Transportation Systems. IEEE Intelligent Transportation Systems Society, Las Palmas de Gran Canaria, Spain, pp. 2745–2750 (2015)
30. Blazquez, C., Celis, M.: A spatial and temporal analysis of child pedestrian crashes in Santiago, Chile. Accid. Anal. Prev. **50**, 304–311 (2013)
31. Blazquez, C., Lee, J.S., Zegras, C.: Children at risk: an initial comparison of child pedestrian traffic collisions in Santiago, Chile and Seoul, South Korea. Traffic Inj. Prev. **17**(3), 304–312 (2016)
32. Haque, M., Chin, H., Huang, H.: Applying Bayesian hierarchical models to examine motorcycle crashes at signalized intersections. Accid. Anal. Prev. **42**(1), 203–212 (2010)
33. Instituto Nacional de Estadística, INE. Censo (2017). https://www.censo2017.cl/. Accessed 18 Apr 2018

Smart Parking Zones Using Meshed Bluetooth Sensor Networks

Paul Seymer$^{(\boxtimes)}$ ⓘ, Duminda Wijesekeraⓘ, and Cing-Dao Kan

George Mason University, Fairfax, VA 22030, USA
{pseymer,dwijesek,cdkan}@gmu.edu

Abstract. Developing seamless smart parking solutions remain an active research area. User coordination burden remains high, and systems based on complex instrumentation are often expensive and costly to maintain. Contemporary parking lot management systems are slow to adopt new technology, particularly in cases where there is no perceived immediate return on investment. We propose the use of a low cost, low power, Bluetooth Low Energy (BLE) based outdoor localization system coupled with a Random Forest classifier and dual-mode Bluetooth mesh network to provide space occupancy detection and sensor data transfer. To balance computational demands with cost, we leverage *fog computing* paradigms to shift computational capability near the sensor network where it can be used without an expensive network back-haul to a data center or cloud. We provide operational experiment results and analysis, and a study on the effects on accuracy from various network complexity and radio map minimization schemes.

Keywords: Smart parking · RF localization · Bluetooth networking

1 Introduction

Contemporary *smart parking* solutions are plagued with enduring problems. First is the excessive cost, due to the need for one sensor per parking space and retrofitting of lots with networking and power. This is a significant problem for large lots and those in remote locations without existing networking support or power. Second is a continued usability concern caused by traffic bottlenecks at ingress and egress payment support points. Those that do not suffer from these problems often use *crowd-sourced* occupancy detection features or rely on smartphone apps that offload the coordination burden directly onto the user and require a complicated technology back-end.

Solutions to these problems require a low cost and low power wireless solution that provides seamless occupancy tracking without the need for significant or expensive lot alterations. To reduce deployment complexity, the solution should cover multiple parking spaces per sensor and provide some degree of vehicle detection and tracking to prevent the need for user-provided payment support.

In past work [32] we presented our zone-based space occupancy and vehicle detection solution over our Bluetooth-based wireless mesh network along with

© Springer Nature Switzerland AG 2021
M. Helfert et al. (Eds.): SMARTGREENS 2019/VEHITS 2019, CCIS 1217, pp. 245–269, 2021.
https://doi.org/10.1007/978-3-030-68028-2_12

experiments and results from the deployment of our system at a parking lot used by the Center for Collision Safety and Analysis (CCSA) on the George Mason University's Fairfax, VA campus. In this work we present an extension of that paper, including an updated prediction model, an ablation analysis detailing the effects of a reduced sensor network and radio fingerprinting schemes on prediction accuracy and mesh network density (Sect. 4) so we may reduce network size and site deployment burdens without making our solution unusable, and an expanded related work section that includes a more direct comparison with our work (Sect. 5). When necessary, we simplified prior work explanations as well as provided additional clarity to tables and figures (citing where appropriate).

2 Solution Overview

We show an overview of our solution in Fig. 1. Our Bluetooth sensor network is deployed to a parking lot and collects Received Signal Strength Indicator (RSSI) measurements of custom Bluetooth Low Energy (BLE) beacons deployed inside parked vehicles. Prior to use, a radio map of RSSI values observed at each sensor node is created for each space in the lot, and used to create a Random Forest machine learning model (each space is a different class in the model). When powered on, our nodes create a self-forming authenticated mesh network to transport this RSSI data back to a central *sink* node.

To balance power hungry and network heavy computation and the use of low-power sensor nodes, we leverage *fog computing* concepts by locating the computational capability necessary to perform occupancy prediction near the sensor network. We divide this computation into two groupings based off of memory, power, and computational demand, where heavy one-time operations such as model training occur in a *cloud* environment and data collection and use of the model occurs in a *fog* network. We simulate our cloud environment, and establish the *fog* network in the CCSA center at the edge of the sensor network. This allows us to offload expensive computation and deploy lower power and lower cost sensor nodes. We depict this arrangement in Fig. 2.

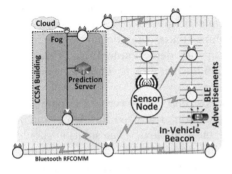

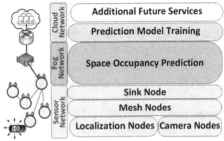

Fig. 1. Solution overview.   **Fig. 2.** Cloud/Fog/Sensor computation.

In addition to occupancy detection, we deploy a BLE-based vehicle ingress and egress detection capability to the entrance to the lot, coupled with an object recognition camera (for comparison).

2.1   Parking Space Occupancy Detection

Our current space occupancy detection system and Bluetooth mesh network is an evolution of prior work [31,32]. This section presents that prior work.

Zone Based Occupancy Detection. Preliminary experiments in prior work had a per-space occupancy detection goal [31]. In that work, training accuracy was above 90% however testing results were significantly less accurate. Several factors influence this outcome, from 2.4 GHz interference from nearby WiFi access points (the CCSA lot has upwards of 35 such access points from a nearby residential community) to vehicle size and orientation differences. To remedy this situation, we shifted from a per-space detection goal to a per-zone one. By creating *zones*, or contiguous parking space areas, we can mitigate small prediction errors due to a difference of a small number of spaces. We constructed zones as shown in Fig. 3. We believe that such a solution remains viable, as parking lot owners may only be interested in the area a vehicle is parked in within a lot, rather than an individual space. We outline the experiments that guided this decision and created an improved prediction model in Sect. 3 (Fig. 4).

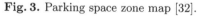

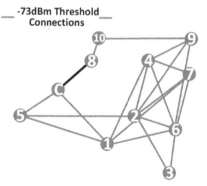

Fig. 3. Parking space zone map [32].   **Fig. 4.** Initial mesh connectivity.

Sensor Node Placement. Mounting locations for sensor nodes must not prevent occupancy of existing spaces nor interfere with vehicle movement. For our target lot, we utilized existing lamp posts, trees, and building window space to provide coverage for all spaces (see Fig. 3). Nodes were mounted at least 8 ft in the air to encourage line-of-sight with a maximum number of spaces. Experiments in prior work [31] gave us some insight into network performance and localization accuracy, causing us to include a redundant communication path from the *sensor* network to the *fog* network inside the building (through nodes "C" and "8"), and add additional sensor nodes. Node 10 is a special mesh-only node that is part of the mesh network but does not observe BLE beacons. Additionally, in this work we performed an ablation analysis on our prediction model determining that several of these nodes could be safely removed without significantly decreasing occupancy prediction accuracy. We detail these outcomes in Sect. 4.

Radio Map Construction. A radio map was constructed of the lot using our in-vehicle beacon and the sensor deployment shown in Fig. 3. Data was collected for each space for a 5 min window. Such a process, however, may be prohibitively time consuming for larger lots. To remedy this, we examine the effects on our model of reducing the number of spaces fingerprinted in Sect. 4.

Radio Fingerprint Feature Selection. Initially, we constructed a model that used a set of features based on descriptive statistics (median, variance, etc.) of all observed RSSI values. After additional analysis and experimentation we concluded that such a feature set was vulnerable to interference, attenuation, and other issues outlined in Sect. 3.1. In many cases these influences are ephemeral, but have severe effects on consistency of values, adding a great deal of noise to our features. We replaced this large unstable featureset with a single, maximum RSSI value observed within a time window at each node. We detail experiments that support this decision in Sect. 3.

2.2 Fogged Bluetooth Mesh Network

Each of our sensor nodes has identical hardware (except for the camera node) and is assigned a specific role (mesh only, sink, localization sensor, camera, etc.) within a configuration file. This role dictates its function, and allows a change in function post-deployment without physically modifying nodes. We use Bluetooth in EDR mode to perform mesh communication so we can partially avoid overlapping frequencies used by our BLE advertising channel-based localization. As Bluetooth has trouble penetrating walls we avoid deploying multiple mesh-only nodes to enable *fog* network communication, and instead communicate over the building's existing wired Ethernet. One mesh node is designated as the *central* sink node, providing a gateway for sensor data to be sent to the prediction system on the *fog* network.

Initially, our mesh network was deployed using a managed flooding approach. After conducting experiments we discovered that the high degree of message duplicates and inter-node connections was compromising our node's ability to receive beacon broadcasts from our in-vehicle beacon. To remedy this, we developed a simple routing algorithm to reduce network links, and a measurement sampling configuration reducing the total number of messages transmitted. We detailed these changes and their effects in Sect. 3.2.

Algorithm 1. RSSI based authenticated meshnet formation [32].

1: **procedure join_network**
2:     **if** node contains "fog" service **then**
3:         do SSDP on Ethernet network (for 20 mins)
4:         **for** each fog node *fn* found **do**
5:             **if** auth_to_fog_network(*fn*) **then**
6:                 initialize message queues for fn
7:         **if** at least one fog node found **then**
8:             launch RESTful API listener (flask)
9:     **if** node contains "edr" service **then**
10:         perform BLE scan (for 20 mins)
11:         **for** each advert bn with matching UUID **do**
12:             **if** bn avg RSSI $\leq$ -75 dBm **then**
13:                 **if** auth_to_ble_network(*bn*) **then**
14:                     known_nodes.append(*bn*)
15:         **if** at least one node *bn* found **then**
16:             broadcast BLE advertisements (for 20 mins)
17:             *gw* $\leftarrow$ *bn* with largest RSSI value
18:             Initialize message queues for *gw*
19: **procedure auth_to_fog_network**(node_info *fn*)
20:     *authmsg* $\leftarrow$ construct_authentication_message
21:     Open RESTful HTTPS connection to *fn*
22:     POST *authmsg*
23:     *authreply* $\leftarrow$ HTTP reply from POST
24:     **if** *authreply* is valid **then**
25:         return True
26:     return False
27: **procedure auth_to_ble_network**(node_info *bn*)
28:     *authmsg* $\leftarrow$ construct_authentication_message
29:     Open RFCOMM connection to *bn*
30:     Send *authmsg*
31:     *authreply* $\leftarrow$ Receive from *bn*
32:     **if** *authreply* is valid **then**
33:         return True
34:     return False

Authenticated Link Formation. Network formation occurs differently on the *fog* and *sensor* networks due to the difference in existing protocols used on Bluetooth and Ethernet networks. For example, node discovery on our *fog* network uses a slimmed-down implementation of SSDP [31], while nodes are discovered on the sensor network using Bluetooth's Service Discovery Protocol (SDP). The *fog* network is flat, while the sensor network is formed outward from the central *sink* node. This allows new sensor nodes to join the network and have a path back to the central node to carry our authentication messages.

Mesh network construction is shown as pseudocode in Algorithm 1 [32]. When each nodes starts up, *join_network* (line 1) repeatedly executes until at least one viable network hop is found. Next-hop discovery for fog-connected nodes is shown in lines 2–8, and for Bluetooth-connected nodes in lines 9–18. Our fog discovery (line 3) is implemented using a simplified SSDP service detailed in [31], and authentication (lines 5–6, procedure outlined in lines 19–27) is performed over a RESTful API written in Python and Flask over HTTPS (line 8). Bluetooth discovery (lines 11–12) uses BLE advertisements over a previously used SDP protocol, to support our signal-strength based routing algorithm outlined in Sect. 3.2. Bluetooth authentication proceeds in line 13. If authentication is successful for at least one node (line 15), a best node is selected (line 17), message queues are initialized (line 18), and the newly joined node begins broadcasting its presence on its respective medium (fog/Ethernet, or Bluetooth mesh) in line 16. This allows for the mesh network to form out from the central *sink* node, as it is the only node to advertise itself on boot, while all other nodes wait for a broadcasting node to come in range. Experiments and analysis that lead us to this algorithm are found in Sect. 3 and prior work [32].

Encrypted Message Transfer. Prior to deployment, each node exchanges and stores AES and HMAC key material with the central node. Our mesh network supports two main types of messages: authentication messages and parking system messages (RSSI data, heartbeats, camera messages, etc). Each message occupies a single AES block (128 bits) composed of a 4-bit *message type* to aid in message processing implementation (0000 for heartbeats, 0001 for RSSI data, etc.), a 16-bit sending node identifier, and 108 bit message text payload. This entire block is encrypted with the AES key and signed with the HMAC key (we implement a SHA-256 HMAC). This block is then pre-pended with a 2 bit mode identifier and 16 bit recipient node identifier and sent out over the network, each to allow for message routing and receipt without every node attempting decryption on every message. This message format is shown in Fig. 5. Additional implementation details can be found in [32].

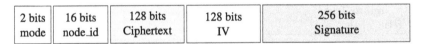

Fig. 5. 530 bit encrypted and signed message [32].

2.3 Vehicle Identification and Tracking

Our solution provides vehicle detection in two ways. First, is a pure wireless solution detailed in Sect. 2.3. For comparison, we include an object recognition camera-based solution in Sect. 2.3 and use it to perform attestations for our BLE beacon (i.e. a particular beacon does indeed belong to a vehicle).

Algorithm 2. BLE Only Vehicle Identification Procedures [32].

 1: **procedure initialize()**
 2:    $parked\_records \leftarrow \{\}$ ▷ init history data structure
 3:    $veh\_entered \leftarrow \{\}$ ▷ init enter records
 4:    $veh\_exited \leftarrow \{\}$ ▷ init exit records
 5:    detect_veh_kill_flag = False
 6:    beacon_measure_intvl = 5min
 7:    start thread **detect-vehicle-enter()**
 8:    start thread **detect-vehicle-exit()**
 9: **procedure detect-veh-enter**(each received beacon b)   ▷ called for each beacon
       central receives
10:       **if** $b.veh\_id$ not in $parked\_records$ **then**
11:          create entry for $b.veh\_id$ in $parked\_records$
12:          notify mgr new vehicle parked ($b.veh\_id$)
13:       $parked\_records[b.veh\_id].last\_seen \leftarrow b.time$
14: **procedure detect-veh-exit()**
15:       **while** detect_veh_kill_flag = False **do**
16:          $n \leftarrow time.now()$
17:          **for each** $veh\_rec \in parked\_records$ **do**
18:             $r \leftarrow parked\_records[b.veh\_id].last\_seen$
19:             **if** $(n - r) > beacon\_measure\_intvl$ **then**
20:                notify mgr new vehicle exited ($b.veh\_id$)
21:          sleep (beacon_measure_intvl)

Algorithm 3. Hybrid BLE/Camera Vehicle Identification Procedures [32].

 1: **procedure initialize**
 2:    Initialize datastructure d
 3:    Start thread to record BLE beacons
 4:    Start thread to record events from camera
 5:    $bt \leftarrow rssi\_threshold$ (set to -70 dBm)
 6:    $td \leftarrow event\_time\_delay$ (set to 5 seconds)
 7:    **if** is nighttime **then**
 8:       Exit, as camera does not function at night
 9:    Start thread to loop through calls to $attest\_veh\_thread(d)$
10: **procedure attest-veh-thread**(datastructure d)
11:    **if** d has new event e **then**
12:       **if** e is a new Beacon event b **then**
13:          Find matching Camera event c
14:       **if** e is a new Camera event c **then**
15:          Find matching Beacon event b
16:       **if** both c and b exist **then**
17:          Send attestation alert (c,b) to central node

Ingress and Egress Tracking. We leverage our localization solution to provide a means to track vehicles traveling into and out of the lot. When our nodes view a beacon that has not been observed in some time, we can assume this is a newly parked vehicle. Similarly, for beacons that are not seen for some time, we can assume the vehicle has left the lot. This forms a basic Bluetooth-only vehicle detection system, which we outline in Algorithm 2. The algorithm performs some setup in lines 8–12, including the data structures it will need to store beacon data. Two threads are launched (line 7–8) that loop through calls to procedures (line 8 and 13) that observe these data structures for changes (lines 9 and 18) in beacon timestamps, making notifications (lines 11 and 19) of vehicle detection when a threshold (initialized in line 6) has been exceeded.

Camera-Based Vehicle Detection and BLE Beacon Attestation. We also compared efficacy of our vehicle detection system to a low power, low cost object recognition camera by locating both at the lot entrance. We used a Jevois-A33 Smart Camera [17] connected via USB to one of our sensor nodes, and configured the camera to use one of it's pre-programmed recognition algorithms (Jevois Darknet YOLO module [16]) to determine if an object was a "car" or some other object. The sensor node was also equipped with our Bluetooth receiver and provided identical functionality to other sensor nodes. In addition to each solution being an independent way of detecting vehicles, we can combine them together so that the camera performs a level of attestation of the beacon it sees, to ensure that it indeed belongs to a vehicle. When a vehicle approaches the entrance to the lot, its beacons are detected by our sensor node. When the vehicle passes in front of the camera, the object recognition function is engaged and determines a "car" has passed in front of the camera. We use timestamps of these events to match them, and make an attestation. We provide an overview of this combined detection and attestation functionality in Algorithm 3. Here we start recording BLE beacon and camera detection events in lines 3–4. Thresholds that we experimentally determined are set in lines 5–6. A third thread is launched in line 9 that continuously runs an attestation procedure that matches new beacon events with new camera events based on timestamps, submits an alert back to the central node in line 17. We conducted feasibility experiments for our implementation of this algorithm in Sect. 3.3.

3   Experiments and Results

Our sensor nodes are constructed with Raspberry Pi 3s and after-market Bluetooth USB adapters [35]. All of our code is written in Python, using pybluez [18] libraries and the Bluez Linux Bluetooth stack [14]. We run a stripped down version of Ubuntu Mate on the Pi, however any Linux operating system compiled for the Pi 3 should perform well. We used Weka [12] and scikit-learn [4] to provide our machine learning libraries.

Table 1. *Offline* lot spaces [32].

Name	Source	Spaces	Rate
Tripod	Tripod	1-84, 89-90 89-90	Constant
350_o	350Z	set 2	Constant
370_o	370Z	1-90	Constant
TL_o	Acura	set 3	Constant

Table 2. *Over Mesh* lot spaces [32].

Name	Source	Spaces	Rate
350_m1	350Z	set 4	Constant
350_m2	350Z	set 1	Constant
350_m3	350Z	set 1	60s sample
370_m	370Z	set 1	60s sample
Rogue_m	Rogue	set 1	60s sample

During the course of our radio map creation and operational experiments, we assembled several training and testing datasets. Initially, we deployed our beacons to tripods in an attempt to create a radio map that was not biased toward a particular vehicle orientation, however we determined through testing of the effects of vehicle attenuation on the beacon's signal that training data produced from a beacon inside a vehicle produced a better model (see Sect. 3.1). As a result, we re-fingerprinted the lot after mounting a beacon behind the rear view mirror of a vehicle, and created several testing sets to explore accuracy when the model is applied to different vehicle shapes and when data is collected in an *offline* mode and over the live mesh network. We summarize each of these datasets in Tables 1 and 2 (sample rates explained in Sect. 3.2). In these tables, *set 1* spaces include 8, 20, 25, 27, 34, 36, 44, 53, 58, 64, 75, and 83. *set 2* spaces includes 25, 27, 29, 34, 36, 38, 39, 56, 58, 60, 62, 64, 67, 70, 71, 75–77, 79–81, and 87–89. *set 3* includes 1–2, 4, 6, 10–13, 18, 20, 24, 31–33, 35, 37, 39–45, 49–50, 53–55, 64, 66, 68, 72, 75, 77–78, 80, 82, and 90. *set 4* spaces includes 25, 27, 29, 34, 36, 56, 58, 60, 71, 72, and 75–76. Earlier work used the entire target parking lot [31], however at the time we conducted our new experiments, there were unmovable objects located in what is shown in Fig. 3 that prevented us from parking in those spaces. As a result, we kept the zone in the figure to prevent the need to renumber spaces, but have removed mention of it in our analysis.

3.1 Improved Prediction Model

We outline improvements to our Random Forest classifier for occupancy prediction in this section. We realized experimentally, that only maximum RSSI values produced consistent results. As a consequence, our first improvement was a reduction in feature-set size from 38 in prior work to 10 features per space, per time interval. In Table 3 we show a summary of results using this new feature-set trained against our tripod model (with both $n = 100$, and $n = 1500$ trees in forest), tested with TL_o, 350_o, and 370_o *in-vehicle* data sets. Training results, 10-fold cross-validated (CV) occupy the first row, while test data occupies the remaining rows.

While our training accuracy was 100% in the optimized tripod model, our success at predicting other vehicle occupancy on a per-space basis ranged 8.94% and 14.05% with the smaller model ($n = 100$) and decreased with the optimized

Table 3. Init. per-space tripod model.

Dataset	n = 100		n = 1500	
	TP	R	TP	R
Training	99.88%	1	100.0%	1
TL_o	11.23%	0.80	10.44%	0.87
350_o	8.94%	0.79	8.18%	0.83
370_o	14.05%	0.74	10.91%	0.82

Table 4. Init. zoned tripod model.

Dataset	n = 100		n = 1500	
	TP	R	TP	R
Training	99.68%	1	99.68%	1
TL_o	42.46%	0.83	38.95%	0.82
350_o	16.06%	0.71	18.48%	0.77
370_o	43.33%	0.81	43.93%	0.82

model to between 8.18% and 10.91%. Even after introducing additional sensors, we were forced to abandon the tripod model and adapt a zone-based approach (outlined in the next subsection) to obtain a viable solution.

Zone Based Occupancy Detection. To explore the effects of a move from per-space to zoned prediction prior to investing in re-fingerprinting the lot, we used the same tripod training data and divided the lot into zones as described in Sect. 2.1. We retrained our model using 6 classes instead of 90, (i.e. 6 zones assembled from all 90 spaces). Our *zoned* training and testing result is shown in Table 4. This was a significant improvement, however well below an acceptable level of accuracy. As a result, we replaced our tripod training set with one constructed from beacons located within a vehicle. We discuss this approach in the next subsection.

In-vehicle Effects on Beacon Attenuation. Upon taking a closer look at the individual measurements of our tripod model and comparing them to data collected from in-vehicle beacons, we saw that the location and orientation of the beacon has a significant impact on it's viability at producing our radio map. When mounted on a tripod, the beacon avoids any attenuation produced by the vehicle's chassis, seats, etc. In past work [31] we attempted to compensate for this by uniformly increasing the RSSI values for beacons, however additional analysis concluded that the attenuation is not consistent in every direction. For example, the rear-view mirror in our vehicles produced a 6 dBm RSSI decrease when measured from the same distance as a 1 dBm RSSI decrease due to a vehicle's front windshield. The errors created by this inconsistency were the limited factor in our model, as artificial compensations produced more problems than they solved. As the line-of-sight between the beacon and each node differs with each space the vehicle is parked in, we had to rebuild our radio map. We discuss our replacement map in the next subsection.

In-vehicle Fingerprinting. We re-fingerprinted the lot using the 370Z due to convenient availability of the vehicle. We then retrained our model and repeated the per-space and zoned tests that we performed for the tripod models. Results

Table 5. Per-space in-vehicle model.

Dataset	n = 100		n = 1500	
	TP	R	TP	R
Training	99.63%	1	99.56%	1
TL_o	42.11%	0.92	40.79%	0.95
350_o	12.78%	0.85	13.19%	0.89

Table 6. Zoned in-vehicle model.

Dataset	n = 100		n = 1500	
	TP	R	TP	R
Training	99.78%	1	99.67%	1
TL_o	89.65%	0.99	89.39%	0.99
350_o	85.28%	1.0	79.86%	1

are shown in Tables 5 and 6. Our trained model evaluated to accuracy above 99% for both per-space and zoned, however the zoned model produce a far superior result in for the smaller (n = 100) model of between 85.28% and 89.65% in our test vehicles. Additionally, the ROC areas increased for this zoned model to 99% and 100%. These tests were performed with data collection in *offline* mode, as they were collected and recovered from the node's directly. We explore the use of collecting data over our active mesh network in the next subsection.

3.2 Over-Mesh Experiments

Our first mesh design used a managed flooding algorithm with no route construction, which created a significantly dense and chatty network. In particular, node 1 (see Fig. 3) became an overloaded single point of failure as all mesh traffic was sent through it. As a result, we found that our Bluetooth radios spent a large amount of time communicating data instead of observing beacons. To remedy this, we deployed an additional sensor node (node 8) to allow for a redundant path, along with a simple route creation technique outlined earlier in Sect. 2.2 and sampling techniques outlined in Sect. 3.2. We discuss the experiments that lead to this change in the following subsections.

Effects of Over-Mesh Data Collection. With our mesh network active and collecting node data at the central *sink* node, we repeated our testing experiments using the 370Z, 350Z, and Acura TL test vehicles. Results are found in Table 7, computed against our zoned model (and per-space model for comparison). We continued to see a large amount of message queuing due to the volume of messages produced by a single beacon, as several beacons broadcasts can be observed by each node, for each time slice. This also produced a delay in assembling all of the required node data to make a prediction at the *sink* node. Results were close to the *offline* results in the last subsection, however there was a notable decrease in accuracy which due to this overload of messages. In some cases, no beacons were observed from nodes that produced data when in *offline* mode.

Effects of Down-Sampling. To improve accuracy and consistency we were forced to determine a means to reduce overall messages transmitted throughout

Table 7. Initial over-mesh results.

Model (Dataset)	TP	R
Zoned (350_m1)	46.33%	0.82
Zoned (350_m2)	61.94%	0.85
Per-Space (350_m1)	1.98%	0.60
Per-Space (350_m2)	9.72%	0.82

Table 8. Prediction using *Single Max*.

Model (Dataset)	TP	R
Zoned (350_m1)	66.67%	0.68
Zoned (350_m2)	75%	0.75
Per-Space (350_m1)	8.33%	0.85
Per-Space (350_m2)	8.33%	0.91

the network. To explore this, we first conducted an experiment where we reduced our mesh-collected test datasets to a single maximum RSSI measurement for each 5 min observation widow. This would be the most extreme reduction of message traffic that would remain within our experimental parameters. Results for prediction using these values is shown in Table 8, which showed an improvement in prediction allowing us confidence in investing in creating a data-sampling scheme at the nodes, and re-collecting new sampled test data.

To further explore sampling prior to making code changes, we took our training set and produced downsampled training sets to determine if an accurate model could still be constructed from a sample per 30 s, 60 s, 120 s, and 300 s (maximum). We show these results in Table 9. We see diminishing returns after a 60 s sample rate, so we coded that into our meshnet and use it moving forward.

Table 9. Down-sampled per-space results [32].

Sample rate	TP	R	Sample rate	TP	R
30 s	99.78%	1	60 s	99.78%	1
120 s	98.33%	1	300 s	97.78%	1

Finalize Design: Sampled and Routed Mesh Results. Before we created our downsampling scheme we attempted to mitigate message overloads with artificial delays so that messages could queue up in nodes and *burst* across to other nodes when connections were made. Our experiments showed, however, that this did not solve the problem. Once we implemented our downsampling and routed configurations, we repeated this measurement for comparison in Fig. 6. We see the routed mesh results are consistently and significantly below the message delays of the initial flooded mesh configuration, and the total messages seen during our experiments were several orders of magnitude less in our new scheme. During this experiment, we set a minimum delay for messages to 100 s to reduce risk of compounding messages and allow for fewer connection establishments when message counts are slow, however in later iterations this delay was removed to speed up availability of occupancy prediction results at the *sink* node.

We then repeated our testing with the 370Z, and added the Nissan Rogue to add diversity in vehicle size and orientation. We were unable to repeat the experiment with the 350Z, however we used downsampled results from the prior over-mesh experiments (350_m2) to form a new dataset for that vehicle (350_m3). These results are listed in the first three lines of Table 10. We also discovered during our experiments that there was a slight increase in accuracy when we used a per-space model, but performed post-processing on the prediction results to match the predicted space to it's corresponding zone. We refer to that in our results as *post zoned* results (lines 4–6 of Table 10). Lastly, we performed an additional post processing step where we determine the final prediction value of the vehicle to be the zone that occurred more than 50% of the time, referred to as *Majority*. We show results from this in the last three lines of the table.

Table 10. 60 s sampled mesh results [32].

Model (dataset)	Default	
	TP	R
370 Zoned(350_m3)	83.33%	0.90
370 Zoned(370_m)	77.08%	0.88
370 Zoned(Rogue_m)	77.08%	0.90
370 60 s Post Zoned (350_m3)	95.83%	–
370 60 s Post Zoned (370_m)	85.41%	–
370 60 s Post Zoned (Rogue_m)	75%	–
370 60 s Post Zoned Majority (350_m3)	100%	–
370 60 s Post Zoned Majority (370_m)	83.33%	–
370 60 s Post Zoned Majority (Rogue_m)	75%	–

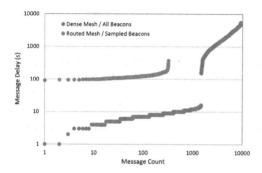

Fig. 6. Message delay comparison [32].

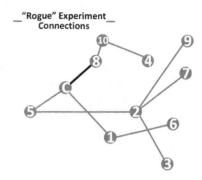

Fig. 7. Routed mesh connections.

3.3   Camera vs. BLE Based Vehicle Entrance/Exit Detection

We compared our BLE-only vehicle ingress/egress detection with outputs from an object recognition camera. To accomplish this, we mounted the camera onto one of our BLE nodes and aimed at the ingress/egress location in our target lot from a window in the near-by building (Fig. 8). We then drove a vehicle into and out of the lot 10 times and compared the outputs from both our node and the object recognition camera. When we analyzed the RSSI values from our node, we determined a consistent threshold for vehicle proximity was a value above −70 dBm. We then counted the number of beacons observed above this threshold. The object recognition camera labeled the vehicle as "car", and timestamps were recovered for each instance where this recognition was made. These outputs are shown in Table 11, along with a range of delays between then the BLE node detected the beacon and when the camera produced a detection output. We see that the camera had a delay of several seconds between the time a beacon was first observed and a recognition event was processed. This is due to the lack of a significant computational demand when detecting the presence of our BLE beacon.

Table 11. Daytime camera recognition vs BLE detection ($\leq$ 70 dBm.) [32]

Vehicle Direction	Observed Beacons	Recog. Objects	Detection Δt
Enter (10)	2–3	1–2 "car"	0–3 s
Exit (10)	1–4	1–3 "car"	2–11 s

Fig. 8. Camera/BLE node rig.

We performed this experiment during daylight hours, and repeated another 10 passes at night. Our solution functions regardless of light levels, while the camera failed to detect any object in darkness. Additionally, for each ingress pass at night, we parked the vehicle in a different parking space within the lot. For spaces that were far from the ingress beacon, there was a clear gap between entrance and exit (Fig. 9) signifying when the vehicle passed by the beacon on its way to a far parking space. For spaces that were near the beacon, there was a much less pronounced difference (Fig. 10), indicating that our BLE-only solution may perform poorly when vehicles park in spaces near the ingress point of the lot. We conclude that a preferred solution leverage all nodes in a lot to perform detection, rather than a single node near the lot's entrance. We will explore this in future work.

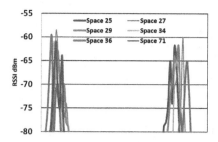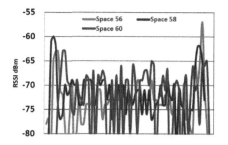

Fig. 9. Far space detection [32]. **Fig. 10.** Near space detection [32].

4 Prediction Model Ablation Study

For very large parking lots, fingerprinting each space may be a prohibitive burden. Furthermore, for zone-based detection, it may not be necessary. To explore the effect of removing sensor nodes (i.e. deploying a smaller sensor network) from the model and removing fingerprinting data (i.e. skipping parking spaces during fingerprinting) from the radio map has on prediction accuracy we conducted an ablation study. This technique exposes certain behaviors of our model for our target environment by removing data from our model piece-by-piece and studying the effects on prediction accuracy. Our goals with this exercise are to study effects and produce a minimum sensor network size (number of nodes) and smallest radio map (fewest spaces fingerprinted).

Each set of experiments begins with the default model from prior work [32], however we found that a small but consistent increase in accuracy was achieved by setting the algorithm to construct a model with random tie-breakers between attributes that are of equal value, and tuned our new model to enable this option.

Effects of Node Reduction. Recall from Sect. 2 that our prediction model is formed by combining maximum RSSI values from each node in the sensor network. For our 10 node deployment, the model is created from 10 values per instance (one for each node). We perform our node reduction experiments by computing attribute importance for each of these values, using the average impurity decrease method implemented in Weka, and remove the least important node. We chose this model as it is model dependent, and not specific to our observations about the physical layout of the sensor network.

Once a node is removed, we retrain our model with the remaining values and compare its accuracy. Each retraining cycle also computes attribute importance to produce a new least important feature, followed by removal of the next least important node, and so on until only a single node is left. This produces 10 accuracy measurements, one for the original model and 9 corresponding to each new model.

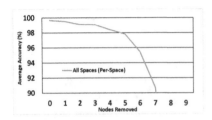

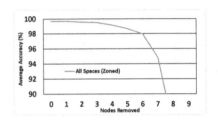

Fig. 11. Effects per-space fingerprinting. (Color figure online)

Fig. 12. Effects zoned fingerprinting. (Color figure online)

We performed this activity for both our per-space model and our zoned model, and show the output in blue in Figs. 11 and 12 (respectively). Here we see the original radio map, with node reduction as explained above, as a blue curve. For both per-space and zoned models, we were able to remove 7 nodes (of 10 total) before accuracy dropped below 90%. Additionally, our zoned model remained about 98% after 6 nodes removed, while the per-space model behaved similarly only up to 4 nodes removed. This makes intuitive sense, as our zoned model effectively masks some prediction errors found in the per-space model, when incorrectly classified nodes produce a prediction that remains in the correct zone. While encouraging, accuracy here is computed only across training data.

To obtain a minimal sensor network size with practical accuracy we must test the models produced with these reduced network size using test data used to validate our original models in Sect. 3.2 (i.e. differing vehicles, sampled and collected over mesh). We tested these reduced node models using the over-mesh 350 and Rogue datasets, and show results in Figs. 13 and 14. The left figure shows how our new model behaves with node reduction, showing consistent results even with removal of 2 to 4 sensor nodes. The right table shows the same result with the *majority* post processing we used in prior work, described in Sect. 3.2. This post processing had a marginal improvement in prediction accuracy, particularly for the *rogue* test set, however in three cases (2 in the *350* set, 1 on the *rogue* set) where this post-processing technique decreased accuracy. These three cases were limited to cases when 6 and 9 nodes were removed, where successful predictions were in the minority of other incorrect predictions.

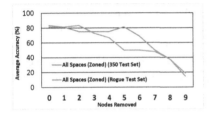

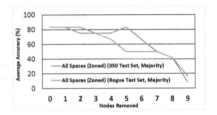

Fig. 13. Node reduction testing results.

Fig. 14. Effects zoned fingerprinting.

When we examine the training and testing results together, we can see that the zoned model maintains performance (e.g. no more than a 10% accuracy loss) when up to 3 nodes were removed. These nodes correspond to nodes 1, 5 and 9. When we examine the network formed by our improved mesh network in Fig. 7, we notice that nodes 1 and 5 are links in the mesh network, and cannot be removed without requiring the network to reform. While we did not perform a network formation experiment with this new arrangement, we know from past data that replacement links between node 4 and 7, and 2 and 6 could have been established instead. We depict this reduced network in Fig. 15.

Effects of Radio Map Reduction. This section includes our analysis of the effects of reducing our radio map size. To remain independent of *a priori* facts about the physical layout of the parking lot or how our nodes behave (after fingerprinting the entire lot), we select spaces to remove from the radio map by simply keeping every 2nd space, and every 4th space. This produces two new radio maps that are half, and one-fourth the size of the original map. Should a balance be achieved between accuracy and space fingerprinting investment, new (perhaps larger) lots can be fingerprinted with less effort.

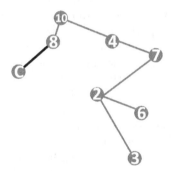

Fig. 15. New *node reduced* sensor network.

We trained two new prediction models, corresponding to each of our planned radio maps: full size (original), 1/2 size, and 1/4 size, and again used our *350* and *rogue* sampled datasets from Sect. 3.2. We show results in Table 12, where we see almost no significant influence on the training set's accuracy but a 20.8333% and 14.5833% decrease in accuracy for *350* and *rogue* testing sets (respectively) with the 1/2 radio map and a 16.6666% and 27.0833% decrease for the 1/4 radio map. Curiously, for the *350* test set, the accuracy counter-intuitively increased with a smaller radio map. We will explore this occurrence in future work. Additionally in the table, we show the outcomes from the "majority" post-processing technique we used in Sect. 3.2 when combining multiple prediction instances. In these cases, accuracy remained the same or was decreased due to rounding error in cases where correct and incorrect predictions totaled the same number (a case we consider a majority "incorrect").

Table 12. Effects of radio map reduction on full-lot accuracy.

Dataset	Full size			1/2 size			1/4 size		
	Acc.	Major.	R	Acc.	Major.	R	Acc.	Major.	R
Training	99.7037	100	1	99.7037	100	1	99.7101	100	1
350_m3	83.3333	83.3333	0.896	62.5	58.3333	0.878	66.6667	66.6667	0.850
Rogue_m	81.25	83.3333	0.899	66.6667	66.6667	0.896	54.1667	50	0.904

Outcomes from these experiments show that decreasing the radio map has a potentially prohibitive effect on prediction accuracy. In these cases, we would need to either combine zones together to further reduce error, or determine a way to perform interpolation on the missing spaces. We believe the latter is a feasibly approach and will explore this in future work.

Balancing Sensor Network and Radio Map Size. When combining a reduced radio map with a reduced sensor network, we are faced with a planning challenge. In the last two subsections, we explored effects of each, however when combining the two techniques together we must be careful not to compound losses in accuracy. We combined our node reduced models together with a reduced radio map, and repeated our training and testing exercises. We show the results in Figs. 16 for training data and Fig. 17 for testing data. Our "majority" post processing technique did not increase accuracy significantly, so we will favor clarity and avoid including those results in this discussion. Additionally our testing data was matched with a zoned model only, as per-space prediction was not possible for a reduced map size (i.e. many of the spaces that correspond to the true location were removed from the map to support the experiment).

Our training data, as expected (per prior discussion), produced a model that evaluated to accuracy above 98% regardless of radio map size up to and including removal of 6 (of 10 total) sensor nodes. Also as expected, the zoned model out performed the per-space model, however accuracy was maintained above 99% up to and including 3 removed nodes. When this process was repeated for testing data in Fig. 17 we see a less pronounced decrease in accuracy across the range of 7 removed nodes. In this case, however, we do see a rank ordering of accuracy with respect to changes in radio map size that favored a larger map. The less fingerprinted spaces, the higher the potential that any test measurement may predict out to the wrong zone. This was expected, however the interest

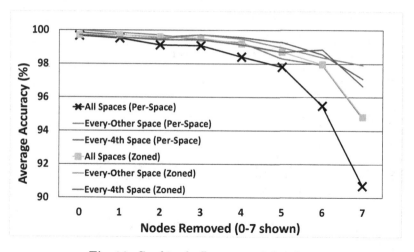

Fig. 16. Combined effects on training data.

here concerns the notion of acceptable losses in accuracy when compared to the deployment time savings of a reduced map and smaller sensor network. We see for both the 350Z and Rogue test sets, reducing the radio map size and a single node improved accuracy. In the case of the rogue dataset, this was maintained for 3 more removed nodes. We suspect that this was due to a specific coincidence where the spaces tested have some values that were creating mis-classification due to less than optimal data in one of the nodes. After examining the model, we noticed that Node 5 was the offending node in this case, and the incorrectly classified spaces were consistently in Zone 1, which happens to be the zone closest to Node 5. This is a bit counter-intuitive as our nodes should be less vulnerable to interference and other attenuation factors with shorter distances from beacon to observing node. In this case, however, a combination of factors are in play. For example, the Rogue is a larger vehicle, with a different internal orientation to the training vehicle, potentially appearing farther away from Node 5's perspective. This part of the lot has fewer observing nodes as well, increasing the effect of Node 5's errors. We seek to explore this topic in future work, and remedy the mis-classification effects from scenarios such as this.

From the data we have assembled, we observe that decreasing radio map size has a significant impact on detection accuracy, while reducing some nodes using the methods we employed can be done with less significant impacts. The *node reduced* sensor network depicted previously in Fig. 15 will still be viable, but at this time must be combined with a full size radio map if accuracy is to be maintained. We will continue to explore this area to improve both our prediction methods, and our node and map downsizing techniques.

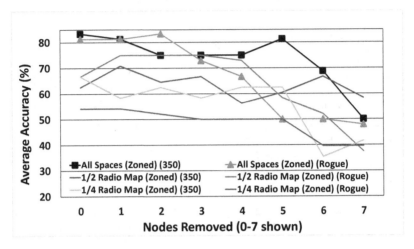

Fig. 17. Combined effects on testing data.

5 Related Work

5.1 Parking Management

Most paid parking lots (and even some free lots) have some degree of parking management deployed, either to collect information on space occupancy or support billing or payment transactions. These often come in the form of a human attendant that handles all aspects of driver and vehicle interaction, or an attendant-less lot with automated ingress and egress ticketing systems.

Crowd-Sourced Space Availability. Many commercially managed lots and street parking owners employ so-called *crowd-sourced* occupancy detection capabilities (ParkMobile [24]) where users of the system indicate when and where they have parked through a smartphone app or near-by electronic kiosk so that fees can be transacted electronically. Similar systems [28,29] often include a means to reserve spaces in advance of parking and often forgo the use of ingress and egress ticketing to speed up this interaction.

There are two main problems, however, with these approaches. First, they rely entirely on the accuracy and trustworthiness of the vehicle operator to correctly indicate where they have parked. Second, they place the entire coordination burden on the end user, substituting the time it takes to get into and out of the lot with time the user must spend indicating where they have parked. Our solution replaces all of these parking system characteristics by removing the ticketing stations entirely, as well as any requirement for the vehicle driver to interact with our system when parking. This represents the optimal *seamless* parking experience.

5.2 Indoor and Outdoor Localization

Outdoor localization is thought to be a solved problem with the deployment of GPS, however fine grained precision of static locations with low cost and low-power hardware continues to face challenges. Contemporary estimates of smartphone GPS accuracy under ideal weather and line-of-sight conditions, for example, is estimated to be just under 5 m [26]. Some research [13] has been performed combining GPS data with historic *crowd-sourced* space occupancy information to provide localization and predict space availability. Systems like these may have a large data storage burden when forced to maintain large amounts of past parking data. There is a larger concern, however, with systems that rely on parked-vehicle provided GPS data: The parking management system is trusting localization data provided to it by the entity that parks. This empowers user-exploitation, particularly when large fees are involved. Parking management systems must perform localization (or verification) from an infrastructure-controlled system, where sensing local to the parking space performs confirmation of vehicle location. Our system does precisely this, however there is a small possibility that the in-vehicle beacons could be manipulated in a way such that malicious activity could focus on directing a signal in such a way at our sensor nodes, that the prediction model would fail or produce incorrect results. We believe, however, that this would be very time-consuming for an adversary and is not something we feel is necessary to defend against at this time.

Indoor localization systems were created to provide location services indoors, where GPS cannot reach. Some solutions on vehicle dead reckoning such as work by Gao et al. that leverages inertial sensors within an in-vehicle smartphone to detect vehicle movement [10]. Liniger [22] combines GPS data with BLE beacons and a vehicle's state obtained from its On-Board Diagnostic (OBD-2) connection to determine is a vehicle is parked or moving. Others use physical detection of occupancy through use of infrared sensors aimed at spaces [38]. Many wireless localization solutions, in contrast, use signal strength measures (often RSSI measures) to perform position prediction using a variety of radio technologies (which can also be used in outdoor environments). For example, Oguejioforo et al. [27] uses RSSI measurements of IEEE 802.15.4 (low-rate wireless Personal Area Networks) radios combined with linear distance estimates, while Fabian [7] provides localization in their parking management solution that uses trilateration. Two problems exist with use of euclidean distance measurements. First, to make use of the estimates, the geography of the environment they are used in must be measured so that some indicated distance from a receiver can be interpreted as a particular location. Second, single sensor measurements are often error prone, and combining several distances to form an accurate single determination of location would compound these errors. An alternative technique is to employ the use of radio maps where sensing remains static but measurements (so called "fingerprints") at predetermined locations are taken and combined together. This modeling can be done and data can be manipulated in many different ways. For example, Faragher and Harle perform develop several localization techniques that compare the use of BLE and WiFi radios [8]. Silver [33] combines various measurement value filtering techniques and compares accuracy of *disc trilateration* and k-nearest neighbor fingerprinting techniques. Daniay et al. [5] leverages RSSI fingerprinting of moving BLE beacons to feed k-nearest neighbor and Neural Network algorithms. Additional works are surveyed in [23].

5.3   Bluetooth and Mesh Networking

Our initial mesh deployment mimicked the Bluetooth SIG BLE mesh specification [3] and other Bluetooth controlled flooding algorithms [19], however such a design quickly became unusable for our purposes as we needed to minimize our use of BLE advertising channels as they were the foundation of our localization solution. This drove us to use Bluetooth *classic* (EDR) in an attempt to minimize the impact on these channels.

Mesh networks are too large of a topic for this section, however we can group mesh network research into two main groups, those that use message flooding [1,15,30] and those that establish fixed or dynamic routes [11,21,25,34]. In contrast, flooding approaches are generally easier to implement and are often broadcast based but produce a lot of duplicate messages while routed approaches are (sometimes) more complicated to implement and often produce some degree of network overhead due to the exchange of routing information between network nodes. Our solution avoids some of this message overhead by producing routes prior to the use of the network, based on a boot-time RSSI measurement of nearby nodes. This prevents the need for network overhead, and remains viable since our sensor network never moves (e.g. the RSSI measurements are network construction will remain the same). Additional routed mesh protocols can be found in [37], and'Bluetooth-specific mesh protocols surveyed in [6,36].

5.4   Random Forest Classifiers

Machine learning techniques are used to find patterns and solve real world problems from malware detection [9] to detecting oils spills in satellite imagery [20]. Any well understood problem that requires a solution involving the determination of patterns within data that are not clearly accessible by manual examination are prime candidates for machine learning algorithms. Random forest classifiers are a type of machine learning algorithm referred to as *ensemble* techniques as they combine multiple models together to form more accurate detection (many other examples of use are surveyed in [2]). Classifiers of this type are easy to interpret and tune, which was out primary driver in considering their use (outside of experimental validation conducted in past work [31].

6   Conclusions

In this work we present an evolution of out Bluetooth based outdoor smart-parking localization solution. We perform a series of validation experiments to produce a prediction model that balances efficacy with simplicity of deployment. With *zone-based* smart parking solutions like ours, outdoor lot owners can leverage new technologies to make parking management more efficient without requiring significant investments in technology.

Acknowledgement. © 2019 The MITRE Corporation. ALL RIGHTS RESERVED. The author's affiliation (pseymer@mitre.org) with The MITRE Corporation is provided for identification purposes only, and is not intended to convey or imply MITRE's concurrence with, or support for, the positions, opinions, or viewpoints expressed by the author. Approved for Public Release 19-2570. Distribution Unlimited.

References

1. Baert, M., Rossey, J., Shahid, A., Hoebeke, J.: The bluetooth mesh standard: an overview and experimental evaluation. Sensors **18**(8), 2409 (2018)
2. Belgiu, M., Dragut, L.: Random forest in remote sensing: a review of applications and future directions. ISPRS J. Photogram. Remote Sens. **114**, 24–31 (2016)
3. Bluetooth SIG Mesh Working Group: Bluetooth mesh profile specification, July 2017
4. Buitinck, L., et al.: API design for machine learning software: experiences from the scikit-learn project. In: ECML PKDD Workshop: Languages for Data Mining and Machine Learning, pp. 108–122 (2013)
5. Daniay, F.S., Cemgil, A.T.: Model-based localization and tracking using bluetooth low-energy beacons. Sensors **17**(11), 2484 (2017)
6. Darroudi, S.M., Gomez, C.: Bluetooth low energy mesh networks: a survey. Sensors **17**(7), 1467 (2017)
7. Fabian, H.: A public parking management system for Zurich. Master's thesis, University of Zurich (2015)
8. Faragher, R., Harle, R.: An analysis of the accuracy of bluetooth low energy for indoor positioning applications. In: Proceedings of the 27th International Technical Meeting of The Satellite Division of the Institute of Navigation (ION GNSS+ 2014), Tampa, Florida, pp. 201–210, September 2014
9. Firdausi, I., Erwin, A., Nugroho, A.S., et al.: Analysis of machine learning techniques used in behavior-based malware detection. In: 2010 Second International Conference on Advances in Computing, Control, and Telecommunication Technologies, pp. 201–203. IEEE (2010)
10. Gao, R., Zhao, M., Ye, T., Ye, F., Wang, Y., Luo, G.: Smartphone-based real time vehicle tracking in indoor parking structures. IEEE Trans. Mob. Comput. **16**(7), 2023–2036 (2017)
11. Guo, Z., Harris, I.G., Tsaur, L., Chen, X.: An on-demand scatternet formation and multi-hop routing protocol for ble-based wireless sensor networks. In: 2015 IEEE Wireless Communications and Networking Conference (WCNC), pp. 1590–1595, March 2015. https://doi.org/10.1109/WCNC.2015.7127705
12. Hall, M., Frank, E., Holmes, G., Pfahringer, B., Reutemann, P., Witten, I.H.: The WEKA data mining software: an update. SIGKDD Explor. **11**(1), 10–18 (2009)
13. Hobi, L.: The impact of real-time information sources on crowd-sourced parking availability prediction. Master's thesis, University of Zurich (2015)
14. Holtmann, M., Hedberg, J.: Bluez - official linux bluetooth protocol stack (2018). http://www.bluez.org/

15. Hortelano, D., Olivares, T., Ruiz, M.C., Garrido-Hidalgo, C., López, V.: From sensor networks to internet of things. Bluetooth low energy, a standard for this evolution. Sensors **17**(2), 372 (2017). https://doi.org/10.3390/s17020372. https://www.mdpi.com/1424-8220/17/2/372

16. Itti, L.: Darknet yolo jevois module (2018). http://jevois.org/moddoc/DarknetYOLO/modinfo.html

17. JeVois Inc: Jevois-a33 smart camera (2018). https://www.jevoisinc.com/pages/hardware

18. karulis: Pybluez - python extension module allowing access to system bluetooth resources (2018). https://github.com/pybluez

19. Kim, H., Lee, J., Jang, J.W.: Blemesh: a wireless mesh network protocol for bluetooth low energy devices. In: 2015 3rd International Conference on Future Internet of Things and Cloud, pp. 558–563, August 2015

20. Leifer, I., et al.: State of the art satellite and airborne marine oil spill remote sensing: application to the BP deepwater horizon oil spill. Remote Sens. Environ. **124**, 185–209 (2012)

21. León, J., Dueñas, A., Iano, Y., Makluf, C.A., Kemper, G.: A bluetooth low energy mesh network auto-configuring proactive source routing protocol. In: 2017 IEEE International Conference on Consumer Electronics (ICCE), pp. 348–349. IEEE (2017)

22. Liniger, S.: Parking prediction techniques in an IoT environment. Master's thesis, University of Zurich (2015)

23. Liu, H., Darabi, H., Banerjee, P., Liu, J.: Survey of wireless indoor positioning techniques and systems. IEEE Trans. Syst. Man Cybern. Part C (Appl. Rev.) **37**(6), 1067–1080 (2007)

24. LLC, P.: Parkmobile (2018). https://parkmobile.io/

25. Mikhaylov, K., Tervonen, J.: Multihop data transfer service for bluetooth low energy. In: 2013 13th International Conference on ITS Telecommunications (ITST), pp. 319–324. IEEE (2013)

26. National Coordination Office for Space-Based Positioning, Navigation, and Timing: GPS accuracy. https://www.gps.gov/systems/gps/performance/accuracy/

27. Oguejioforo, S., Okorogu, V., Abe, A., Osuesub, O.: Outdoor localization system using RSSI measurement of wireless sensor network. Int. J. Innov. Technol. Exploring Eng. **2**, 1–6 (2013)

28. Parking Panda. https://www.parkingpanda.com/

29. Passport Labs, INC.: Passportparking. https://www.passportinc.com/

30. Reddy, Y.K., et al.: A connection oriented mesh network for mobile devices using bluetooth low energy. In: Proceedings of the 13th ACM Conference on Embedded Networked Sensor Systems, pp. 453–454. ACM (2015)

31. Seymer, P., Wijesekera, D., Kan, C.D.: Secure outdoor smart parking using dual mode bluetooth mesh networks. In: Proceedings of the 89th IEEE Vehicular Technology Conference (VTC 2019-Spring), April 2019

32. Seymer, P., Wijesekera, D., Kan, C.D.: Smart parking zones using dual mode routed bluetooth fogged meshes. In: Proceedings of the 5th International Conference on Vehicle Technology and Intelligent Transport Systems, May 2019

33. Silver, O.: An indoor localization system based on BLE mesh network. Master's thesis, Linkoping University (2016)

34. Sirur, S., et al.: A mesh network for mobile devices using bluetooth low energy. In: 2015 IEEE SENSORS, pp. 1–4, November 2015. https://doi.org/10.1109/ICSENS.2015.7370451

35. StarTech: Mini usb bluetooth 4.0 adapter - 50m (165ft) class 1 edr wireless dongle (2018). https://www.startech.com/Networking-IO/Bluetooth-Telecom/USB-Bluetooth-4-Dongle~USBBT1EDR4

36. Todtenberg, N., Kraemer, R.: A survey on bluetooth multi-hop networks. Ad Hoc Netw. **93**, 101922 (2019)

37. Waharte, S., Boutaba, R., Iraqi, Y., Ishibashi, B.: Routing protocols in wireless mesh networks: challenges and design considerations. Multimedia Tools Appl. **29**(3), 285–303 (2006)

38. Yee, H.C., Rahayu, Y.: Monitoring parking space availability via zigbee technology. Int. J. Future Comput. Commun. **3**(6), 377 (2014)

Heterogeneous Infrastructure for Cooperative Driving of Automated and Non-automated Connected Vehicles

Rico Auerswald[1], Markus Dod[3], Lars Franke[5], Richard Fritzsche[1],
Mathias Haberjahn[5], Alexander Jungmann[2], Michael Klöppel-Gersdorf[1(✉)],
Josef F. Krems[4], Sven Lorenz[3], Isabel Kreißig[4], Franziska Schmalfuß[2],
and Sabine Springer[4]

[1] Fraunhofer IVI, Fraunhofer Institute for Transportation and Infrastructure Systems, Dresden, Germany
{rico.auerswald,richard.fritsche,
michael.kloeppel-gersdorf}@ivi.fraunhofer.de
[2] IAV GmbH, Chemnitz, Germany
{alexander.jungmann,franziska.schmalfuss}@iav.de
[3] Mugler AG, Oberlungwitz, Germany
{markus.dod,sven.lorenz}@mugler.de
[4] Cognitive and Engineering Psychology, Chemnitz University of Technology, Chemnitz, Germany
{josef.krems,isabel.kreissig,sabine.springer}@psychologie.tu-chemnitz.de
[5] Preh Car Connect GmbH, Dresden, Germany
{lars.franke,mathias.haberjahn}@preh.de

Abstract. Automated driving is an active topic of research, while first results have already found their way into productive use. Nonetheless, nearly all of today's vehicles are still non-automated. Most modern vehicles, however, are equipped with communication capabilities. Hence, combining these two developments and enabling sophisticated cooperative maneuvers is an important step in the development of Intelligent Transport System (ITS). In this work, we describe a heterogeneous architecture that enables connected vehicles to access ITS services both via a mobile communication system and via the road-side infrastructure. The introduced ITS is designed to realize cooperative maneuvers in mixed traffic scenarios using heterogeneous cloud infrastructure systems. This work shows the Automated Connected Vehicle (ACV) concept used and the human factors while driving an ACV as well as driving a Non-Automated Connected Vehicle (NACV) that interacts with an ACV. Furthermore, we show that the system works well in real traffic scenarios by presenting insights of demonstrations.

Keywords: Cooperative driving · Mixed traffic · Hybrid communication HMI design · Modular system · ITS-G5 · C-V2X · Cloud computing

Supported by project HarmonizeDD funded by the Federal Ministry of Transport and Digital Infrastructure under the grant 16AVF1024.

M. Helfert et al. (Eds.): SMARTGREENS 2019/VEHITS 2019, CCIS 1217, pp. 270–296, 2021.
https://doi.org/10.1007/978-3-030-68028-2_13

1 Introduction

Vehicle-to-Everything (V2X) communication is one of the main enabling technologies for employing Intelligent Transport System (ITS) in public traffic [18]. While an extensive information exchange has the potential to increase road safety, traffic efficiency, and comfort aspects for all road users, Automated Driving (AD) applications are of particular interest of recent ITS research and development activities. The goal of fully autonomous vehicles will be achieved in a gradual process, where in the beginning only a few vehicles will be able to drive autonomously. As a result, mixed traffic scenarios with both Automated Connected Vehicles (ACVs) and Non-Automated Connected Vehicles (NACVs) will be the prevailing situation on public roads for several years.

In this regard, V2X communication is seen as a key technology for a seamless integration of ACVs by supporting the interaction of both vehicle types. Human drivers of NACVs equipped with advanced Human-Machine-Interfaces (HMIs) benefit from communications with ACVs by better understanding its driving behavior, which can differ from that of a human driver in specific situations. Moreover, communication in mixed traffic is also supporting the ACV in terms of reacting on the human driver behavior more foresighted and enables considerate interactions [37]. Of particular interest is the introduction of cooperative maneuvers that help to clarify ambiguous situations, which can result in unnecessary congestion or even safety critical cases.

While cooperative maneuvers can be negotiated among vehicles themselves, the infrastructure has the ability to support road users by recommendations and information generated by cooperative ITS cloud services using comprehensive perception and additional information obtained from the traffic control system. The underlying communication technology employed for ITS services was subject to extensive discussions for the last years. These discussions are still ongoing. While the design process of ITS protocols is based on direct communication with 802.11 amendment p, cellular based communication technologies become more present within the ITS community [13]. Cellular-V2X is a direct communication technology, which has been designed as an alternative to 802.11p, with several innovative features. In addition, conventional cellular communications is also a candidate for exchanging ITS messages [7,16]. While each of the candidate technologies has its up- and downsides, an asserting technology is not yet foreseeable. As a result, current ITS deployments need to consider each of the candidates and deal with heterogeneity of the communication systems.

In this work, we introduce an ITS concept which supports heterogeneous communication and cloud infrastructure applicable in mixed traffic scenarios. We present novel message formats for maneuver coordination between vehicles as well as for maneuver recommendations from the infrastructure side. Based on the use case of a cooperative lane change, we give insights w.r.t. the ACV and NACV architecture and illustrate insights w.r.t. an actual demonstration in public traffic.

This is an extended version of a previously published article [2]. In contrast to the previous article, we now examine a more involved use case (i.e., cooperative lane change), which necessitates the introduction of new message formats, also described here. Furthermore, we have conducted several new field tests and report corresponding results.

The remainder of this article is structured as follows. First we present the system architecture in Sect. 2 followed by a description of the cooperative lane change use case in Sect. 3. We give more insights in Sect. 4, 5, and 6, by presenting the communications system, the infrastructure, and the vehicle side, respectively. We show an overview of a first live demonstration in Sect. 7, before we conclude the work in Sect. 8.

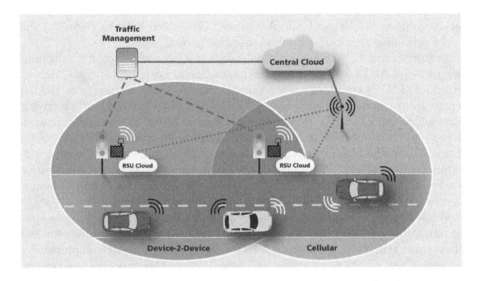

Fig. 1. Overall system architecture [2].

2 System Architecture

This work is based on an ITS system architecture with three main components: the vehicles, the infrastructure, and the communication system, as illustrated in Fig. 1. Each of the components is characterized by heterogeneity. The communication system is the key enabler to connect vehicles among each other as well as with the traffic infrastructure. Moreover, it is required to share information among infrastructure components. For V2X communication, there are multiple candidate technologies under discussion for the exchange of ITS messages. Two incompatible competing Device-to-Device (D2D) communication technologies (802.11p, Cellular V2X (C-V2X)) claim to access the free 5.9 GHz spectrum, reserved for ITS applications, while communication via the cellular network is another option, preferred by several stakeholders. In order to transmit messages in specific geographical areas, cellular communication is extended by a geographical messaging service, the so called GeoMessaging service. In the presented architecture, all three technologies are integrated and can be used exclusively as well as in parallel.

Closely coupled with the communication technologies are the infrastructure components. Applications are executed on the Road-Side Unit (RSU), which can exchange ITS messages with vehicles utilizing each of the three communication technologies. The RSU is characterized by its close connection to the traffic light system but also has the ability to access information from local infrastructure sensors. The local view at the road side can be extended by connecting multiple RSUs among each other (typically via the cellular network or beam radio) or by connecting it with a central cloud, which has access to a wider information base and is connected to the traffic management system, too. Since the central cloud is not located at the road side, it is connected to the RSUs but also to the vehicles via cellular communication in combination with GeoMessaging.

Heterogeneity is available on the vehicle side, too. Beyond the fact, that they are connected to a heterogeneous cloud system via multiple communication technologies, the vehicle types itself are distinguished between ACVs and NACVs. The interaction of those two vehicle types is subject of this article, focusing on the exemplary use case of a cooperative lane change (see Sect. 3). While vehicles could, in principle, support all communication options, we assume that vehicles are typically equipped with only a subset of the three mentioned communication technologies. Cellular communication is assumed to be integrated in each connected vehicle. This assumption is consistent with the assumption of current car manufacturers, and is supported by the fact, that the connection to the Pubic Key Infrastructure (PKI) is typically established via cellular.

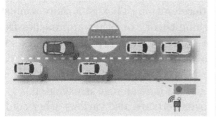 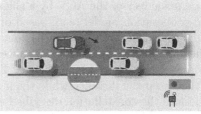

(a) RSU recommends lane change to blue vehicle via MRM.

(b) Blue vehicle communicates its intention to change lane and requests a larger gap.

Fig. 2. Example use case for cooperative driving: Cooperative lane change.

3 Application Scenario for Cooperative Driving

Existing ITS message formats can usually only be used to relay status information (e.g., Cooperative Awareness Message (CAM), Decentralized Environmental Notification Message (DENM)), with the exception of the Signal, Phase and Timing Extended Message (SPATEM), which may also contain speed recommendations. In order to enable cooperative driving maneuvers beyond purely status-based ones, we introduce two new message types: Maneuver Coordination Message (MCM) and Maneuver Recommendation Message (MRM) (see Sect. 4). The MCM is transmitted between vehicles in order to inform each other about planned and ongoing maneuvers, but can be also utilized to request maneuvers from other vehicles. The message is currently studied in ETSI ITS standardization, where several approaches are discussed. Based on the MCM, we additionally introduce the MRM, sent out from the infrastructure side in order to support vehicles in their driving decisions.

An exemplary driving scenario where MRM and MCM take effect would be an approach of multiple connected vehicles, one of them is also automated (ACV), on an urban road with two lanes to an intersection (cf. Fig. 2a). The junction is equipped with traffic lights and a RSU. Due to speed recommendations provided by the RSU, the group of vehicles will arrive at the junction right at the end of a red phase. It is assumed that the lane of the ACV is already occupied by several vehicles waiting for green. In order to distribute the traffic more evenly among the lanes, the RSU sends a MRM with a recommendation for a lane change directly to the ACV before the ACV reaches the waiting vehicles in front.

It is assumed that the ACV is willing to follow the received MRM but unable to execute the automated lane change maneuver directly due to a NACV right next to it occupying the required space on the targeted lane. Therefore, the ACV communicates its intention for a lane change not only by its turn indicators, but also via a MCM message initiating a cooperative lane change maneuver.

Within this constellation, the ACV requests the adjacent NACV to form a sufficiently sized gap for the sake of cooperation – either by accelerating or decelerating (cf. Fig. 2b). For the remainder of this work, we assume that the NACV is always willing to cooperate and forming a gap for the intended lane change maneuver of the ACV by a slight deceleration. That is, a more sophisticated cooperation model (e.g., based on game theory or other approaches from the multi-agent system domain) is out of scope of the work at hand. As soon as the gap plus required safety distances is large enough for the ACV, the ACV performs an automated lane change. The NACV is requested by the ACV via MCM to keep the distance while the automated lane change is executed.

Besides the constellation described above there are also various other configurations possible, e.g.:

1. The vehicle which intends to change the lane is a NACV. A human driver triggers MCM messages (e.g., with the indicators) and performs the lane change manually. The vehicle, which serves as the cooperation partner, is an ACV. It automatically reacts to the MCM received from the NACV by forming the gap.
2. Both cooperation partners are ACVs. The cooperative driving behavior is similar to triggers and actions of the ACV described in both scenarios above.

In the following sections, we show how the exemplary use case of a cooperative lane change initiated by driving recommendations from a RSU can be implemented in a practical system, incorporating among other heterogeneous communication technologies as well as a vehicle-centric Automated Driving System (ADS).

4   Communications

Within the ITS community a couple of standardization activities w.r.t. V2X communications are spread over several international committees (ETSI, IEEE, 3GPP or SAE), who agreed on a common understanding of the principle stack design, illustrated in Fig. 3. This article addresses access technologies and ITS facilities in this section and ITS applications within the next sections. While this work is based on standardized and pre-standardized ETSI ITS-G5 messages [12], we also look at a new message formats for cooperative driving. The MCM is exchanged among vehicles in order to coordinate or even negotiate maneuvers. The message introduced in this work is designed on a tactical level, including driving intentions and requests to cooperation partners. A respective study item is established in ETSI-ITS with several proposals of concepts for message formats and protocols. In addition to current standardization activities, a further message, the MRM is introduced, utilized by the traffic infrastructure to distribute recommendations based on a more comprehensive picture of the overall traffic situation.

While ITS facilities messages and protocols have been initially designed with the assumption of IEEE 802.11p as the underlying access technology, the protocol layer is intended to be reused for C-V2X as well as for cellular based message exchange. Note that for transport and network layer we assume Basic Transport Protocol (BTP) [11] plus geo-networking [10] for D2D, and TCP/IP with geo-based addressing for cellular communications. The next two subsections give more details about the ITS facilities messages and access layer technologies.

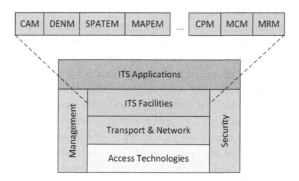

Fig. 3. ITS communication stack including the medium access technologies, network & transport protocols and the ITS facilities layer [2].

For more details on network and transport layer we refer to ETSI-ITS WG3 activities, e.g., [11].

4.1   ITS Facilities Messages

ITS applications implemented in today's available On-Board Units (OBUs), RSUs, or central cloud services are mainly focusing on day 1 and day 1.5 use cases [6]. Respective messages for implementing those applications are, e.g., CAM, DENM, SPATEM, and Map Extended Message (MAPEM). A prominent service in current ITS research and standardization is the collective perception service with its message Collective Perception Message (CPM), which allows a vehicle or the infrastructure to share its view of the surrounding via a dynamic object list, obtained from local sensor information. The intensive standardization process in ETSI ITS lasted for about two years and is still on going.

An additional application, subject of recent discussions, is the maneuver coordination service with its message format MCM. While some research and development activities focus on a trajectory based approach, this work presents a message design based on tactical information. An overview of the MCM format utilized in this work is given in Fig. 4. Besides header and time stamp information, which correspond to existing message formats, the key part is within the "mcmParameters" container. The message offers the possibility to communicate a certain strategy a vehicle is pursuing and to inform about its route or at least the next route points. However, in this work we focus on the maneuver containers for ego maneuvers as well as for requested maneuvers, where each of the two consists of a maneuver list. A maneuver itself is characterized by the attributes listed in Fig. 4. Besides several time and position descriptions, the maneuver type can be described by choosing one of the six options: turn, changeLane, accelerate, targetSpeed, distance, and pass. For each type more detailed information can be included.

The Maneuver data type is used for ego maneuvers as well as for requested maneuvers, where some of the maneuver attributes have a slightly different meaning depending on the type of container the maneuver is included. The basic concept is that with ego maneuvers a vehicle can communicate its current as well as its intended maneuvers. If a vehicle requires cooperation of another vehicle it can communicate this matter utilizing the requested maneuver container. An important feature of this proposal is the ability to reference maneuvers, e.g., via the cause field. An ego maneuver communicated by vehicle A can be caused by an ego maneuver of vehicle B or even by a maneuver request of vehicle B.

In this work, we do not go into more detail about the message format but explain the principle use based on an example of the cooperative lane change, described in Sect. 3. In this use case, the ACV broadcasts its intention of changing the lane to the left and can include parameters for describing time and space requirements. If the ACV observes other vehicles for which this information might be relevant, their station IDs can be explicitly noted in the field "stations". This is useful to give other vehicles the chance to adapt their future maneuvers accordingly. In the example use case, however, the NACV already blocks the lane change intention of the ACV. In this case, the ACV can explicitly emphasize that an action of the NACV is required. In principle, if a vehicle wants to respond to a request, it can include the id of the requested maneuver within the cause field of its ego maneuver, so that the intention to cooperate or not to cooperate can be signalized. However, an NACV might not be able to transmit such information, since the human driver would need to tell its vehicle.

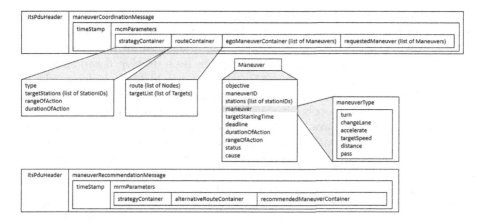

Fig. 4. Message format of the maneuver coordination message (MCM) as well as of the maneuver recommendation message (MRM).

In addition to the exchange of maneuver information among vehicles, also the infrastructure interact with road users by giving recommendations, described with the MRM. The message format is illustrated in Fig. 4 as well. It can be observed that its very similar to the MRM format. Beside recommendations about driving strategies and route adjustments, it can suggest certain maneuvers to particular road users or groups of road users. Referring to our example use case, the infrastructure can initiate the lane change via a recommendation to the ACV, e.g., because of a more distant blocking situation, which the vehicle itself is not aware of. When the ACV reacts on that recommendation and transmits a respective ego maneuver, it can refer to the former recommendation of the infrastructure. In addition, the NACV can also obtain a recommendation, e.g., to decelerate in order to cooperate with the ACV.

4.2   Access Technologies

In order to realize the cooperation among road users and also include support from the infrastructure, ITS messages need to be transmitted into particular geographical areas. Such area typically corresponds to the surrounding of the transmitter, where road users are located, which might be affected by the transmitting vehicle. Naturally, an intuitive approach is a direct communication technique offering a broadcast mechanism. Due to the competition between 802.11p and C-V2X and the following uncertainty regarding the applied technology, car manufacturers are reluctant to invest in V2X technologies. On the other hand, cellular communication technology is already integrated in one third of today's vehicles [33]. Although, the intended application has been accessing backend services, current discussions suggest to use cellular for exchanging ITS messages as well [1].

Direct Communication. Direct communication has already been motivated in the previous paragraph by the receiver location. Another argument for a direct communication technology is that there is no need for a network access required. Based on that motivation, 802.11p has been developed and standardized. which is an adaptation of 802.11a. It supports higher vehicle speeds, is based on broadcasting and works without any initialization procedures. Based on 802.11p higher layer protocols have been developed in standardization processes. While 802.11p has been available for several years, the alternative communication technology C-V2X was developed and integrated into the 3GPP standard. It allows for exchanging information directly among road users, similar to 802.11p, but is based on the cellular frame structure, utilizes the PC5 interface for D2D communication and introduces specific synchronization and congestion control mechanisms. Moreover, C-V2X offers a dedicated mode for network availability, with central resource allocation, which leads to an increase in spectral efficiency or reliability [14]. Due to incompatible congestion control mechanisms, a coexistence of both technologies in the same frequency band comes with several conflicts and would result in inefficient resource usage. Note that it is technically not possible to receive a message via C-V2X, which has been send via 802.11p and vice versa. Hence, if differently equipped vehicles are in the surrounding, transmitting ITS-messages via cellular in parallel might be a solution for reaching each of the relevant vehicles.

Cellular Communication. As already mentioned, a major motivation of using classical cellular communication, is the availability of modems integrated in today's vehicles. Moreover, it is assumed that for vehicles, which will be equipped with direct communication technology, cellular modems will be integrated in any case. Especially, with the introduction of 5G, lower latency and higher reliability might lead to higher attraction of using cellular for V2X communication. On the down side, network availability is constantly required for a reliable provisioning of V2X services. A main question of using cellular for broadcasting ITS messages is how to transmit them in the required areas. Therefore, the presented architecture utilizes a geo-based addressing mechanism, which is integrated into the cellular network as well as in the vehicle and RSU side. The mechanism is based on IP-multicast and can also be used to transmit ITS messages from the central cloud into specific areas.

Note, that the presented architecture has the ability to transmit ITS message with each of the two direct as well as via cellular communication technology.

This can be selective or in parallel and allows advanced hybrid communication algorithms, e.g., in order to increase reliability, range or reduce the load.

5   Infrastructure

Beside the communication among vehicles themselves, a key aspect are the ITS services provided by the infrastructure. In the presented system, we extend basic infrastructure-services (e.g., via SPATEM) by collective perception service via CPM as well as recommendations via MRM in order to support cooperative maneuvers and foresighted driving. Due to the heterogeneous communication technologies, a heterogeneous cloud infrastructure is established for providing services for both vehicles equipped with direct communication and those equipped with cellular communication. While direct communication based services can be provided by the RSU cloud, cellular users primarily refer to the central cloud. Note that RSU cloud usage is also possible for cellular users via geo-messaging. For the following discussions cellular means Long Term Evolution (LTE).

5.1   RSU Cloud

The RSU clouds use a modular and hybrid system concept. The central element is the hybrid communication unit, which is responsible for the message transfer between the ITS facilities and the communication interfaces. The RSU itself consists of various communication interfaces (like 802.11p, C-V2X, and LTE), the ITS facilities and the ITS applications. The hybrid communication unit separates the ITS facilities from the communication interfaces and the software stack of the RSU cloud. The hybrid communication control handles the distribution and reception of the messages. Therefore, it is possible to send one message simultaneously over more than one communication interface without involvement of the ITS facilities or the ITS applications. On the other hand, all the received messages will be forwarded to the facilities-layer, no matter from which interface they were received. With this concept it is possible to reach more road users over various communication technologies, or achieve a safer transmission by using redundant paths.

The current system concept of the RSU cloud contains various communication interfaces to enable different applications. The LTE interface realizes the connection to the backbone. Furthermore, this interface is used to distribute messages to all vehicles in a given region via GeoMessaging. The two interfaces 802.11p and C-V2X are used to directly communicate with the road user.

All the ITS applications run in Docker-Containers [29] so that they are separated from each other. This strengthens safety and security, facilitates an easy roll out of the software components, and makes them independent from the hardware. This concept enables different partners to run their own applications on the RSU cloud without causing interference to other applications (see [30] for an analysis from the resource management point of view). Each ITS application

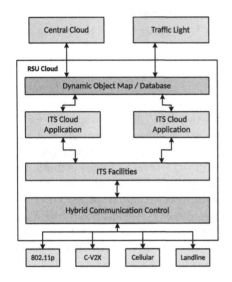

Fig. 5. System concept of RSU cloud [2].

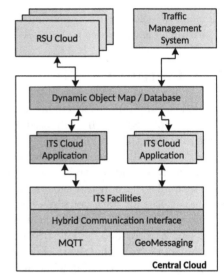

Fig. 6. Architecture of the central cloud [2].

has the possibility to subscribe for messages and information from the ITS-Facility-Layer and from the Dynamic Object Map (DOM) to realize its services. The RSU cloud hardware, namely a NVIDIA®Jetson™ TX2, is a powerful embedded computation unit, which also contains a GPU to support parallel computation and AI algorithms.

The system concept of the RSU cloud is shown in Fig. 5. Components that are also used in the central cloud are marked grey, while components that are unique to the RSU cloud are marked blue. Although both central and RSU cloud employ a Dynamic Object Map (DOM) and Hybrid Communication Controls/Interfaces, both components differ significantly in either RSU or central cloud. In the case of the communication control, the difference lies in the addressed interfaces (802.11p, C-V2X, etc. for the RSU cloud vs. MQTT/GeoMessaging in case of the central cloud), whereas for the DOM the difference is the contained information and structure (local view for the RSU cloud vs. a general overview in the central cloud). Due to the modular structure the concept is future-proof. Obsolete interfaces can be easily replaced by new state-of-the-art interfaces and additional interfaces can be added. It enables the simulcast operation for backward compatibility.

The software stack in the RSU cloud shares the concept of modularity already found in the hardware layout. It consists of a number of micro-services, which communicate using gRPC [15]. This approach offers flexibility for future extensions and allows to quickly exchange single components, e.g., for bug fixing or version updates. The core system is the DOM, which stores dynamic (e.g., vehicle positions, traffic light state) and static (e.g., maps) information. Data ingress happens through ITS messages (especially CAM, CPM, but also MCM) as well as backend systems (e.g., prognoses for traffic lights) and the TLS (current traffic light state). Before information is passed into the DOM, there is an additional processing step of data fusion and validation. This ensures that only valid entries are inserted. Furthermore, data fusion ensures that objects, which were detected by more than one method (e.g., via its own CAM and the CPM of another vehicle), are inserted only once. Data egress mainly concerns the generation of MAPEM and SPATEM and the communication with backend systems as described above. In addition, the information stored in the DOM can be used to generate maneuver recommendations, e.g., lane change recommendations as described in Sect. 3 or Green-Light Optimized Speed Advisory (GLOSA) [21]. These recommendations are transmitted using the appropriate message formats, e.g., MRM for the lane change and SPATEM for the GLOSA recommendation.

5.2   Central Cloud

In addition to the decentralized cloud environments provided by the individual RSUs, we also consider the usage of a centralized cloud-based solution, termed central cloud in the scope of this project. A high-level view of the architecture is provided in Fig. 6, where the components specific to the central cloud are highlighted in blue. As noted above, DOM and Hybrid Communcication interface differ significantly in contrast to their counterparts in the RSU cloud.

While, in principle, the services provided via the central cloud address the same ITS applications as the RSU, there are some key differences. The only communication channel between the connected vehicles and the cloud services is provided by a cellular data connection. In order to evaluate different communication schemes, two distinct means of transporting ITS messages via the cellular connection are supported. For the first scheme, the standardized communication protocol MQTT [19] is used to connect to a central message broker deployed as part of the central cloud in order to transport the ITS messages between the communicating parties. The messages are routed by the message broker according to a topic-based publish-subscribe pattern. Here, a careful choice of topics (e.g., geographical area) allows addressing only a subset of participants, which reserves bandwidth and provides certain information only where it is necessary (e.g., GLOSA is only relevant for vehicles approaching a certain intersection). Alternatively, a GeoMessaging solution, implemented by means of IPv6 multicast, which is deployed in the core of the cellular network, is used. This is done in order to allow for an efficient and scalable communication without a central message broker. The interface between the communication channels and the applications is provided by the ITS facilities layer, which allows for a complete decoupling of the mode of communication from the actual ITS applications.

The software architecture of the central cloud is similar to that of the RSU cloud, i.e., the individual services are implemented as micro-services and are coupled via a high-performance messaging bus and gRPC APIs [15]. Due to the centralized nature of the central cloud, the deployed ITS applications have a larger pool of information available, as information is ingested from a wider geographical area. Specifically, the central cloud services are connected to all equipped vehicles and RSUs in the target region. This allows the ingestion of real-time data provided by the RSUs, including the status of the traffic lights and sensor data, as well as additional information made available via the Traffic Management System (TMS) of the city of Dresden, VAMOS [22]. The TMS provides predictions for both the signal state and the length of queue for each signal at the relevant intersections. This information is pushed from the TMS to the respective service in the central cloud using the well-established DATEX II [8] interface. The information provided by the various sources is combined into a coherent dynamic object map and, after fusion with static information such as HD maps, provides the basis for the ITS applications. The messages generated by the cloud applications are processed by the ITS facilities and transmitted, either via cloud-based MQTT or GeoMessaging, to the connected vehicles. The messages generated by the vehicles take the reverse path and are forwarded to the appropriate cloud application, based on the type of the message and other factors such as the location of the originating vehicle.

5.3 Cooperative Lane Change

In the following, the generation of a MRM to request an ACV to change lane will be analyzed in detail, both from the side of a RSU cloud and the central cloud.

Starting with the RSU cloud, the example processing steps could be as follows:

1. RSU receives information from its sensors that an egress lane is blocked due to an emergency and stores this information in the Dynamic Object Map (DOM).
2. RSU receives the CAM of an ACV driving on an ingress lane leading to the blocked egress lane and stores this data in the DOM. Due to the hybrid communication control, the RSU does not (and does not need to) know from which communication channel the message originated.
3. Based on the data stored in the DOM, an ITS cloud application computes that it would be beneficial if the ACV changed lane before crossing the intersection. Acting on this computation, a MRM is generated, which addresses the ACV and recommends the lane change. Reasons for evaluating the lane change as beneficial could be safety aspects, i.e., avoiding a possible hard brake before the obstacle, or also environmental reasons, i.e., avoiding the emissions related to a hard brake and the following acceleration phase. Please note that this requires a good understanding of the current traffic situation, which could be gained by sensors at the intersections but also via CPM.
4. Finally, the message is generated and sent using all available channels.

The processing steps in the central cloud are quite similar, except for the first step. As the central cloud has no direct access to sensors at the infrastructure, it has to ingest this information either from one of the RSU clouds or from the Traffic Management System. Also note that the communication paths are different in steps 2 and 4, as the central cloud uses several LTE-based protocols but no direct V2X messaging.

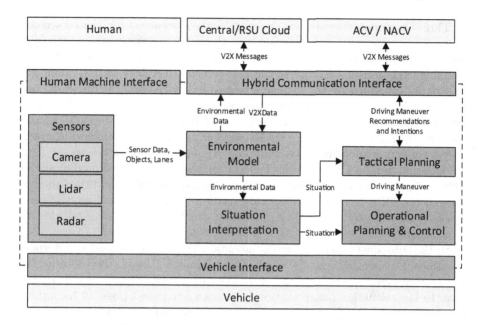

Fig. 7. Automated Driving System and its integration into the overall architecture [2].

6   Vehicles

Cooperative driving in real traffic cannot be accomplished by focusing on automated vehicles alone. In our work, we assume that all automated and non-
automated vehicles are connected and share information.

6.1   Automated Connected Vehicle

Each ACV implements an ADS that enables the vehicle to operate without
intervention of a human driver in a defined Operational Design Domain (ODD).
Briefly speaking, an ODD defines environmental and time-of-day conditions and
restrictions, respectively, the presence or absence of certain traffic, and roadway
characteristics. Furthermore, in order to facilitate cooperation during dynamic
driving tasks, each ADS is embedded into the overall architecture, as presented
in Sect. 2. That is, each ADS can rely on information from other ACVs as well as
NACVs while simultaneously providing information such as driving maneuver
intentions or sensor objects to both other traffic participants and infrastructure services. Figure 7 gives a broad overview of the implemented ADS and its
integration into the overall architecture.

Three components serve as major input for the system: vehicle-centric sensors (cameras, lidar sensors, and radar sensor), the hybrid communication interface, and the vehicle interface. Sensor data is used to create a local view of the surrounding environment - relative to the host vehicle. Host data such as odometry information provided by the vehicle interface is incorporated for properly validating and fusing data from different sensors and sensor types. Furthermore, the environmental model integrates external data such as static map data and dynamic environment data (e.g., CAMs and CPMs from other vehicles) from the hybrid communication interface. For properly associating relative sensor data and external data, a highly precise localization mechanism based on differential GPS is applied. Needless to say, that, depending on the ODD and the inherent flaws of the GPS technology, other localization approaches such as landmark based localization techniques (e.g., based on cameras or lidar sensors) have to be considered.

In the subsequent step, the environmental model's data is used to interpret situations. Put another way, the environmental model's data is used to generate a more comprehensive view of the overall situation beyond plain object or lane data. In fact, situation interpretation is necessary to detect possibly hazardous situations, to obey traffic regulations, or to optimize other metrics such as long-term fuel consumption. The output of the situation interpretation process can be considered as the environmental model's original data enriched by

- information that was originally hidden but derived by means of prediction or inference techniques, and
- a more abstract (e.g., symbolic) description of the situation in order to facilitate high-level planning and decision-making.

Depending on the current situation, a tactical planner is subsequently selecting and planning discrete driving maneuvers such as lane changes, speed adjustments, or even parking maneuvers. For cooperation, the tactical planner simultaneously takes MRMs from the infrastructure as well as MCMs from other traffic participants into account. Furthermore, the tactical planner uses the hybrid communication interface to inform adjacent vehicles about maneuver requests such as lane changes. An operational planner subsequently translates the current driving maneuvers into time-dependent trajectories, while taking the environmental model's data into account in order to avoid collisions. A control component finally subdivides the trajectory into multiple control sequences for the vehicle interface. More concretely, it computes throttle and brake commands as well as the steering angle for the car actuators.

Cooperative Lane Change. In the following, we assume that the vehicle that wants to change the lane is an ACV (denoted as V_1) while the vehicle that is blocking the adjacent lane is a NACV (denoted as V_2). Both vehicles are broadcasting CAMs. Vehicle V_1 is automatically following its current lane based on lane data perceived by its sensors and fused by its perception processes. Simultaneously, V_1 detects V_2 by means of its sensors. The CAMs broadcasted by V_2 is received by V_1 via the hybrid communication interface. Corresponding CAMs and sensor objects are associated in the environmental model. Based on the environment model's data, the situation interpretation component, in turn, distinguishes three basic situations:

1. V_1's adjacent lane is not blocked,
2. V_1's adjacent lane is blocked, but the blocking vehicle has no communication capabilities (i.e., the corresponding sensor object could not be associated with any CAM), and
3. V_1's adjacent lane is blocked and the blocking vehicle has communication capabilities (i.e., the corresponding sensor object was successfully associated with the corresponding CAM).

Depending on the derived situation, the tactical planner either

1. directly initiates the lane change maneuver and triggers the subsequent components such as the operational planner to perform the lane change, or
2. completely refuses the lane change maneuver, or
3. initiates and orchestrates the *cooperative* lane change maneuver.

In case the cooperative lane change is initiated, the tactical planner starts to broadcast MCMs. The recipient Id within the MCMs corresponds to the V2X station Id of the CAM, which was associated to the sensor object. Subsequently, the tactical planner observes whether V_2 is reacting to the broadcasted MCMs (i.e., whether V_2 is cooperating) by evaluating if the gap on the adjacent lane is increasing or not. For properly informing the driver of V_2 (cf. Sect. 6.2), the tactical planner is continuously broadcasting an MCM containing the current and desired size of the gap. As soon as the gap is big enough (i.e., the lane is not blocked anymore), the tactical planner triggers the operational planner to perform the lane change. As soon as the lane change maneuver was finished, vehicle V_1 continues to automatically follow the current lane.

6.2   Human Factors While Driving Connected Vehicles

The road-vehicle-user system changes when connected vehicles become a part of the traffic [23], because new opportunities of interaction and information exchange are enabled by the new connectivity. Connected traffic carries potential benefits such as reduced pollution, increased safety, and traffic flow, but they can only be achieved if the resulting new interaction possibilities are accepted and utilized by the car users. It has to be assured that ACV users still feel comfortable and trust the vehicle when the automated vehicle adapts its driving maneuvers to incoming ITS messages [9]. Assuming the cooperative lane change with an NACV as gap-building vehicle, the ACV driver might get confused or even take over control, because the own car wants to change lanes without any obvious reason.

Additionally, the NACV driver could be less cooperative if he/she does not know the reason for the other car's lane changing intention that seems not necessary at that moment. Therefore, it is important to investigate whether the ACV and the NACV user needs information and if so, which information these are in order to reach compliance and goals of connectivity regarding increased traffic flow. In the scenario of connected vehicles, drivers should react to incoming information and adapt their behaviors. In case of the cooperative lane change (see Fig. 2), the driver may get the information that he/she should open a gap for the oncoming ACV. First, the driver needs to perceive and understand the ITS message, and second, is expected to accept a request or just react according to the message (e.g., open gap for requested lane change of other vehicle). Otherwise, cooperation fails and expected benefits will not be achieved. In cooperation scenarios including ACV, implicit communication is probably reduced and so, one source of information for the NACV driver is missing. Thus, alternative communication channels are needed. Thinking of a modified scenario of the cooperative lane change in which the ACV opens a gap, the NACV driver might still need feedback that the ACV is aware of the NACV in order to feel safe to execute the lane change.

When traffic indeed becomes a mix of ACV and NACV, drivers of conventional cars interact with ACV and might become insecure, as experience with ACV will be limited. Especially in the early stages of the mixed traffic, the lack of trust in the other, new road user, the ACV, will pose a problem. According to Lee and See [24], trust in automation can increase when information of the system are available for the user, for instance, via a display. Information of planned behavior of the ACV sent via V2X and presented visually in the NACV carries the potential to increase trust in ACV. Designers of innovative technologies that enable connected, cooperative driving should take into account that driver's behavior is based on mental models that represent knowledge and learning experience with the system [36]. Thus, providing feedback via a Human-Machine-Interface (HMI) regarding the planned actions of the ACV to the NACV driver carries the potential to increase NACV knowledge about the ACV and its actions and supports building a better mental model of ACV. That is, HMI play an important role for the successful realization of cooperative maneuvers. Research regarding specific information needs for mixed, urban, connected traffic is limited. In reviewed literature, V2X information identified as relevant for the user focus on safety-relevant aspects such as accidents, road construction, or endangering weather conditions (e.g. [25]). Payre and Diels [28], for instance, investigated V2X signs to realize four safety related features, namely, the Emergency Electronic Brake Lights, Traffic Condition Warning, Emergency Vehicle Warning, and Road Works Warning. However, cooperation between automatically driven and conventional vehicles is rare. Identifying such needs was part of the project and one first important step in the development process of the HMIs.

Identifying Information Needs. As a first step, focus group discussions were conducted for capturing informational needs for NACV and ACV users in urban mixed traffic scenarios. A detailed description of the focus groups can be found in [32]. In total, five participants focused their discussions on the NACV perspective and various use cases [2, 32] built the basis for the discussion. Afterwards, participants rated the importance of each collected piece of information using a point system. As an overall result, potential NACV users expect support from the HMI regarding situation recognition as well as action recommendations. In detail, the situation recognition includes traffic signal status, information about the remaining time of the green and red phase, information about dynamic objects and their heading direction, traffic density, and location. Regarding maneuver recommendation, participants would appreciate to get advice regarding speed choice, lane choice, and navigation. For cooperation, the information exchange, maneuver agreement and commitment were requested. With the focus on the use case cooperative lane change, participants expressed the need for additional information about an approaching emergency vehicle as one possible reason for lane change recommendation (e.g., its position relative to the driven NACV). With regard to further information needs, selected information such as the duration of the green and red phase have been implemented and tested in former research [4], but design concepts of other discussed information needs are sparse.

Prototype Evaluation. Based on the results of a preliminary HMI-workshop with usability experts, a prototypical, dynamic and more realistic version of a Head-up Display (HUD) was developed and evaluated. The HUD system, which has been provided by *Noritel Mobile Kommunikation* within HarmonizeDD, is connected to the central processing unit of the NACV via LIN protocol. Similar to the NACV-App, which is further described in Sect. 7, a new HMI was developed to assist the driver within cooperative lane change maneuver (see Fig. 9).

Within a laboratory study, standardized videos of several simulated drives in an urban area were presented to $N = 23$ participants ($M_{age} = 25.6$ years; $SD_{age} = 4.8$) from a driver's perspective. For generating the videos, the driving simulator software STISIM Drive [34] was used. In addition to the simulated driving scenarios, the videos contained an animated, dynamic HUD in the downright position, which showed the cooperation process for cooperative lane changing maneuvers. The implemented lane change scenarios were manipulated as follows: they were (a) either successful (other car opened an acceptable gap, e.g., confirmed cooperation) or not (ego-car is forced to decelerate) and (b) were performed by either the ego-car or another car that changed towards the lane where the ego-car was located. Needs for a lane change were given by positioning obstacles on the road, gauge narrowing, or by an occurring emergency vehicle (EV) on active service.

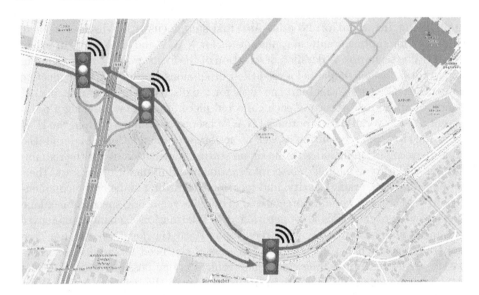

Fig. 8. Schematic setup for an exemplary driving test of connected and automated driving functions on a test corridor in the Digital Testbed Dresden (source: Open-StreetMap, [2]).

Fig. 9. HMI for cooperative lane change maneuver presented on a combiner HUD (i.e., a HUD, which uses a small plastic screen instead of the windshield to project the information) by Noritel.

Implementing a within subjects design, participants were instructed to use the think aloud method [26] while watching the videos, i.e., they should speak out loud how they interpret the presented situation and what they see in the HUD. Participants were asked to move the steering wheel and/or press the brake or gas pedal in case they would drive differently from the presented drive. During a post-interview, participants answered questions on, for instance, the comprehensibility of the HUD, potential of improvement and amount of information. At the end of the experiment, participants completed a standardized questionnaire on the experienced workload, acceptance of the HUD, its usability and user experience (UX). Assessing usability comprises the extent of effectiveness, efficiency, and satisfaction of a product (e.g., the HMI) to enable users achieving predefined goals (e.g., keeping the user in the loop). User experience, in turn, comprises not only usability but also every user expectation, perception, and reactions that he/she experiences before, while and after usage. The subjectively experienced workload was estimated on average range ($M = 49.9$, $SD = 14.3$, scale range: 0 to 100, [17]), which means that the participants' effort of fulfilling the task of watching the simulated drives, interpreting, and verbalizing the presented information in the HUD was acceptable. The HUD's usability ($M = 59.1$, $SD = 17.5$, scale range: 0 to 100, [5]) as well as its overall user experience were rated neutrally to slightly positively ($M = 0.6$, $SD = 0.6$, scale range: -3 to 3, [31]). These values can be interpreted as a marginal usability and user experience of the HUD. In turn, this means that the HMI bears some potential of improvement in order to support drivers during cooperative maneuvers appropriately. Besides, looking at participants' estimations on the van der Laan scale, the HUD's acceptance was rather poor ($M_{usefulness} = -0.57$, $SD_{usefulness} = 0.83$; $M_{satisfaction} = -0.28$, $SD_{satisfaction} = 0.83$, scale range: -2 to 2, [35]). The results reveal that the HMI neither satisfied the participants' needs nor was it rated useful, which implies a big potential of improvement, especially w.r.t. the purpose of introducing it onto the market.

Qualitative data derived from interviews provides further insight into these findings: Generally, it was found that informing drivers on upcoming events and giving them information on cooperation status is appreciated. Furthermore, most of the participants did not have any problems in understanding the illustrated cooperation in the HUD in general and almost all elements of the HUD were correctly understood. Nevertheless, interview data revealed some need for improvement of the HMI. For example, 7 out of 23 participants interpreted the request for a cooperative lane change as navigational hint. Moreover, participants hardly mentioned the little triangles on the bottom as a sign for lane usage during the think aloud part. Perhaps, this piece of information was dispensable. Besides, it was stated that the direction of the green thumb indicating the cooperation approval in general (not for one sole cooperation partner) was unclear. Moreover, some participants mentioned to be confused due to the redundant pieces of information given and therefore argued for reducing the amount of informational elements visualized in the HUD. In contrast to this opinion, other participants asked for further information that provides a reason for untypical system behaviors via text.

Results of the laboratory study showed that the development is on a good path in general. Making cooperative maneuvers possible by informing the human driver on cooperation status is realizable following the proposed approach. However, in the next developmental step, the amount of information presented in the HUD should be reduced as it caused confusion. Additionally, some symbols used to show different cooperative statuses should be designed more directionally (e.g., the green thumb). Furthermore, text could be added to help understand the maneuver recommendations.

7   Field Tests and Evaluations

Major parts of the outlined architecture and the interaction of its systems and components were initially demonstrated as part of a test event in November 2018 on the Digital Testbed Dresden. The test corridor in the north of the city of Dresden near the Dresden International Airport was utilized as test and demonstration course. The corridor is equipped with RSUs at five traffic light coordinated intersections, whereof three were part of the test course (Fig. 8). The road infrastructure itself is well developed, with two lanes per direction allowing cooperative driving maneuvers and minimizing possible interference with public road traffic. The equipped RSUs are connected to the respective traffic light control unit and to the central cloud. At the time of the test event, the RSUs supported V2X communication via 802.11p. An account of these initial demonstrations can be found in [2].

To date, further field tests were conducted as part of the enhancement of existing as well as the addition of new components to the outlined architecture. One substantial milestone was achieved in a test session in June 2019, in which the sequence of a cooperative lane change between an ACV, which intends to change lane, and a NACV, which is requested to form the required gap, was successfully tested. The core objective of the test session was to evaluate the interaction of the ACV and the NACV within a jointly operated maneuver, in particular to test:

- The initialization and execution of the automated lane change function in the ACV
- The generation/initialization of MCMs (intending to change lane and requesting to form a gap) in the ACV as well as the sending via 802.11p
- The receiving of MCMs in the NACV and the visualization within the HMI application
- The sequence of the cooperative lane change, e.g., the different cooperation phases (requested, in cooperation, finished/canceled)

The underlying test cases primarily comprised function tests. As a result, all the tested components revealed the intended system behaviour. Furthermore, the cooperative lane change scenario was evaluated regarding human factor aspects (see next subsection).

In forthcoming field tests, additional elements of the use case described in Sect. 3 will be tested, e.g., the triggering of MCMs in the ACV due to lane change recommendations via MRM sent from a nearby RSU as well as the integration of heterogeneous communication technologies like C-V2X and GeoMessaging in addition to 802.11p.

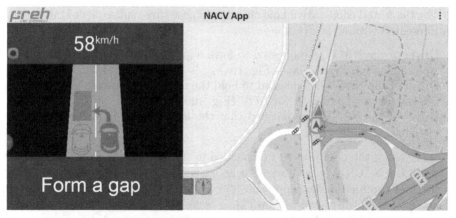

(a) Request to form a gap for lane change maneuver from ACV (purple vehicle).

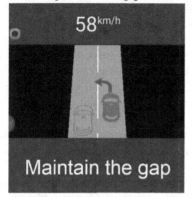
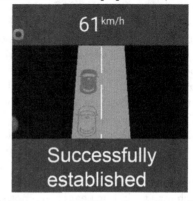

(b) Request to hold the gap for lane change maneuver from ACV.

(c) Info on successful cooperation and lane change maneuver.

Fig. 10. NACV app at certain stages of the cooperative lane changes

7.1   Human Machine Interface

In order to keep the NACV driver in the loop and to support the cooperative lane change, a prototypical HMI based on Android was developed, which should be evaluated in the scope of the field test: The NACV-App (cf. Fig. 10). The HMI context is divided into two parts: Map and event view. The right-handed map view presents the map-matched ego position and the sensed driving-situation around the NACV. Here, simple V2X messages or situations like EEBL (Electronic Emergency Brake Light), RWW (Road Works Warning), EVW (Emergency Vehicle Warning) or other DENM messages are directly presented. In case of incoming V2X messages, indicating complex maneuver situations like a GLOSA event or a request for a cooperative lane change, the event view is overlayed on the left side of the context.

For the tested cooperative lane change use case three subsequent HMI states are presented within the event view:

1. Driver of the NACV is requested to form a gap if the ACV ahead aims for a lane change into NAVC lane (Fig. 10a)
2. Driver of the NACV is requested to hold the minimum gap distance to enable the lane change maneuver for ACV (Fig. 10b)
3. Driver of the NACV gets notified that the lane change maneuver was completed successfully (Fig. 10c)

The goal of the brief user test embedded in the field test in June 2019 was to evaluate the NACV-App prototype in an early stage of development according to the user centered design approach [27]. For this purpose, a total of $N = 10$ members of the project consortium ($M_{age} = 36.1$ years; $SD_{age} = 7.5$), who had comparatively high level experience in context of automated driving, participated in a user test. For safety reasons participants sat on the passenger seat, but were instructed to look at the HMI as well as surrounding traffic (i.e., to glance as if they had to carry out the driving task). During the 10 min test drive in real traffic each participant experienced at least two successfully performed cooperative lane changes. Afterwards participants were asked to assess the HMI regarding usability (SUS; [5]), UX (UEQ; [31]) and trust [20] via standardized questionnaires and answered questions about comprehensibility and optimization potential in a short interview.

Results of the SUS data revealed mean usability-scores of $M = 74.00$ ($SD = 15.38$; scale range: 0 to 100; [5]). This could be interpreted as a marginal to acceptable [3] usability of the NACV-App, which in turn means that the HMI is appropriate for the purpose to support drivers of a NACV in a cooperative lane change task, but bears some potential of improvement. Participants' overall scores regarding user experience are in a neutral range ($M = 0.73$, $SD = 1.10$; scale range: -3 to 3; [31]). While pragmatic quality, which aims at an effective and efficient accomplishment of a task, scores neutral to marginally positive ($M = 1.20$, $SD = 1.28$), hedonic quality, which aims at creativeness and the fun-factor of an HMI, scores clearly in the neutral range ($M = 0.25$, $SD = 1.28$). Thus, results regarding UX show the biggest potential for improvement of the NACV-App regarding aspects of hedonic quality. Besides, trust ratings resulted in medium to high scores ($M = 5.13$, $SD = 0.98$; scale range: 1 to 7; [20]), which could be seen as an indicator that the implemented HMI-prototype displays trustworthy and reliable information. Participants' answers in the interview revealed that the NACV-App was intuitively comprehensible in general. Simplicity and clarity were highlighted as positive characteristics. Furthermore, the combination of displaying real-time information of the traffic situation on the one hand and the maneuver process on the other hand was appreciated by participants. One major issue raised in the interviews was the position of the HMI in the center console, which was considered critical and demanding. Instead, it was supposed to display the information rather via HUD. Beyond that, there were several hints throughout the interviews that wording used for action recommendations should be improved in terms of giving clearer instructions.

When interpreting the results, it should be kept in mind that the user test was carried out with a small group of highly involved users, who are familiar with the topic of connected and automated driving. Therefore evaluating different refined HMI-designs with potential end users is recommended.

In sum, results of the user study in a real traffic set-up delivered differentiated results identifying advantages and potentials of the developed user interface prototype. Following a user-centered design approach, these results will be taken into account in the further development process. This contributes to usability and user experience of the real-time functional HMI and therefore potentially fosters traffic safety, comfort, and smooth cooperation in mixed traffic of the future.

8 Conclusions and Outlook

In this work we presented an ITS system concept for supporting cooperative driving in mixed traffic scenarios, i.e., considering automated and non-automated vehicles, taking into account the several available communication technologies in form of 802.11p, C-V2X and LTE. We especially emphasized the ability of the system to incorporate vehicles equipped with heterogeneous communication capabilities by introducing a heterogeneous cloud architecture that makes it possible to support connected vehicles with ITS services, e.g., recommendations regarding cooperative maneuvers or foresight driving. We gave insights into the design and the interaction of the heterogeneous components, the automated vehicle, and the HMI concepts.

We carried out several live demonstrations, which showed the viability of our approach and the soundness of our technological implementation in real mixed traffic scenarios. Our research also pointed out the importance of informing the driver (in case of an NACV) or the passengers (in case of the ACV) about the current situation, especially with regard to cooperative maneuvers. While the proposed HMI and NACV app are able to carry out this task, user studies suggest that improvements may be possible. Our goal is to end up with a user-friendly, reliable system that can cover the identified use cases and help to reach long-term goals such as reduced traffic jams, reduced pollution, and increased traffic safety.

References

1. 5GAA: 5G Automotive Association project page (2018). https://5gaa.org. Accessed 20 Feb 2019
2. Auerswald, R., et al.: Cooperative driving in mixed traffic with heterogeneous communications and cloud infrastructure. In: Proceedings of the 5th International Conference on Vehicle Technology and Intelligent Transport Systems - Volume 1: VEHITS, pp. 95–105. INSTICC, SciTePress (2019). https://doi.org/10.5220/0007682900950105

3. Bangor, A., Kortum, P.T., Miller, J.T.: An empirical evaluation of the system usability scale. Intl. J. Hum.-Comput. Interact. **24**(6), 574–594 (2008)
4. Bradaï, B., Garnault, A., Picron, V., Gougeon, P.: A green light optimal speed advisor for reduced CO2 Emissions. In: Langheim, J. (ed.) Energy Consumption and Autonomous Driving. LNM, pp. 141–151. Springer, Cham (2016). https://doi.org/10.1007/978-3-319-19818-7_15
5. Brooke, J.: Sus-a quick and dirty usability scale. Usability Eval. Ind. 189, 194 , 4–7 (1996)
6. C-ITS Platform: Final report. Technical report, C-ITS Platform, January 2016. Accessed 12 Feb 2019
7. Cecchini, G., Bazzi, A., Masini, B.M., Zanella, A.: Performance comparison between IEEE 802.11p and LTE-V2V in-coverage and out-of-coverage for cooperative awareness. In: 2017 IEEE Vehicular Networking Conference (VNC), pp. 109–114, November 2017. https://doi.org/10.1109/VNC.2017.8275637
8. CEN/TC 278: Intelligent transport systems - DATEX II data exchange specifications for traffic management and information - Part 1: Context and framework. Standard (2018)
9. Elbanhawi, M., Simic, M., Jazar, R.: In the passenger seat: investigating ride comfort measures in autonomous cars. IEEE Intell. Transp. Syst. Mag. **7**(3), 4–17 (2015). https://doi.org/10.1109/MITS.2015.2405571
10. ETSI EN 302 636-4-1 V1.3.2 (2017–08) Intelligent Transport Systems (ITS); Vehicular Communications; GeoNetworking; Part 4: Geographical addressing and forwarding for point-to-point and point-to-multipoint communications; Sub-part 1: Media-Independent Functionality. Standard, ETSI, August 2017
11. ETSI EN 302 636-5-1 V2.1.1 (2017–08) Intelligent Transport Systems (ITS); Vehicular Communications; GeoNetworking; Part 5: Transport Protocols; Sub-part 1: Basic Transport Protocol. Standard, ETSI, August 2017
12. ETSI EN 302 637–2 V1.3.2 (2014–11) Intelligent Transport Systems (ITS); Vehicular Communications; Basic Set of Applications; Part 2: Specification of Cooperative Awareness Basic Service. Standard, ETSI, November 2014
13. Festag, A.: Cooperative intelligent transport systems standards in Europe. IEEE Commun. Mag. **52**(12), 166–172 (2014). https://doi.org/10.1109/MCOM.2014.6979970
14. Fritzsche, R., Festag, A.: Reliability maximization with location-based scheduling for cellular-v2x communications in highway scenarios. In: 2018 16th International Conference on Intelligent Transportation Systems Telecommunications (ITST), pp. 1–5, October 2018. https://doi.org/10.1109/ITST.2018.8566935
15. Google: gRPC project page (2018). https://grpc.io. Accessed 23 Jan 2018
16. Hameed Mir, Z., Filali, F.: LTE and IEEE 802.11p for vehicular networking: a performance evaluation. EURASIP J. Wireless Commun. Netw. **2014**(1), 89 (2014). https://doi.org/10.1186/1687-1499-2014-89
17. Hart, S.G.: Nasa-task load index (nasa-tlx); 20 years later. In: Proceedings of the Human Factors and Ergonomics Society Annual Meeting, vol. 50, pp. 904–908. Sage publications Sage CA. Los Angeles, CA (2006)
18. Hobert, L., Festag, A., Llatser, I., Altomare, L., Visintainer, F., Kovacs, A.: Enhancements of v2x communication in support of cooperative autonomous driving. IEEE Commun. Mag. **53**(12), 64–70 (2015). https://doi.org/10.1109/MCOM.2015.7355568
19. ISO/IEC 20922:2016 Information technology - Message Queuing Telemetry Transport (MQTT) v3.1.1. Standard, ISO, June 2016

20. Jian, J.Y., Bisantz, A.M., Drury, C.G.: Foundations for an empirically determined scale of trust in automated systems. Int. J. Cogn. Ergonomics **4**(1), 53–71 (2000)
21. Kloeppel, M., Grimm, J., Strobl, S., Auerswald, R.: Performance evaluation of GLOSA-algorithms under realistic traffic conditions using C2I-communication. In: Nathanail, E.G., Karakikes, I.D. (eds.) Data Analytics: Paving the Way to Sustainable Urban Mobility. CSUM 2018. Advances in Intelligent Systems and Computing, vol. 879, pp. 44–52. Springer International Publishing, Cham (2019). https://doi.org/10.1007/978-3-030-02305-8_6
22. Krimmling, J.: Das Dresdner Verkehrsmanagementsystem VAMOS. In: Sandrock, M., Riegelhuth, G. (eds.) Verkehrsmanagementzentralen in Kommunen: Eine vergleichende Darstellung, pp. 157–197. Springer Fachmedien Wiesbaden, Wiesbaden (2014)
23. Kulmala, R., Rämä, P.: Definition of behavioural adaptation. In: Rudin-Brown, C., Jamson, S. (eds.) Behavioural adaptation and road safety : theory, evidence, and action, pp. 11–22. Boca Raton, Florida CRC Press, June 2013. https://doi.org/10.1201/b14931-5. http://alltitles.ebrary.com/Doc?id=10798605. formerly CIP
24. Lee, J.D., See, K.A.: Trust in automation: designing for appropriate reliance. Hum. Factors **46**(1), 50–80 (2004). https://doi.org/10.1518/hfes.46.1.50_30392
25. Malone, K., et al.: Deliverable d11.4. impact assessment and user perception of cooperative systems. Technical report, Drive c2x, July 2014. Accessed 23 July 2019
26. Nielsen, J., Clemmensen, T., Yssing, C.: Getting access to what goes on in people's heads?: reflections on the think-aloud technique. In: Proceedings of the second Nordic conference on Human-computer interaction, pp. 101–110. ACM (2002)
27. Norman, D.A.: The Psychology of Everyday Things. Basic Books, United States (2013)
28. Payre, W., Diels, C.: Human-machine interface design development for connected and co-operative vehicle features. In: International Conference on Applied Human Factors and Ergonomics, pp. 415–422. Springer (2017)
29. Rad, B.B., Bhatti, H.J., Ahmadi, M.: An introduction to Docker and analysis of its performance. Int. J. Comput. Sci. Netw. Secur. (IJCSNS) **17**(3), 228 (2017)
30. Salahuddin, M., Al-Fuqaha, A., Guizani, M., Cherkaoui, S.: RSU cloud and its resource management in support of enhanced vehicular applications. In: 2014 IEEE Globecom Workshops, GC Wkshps 2014, pp. 127–132. IEEE, December 2014. https://doi.org/10.1109/GLOCOMW.2014.7063418
31. Schrepp, M.: User experience questionnaire handbook. all you need to know to apply the UEQ successfully in your projects (2015)
32. Springer, S., Schmidt, C., Schmalfuß, F.: Informationsbedarf von Nutzern konventioneller, vernetzter und automatisierter, vernetzter Fahrzeuge im urbanen Mischverkehr. In: VDI (ed.) Fahrerassistenzsysteme und automatisiertes Fahren 2018, VDI-Berichte 2335, pp. 391–406. VDI-Verlag GmbH, Düsseldorf (2018)
33. Statista: Connected car report 2018 (2018). https://www.statista.com/outlook/320/109/connected-car/united-states. Accessed 20 Feb 2019
34. Systems Technology: STISIM Drive - Scenario Definition Language (SDL). http://web.mit.edu/16.400/www/auto_sim/Help/SDL.htm. Accessed 20 Jun 2019
35. Van Der Laan, J.D., Heino, A., De Waard, D.: A simple procedure for the assessment of acceptance of advanced transport telematics. Transp. Res. Part C: Emerging Technol. **5**(1), 1–10 (1997)

36. Wilson, J.R., Rutherford, A.: Mental models: theory and application in human factors. Hum. Factors **31**(6), 617–634 (1989). https://doi.org/10.1177/001872088903100601
37. Zhang, L.: Cooperative adaptive cruise control in mixed traffic with selective use of vehicle-to-vehicle communication. IET Intell. Transp. Syst. **12**(10), 1243–1254 (2018)

PFARA: A Platoon Forming and Routing Algorithm for Same-Day Deliveries

Sînziana-Maria Sebe$^{(\boxtimes)}$ and Jörg P. Müller

Institute of Informatics, Clausthal University of Technology,
Clausthal-Zellerfeld, Germany
`sinziana-maria.sebe@tu-clausthal.de`

Abstract. Platoons, vehicles that travel very close together acting as one, promise to improve road usage on freeways and city roads alike. We study platoon formation in the context of same-day delivery in urban environments. Multiple self-interested logistic service providers (LSP) carry out same-day deliveries by deploying autonomous electric vehicles that are capable of forming and traveling in platoons. The novel aspect that we consider in our research is heterogeneity of platoons in the sense that vehicles are equipped with different capabilities and constraints, and belong to different providers. Our aim is to examine how these platoons can form and their potential properties and benefits. We present a platoon forming and routing algorithm, called PFARA, that finds longest common routes for multiple vehicles, while also respecting vehicle preferences and constraints. PFARA consists of two parts, a speed clustering step and a linear optimisation step. To test the approach, a simulation was used, working with realistic urban network data and background traffic models. Our results showed that the performance of our approach is comparable to a simple route-matching one, but it leads to better utility values for vehicles and by extension the LSPs. We show that the grouping provided is viable and provides benefits to all vehicles participating in the platoon.

Keywords: Platoon · Heterogeneous groups · Route matching · Group building optimisation · Simulation

1 Introduction

Platooning is a topical subject researched by many scientist especially in the context of automated driving. Relying on a leader to make the driving decisions and then mirroring them is one part of how this automation can be achieved. Research on platooning has been conducted since the 1950's [21,32] and has been gaining momentum since. Most platooning research tends to focus on highway scenarios [36] with large freight transports in mind e.g. SARTRE [27]. However, with recent developments in technology, urban platooning appears promising with respect to the better utilisation of the scare resource of urban space. However, current research on urban platooning focuses on stability, manoeuvring,

© Springer Nature Switzerland AG 2021
M. Helfert et al. (Eds.): SMARTGREENS 2019/VEHITS 2019, CCIS 1217, pp. 297–320, 2021.
https://doi.org/10.1007/978-3-030-68028-2_14

and control (see e.g., [1,26,31]), and, to a lesser extent, on the traffic management perspective [13,22].

Same-day deliveries in the scope of logistic traffic is a novel use case for platooning. Due to the growth of online shopping, and the desire of customers for immediate shipping, logistic companies have to restructure the way they carry out their deliveries. *On the one hand*, the distribution network has to be adapted. To support such orders, Crainic et al. developed a two-tier network architecture [6,8], with hubs, satellites and customers being the main transitional points. Goods are first carried from a large hub, located mostly outside the urban area, to multiple smaller locations called satellites, which are scattered inside the city, each catering to about 20 to 25 customers [7]. From the satellite, the goods are transported to the customer, the so-called last mile delivery, which accounts for the majority of the costs of said delivery [10].

On the other hand, the way orders are handled has to change. Usually, logistic companies plan and schedule deliveries in a way that minimises cost and maximises order completion. This process is costly in time and computational resources, making it an unviable approach for same-day orders. Immediate deployment of received orders, combined with having small autonomous electric vehicles carry out the costly last-mile stretc.h would be a possible solution. These vehicles are flexible and do not contribute as much to traffic congestion and toxic emissions, but sending multiple such vehicles in an already busy network does not alleviate the situation entirely.

Combining the logistic same-day deliveries into platoons could benefit urban traffic by streamlining deliveries, removing large trucks from the inner city and potentially decongesting some intersections. However, this subject has not been thoroughly researched thus far, with only a few publications existing (e.g. [13,30]) and to our knowledge, none that looks into how vehicles are grouped into platoons, especially with vehicles belonging to different service providers. We refer to Sect. 2 for a more in depth analysis of the state of the art.

For our research we assume the context of logistic traffic, with multiple service providers, each with their own fleet of vehicles that carry out deliveries to customers. We also assume that platooning is incentivised by the traffic management authority, providing platooning vehicles with subsidies. Platoons form in a spontaneous way, at intersections where more than two vehicles meet. A vehicle only forms/joins a platoon if its perceived utility for joining is better than if it were to travel alone. In order to gain the most benefit from platoons, we assume that logistic service providers are willing to form mixed platoons with each other. This leads to a high degree of heterogeneity, not only in the vehicles and destinations sense, but given the self-interested nature of all providers; in valuation functions, restrictions and preferences as well. This research presents a grouping and routing algorithm that fosters this type of cooperation while respecting the limitations imposed.

Our previous work [33] presented a first and simple optimisation approach to solve the problem of cross-provider platoon formation. In this work the optimisation algorithm only included a distance limitation, and since the model did not have an explicit representation of time, it could not express nor solve dynamic problems, e.g. including speed preferences or delivery windows. In [33], we showed that the algorithm computes accurate and promising results, but has very limited expressiveness. This paper presents a substantially enhanced version of the grouping algorithm that accounts for important aspects of travel, including distance, time, speed, and cost. The model has been finalised, and simulated movement of vehicles has been introduced allowing us to model dynamic situations, where the grouping algorithm is run every time one or more vehicles or platoons meet at intersections.

The structure of the paper is as follows; in Sect. 2 we give an overview of the state of the art regarding platoons as well as other group building algorithms. Section 3 presents our proposed platoon forming and routing algorithm whose goal is finding the longest common route, while respecting, length, time, speed and cost restrictions. A simulation developed to test the approach is also presented here. Section 4 presents multiple simulation experiments, which show good results regarding solution quality and algorithm runtime performance. We follow with a discussion in Sect. 5 where we also address the future developments of this research. Lastly we present our conclusion in Sect. 6.

2   Literature Review

The concept of platooning, where vehicles drive in a line close to each other and behaving as one unit, has been a topic of great interest in research due to it's promising outlooks for road usage on heavy-duty transports on freeways [3–5]. Since vehicles travel more closely together in platoons than in usual traffic, the resource of road space is better utilised, which in turn has a positive effect on network flow. Another reason why platooning on freeways is seen as positive is the reduction in fuel consumption [20]. Because of the reduced gap between vehicles, the wind drag does not have as high of an effect, which means that less fuel is used to maintain a constant speed. However, more recent studies and experiments have shown that although platooning did increase safety, the effect on the fuel-consumption was less than what was expected, with just a three to four percent reduction [19]

Other research on platooning deals more with control, manoeuvres (merging, splitting, travelling), stability and safety. Ploeg et al. [26] calculated the needed time headway to achieve string stability and safety in platoons. This distance can be used in all scenarios, both urban and highway to calculate the spacing needed between platooning vehicles depending on speed. Another piece of research looks into cooperative manoeuvres, as an extent to platooning that again Ploeg et al. [25] studied for highway scenarios. They present a layered control architecture for such manoeuvres, which was also the basis for the Grand Cooperative Driving Challenge.

Transitioning to an urban environment, the focus still seems to be on control, stability and manoeuvres. To increase stability on curved roads and to account for the different speeds in an urban scenario, lateral and longitudinal control have to function independently according to Ali et al. [1]. A third control mechanism responsible for the platoon must also be put into place thus giving us a controller for each movement type. In [16], Khalifa et al. show that stability is guaranteed even with limited of communication between vehicles, through a consensus-based control mechanism for longitudinal movement. Stability of platoons is addressed in [31] by making use of multiple state machines to ensure flexibility. There is one state machine for each of the logic elements of platooning: messaging, forming and distance.

Other benefits of platooning arise from a traffic management perspective in slower urban traffic. Lioris et al. [22] have found that bottleneck-prone places, such as intersections, could benefit from platooning. By using adaptive traffic lights, and allowing platoons to pass uninterrupted, the throughput (measured in number of vehicles) of the intersection can be doubled.

Most work focusing on platoons does not touch on the aspect of how vehicles decide to platoon and who to platoon with. The study presented in [31], details just the actions needed to join or form a platoon. The aspects of how the vehicles would form a logical group and what characteristics are important in making the platooning decision lack in research.

An interesting use-case for platoons is logistic transport, from large freight shipments, which we have already addressed, to small singular same-day deliveries. Urban platooning in the case of logistic same-day deliveries was addressed in [30] with a focus on network design. Assuming that fully autonomous platoons cannot travel on all edges of a network, human-lead platoons have to drive through those inaccessible areas. The authors goal is to minimise the costs across all vehicles in the delivery fleet of a single logistic service provider. Given the circumstance, the algorithm for vehicle grouping is not addressed, perhaps because of the large overlap in the different vehicle capabilities and objectives, as well as due to the strategic level on which the problem operates. In a similar vein, Haas and Friedrich [13] look at platoons in a city-logistic scenario from the traffic managers point of view. They focus on the microscopic/operational level focusing on the number of vehicles in platoons and the number of platoons in a network during the course of a single day. They consider autonomous delivery vans, that rely on platoons to travel through the network. This means that they are stationary when alone and can only drive autonomously during splitting and merging operations. They do note that the vans only join a platoon if they can be brought further to their destinations, if not they wait for another. Otherwise the authors tend to focus on developing an interaction model for platoons in a roundabout scenario, where determining who has the right-of-way is not as obvious as it is with normal traffic.

Group building algorithms have been studied for a long time and there are many variants each depending on the field of application. General approaches are presented in [2]. Other publications address specific algorithms such as [40] for Walds SPRT Algorithm, [14] which identifies important criterion and then sorts accordingly, maximum likelihood algorithms, [11] for Wertheimers laws of grouping, [23] for hierarchical grouping and algorithms that find the maximum consistency between the data and the group appointment.

Switching to a more specific field, namely that of traffic, we are faced again with more aspects to consider. A pre-requisite for any sort of group formation and disbandment is the ability to communicate; so Taleb et al. [37] proposed that a group of vehicles could only exist if the communication line is maintained. This resulted in vehicles being grouped by their velocity headings; all going in the same direction, while matching the speed within the group to maintain inter-vehicular distances, and therefore the communication link. This sole criterion is not enough when formulating platoons, but does matter when considering the maintenance of one.

Ways to pair drivers with passengers while also considering schedules and routes are presented in [15]. The problem they formulate is a many-to-many advanced reservation travel problem. Important characteristics upon which potential pairs can be made are found and studied, namely: the location of origins and destinations, the passenger type and trip purpose, closeness of desired departure times, number and capacity of available vehicles and the direction of the trips. With normal routing algorithms the focus is on cost minimisation for the company (in the form of length of route or lack of empty trips) and not enough focus is given to the passenger and their preferences. To combat this, the authors use a fuzzy relation to find similar trips. This work can be used as a base for our own criteria definition, although our focus is not on the match between passenger and vehicle, but rather the compatibility between vehicles.

Sanderson et al. propose a consensus based approach to clustering vehicles, in their work [28]. They use their own IPCon algorithm [29] to provide collective arrangements taking preferences and constraints into account through role-associated power of the participants (vehicles in this case). Similarly, Dennisen and Müller [9] propose preference-based group formation through iterative committee elections. They assume the context of a ride-sharing service that drives to different sights within a city. Passengers have to choose which sights to visit and be sorted into the autonomous vehicle based on their preference. The algorithm works by removing the unhappiest passenger using the Minisum or Minimax approval committee rules. The votes are then recounted and the process started again until a suitable solution is found. When considering our case, there is overlap in the fact that finding the best common route is the goal, but since we are dealing with autonomous machines and not humans, an informed vote does not seem obvious.

More related to our research field is the work of Khan and Boloni [17] which spontaneously groups vehicles driving on freeways using a utility function based on speed. The focus is on the manoeuvres that come with convoy driving: joining, staying and splitting; but not the actions needed, but rather the utility that comes with each one. While this might be sufficient in a highway scenario, where all vehicles are driving in the same direction, it is not the case for an urban environment where vehicle routes differ greatly.

To conclude, there is only limited research activity at the intersection of the two research fields of platooning and grouping algorithms; in particular, it does not adequately address highly heterogeneous scenarios like urban logistic traffic. PFARA, described in the following section aims to address this research gap.

3   The Platoon Forming and Routing Algorithm (PFARA)

Based on the literature, the decisive constraints and aspects of the heterogeneous group building problem need to be determined. Taking the different elements of traffic, urban environments and logistics into account, the heterogeneity of agents and their preferences makes platoon formation and routing highly complex. First the logistic service providers will want to keep their cost minimal while reaching their target number of orders as well as keep cooperation only with some but not all other companies. The vehicles are bound by their battery life, thus restricting the route, as well as speed, be it legal limits or individual speed capabilities. And last, but most important, we have the client which selects a specific delivery window that must respected.

The problem of heterogeneous platoon building can be solved through a linear optimisation problem using the aforementioned preferences. They are used as linear constraints in the optimisation problem that has the goal of minimising total costs. This is turn has a positive effect of both travel time and length of route. We refer to Subsect. 3.5 for a more detailed description of the algorithm, but we do note that it is deterministic offering multiple best solutions.

Attempting to solve this problem with the aforementioned fuzzy theorem would not yield good results given the different weights given to the aspects for each vehicle or logistic service provider. For example some might prioritise battery life over speed, or some might want to wait for platoons rather than drive alone, or completely disregarding platoons if not readily available to save up on time. So while the restriction criteria are the same for all vehicles, their weight or importance will differ in the problem.

If our algorithm fails to find a singular best solution, which could happen in networks that follow a grid-type pattern, the aforementioned voting approaches could act as fail-safe methods of selecting the grouping and route. This guarantees that the decision is not made by a singular element, but rather all potential vehicles in the platoon.

3.1   Input Data

The urban network is transformed into a graph to allow for routing. Intersections are transformed into vertexes and the streets into edges. Traffic demand is the sum of routes over all origin and destination points in the network, or how many cars use each edge in a given time-span. This is meant to represent background traffic which will affect our platoon routing.

$$Q(x,t) = \frac{\Delta N}{\Delta t} \tag{1}$$

where $Q(x,t)$ is the traffic demand, ΔN is the number of vehicles and Δt the time-span. [39]. From here we can find the traffic density, by normalising through division over the edges length.

$$\rho(x,t) = \frac{\Delta N}{\Sigma_\alpha d_\alpha} \tag{2}$$

where $\Sigma_\alpha d_\alpha$ is the length.

The resulting traffic density is given as each edge's weight, and act as the cost to minimise in the optimisation problem. We consider traffic density the "cost" because of its direct translation into time-savings; the freer an edge, the faster it is to transverse it, the quicker the vehicle delivers its package and can return to be dispatched again. Given the electric nature of the vehicles considered, the more time they spend away from the satellite, the longer they will need to charge, thus reducing the amounts of orders they can fulfil in a day.

Having the environment defined, vehicles can then be added and their routes calculated by PFARA. Each vehicle has an origin, a destination and a set of preferences; minimum acceptable speed for platooning, maximum speed, maximum length of route, maximum travel time and maximum cost.

3.2   Assumptions

The vehicles are assumed to function autonomously, all the while attempting to form a platoon. In order for a platoon to exist, a minimum of two vehicles is necessary. They must be at the same vertex at the same time to do so. For now vehicles do not wait at intersections for other vehicles or platoons, even if their preferences allow it. Platoons form spontaneously and organically with vehicles that would benefit from platooning. A vehicle would not participate in a platoon if the cost to do so is larger than travelling alone, or its distance, time, speed and cost restrictions are not respected. After a platoon forms, all vehicles in it drive with a uniform speed. As pointed out in the literature review, vehicles must have communication capabilities, based on [37] and [16]. Each vehicle sends its destination and restrictions to a local agent which performs PFARA. The results (route, expected cost, expected length and group) are then communicated back to each vehicle.

For a visual representation of how platoons would form, please see Fig. 1. Two platoons approach the same intersection, but the vehicles comprising them follow different headings, denoted by the different opaque colours. The vehicles communicate their destination, preferences and limitations to the local agent denoted by the broadcast tower, which runs PFARA and forms two new platoons, denoted by the slightly more transparent vehicle formations.

To encourage the penetration rate of platoons, they are treated as one vehicle, since logically they perform as one. All members of the platoon share a common route and contribute equally to its cost. This leads to a reduction of individual costs for all vehicles and encourages the formation of larger platoons. The cost of a route is considered as the sum of weights for all edges used in it.

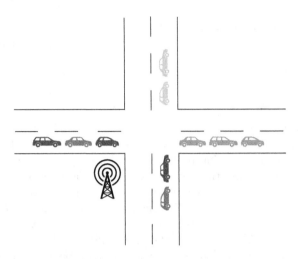

Fig. 1. Vehicle interaction and group formation.

3.3 Notations

For ease of understanding, all symbols to be used in the formal description of the algorithm and their meaning is presented in Table 1.

Table 1. Symbols and meaning [33].

Symbol	Definitions
$G = (V, E)$	graph
$n \in V$	vertices
$e \in E$	edges, $e \equiv (i, j)$
$d(e)$	traffic density of edge e
$l(e)$	length of edge e
s	speed of the platoon
v	vehicle
$dest_v$	destination vertex of vehicle v , fixed
K_v^*	maximum costs for vehicle v
Ω_v	maximum delivery time for vehicle v
Λ_v	maximum length of route for vehicle v
$p(e)_v$	price vehicle v pays for edge e
NP	the number of vehicles in the platoon

3.4 PFARA: The Speed-Clustering Step

Given that all vehicles in a platoon must travel with the same speed to maintain stability, an initial speed clustering has to be put in place. A minimum acceptable speed for platoons as well as the maximum speed is specified in the vehicles preferences. To form a grouping based on speed, the maximum minimum speed within the group is first selected. All vehicles whose maximum speed is greater than it are grouped and their destination and preferences directed to the second step: the optimiser. If not all vehicles in the original group were selected, the next greatest minimum speed is taken, and the same procedure applied, to be repeated until all vehicles are grouped, or it is determined that they must travel alone. This can be written as:

```
while not (all vehicles grouped or excluded)
{
  find maximum minimum speed;
  for each vehicle
  {
    if (maxspeed >= maxminspeed)
      group vehicle;
  }
}
```

While determination of the platoon's speed could be written as a linear constraint in the following step, we believe that this approach would be restrictive. The common speed calculated would be lower than an ideal speed and could possibly deter vehicles from joining. This means that our algorithm has to be repeated with a smaller group of vehicles which not only takes time, but also provides less cost savings.

3.5   PFARA: The Optimiser Step

The objective for this step is to find the route with the most overlap between vehicles that also respects their restrictions. This can be achieved by adapting the shortest path algorithm (presented by Eq. 3,4 and 5) to fit multiple vehicles instead of one.

$$min \sum_{(i,j)\in E} x(i,j) * d(i,j) \tag{3}$$

$$x(i,j) \in 0,1 \,\forall\, edge \ (i,j) \tag{4}$$

$$\sum_{j} x(i,j) - \sum_{j} x(j,i) = \begin{cases} 1 & \Longleftrightarrow \quad i = Origin \\ -1 & \Longleftrightarrow \quad i = Destination \\ 0 \ otherwise. \end{cases} \tag{5}$$

x is the variable associated with an edge, defined between vertices i and j. It has the value 0 if its edge is not in the shortest path, or 1 if it is (4). The flow constraint enables the vehicles to pass through intermediary nodes and is defined with the three cases (5). Naturally the objective is to minimise the costs which we measure in traffic density (3).

When transposing this to platooning, we introduce a new variable y to signify the platoon. This variable acts in a similar fashion to how x did in the classic problem: $y = 0$ if it is not part of the route of any vehicle and $y = 1$ if it is (7). y is used in the objective function to be minimised (6). To ensure that the route covers all vehicles, we add a restriction that states that y can have the value of one only if there is at least an x with the value of one (8). The flow constraint remains unchanged (9). To these restrictions we add the ones for length of route (10), delivery time (11), and maximum cost (14). Incentivising platoons is done by giving a reduction in costs. Since all vehicles contribute to the cost (13), the more vehicles in a platoon, the less they have to pay for each edge. Therefore the platooning optimisation problem would be formulated as such follows:

Definition 1. *Given a group of vehicles, being at the same vertex O in the graph at the same time; let the routes for all the vehicles be given by $y(i,j)$, and the individual vehicle routes by $x(i,j)_v$ where*

$$min \sum_{(i,j)\in E} y(i,j) * d(i,j) \tag{6}$$

$$y(i,j), x(i,j) \in \{0,1\}, \forall edge\ (i,j) \tag{7}$$

$$x(i,j)_v \leq y(i,j) \forall edge\ (i,j), \forall vehicle\ v \tag{8}$$

$$\sum_j x(i,j)_v - \sum_j x(j,i)_v = \begin{cases} 1 & \Longleftrightarrow\ i = O \\ -1 & \Longleftrightarrow\ i = dest_v \\ 0 & otherwise. \end{cases} \quad \forall v,\ \forall (i,j) \in E \tag{9}$$

$$\sum_{x(i,j)_v=1} l(i,j) \leq \Lambda_v \forall\ v \tag{10}$$

$$\sum_{x(i,j)_v=1} \frac{l(i,j)}{s} \leq \Omega_v \forall\ v \tag{11}$$

$$p(i,j)_v \geq 0 \ \forall\ v\ and\ edge\ (i,j) \tag{12}$$

$$p(i,j)_v = \frac{d(i,j)}{NP_{(i,j)}} \forall\ v\ where\ NP_{(i,j)} = \sum_v x(i,j)_v \tag{13}$$

$$\sum_{(i,j):x(i,j)_v=1} p(i,j)_v \leq K_v^*, \forall\ v. \tag{14}$$

A similar but much less expressive model was presented in [33]. It only addressed the optimisation problem limited strictly by a length of route constraint. Also the analysis of the grouping algorithm was done statically since the model did not feature time, and by extension, speed. Without those elements a complete solution accounting for the four most important aspects of travel (length, time, speed and cost) was not possible.

This work features all the aforementioned aspects and takes into account the time of meeting, speed matching and the cost restrictions. This ensures the solution provided is complete and can be applied to all vehicles regardless.

3.6   Simulation

The simulation was formulated to study the effectiveness of PFARA and its effects on the valuation of cooperation between vehicles. Its performance is also tested to ensure that it is applicable and appropriate for real-life scenarios.

Framework. To analyse PFARA, a simulation was designed using Java. Each separate component has a specific framework. Jung [24] is used to generate the environment due to its powerful library that models data into a graph, its visualisation options, routing and analysis capabilities. To visualise the routes and traffic densities, we employed the use of a heat-map using the colour schemes provided by [18]. The actual drawing of routes was done with a JXMapViewer2 painter, modelled after a pre-existing examples [35]. For the optimisation part, Gurobi [12] was used, a powerful commercial solver. It was extremely easy to implement into the simulation as an external jar file and the problem definition process was also simple. To write the problem we start by defining as many x variables as we have vehicles in the potential platoon, and one y variable. Then the objective function is written based on the y and weights (traffic density) of the edges with minimisation being the goal. Then for each of the criteria defined above (Eqs. 8, 9, 10, 11 and 14), a linear constraint is written. Since speed is already addressed before running the optimiser, we do not need to include it here. After running and finding a solution, the results are saved in a separate data structure, available at any time and the optimiser object made redundant to save up on computational resources.

Methodology. Simulation starts with creating the environment and the vehicles from an input file. The vehicles each have their set of preferences as well as a starting satellite and a destination. Then the internal clock starts and after running instances of the optimiser for each satellite to group the vehicles, they begin moving through the environment. They go along their given route, attempting to form new platoons whenever they encounter new vehicles/platoons. If a vehicle or a platoon intersects with other vehicles or platoons, they go through the grouping process (first by speed and then by optimiser). The algorithm finds the best group, their routes (both common and separate until their destination) and expected cost for each vehicle. After grouping, the vehicles travel together until the end of their common route, where they split and continue their trip towards their destination, or attempt to form a new platoon with some of their former co-platooners. To ensure that the selected route is constantly the "best" one, given that urban traffic tends to shift quite rapidly, PFARA can be performed at some or all intermediary nodes. To account for the distance and time travelled as well as the cost of the route, and update of the preferences is performed at each intermediary node. The length of the edge travelled is subtracted from the maximum distance, and the same goes for the maximum time and cost. This ensures that a new instance of the optimisation part of the algorithm sets the restrictions to a current version of the preferences, and not to the ones at the start of travel. The simulation completes with the vehicles reaching their respective destinations. Afterwards, an output file is written detailing each action of each vehicle, their cost, length of route and time of arrival. Lastly a heat map of the network is generated allowing us to see which edges were used by the vehicles and of how many of them were on each edge.

Baseline Algorithm: Overlapping. To have a benchmark comparison for our approach we decided to conceptualise the most obvious version of a platooning grouping algorithm, which is simple best route matching. Considering each vehicles current position as the origin point, the already-existing routing algorithm present in Jung is used to find the fastest route. By aggregating the routes for all vehicles, we can find where they would travel together (considering constant speed). By counting the number of times an edge was used, we determine the potential size of the platoon travelling on it as well as knowing which vehicles make up the platoon. This approach however does not take into account the possible restrictions, re-routings and above all, vehicle preferences. It is on the other side extremely easy to calculate and straightforward. To ensure we are just comparing the optimisation part to this simple overlapping approach, all other aspect of the simulation were used in the overlapping algorithm as well. Therefore we have the time counter, the vehicles' movement throughout the environment, and most importantly, the preliminary speed clustering.

Input Data. To simulate scenarios we employed data from [34], namely the Berlin Tiergarten neighbourhood. The data set is finely granular enough to use and comes with a very rough account of traffic demand. It was not given for each edge in particular, but rather as an aggregation of trips based on zones in the neighbourhood. So to get accurate weights for our problem, individual trips needed to be generated. The vertices were divided into zones and random ones pulled to act as origins and destinations. Routes were calculated, aggregated for the whole instance, and then normalised by dividing through each edges length (according to the definition given by Eq. 2), thus giving us traffic density to act as the edges weights for our algorithm. An example of this process would be having thirteen trips from zone 2 to zone 9, pulling a random node from zone 2 and one from zone 9, finding the best route between them, saving the results and repeating the process another twelve times aggregating the edges taken for all. This process does not offer constant results, but they are similar enough between runs to be considered consistent.

We also created a synthetic smaller network of a five-by-five grid network to follow the routes and examine the driving behaviour more closely. Factors like traffic density, positioning of satellites and vehicle preferences were varied to ensure the generality of PFARA.

Output Data. As mentioned before, after each run the simulation provides output in the form of a log file and a heat map visualisation. The colours selected to display it (Inferno palette) were chosen due to the cognitive ease of understanding it by the viewer [38] (yellow for hot to dark purple for cold). A light yellow edge means it was the most used, whereas dark purple indicates it was a part of the route of a single vehicle. A colourless edge signifies it not being a part of any vehicles' route.

The log file consists of the events of all vehicles. The time step and location of each event is specified. The event types are:

1. Creation. Takes place at the satellite vertex.
2. Departure. Happens for satellite and intermediary vertices.
3. Arrival. Happens for intermediary vertices as well as the destination.
4. Completed. Accompanies the arrival event to denote the completion of the route.
5. Formed. When a vehicle joins a platoon and who they join with.
6. Split. When a vehicle disbands from the platoon. Can be due to completion or because the end of the common route was reached.

Besides the events, upon completion the following is specified:

1. the cost accumulated
2. length of route taken
3. the allowance left for length, time and cost for all vehicles.

The overlapping algorithm provides the same result structure; a heat map and a log file.

4 Results

To check the validity of our algorithm, we ran experiments on real and synthetic environments. The real environment was the Berlin Tiergarten neighbourhood that also has realistic traffic density. The synthetic one is represented by a five by five Manhattan grid network. To validate all aspects of the algorithm, multiple experiments were run varying things like traffic density, satellite placements, and vehicle preferences. The algorithm did well in all cases and all groupings and routes were correct and respected the restrictions.

By looking at the heat maps, we get an idea of how the placement of satellites and traffic density affect the deliveries, and where joining and splitting could occur across the platoons. The colours show how many vehicles use a specific edge and a change in colour from one edge do the next may denote vehicle/s splitting (if it shifts colder) or joining (if it shifts warmer). However, due to fact that the heat map is generated statically at the end of the simulation, it cannot serve as a definite way of determining said points. The colour of the edge changes with how many vehicles use it and not necessarily just with platoons. However we will present a case where the split and join points can be clearly identified.

We take the example of the five by five Manhattan grid network, with the outside edges having higher traffic density, which decreases towards the centre. We simulate five different logistic service providers, each with a fleet of five

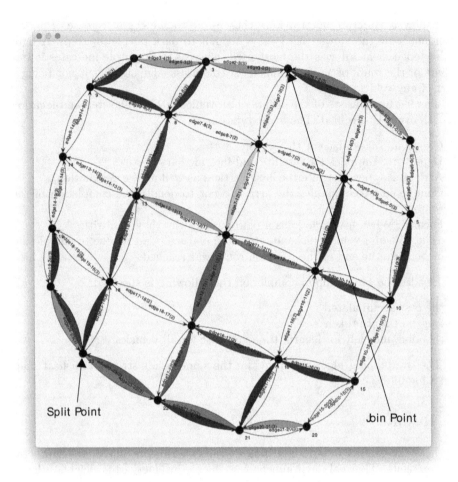

Fig. 2. Heat map depicting split and join points.

vehicles, each having a random destination node. The locations of the satellites are the four corners of the network and the central node. All the vehicles start at the same time (the starting time of the simulation) and travel at the same speed. Split points can be identified by a transition of the edge colour from warm to cooler when looking at Fig. 2. That is the case at node 23 where a vehicle splits from the five vehicle platoon coming from node 24 and continues alone towards node 18, with the other four continuing their journey in the platoon towards node 22. Joining points like node 2 can be identified by the transition of the edge colour from cooler to warmer. Two platoons, one coming from node 3 containing five vehicles, and the other coming from node 1 containing four vehicles, meet and join at node 2 in a larger seven vehicle platoon (node 2 was the destination for two vehicles) travelling toward node 7.

4.1   Numerical Results

To analyse the numerical results as best as possible we compared our approach to independent travel and the overlapping algorithm. Pinning the two grouping algorithms agains one another allows us to see how viable our design is. The real environment of Berlin Tiergarten Neighbourhood was used to guarantee the results are as realistic as possible. To resemble real traffic we assumed the satellites are located at intersections where most of the traffic takes place (number of vehicles leaving the intersection is highest) and the vehicle destinations we selected the nodes where the number of vehicles arriving would be highest, both based on traffic density information. We have two providers, each with one satellite and 15 and 10 vehicles respectively, each with a different destination. With the origin and destination points set, both algorithms were run and the resulting costs analysed.

From Fig. 3 we can see what sort of cost savings we accrue from using the two grouping algorithms. In the case of the first provider (pod 1 to pod 24), both the overlapping and the PFARA approach mostly give the same results. The only two exceptions are pod 13 and 24, which have less costs with PFARA. This shows us that this approach found an alternative route that allows for longer platooning for at least one of the vehicles, but which benefits both. This is confirmed when analysing output log file.

In the case of the second provider (pod 30 to pod 44) we have more variety in the results. Again, both algorithms are far superior than the alone-travel alternative, but when comparing them to each other we have an array of relations. In some cases, like pod 43, pod 32, the cost is the same. Pod 40 and pod 30 have a significantly better result with PFARA. The most interesting result is pod 42, whose costs for both grouping algorithms are lower than travelling alone, but PFARA does considerably worse than the overlapping alternative. This means the route given by PFARA for this vehicle is longer, but when considering the global cost of this provider, it might be worth it. The total costs for this logistic service provider are:

- Alone: 198761
- Overlap: 121897.97
- Optimiser: 102558.95

We can see that even if some vehicles take detours, it might be worth for the service provider to go for the PFARA approach anyway. The influences and weights of each of these factors (cost, length and time) need to be calculated and specified by each of the service providers, and adjusting the vehicles preferences and restrictions accordingly. Table 2 shows a more detailed view of the results for the specific cases mentioned above.

Another experiment is ran on the synthetic five-by-five grid network to present an easier to understand set of results, which is not possible with the Tiergarten neighbourhood due to its size. In this case there are five logistic service providers each with five vehicles.

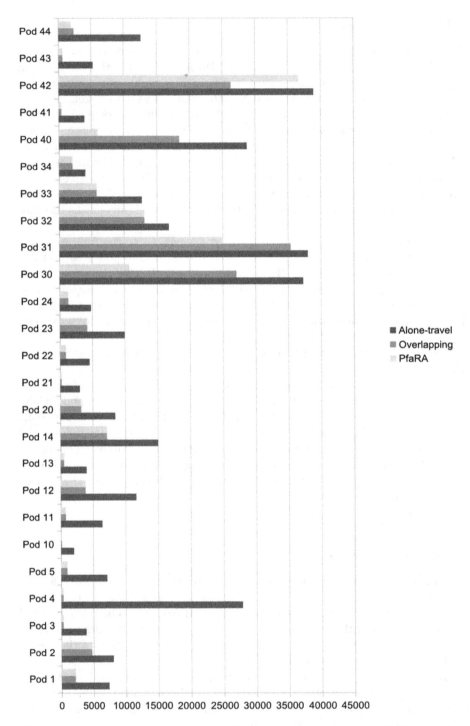

Fig. 3. Cost comparison of the two algorithms with alone-travel on realistic network.

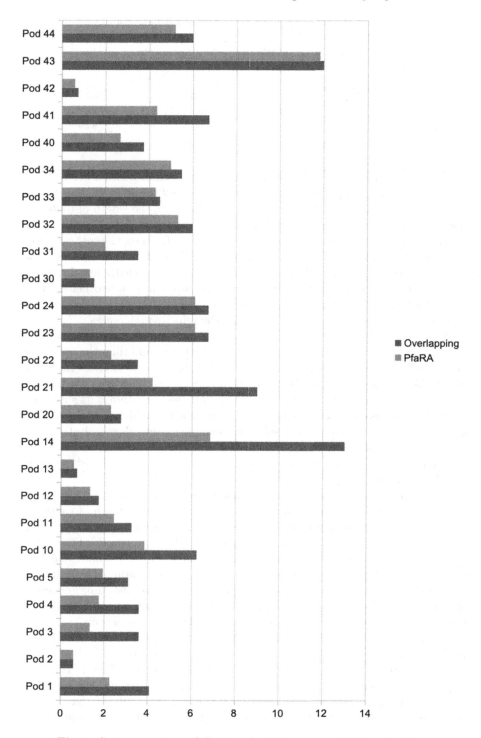

Fig. 4. Cost comparison of the two algorithms on synthetic network.

Table 2. Result comparison of the two algorithms, detailed.

Vehicle	$Cost_{Overlap}$	$Time_{Overlap}$	$Length_{Overlap}$	$Cost_{PFaRA}$	$Time_{PFaRA}$	$Length_{PFaRA}$
pod 43	633.87	45	3.74	633.87	45	3.74
pod 32	13154.73	27	1.29	13164.73	27	1.29
pod 40	18482.71	81	6.01	6013.36	81	6.01
pod 30	27100.71	101	6.85	10816.02	101	7.44
pod 42	26364.71	93	7.40	36673	107	8.09

We can tell from Fig. 4 that the optimiser approach provides a better result than the overlapping approach for all vehicles. Usually the vehicles do not stray from their best route, which is shown by observing both the length of route and travel time given in the output file. The only exception is vehicle 43, which takes a rather considerable detour to travel with a platoon. Even so, the cost it accrues is still lower than the alone travel alternative, which is 12. One could argue that this cost saving is not worth the extra time and distance traveled, since the vehicle could have returned to the satellite and been re-dispatched on another delivery. As mentioned before the cost-time-length valuation is up to each logistic service provider to decide and implement it through the vehicles preferences.

When looking at the results for both scenarios, we can see that sometimes the simplistic overlapping approach does offer better results than the optimiser, but globally it is not the best solution. The optimiser guarantees us the group specific best solution, so the minimal cost for all vehicles considered, leading to a Pareto-type solution. Another fault of the overlapping algorithm is its simplicity, none of the preferences and limitations imposed on the vehicles are considered, leading to a possible incomplete solution. The optimiser takes limitations and preferences into account, giving not the universal (impossible to calculate on a large-scale scenario), nor the user (vehicle) best solution, but somewhere in the middle, with a group specific best.

Besides the improvement in cost, we also tested the influence that the preferences of the vehicle have in PFARA. Restrictions in speed, length of route and time of travel affect the grouping of vehicles in the form of the preliminary clustering (speed) as well as in the optimisation problem (time and length). For that we modified the scenario presented previously, and made vehicle 5 slower, vehicle 41 to have a length limitation and vehicle 43 to have a time limitation. The results are presented in Table 3 having the first three columns with the cost, time and length of the route for the PFARA without restrictions and then the last three columns he cost, time and length of the route for the PFARA with restrictions.

We can see that the vehicles 30 to 34 and 10 to 14 are not affected by the preference modifications. Vehicles 1 through 4 are affected by the lack of vehicle 5 in the platoon, it being excluded due to its lower speed. This is turn also slightly affects the cost of vehicles 20, 22, 23 and 24. Given vehicle's 43 time and 41's length restrictions the previous formation and route of that platoon completely changes. Instead of a five vehicle platoon, we have two platoons, of two and three vehicles respectively.

Table 3. Comparison of PFARA on synthetic network, with and without different vehicular preferences.

Vehicle	$Cost$	$Time$	$Length$	$Cost_{Pref}$	$Time_{Pref}$	$Length_{Pref}$
pod1	2.27	55	500	2.783	55	500
pod2	0.6	11	100	0.75	11	100
pod3	1.35	22	200	1.75	22	200
pod4	1.77	33	300	2.25	33	300
pod5	1.945	44	400	9	67	400
pod10	3.85	44	400	3.85	44	400
pod11	2.35	33	300	2.35	33	300
pod12	1.35	22	200	1.35	22	200
pod13	0.6	11	100	0.6	11	100
pod 14	6.85	55	500	6.85	55	500
pod20	2.295	55	500	2.4	55	500
pod21	4.2	33	300	4.2	33	300
pod22	2.295	55	500	2.9	55	500
pod23	6.128	77	700	6.23	77	700
pod24	6.128	77	700	6.23	77	700
pod30	1.3	22	200	1.3	22	200
pod31	2	22	200	2	22	200
pod32	5.3	33	300	5.3	33	300
pod33	4.3	33	300	4.3	33	300
pod34	5	33	300	5	33	300
pod40	2.683	44	400	4	44	400
pod41	4.35	33	300	7.5	33	300
pod42	0.6	11	100	1.5	11	100
pod43	11.183	88	800	8	44	400
pod44	5.183	66	600	6.5	66	600

4.2 Performance

Figure 5 shows both algorithms' performance, representing the runtime of the PFARA and the overlapping algorithm respectively for the number of vehicles specified. These experiments were run on the realistic environment of the Berlin neighbourhood to guarantee PFARA could be applicable in a real-life scenario.

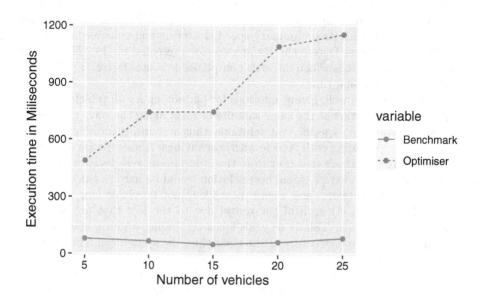

Fig. 5. Performance analysis.

When looking at the runtime of the algorithms, an evident increase happens with raising the number of vehicles. Even so, with 25 vehicles being considered for platooning at the same time, a result is still found in under two seconds. Considering that vehicles must not only be physically near each other to platoon, but also close time-wise, we can safely assume that in a real traffic scenario, no more than 20 vehicles would attempt platooning. In the case where a large platoon would meet another, due to them logically being one vehicle, PFARA is also easily solvable. With the more likely case of having five or ten vehicles, PFARA does really well, finding the best solution in 0.5 and 0.75 s respectively.

5   Discussion and Future Work

The algorithm presented in this paper provides a viable solution to the platoon forming and routing problem, for vehicles that are heterogeneous in nature and have limited capabilities.

When comparing our approach to the state of the art, PFARA takes into account multiple aspects aspect of travel (speed, time, length and cost). It does slightly underperform when comparing it to a more straightforward route-matching approach, but respects individual preferences and restrictions of vehicles and hence allows us to consider cross-provider platooning. To the best of our knowledge there are no other approaches to group vehicles in a platoon from a logical standpoint; as mentioned before, focus tends to be on the manoeuvres necessary to form, rather than what makes the vehicles form.

When comparing to the results in our previous work, having the same input data, we can see that the inclusion of time, speed and movement has a significant influence on the costs. More limitations on the system means less flexible grouping; but this also means that the groups are robust and a spontaneous change of route that could lead to disbandment is less likely. The new additions to the model have not affected the runtime of the algorithm negatively; on the contrary, PFaRA, with its preliminary speed clustering and enhanced optimisation problem performs faster than its predecessor presented in [33]. This is due to the added restrictions which discards non-plausible routes faster, significantly reducing computational time.

PFARA performs well, giving solutions for platooning for all vehicles considered; whether they start at the same satellite or meet along the way. The routes provided are the group specific best solutions, thus accounting for heterogeneity of the vehicles, providing each vehicle with cost savings. A user specific optimum would most likely exclude that user from the group because it deviates from the Pareto solution provided. A global best solution would be hard to calculate, due to the size of the network, and would most likely not be viable long term (for example for the entire length of the route) due to the fact that urban traffic is considerably volatile. This is why we focus on finding a group specific best solution and due to the structure of the algorithm, the system can be relaxed or restricted by removing or adding in constraints.

Our approach can be applied to arbitrary platoons and is not restricted to just logistic traffic. It is general enough for all types of vehicles and environments given that the vehicles preferences are known. One limitation of our current approach is that it does not consider the physical size of the vehicles. In urban traffic space is limited, and while heterogeneous platoons also include differently sized vehicles, one must guarantee that there is enough space to accommodate it. This is where the time headway proposed in [26] can be used to calculate the physical size of the platoon based on it's speed and the sizes of the vehicles included in it. We are planning to address this aspect in future research.

A further important extension of our model will include adding a negotiation algorithm that allows for vehicles to arrange further travel in a platoon through monetary exchanges at the end of their common route. This means that any vehicle accepting will be taking a detour from their ideal (selfish) route. The trade-off between cost reduction and travel limitations is up to each vehicle to calculate. Moreover due to the competitive nature of the LSPs, the compensations offered need to be high enough to be profitable for competitors in order to convince them to participate, while also being low enough for the offerer to maintain an upper hand in the market. Problems usually associated with this type of scenario such as deliberately accepting less than favourable routes to financially "hurt" the competition which also means waste of resources should be avoided.

6 Conclusion

The use of autonomous electric vehicles for last-mile deliveries in urban areas can bring benefits to customers, traffic managers and logistic service providers alike. They no not create emissions, can navigate through traffic alone and remove the need of a human driver. But the advantages they bring can be increased by having them travel in platoons when possible.

To guarantee the formation of platoons, all delivery vehicles from different logistic service providers should be willing to cooperate, thus creating heterogeneous groups. The vehicles have preferences (the minimum speed they are willing to accept for the platoon), restrictions (the end of the delivery time window, or travel distance manageable with their battery autonomy) and characteristics (maximum speed they can achieve) that have to be taken into account.

Our contribution is a grouping and routing algorithm for heterogeneous vehicles with same-day delivery in mind. The vehicles go through two grouping stages; one based on speed and another based on route and restrictions. The second stage is an optimisation problem that looks for the largest route overlap between the vehicles, while respecting their limitations (in the form on linear constraints). The objective is to minimise the cost of the vehicles considered, which is measured in traffic density. This approach offers feasible groups and routes, while maintaining the possibility of further relaxation or limitation of the system.

The proposed PFARA performs well in terms of solution quality (cost) and runtime performance, offering a viable and robust grouping and routing for all vehicles, independent of when and where they meet.

Acknowledgements. This work has been funded by the Deutsche Forschungsgemein-schaft (DFG, German Research Foundation) under Grant 227198829/GRK1931. The focus of the SocialCars Research Training Group is on significantly improving the city's future road traffic, through cooperative approaches. We also acknowledge Nelly Nyeck for her help with gathering results, Philipp Kraus for suggesting frameworks and Stephan Westphal for guidance towards a correct optimisation formulation.

References

1. Ali, A., Garcia, G., Martinet, P.: Urban platooning using a flatbed tow truck model. In: 2015 IEEE Intelligent Vehicles Symposium (IV), pp. 374–379. IEEE (2015)
2. Amir, A., Lindenbaum, M.: A generic grouping algorithm and its quantitative analysis. IEEE Trans. Pattern Anal. Mach. Intell. **20**(2), 168–185 (1998)
3. Amoozadeh, M., Deng, H., Chuah, C.N., Zhang, H.M., Ghosal, D.: Platoon management with cooperative adaptive cruise control enabled by vanet. Veh. Commun. **2**(2), 110–123 (2015)
4. Bengtsson, H.H., Chen, L., Voronov, A., Englund, C.: Interaction protocol for highway platoon merge. In: 2015 IEEE 18th International Conference on Intelligent Transportation Systems (ITSC), pp. 1971–1976. IEEE (2015)
5. Biswas, S., Tatchikou, R., Dion, F.: Vehicle-to-vehicle wireless communication protocols for enhancing highway traffic safety. IEEE Commun. Mag. **44**(1), 74–82 (2006)
6. Crainic, T.G.: City logistics. In: State-of-the-Art Decision-Making Tools in the Information-Intensive Age, pp. 181–212. INFORMS (2008)
7. Crainic, T.G., Perboli, G., Mancini, S., Tadei, R.: Two-echelon vehicle routing problem: a satellite location analysis. Procedia-Soc. Behav. Sci. **2**(3), 5944–5955 (2010)
8. Crainic, T.G., Sgalambro, A.: Service network design models for two-tier city logistics. Optim. Lett. **8**(4), 1375–1387 (2013). https://doi.org/10.1007/s11590-013-0662-1
9. Dennisen, S.L., Müller, J.P.: Iterative committee elections for collective decision-making in a ride-sharing application. In: ATT@ IJCAI (2016)
10. Gevaers, R., Van de Voorde, E., Vanelslander, T.: Characteristics and typology of last-mile logistics from an innovation perspective in an urban context. City Distribution Urban Freight Transp. Multiple Perspect. Edward Elgar Publishing, 56–71 (2011)
11. Gordon, I.E.: Theories of Visual Perception. Psychology Press, United Kingdom (2004)
12. Gurobi: Gurobi optimization (2018). https://www.openstreetmap.org
13. Haas, I., Friedrich, B.: An autonomous connected platoon-based system for city-logistics: development and examination of travel time aspects. Transportmetrica A: Transp. Sci. 1–18 (2018)
14. Havaldar, P., Medioni, G., Stein, F.: Extraction of groups for recognition. In: Eklundh, J.-O. (ed.) ECCV 1994. LNCS, vol. 800, pp. 251–261. Springer, Heidelberg (1994). https://doi.org/10.1007/3-540-57956-7_30
15. Kagaya, S., Kikuchi, S., Donnelly, R.A.: Use of a fuzzy theory technique for grouping of trips in the vehicle routing and scheduling problem. Eur. J. Oper. Res. **76**(1), 143–154 (1994)

16. Khalifa, A., Kermorgant, O., Dominguez, S., Martinet, P.: Vehicles platooning in urban environment: consensus-based longitudinal control with limited communications capabilities. In: International Conference on Control, Automation, Robotics and Vision (2018)

17. Khan, M.A., Boloni, L.: Convoy driving through ad-hoc coalition formation. In: 11th IEEE Real Time and Embedded Technology and Applications Symposium, pp. 98–105. IEEE (2005)

18. Kraus, P.: Colormap (2018). https://github.com/flashpixx/colormap

19. Krempl, S.: LKW platooning; sicher aber nicht so sparsam wie erwartet (2019). https://www.heise.de/newsticker/meldung/LKW-Platooning-Sicher-aber-nicht-so-sparsam-wie-erwartet-4419922.html

20. Larson, J., Liang, K.Y., Johansson, K.H.: A distributed framework for coordinated heavy-duty vehicle platooning. IEEE Trans. Intell. Transp. Syst. **16**(1), 419–429 (2014)

21. Lewis, B.J.: Platoon movement of traffic from an isolated signalized intersection. Highway Res. Board Bull. (178) (1958)

22. Lioris, J., Pedarsani, R., Tascikaraoglu, F.Y., Varaiya, P.: Platoons of connected vehicles can double throughput in urban roads. Transp. Res. Part C: Emerging Technol. **77**, 292–305 (2017)

23. Mojena, R.: Hierarchical grouping methods and stopping rules: an evaluation. Comput. J. **20**(4), 359–363 (1977)

24. O'Madadhain, J., Fisher, D., Nelson, T.: Jung, java universal network/graph framework (2018). http://jung.sourceforge.net/index.html

25. Ploeg, J., et al.: Cooperative automated maneuvering at the 2016 grand cooperative driving challenge. IEEE Trans. Intell. Transp. Syst. **19**(4), 1213–1226 (2017)

26. Ploeg, J., Van De Wouw, N., Nijmeijer, H.: LP string stability of cascaded systems: application to vehicle platooning. IEEE Trans. Control Syst. Technol. **22**(2), 786–793 (2013)

27. Robinson, T., Chan, E., Coelingh, E.: Operating platoons on public motorways: an introduction to the sartre platooning programme. In: 17th World Congress on Intelligent Transport Systems, vol. 1, p. 12 (2010)

28. Sanderson, D., Busquets, D., Pitt, J.: A micro-meso-macro approach to intelligent transportation systems. In: 2012 IEEE Sixth International Conference on Self-Adaptive and Self-Organizing Systems Workshops, pp. 77–82. IEEE (2012)

29. Sanderson, D., Pitt, J.: Institutionalised consensus in vehicular networks: executable specification and empirical validation. In: 2012 IEEE Sixth International Conference on Self-Adaptive and Self-Organizing Systems Workshops, pp. 71–76. IEEE (2012)

30. Scherr, Y.O., Neumann-Saavedra, B.A., Hewitt, M., Mattfeld, D.C.: Service network design for same day delivery with mixed autonomous fleets. Transp. Res. Procedia **30**, 23–32 (2018)

31. Schindler, J., Dariani, R., Rondinone, M., Walter, T.: Dynamic and flexible platooning in urban areas. In: AAET Automatisiertes und vernetztes Fahren Conference 2018 (2018)

32. Schuhl, A.: The probability theory applied to distribution of vehicles on two-lane highways (1955)

33. Sebe, S., Kraus, P., Müller, J.P., Westphal, S.: Cross-provider platoons for same-day delivery. In: Proceedings of the 5th International Conference on Vehicle Technology and Intelligent Transport Systems - Volume 1: VEHITS, pp. 106–116. INSTICC, SciTePress (2019). https://doi.org/10.5220/0007689601060116

34. Stabler, B., Bar-Gera, H., Sall, E.: Transportation networks for research (2018). https://github.com/bstabler/TransportationNetworks
35. Steiger, M.: jxmapviewer2 github (2012). https://github.com/msteiger/jxmapviewer2
36. Swaroop, D., Hedrick, J.K.: Constant spacing strategies for platooning in automated highway systems. J. Dyn. Syst. Meas. Control **121**(3), 462–470 (1999)
37. Taleb, T., Sakhaee, E., Jamalipour, A., Hashimoto, K., Kato, N., Nemoto, Y.: A stable routing protocol to support its services in vanet networks. IEEE Trans. Veh. Technol. **56**(6), 3337–3347 (2007)
38. Thyng, K.M., Greene, C.A., Hetland, R.D., Zimmerle, H.M., DiMarco, S.F.: True colors of oceanography: guidelines for effective and accurate colormap selection. Oceanography **29**(3), 9–13 (2016)
39. Treiber, M., Kesting, A.: Trajectory and floating-car data. In: Traffic Flow Dynamics, pp. 15–18. Springer (2013)
40. Wald, A., Wolfowitz, J.: Optimum character of the sequential probability ratio test. Ann. Math. Stat. 326–339 (1948)

Intrusion Response System for Vehicles: Challenges and Vision

Mohammad Hamad$^{(\boxtimes)}$ ⓘ, Marinos Tsantekidis ⓘ, and Vassilis Prevelakis ⓘ

TU Braunschweig, Institute of Computer and Network Engineering,
38108 Braunschweig, Germany
{mhamad,mtsantekidis,prevelakis}@ida.ing.tu-bs.de
https://www.ida.ing.tu-bs.de/en/research/embedded-security/

Abstract. Recently, significant developments were introduced within the vehicular domain, making the modern vehicle a network of a multitude of embedded systems communicating with each other, while adhering to safety-critical and secure systems specifications. Many technologies have been integrated within modern vehicles to give them the capability to interact with the outside world. These advances have significantly enlarged the attack surface. We already have numerous instances of successful penetration of vehicular networks both from inside the vehicle and from the outside. To face these attacks, many intrusion prevention and detection mechanisms were implemented inside a vehicular system. Nonetheless, even if all security mitigation is adopted, an attack still can happen. In critical-safety environments, such as the vehicle, the response to the attack is as essential as detecting the attack itself. Although Intrusion Response Systems (IRSs) have been adopted in other domains to add an extra layer of security, there is a lack of such systems in the vehicular field. In this work, we investigate the challenges and identify the requirements for integrating such a mechanism within the vehicle system. Besides, we present an IRS framework, which meets the identified requirements. Also, we discuss the integration of IRS through the vehicle system development and the different aspects which support such a process. Finally, we use the automated obstacle avoidance system to explain how we could develop intrusion response strategies and to measure the overhead of such security system.

Keywords: Security · Automotive security · Intrusion response system intrusion detection system

1 Introduction

The notion of securing intra-vehicle systems was based on the fact that a vehicle is physically protected. The only way to hack the car is to have physical access to it and to benefit from the external interfaces which give the attacker direct access to the internal network. The ODB-II port used to be the most common interface to give an attacker such direct access. Other interfaces such as CD/DVD players

ⓒ Springer Nature Switzerland AG 2021
M. Helfert et al. (Eds.): SMARTGREENS 2019/VEHITS 2019, CCIS 1217, pp. 321–341, 2021.
https://doi.org/10.1007/978-3-030-68028-2_15

or USB ports (which are used to connect external devices, e.g. a smartphone) can also be leveraged to the same effect [7]. However, the newly introduced technologies which enable the car to interconnect with the outside world, made the physical isolation of the intra-vehicle network obsolete. Nowadays, attackers are able to exploit various vulnerabilities within the automotive system, hack and gain control of the vehicle remotely.

Traditionally, the intra-vehicle bus systems have been developed to fulfill safety, cost and efficiency requirements without considering any security risks. For example, Controller Area Network (CAN) messages are broadcasted in clear text and without any real proof about their integrity [28]. Consequently, any malicious Electronic Control Unit (ECU) can pretend to be any other legitimate ECU (i.e., *masquerade attacks*), intercept all the exchanged messages among the different ECUs (i.e., *man-in-the-middle attacks (MITM)*), manipulate the transmitted data (i.e., *spoofing attacks*) or fraudulently delay or re-transmit previous messages (i.e., *replay attacks*). In addition, the malicious component can flood the bus with fake high-priority messages to disrupt the other communications (i.e., *Denial of Service (DoS) attacks*) [34]. However, these issues are not limited only to the CAN bus. Other bus systems (i.e., Ethernet [39], FlexRay [38], LIN [46]) suffer from similar deficiencies, and they used to and still present targets of many attacks.

Wireless networking, which is used by multiple applications in the vehicle, is not in better condition when it comes to security. Many attackers are targeting systems which depend on the wireless communications. For example, Roulf et al. [24] investigated the Tire Pressure Monitoring System (TPMS). They found that the sensors transmitted messages without any security protection. Other evidence showed that the attacker could open a vehicle's doors without the key [15,47] by replaying wirelessly transmitted messages between the car and the smart key.

Prevention mechanisms represent the first line of security defense for the automotive system, which aims to prevent the occurrence of attacks proactively. Many prevention mechanisms were adopted to guarantee data confidentiality, data integrity, and to prevent unauthorized third parties from accessing services and communication channels on-board the vehicle. These mechanisms include:

- The secure development of the automotive software components, to impede the attacker from exploiting software vulnerabilities.
- The development of hardware security mechanisms, to support the reliable execution and isolation of these components, to prevent the attacker from controlling the whole system in case they succeeded compromising one part.
- The definition of a secure link and a proper access control mechanism, to support the secure communication among these components while they are running and prevent any malicious third party from interfering with their interactions.
- The development of a reliable framework to update these components, to prevent malicious parties from introducing new vulnerabilities.

Despite the adoption of all the proactive security mechanisms mentioned in the previous section, there is no guarantee that the system becomes secure and that no attacker can strike it. There is no absolute security of a system, and the proof is that despite all these mitigation mechanisms, attackers were able to exploit these vulnerabilities and mount severe attacks against a vehicle [7,24,28]. Therefore, another layer of protection was introduced (i.e., Intrusion Detection Systems (IDSs)) to monitor the vehicular system and its network, and to detect any violation of a predefined security policy or any malicious behavior of the system components during operation [19,29].

Since a vehicle is a safety-critical system, the detection of an attack is as pivotal as the response to the attack itself. When an attack against a component is detected, one way to respond to this attack is by restarting the affected component [45], in hope that the resulting failure was a transient one. When considering safety-critical systems, a component that is important to the operation of such a system may cause physical damage if it becomes non-functional, so this option is not optimal or even desired [30]. High system resilience and safety are two fundamental aspects that need to be always guaranteed by several response strategies, which the security policy of the vehicle implements. These response strategies are implemented through an IRS. Generally - and even more so in the vehicular domain - IRSs have received less attention and research effort compared to IDSs [44] until now.

In this chapter, we try to investigate the main requirements and challenges that face the adoption of IRSs in the vehicular domain. Also, we present an IRS framework, which meets the identified requirements. Furthermore, we discuss the integration of IRS through the vehicle system development and the different aspects which support such a process. Finally, we use the automated obstacle avoidance system to explain how we could develop intrusion response strategies and to measure the overhead of such a system. This work is an extension of our previous work [20] where we revised the requirements and challenges section. Also, we have expanded the framework description and introduced intrusion response exchange protocol. Finally, we measured the added overhead of the proposed protocol.

The rest of the chapter is organized as follows. Section 2 mentions the current state of affairs concerning IRSs. In Sect. 3, we present the challenges which face IRSs in a vehicular context and the requirements of such a system. In Sect. 4, we present our intrusion response framework for in-vehicle system. The development of this framework and the different related aspects are explained in Sect. 5. In Sect. 6, we discuss the development process as well as the proposed responses using autonomous driving as a use case. We evaluate our prototype system in this section too. Finally, we conclude our chapter in Sect. 7.

2 Intrusion Response Systems

As the advancement of technology offers capabilities which result in attackers on every level getting more competent and effective, attacks have become more elaborate. Therefore, we need to establish an adequate level of security in software systems. Complete security of a system is unfeasible and so it becomes imperative to detect a situation where an attack might be unfolding and take some action to respond to it. Consequently, intrusion prevention mechanisms (firewalls, cryptography, access control, etc.) alone are not sufficient to mitigate these attacks. IDSs were widely developed to detect, analyze and report intrusions in a computing system. Whenever a task behaves abnormally or violates a predefined security policy, the IDS considers this task as a malicious one. Some IDSs have already implemented limited static responses, such as generating an alarm or report [27]. However, with increasing levels of attacks' complexity and targeted domains, more comprehensive response strategies are required. These strategies could be implemented through an IRS.

Authors in [13,23,43,44] have surveyed the existing IRSs. They have proposed a taxonomy of these systems according to different characteristics:

Activity of Triggered Response: This feature determines the activity of the selected response. IRSs can issue a response which aims to limit the effect of the attack and minimize further damage (i.e., active response). Another IRSs could respond only by notifying (or alarming) the system of the existing attack (i.e., passive response).

Time Instance of the Response: This aspect determines when the responding action should take place. IRS either activate the response after the occurrence of the attack (delayed response) as in [31] or take action before the attack has affected the system resources (proactive response), such as [14].

Level of Automation: This characteristic defines how the response occurs. Some IRSs require the interference of the system administrator in order to apply the predefined response (manual response), while others are totally independent and do not require any human interaction to react to an intrusion (automatic response).

Ability to Adjust: This is used to distinguish between the different IRSs based on the way these systems choose the applied responses. Most of the IRSs use a fixed predefined response for a certain alert (static response) [32,40]. A number of IRSs choose the response based on attack metrics, therefore the response for the same attack could be different from one instance to another (dynamic response) such as [2,48].

Cooperation Capabilities: This characteristic determines how the IRS acts during the attack. This includes whether it works alone and applies its chosen response locally (stand-alone system) such as [2], or it collaborates with other coexisting IRSs to apply the selected response locally and globally (collaborative), such as [31].

3   Vehicular Intrusion Response System

In the vehicular domain, many authors have mentioned the need for an effective intrusion response mechanism for the vehicle system [12,42]. However, very few authors have investigated the design of such a system; even in these few proposals, authors have looked at the response as a part of the intrusion detection framework [11, 21]. Recently, Völep et al. [50] have proposed an intrusion-tolerant architecture to tolerate partial compromise of software components of an autonomous vehicle. In other cases, e.g. [36], an intrusion detection and adaptive response mechanism was designed to detect a range of attacks and to provide an effective response for Mobile Ad-hoc Networks (MANETs).

3.1 Challenges

The vehicle, which is considered as a safety-critical system, has its own special properties and restrictions which limit the adoption of the existing IRS of the other domains. Automotive systems are different from the conventional networks from many perspectives. In this section, we explain some of these challenges which affect the design of any intrusion response framework for the in-vehicle system.

- **Highly Interconnected Architecture:** A modern vehicle contains more than 70 microcontroller-based computers (ECUs) which are distributed all over the vehicle, communicating among themselves via different types of networks such as CAN, Flexray and Ethernet [5]. In order the vehicle function properly and safely, these ECUs must exchange data, therefore many of them share the same bus system. Besides safety considerations, a vehicle must also provide comfort to its passengers (e.g. infotainment, air conditioning, etc.), which is serviced by separate ECUs. The unrestricted interaction among all those ECUs puts the whole system in danger. An attacker could launch a stepping-stone attack, where they compromise a less important ECU with weaker security (e.g., the entertainment system), in order to gain control of a more crucial one (e.g. engine system) [28]. Consequently, any response or mitigation mechanism should consider the highly interconnected and distributed nature of a vehicular environment.
- **Limited Resources:** The computational power of the embedded ECUs inside a vehicle is far lower compared to the capabilities of computers and servers in traditional networks. This limits the possibility of porting strategies which are already in place in those networks, because the limited-resources ECUs will not be able to cope with them.
- **Ever-changing Scenery:** Current and future vehicles are ever-changing environments where changes may take place after their production. Cars are designed to work for an average of 12 years [33]. So, a car in its lifespan may have updates for both its hardware and software components. This means that the rules of the security policies in an IRS cannot be static, but must be defined as dynamic and changing in order to accommodate the behavior of the newly introduced components.
- **Autonomous and Semi-autonomous Nature:** In a traditional IT environment, a human administrator would be expected to approve and apply responses. Nowadays, some might consider the driver as the administrator of

the vehicular environment. However, for safety reasons, the driver's attention must not be diverted while driving. Moreover, a driver may not have the technical knowledge to address an attack underway or the required response, so must not deal with such decisions. Furthermore, in the case of an autonomous car, these actions will be performed automatically, without any input from the driver.

3.2   Requirements

The existing IRSs, which are deployed on other domains, deal with only a subset of the aforementioned challenges. Therefore, based on both the challenges of the vehicular domain and the general IRS taxonomies (see Sect. 2), we explain here the desired properties for any proposed IRS for an intra-vehicle system. The proposed IRS should be:

Predictive: The IRS should predict an attack on the system and not wait until after the attack takes place to detect it. Early prediction provides the system with a sufficient amount of time to respond in an effective manner. However, false positives are of notable concern here. Unfortunately, as the security constraints are tightened, the likelihood of false positives increases.

Reactive: The proposed system should react in a way that mitigates the damage caused by the attack and prevents its propagation to other subsystems. In addition, it must consider issues such as containment, continued availability, interaction with other subsystems and, in certain cases, latency. These requirements are in many cases in conflict with each other; for example, security and availability often work against one another [49].

Proper: The IRS should react properly, based on the type and target of the potential attack. In a case where the IRS detects that a component is acting off-nominally, it responds to that behavior by terminating (killing) the running process and executing a new instance. However, such a response is not preferable because it may cause an accident. Moreover, because of the lack of direct interaction with the driver to solve the security issue, terminating the malicious task without any relevant information about vulnerability may not be the right course of action, as an attacker could use the same obscure vulnerability to break the newly instantiated task repeatedly.

Diverse: The IRS should be designed to respond in multiple ways, including a fully automated response. When a task is terminated, regardless of the cause of termination (security related or otherwise) the system should respond to the failure by (i) using a redundant component to provide the functionality that is lost with the demise of the failed task, (ii) determining whether the system can continue running without this functionality (fail-continue), or (iii) forcing the system into a fail-safe condition, i.e. it goes into a mode where the safety of the vehicle and passengers is assured even if the system can no longer continue to operate. Although current regulations ensure that safety decisions must only be taken by the driver [22], the situation may need to be changed to reflect the rise of autonomous and self-driving technology.

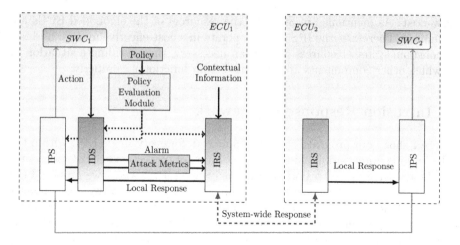

Fig. 1. Intrusion response system and the relation with IDS and IPS.

In the meantime, a semi-automated response which requires partial interaction with the driver could be adopted.

Changing: The IRS must be able to differentiate its response to the same attack based on several factors, such as contextual information during the vehicle's different operational modes, the attack severity, the subsystem targeted and other dependent systems. However, creating static security rules or a decision table for all these different specifications is not a trivial task. Therefore, the use of a dynamic security policy to express these parameters could be a preferable solution [9,18].

Deactivable: Any security measure employed to counter a malicious attempt comes at a price. As such, the IRS introduces overhead on the system's performance, based on the type and duration of the response. To minimize this overhead, any proposed IRS should be able to deactivate the response mechanism when specific, predefined conditions specified within the security policy are met [26].

Localized: Each ECU should be protected by its own IRS. When a component is potentially under attack, the corresponding IRS detects the malicious attempt and decides locally how to deal with it. Although this decision may address the attack against the specific component, it may not be optimal for the overall system. Each individual component should be able to implement a response strategy locally which, however, must be defined for the system as a whole.

Responsive: Activating the response action should take place immediately after the attack is detected. If a significant amount of time passes, the damage might already be done, negating the existence of the IRS. Therefore, the proposed IRS should evaluate the security policy as well as any other inputs with minimal delay.

Low-cost: As mentioned in Sect. 3.1 the resources of the embedded ECUs are limited. Therefore, the IRS should operate in a cost-effective manner and not consume system resources more than necessary, thus avoiding a situation in which other components are prevented from functioning properly.

4   Intrusion Response Framework

Figure 1 shows our proposed security framework for every single ECU within the vehicle. This framework includes different layers of protection against intrusions. The first layer is the intrusion prevention system (IPS), where we proposed the use of a firewall to intercept the communications of each software component (SWC). Besides IRS, The framework depends on IDS to monitor the behavior of the software components to notify the IRS about the intrusion existence. The IRS represents the last layer of protection. It used to determine the actions when a security violation is detected either by IDS or IPS. The main aim of this layer is protecting the vehicle from entering unstable states as a result of the discovered attack.

The IRS requires inputs from the different system components (such as the properties of the detected attack or off-nominal behavior) which is delivered by the IPS or the IDS as a part of the alarm message sent to the IRS whenever an incident is detected. The security policy is also needed for this layer since it includes the possible responses to different attacks. Contextual and operational information is also gathered by a detective service and delivered to the IRS when it is required. The IRS contains a repository which is used to store the collocated characteristics of attacks (i.e., aim, scenario, severity, etc.). This information is used as feedback or input for the next threat modeling process.

Improving the response strategies of any security mechanism is dependent on early detection (i.e., early prediction) of a potential attack. The early prediction provides the system with a sufficient amount of time to initiate recovery actions to respond effectively. Figure 2 shows the timeline of the malicious event (normal, suspicious, and malicious) and the significant role which the IDS can play to give the IRS a large period to react. It also shows how the security attack will turn by the time into a failure which requires the interference of the safety countermeasures (i.e., Fault Tolerance System (FTS)).

The IDS is used to monitor and evaluate the behavior of the different vehicle software components within each ECU depending on predefined security policies. Each policy specifies the correct functioning of the given component. Any violation of this policy is used as a prediction of a potential security breach. At this point, the task enters becomes suspicious. The activation of any response mechanism is triggered as soon as the IRS receives an alarm from the IDS about a detected potential attack. Whenever the IDS detect a suspicious, the IRS is responsible for activating local and system-wide responding strategies.

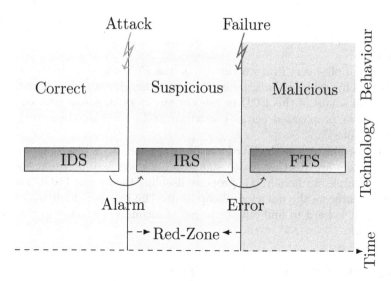

Fig. 2. The relation between different technologies to handle the different behaviors of software component.

4.1   Local Response Strategies

The local tactics are used to respond to an attack against a component, other components on the same ECU, as well as the whole ECU itself. The local response to the *malicious component* can be:

- **Suspicious/Malicious Operational:** Although the task is considered malicious, the IRS leaves the task running until a certain limit. While it is executing, the IRS starts a series of possible responses, e.g., the component could be isolated and its communication with the other components on the same ECU or with other sub-systems becomes very limited and begins to be traced. The logged information can be used later to design a proper mitigation mechanism. Moreover, the trust level of the component is degraded, so other components become more cautious about the information delivered to/from this component.
- **Suspicious/Malicious Silent:** The IRS kills the process whenever it exceeds the ultimate bound since the component will suffer from a security failure at this point [1]. Although the IRS may stop the component at the end, which could be the goal of the attacker by causing a DoS, the IRS has plenty of time to activate other response strategies ahead of this point. On the other hand, the IRS can implement a response which ensures that a new healthy instance of the malicious component is initiated with all of its state reverted back to a specific point where it was executing correctly before killing the malicious one.

All mentioned tactics for the infected component affect the *other components on the same ECU* as well. For example, some less critical software components which are mapped to the same ECU where the malicious component is running on, may have to become silent/inactive to save resources for the system to audit and recover.

The IRS applies very firm restrictions on the *ECU which hosts the malicious component*. This could include performing more security auditing operations on the communications of this ECU to prevent any stepping-stone attacks. In case the attack was propagated across the whole ECU, total isolation of the ECU could be adopted.

It is important to note that the location where the IRS is placed as well as the targeted system architecture play a significant role in choosing the proper reaction. For example, authors in [11] propose disabling the targeted ECU instead of the one which hosts the malicious component. The reason behind such a selection is that it is hard to find out the origin of incoming messages in the case of CAN network.

4.2 System-Wide Response Strategies

System-wide responses are implemented by other IRSs on different dependent ECUs within the vehicle. Such responses are activated as soon as a notification from the IRS where the suspicious component exists, is initiated. We can look at these response strategies as an extension of the local ones. Here we summarize some of these possible responses based on the locally applied response:

- **Reallocation:** As we mentioned before, IRSs aim to ensure the availability of the different components by initiating at least one new healthy instance of the malicious component (more than one replica can be used at the same time). The place where the new instance is mapped is critical for the other dependent system components. In case the new replica is mapped to a new ECU, other components that depend on the misbehaving one need to communicate with the newly initiated component instead. This requires the use of a new communication configuration to adjust the reallocation.
- **Degradation and Propagation:** as a result of stopping certain non-critical software components on the malicious ECU to support the adoption of local responses. The same strategy has to be applied to other interrelated ECUs which include components dependent on the silent ones. In the same manner, if the trust level of the provided data by the malicious component gets reduced, the trust level of the other elements which use this data needs to be adjusted accordingly.
- **Combination:** The IRS could adopt a combination of the aforementioned tactics to achieve the best possible protection.

4.3 Intrusion Response Exchange Protocol

Intrusion Response eXchange Protocol (IRXP) is used to exchange the attack information and the system-wide response strategies among the different IRSs.

Figure 3 represents the different steps of IRXP. The protocol is activated whenever the IDS or IPS on an ECU detect a violation of the security policy of any software components on that ECU. The IDS or IPS pass the information of this violation as an alarm to activate the local IRS. This alarm includes detailed information about the attack (or the suspicious action). This information includes the targeted component, the attack details, and attack detection time and transmitted using a predefined format similar to the alarm format proposed in [8].

This information is used by the local IRS to determine the required local response for this attack. Policy Evaluation Module (PEM) is used to support identifying such responses based on the attack metrics as well as the local system policy. The IRS takes these responses and sends them to the suitable component to be executed. For example, it could be a new communication rule which needs to be added to the decisions repository of the security module. Later, these attack metrics can be customized and sent to the other IRSs hosted by other ECUs which could be affected by the local response. Besides the basic information about the attack, the applied local responses are also propagated to ensure the adoption of the system-wide response. we refer to these information as a message (Msg).

In order to prevent any malicious third parties from manipulating the transmitted message, the IRS uses the ECU's private key to sign the message (in our case IRS uses ECU_{1SK}). Also, a monotonic counter value can be used to prevent replay attacks by ensuring the IRS response freshness. IRS on the remote ECU (i.e., ECU_2) uses the received public key of the other ECU (ECU_{1PK}) to validate the message which will be used to feed PEM (on ECU_2) with the required information to determine its local response. At this point, the IRS on ECU_2 repeats the steps that the IRS on ECU_1 has already performed.

5   Development Process of Vehicular IRS

Developing the response strategies to cover the large number of distributed components is a difficult task, requiring detailed knowledge of possible interaction paths and the dependencies among all those components, as well as the security threats that could target them along with the possible attack scenarios. When considering an evolving system, which shall be updateable (where component interactions may change), this task becomes even more difficult and requires a framework which offers IRS support under concurrent change. Therefore, the development of the response strategies has to be well planned through the design and life-cycle of the system (i.e., it should be part of the different stages the V-model).

In this section we show how to integrate the development of the IRS within the whole development process of the vehicular system. In addition, we discuss the various aspects of the system which affect the design and implementation of the IRS. Figure 4 shows the general scheme to develop the IRS. Here, we explain the different aspects which need to be considered during the development of the different responses.

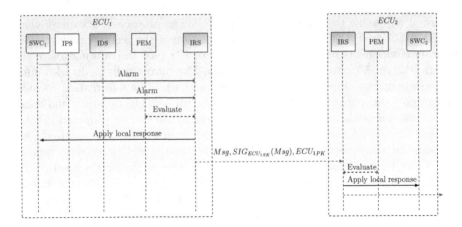

Fig. 3. Intrusion response exchange protocol.

5.1   Threat Model

Threat modeling is a systematic approach for describing and classifying the security threats that a system faces. Moreover, it provides significant information that would help to safeguard the target system and to develop effective response strategies against any attacks. During the design stage of the V-model, security requirements are defined to address all existing vulnerabilities identified

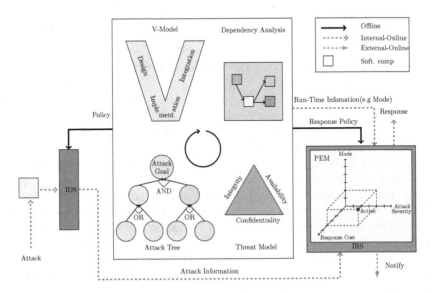

Fig. 4. General scheme of IRS development [20].

by the threat model. At the same time, the response actions for violating these requirements are defined in an abstract view. At a later stage (i.e. implementation and integration) the response actions become more detailed to reflect the final system architecture and keep complying to the initial actions.

Generally, an attacker aims to violate one or more of the next requirements:

- Confidentiality: unauthorized disclosure of the content of data (i.e. saved data or exchanged messages) by unauthorized actors.
- Integrity: unauthorized change of the software component itself, the runtime environment, saved data, or exchanged messages among the different components.
- Availability: loss of the ability to reach a component or service as a result of unintended or malicious actions.

In addition, threat modeling provides us with a good comprehension about the prospective attackers, their capabilities and their objectives. This information is used by the attack tree to perform a risk assessment of each attack which affects the selection of the response strategy based on the attack severity.

5.2   Attack Tree

As we mentioned above, the main goal of the attackers is to violate the security requirements via different tools and scenarios. An attack tree [41] is used to investigate most of these scenarios in a tree structure. The root of the tree represents the attacker's essential goal (e.g. make one component unavailable), while the intermediate nodes of the tree (sub-goals) define different stages to achieve this goal. The success of an attack depends on the subsequent success of interrelated attack steps. By using an attack tree, we can model the path that an attacker can use to reach their ultimate goal. This path may require compromising other components, which could be mapped to the same ECU where the target component is located or in a different one (stepping-stone attack).

The attack tree is created off-line for each system asset (e.g. hardware, software, data) [17]. Then, the defined attack trees are used to evaluate the security risks, to calculate the probability of a successful attack and to measure the defense (local response) cost [10]. Calculating these metrics depends on different aspects [25], as well as the information provided by the threat model. The attack information, which is delivered by the IDS to the IRS after detecting the security violation, is used as an input for the IRS to choose the appropriate response.

5.3   Dependency Analysis

Another important aspect of implementing the response mechanism is to determine all dependency relations between other components and the malicious one. We call a task *dependent* on another task when it uses a service provided by that task. These relationships can be denoted in a dependency tree [48]. Then the direct and indirect dependencies are specified.

Moestl et al. [35] have proposed a cross-layer dependency analysis to detect dependencies between the different components across the different architectural model layers in safety-critical systems such as a vehicle. By defining the dependencies, the IRS on the local platform can notify all other dependent subsystems about the attack, thus response mechanisms on other platforms are also deployed. In addition, the system-wide response cost can be evaluated by using the dependency analysis.

5.4 Security Policy

A security policy is used to define the response of the system when a task becomes suspicious, the conditions under which a monitored task may return to normal state and, finally, the response to a task breaching its ultimate limit (i.e., causes a failure). The main challenge in this context is to define a comprehensive security policy to manage the various responses in the in-vehicle system after the final integration phase in the development process. This challenge originates from the large number of integrated ECUs in the vehicle, the complexity of the dependencies between the different components on each ECU and the various actors who participate in the development process of these components. Additionally, another challenge comes from the need to update the response strategies in a later stage to reflect the changes on the actual system architecture after a system update or upgrade. Therefore, the response policy is developed in an abstract way and is gradually detailed during the different development phases (design, implementation, integration) similar to [18]. The defined policy is separated from the service itself, which facilitates the independent update of both.

Listing 1.1. Security Policy Structure.

```
if (property = = normal)
  do (allow)
else //suspicious
  if (property = = suspicious)
    if (attack_severity= = high)
      if(mode = = startup)
        do(response)
  else //malicious
    do(response)
```

Listing 1.1 shows the structure of the security policy. Based on a certain property of a component, such as execution time, power consumption, system call distribution or bit-rate of message exchange, the boundary of the activating IRS is determined in the policy and the response action within each zone is defined. Other properties such as the system operational modes (e.g. vehicle at startup mode) as well as the attack severity could affect choosing the response action. All this information is collected while the system is running and evaluated using the PEM to choose an action dynamically.

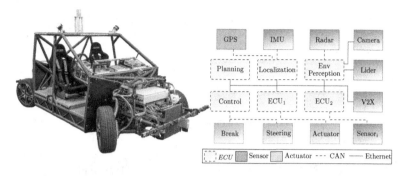

Fig. 5. MOBILE (left) and a simplified hardware architecture and software components for autonomous driving system (right).

6 Use-Case

In this work, we consider the research vehicle MOBILE (see Fig. 5), built at the Institute of Control Engineering [3] to be used as a demonstrator platform with which we can describe and check the applicability of our proposed IRS.

We will use the automated obstacle avoidance system to explain how we could develop intrusion response strategies. The obstacle avoidance system is one of the vital features which aims to ensure safe vehicle operation and ride comfort of the autonomous vehicle. Figure 5 depicts the simplified hardware architecture of the autonomous vehicle driving system as well as the network architecture for the main subsystems which support the implementation of the automated obstacle avoidance system.

One important functionality which is needed for this system is the localization. This functionality gives the vehicle the ability to determine its position with respect to the environment. The main information resource for this functionality is provided by the Global Position System (GPS). We want to focus on this functionality to show how we could develop response strategies when a security violation targets it and discuss all the aspects presented in previous Section. Figure 6 shows part of the final integration of that system on the actual ECUs. Also, it presents the communication between the different components on these ECUS.

In the first stage, the security requirements for the relations between this functionality and other ones are defined: (a) availability and (b) integrity. Any violation of these requirements demands the adoption of the proper responses. Attack trees are developed to identify all the attack scenarios which could violate these two requirements. Attacks such as spoofing data attack, jamming attack, and many others are defined [6, 37]. Based on the attack details, detection mechanisms are defined and stated in the security policy to identify those attacks while the system is on-line.

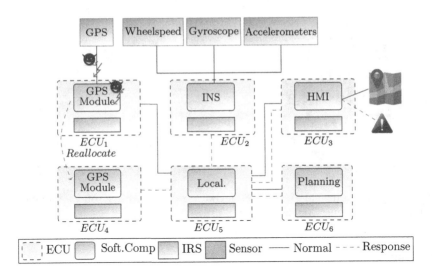

Fig. 6. Response strategies in the presence of security attack on localization functionality of autonomous vehicle use-case.

The responses to these attacks are also defined. One response is receiving the service from anther source. The Inertial Navigation System (INS) could be used as a temporary resource for providing localization information. Another response option is to reallocate the GPS module (in case of the Receiver Software Attack [37]) either within the same ECU or on another one (ECU_4 on our use-case). Both strategies require the communication reconfiguration for the directly dependent components. Dependency analysis shows that the localization component (*Local.*), which is mapped to ECU_5, directly depends on the GPS module. Therefore, the security policy related to this component (i.e., *Local.*) on ECU_5 should enable two communication paths with ECU_2 and ECU_4 whenever the *GPS Module* is behaving maliciously.

It can also disable the link with ECU_1 to prevent the attack propagation, while the *HMI* component, which is mapped to ECU_3 and indirectly dependent on the *GPS module*, can keep displaying the given data on the map, but with an alarm sign activated to express the low level of GPS data trust as shown in Fig. 6

Implementation: We implemented a prototype of our IRS on a single platform. We used a Raspberry Pi 3 (RPi) running a mickrokernel-based operating system (Genode) to give us more capabilities to control the communication among the different components on the same platform as well as the isolation mechanism for the tasks. We used Keynote Trust management [4] to express the security policy and to evaluate it later.

We measured the required time for choosing the proper response when one component becomes malicious. This time includes the evaluation time of the security policies of all dependent components in the same platform. Figure 7, shows the measured time when 1 to 6 components are involved.

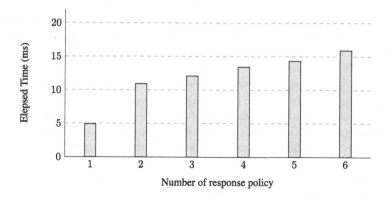

Fig. 7. Required evaluation time for dependent components on the same RPi [20].

Also, we measured the required time to transmit the security policies which contain the proposed response between tow different ECUs (i.e., RPIs). Figure 8 shows the result of this measurement. The result indicate that the increase of policy numbers lead to high latency.

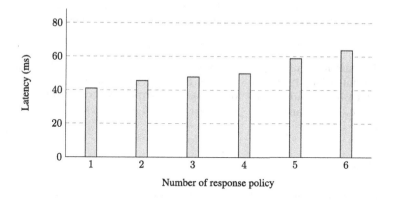

Fig. 8. Transmission time as a function of the response policy number.

7   Conclusion

We propose to develop an IRS framework under which response strategies are implemented in a specific time-frame whenever a component faces a cyber-attack, after the detection of which the IDS notifies the IRS to be activated. The proposed IRS is **predictive**, since it identifies when a task enters a suspicious zone for a period before it reaches its ultimate bound and causes any harm. Two factors influence the length of this period: (a) the upper bound under nominal behavior and (b) the monitored property. The temporal property can be used as an indication to predict an attack at an early stage, before violating the ultimate temporal boundary (i.e. deadline) [16] . However, false positives are of concern, because the likelihood of one manifesting increases as the security constraints get tightened.

During the response time-frame, the IRS is able to activate a first level of response (e.g. system notification, etc.). After that, a second set of actions can be applied (e.g. supervision of the task). The security policy can set several other response options. Another level of response could be adopted whenever the behavior of the task become malicious and lead to system failure. All these different approaches show that our system is **diverse** and **reactive** complying with the respective requirements.

A different instance of the IRS is running on each ECU in the system (i.e. **localized**). Performance overhead measurements have shown that even in resource-constrained environments our framework runs in a cost-effective manner. IRSs are designed to use a predefined security policy in different strategies. We have extended the security policy, which was used in our previous work [18] to define IDS rules, to include these strategies. At runtime, the policy evaluation framework evaluates the policies and enforces them at two different points.

The framework must implement the **proper** response defined in the security policy when a task becomes suspicious. The decision for the correct response is based on (*i*) the system states as well as the attack severity (**changing**), (*ii*) the conditions under which a suspicious task may return to its normal state (**deactivatable**) and, finally, (*iii*) the response to a task breaching its ultimate limit.

Acknowledgment. This work is partially supported by the European Commission through the following H2020 projects: THREAT-ARREST under Grant Agreement No. 786890, I-BiDaaS under Grant Agreement No. 780787, CONCORDIA under Grant Agreement No. 830927 and SmartShip under Grant Agreement No 823916.

References

1. Avizienis, A., Laprie, J.C., Randell, B., Landwehr, C.: Basic concepts and taxonomy of dependable and secure computing. IEEE Trans. Dependable Secure Comput. **1**(1), 11–33 (2004)
2. Balepin, I., Maltsev, S., Rowe, J., Levitt, K.: Using specification-based intrusion detection for automated response. In: Vigna, G., Kruegel, C., Jonsson, E. (eds.) RAID 2003. LNCS, vol. 2820, pp. 136–154. Springer, Heidelberg (2003). https://doi.org/10.1007/978-3-540-45248-5_8
3. Bergmiller, P.: Towards Functional Safety in Drive-by-Wire Vehicles. Ph.D. thesis (2014)

4. Blaze, M., Feigenbaum, J., Ioannidis, J., Keromytis, A.D.: The keynote trust-management system version 2. RFC **2704** (1999)
5. Broy, M.: Challenges in automotive software engineering. In: Proceedings of the 28th International Conference on Software Engineering, pp. 33–42. ACM (2006)
6. Carroll, J.V.: Vulnerability assessment of the US transportation infrastructure that relies on the global positioning system. J. Navig. **56**(2), 185–193 (2003)
7. Checkoway, S., et al.: Comprehensive experimental analyses of automotive attack surfaces. In: USENIX Security Symposium (2011)
8. Debar, H., Curry, D., Feinstein, B.: The intrusion detection message exchange format (idmef). Technical Report (2007)
9. Debar, H., Thomas, Y., Cuppens, F., Cuppens-Boulahia, N.: Enabling automated threat response through the use of a dynamic security policy. J. Comput. Virol. **3**(3), 195–210 (2007)
10. Edge, K.S., Dalton, G.C., Raines, R.A., Mills, R.F.: Using attack and protection trees to analyze threats and defenses to homeland security. In: MILCOM 2006-2006 IEEE Military Communications Conference, pp. 1–7. IEEE (2006)
11. Fallstrand, D., Lindström, V.: Applicability analysis of intrusion detection and prevention in automotive systems. Master's thesis, 53 (2015)
12. Fallstrand, D., Lindström, V.: Applicability analysis of intrusion detection and prevention in automotive systems. Master's Thesis in Computer Systems and Networks on the Chalmers University of Technology Goteborg (2015)
13. Foo, B., Glause, M.W., Howard, G.M., Wu, Y.S., Bagchi, S., Spafford, E.H.: Intrusion response systems: a survey. In: Qian, Y., Joshi, J.,Tipper, D., Krishnamurthy, P. (Eds.), Information Assurance: Dependability and Security in Networked Systems, pp. 377–412 (2008)
14. Foo, B., Wu, Y.S., Mao, Y.C., Bagchi, S., Spafford, E.: Adepts: adaptive intrusion response using attack graphs in an e-commerce environment. In: 2005 International Conference on Dependable Systems and Networks (DSN'2005), pp. 508–517. IEEE (2005)
15. Francillon, A., Danev, B., Capkun, S.: Relay attacks on passive keyless entry and start systems in modern cars. In: Proceedings of the Network and Distributed System Security Symposium (NDSS). Eidgenössische Technische Hochschule Zürich, Department of Computer Science (2011)
16. Hamad, M., Hammadeh, Z.A., Saidi, S., Prevelakis, V., Ernst, R.: Prediction of abnormal temporal behavior in real-time systems. In: Proceedings of the 33rd Annual ACM Symposium on Applied Computing, pp. 359–367. ACM (2018)
17. Hamad, M., Nolte, M., Prevelakis, V.: Towards comprehensive threat modeling for vehicles. In: The 1st Workshop on Security and Dependability of Critical Embedded Real-Time Systems, p. 31 (2016)
18. Hamad, M., Nolte, M., Prevelakis, V.: A framework for policy based secure intra vehicle communication. In: 2017 IEEE Vehicular Networking Conference (VNC). IEEE (2017)
19. Hamad, M., Schlatow, J., Prevelakis, V., Ernst, R.: A communication framework for distributed access control in microkernel-based systems. In: 12th Annual Workshop on Operating Systems Platforms for Embedded Real-Time Applications (OSPERT16), pp. 11–16, July 2016
20. Hamad, M., Tsantekidis, M., Prevelakis, V.: Red-zone: towards an intrusion response framework for intra-vehicle system. In: The 5th International Conference on Vehicle Technology and Intelligent Transport Systems (VEHITS). Crete, Greece, May 2019

21. Hoppe, T., Kiltz, S., Dittmann, J.: Adaptive dynamic reaction to automotive it security incidents using multimedia car environment. In: 2008 The Fourth International Conference on Information Assurance and Security, ISIAS'2008, pp. 295–298. IEEE (2008)

22. Hoppe, T., Kiltz, S., Dittmann, J.: Applying intrusion detection to automotive it-early insights and remaining challenges. J. Inf. Assurance Secur. (JIAS) **4**(6), 226–235 (2009)

23. Inayat, Z., Gani, A., Anuar, N.B., Khan, M.K., Anwar, S.: Intrusion response systems: foundations, design, and challenges. J. Netw. Comput. Appl. **62**, 53–74 (2016)

24. Ishtiaq Roufa, R.M., et al.: Security and privacy vulnerabilities of in-car wireless networks: a tire pressure monitoring system case study. In: 19th USENIX Security Symposium (2011)

25. nformation technology - Security techniques - Methodology for IT security evaluation. Standard, International Organization for Standardization, August 2008

26. Kanoun, W., Samarji, L., Cuppens-Boulahia, N., Dubus, S., Cuppens, F.: Towards a temporal response taxonomy. In: Di Pietro, R., Herranz, J., Damiani, E., State, R. (eds.) Data Privacy Management and Autonomous Spontaneous Security, pp. 318–331. Springer, Berlin, Heidelberg (2013)

27. Kemmerer, R.A., Vigna, G.: Intrusion detection: a brief history and overview. Computer **35**(4), supl27-supl30 (2002)

28. Koscher, K., et al.: Experimental security analysis of a modern automobile. In: 2010 IEEE Symposium on Security and Privacy (SP), pp. 447–462. IEEE (2010)

29. Larson, U.E., Nilsson, D.K., Jonsson, E.: An approach to specification-based attack detection for in-vehicle networks. In: 2008 IEEE Intelligent Vehicles Symposium, pp. 220–225. IEEE (2008)

30. Le Lann, G.: The ariane 5 flight 501 failure-a case study in system engineering for computing systems. Ph.D. thesis, INRIA (1996)

31. Lewandowski, S.M., Van Hook, D.J., O'Leary, G.C., Haines, J.W., Rossey, L.M.: Sara: survivable autonomic response architecture. In: Proceedings DARPA Information Survivability Conference and Exposition II. DISCEX'2001, vol. 1, pp. 77–88. IEEE (2001)

32. Locasto, M.E., Wang, K., Keromytis, A.D., Stolfo, S.J.: Flips: hybrid adaptive intrusion prevention. In: International Workshop on Recent Advances in Intrusion Detection, pp. 82–101. Springer (2005)

33. Markit, I.: Vehicles getting older: average age of light cars and trucks in U.S. rises again in 2016 to 11.6 years, IHS markit says, November 2016. https://news.ihsmarkit.com/press-release/automotive/vehicles-getting-older-average-age-light-cars-and-trucks-us-rises-again-201

34. Miller, C., Valasek, C.: Remote exploitation of an unaltered passenger vehicle (2015)

35. Moestl, M., Ernst, R.: Cross-layer dependency analysis for safety-critical systems design. In: Proceedings ARCS 2015-The 28th International Conference on Architecture of Computing Systems, pp. 1–7. VDE (2015)

36. Nadeem, A., Howarth, M.P.: An intrusion detection & adaptive response mechanism for manets. Ad Hoc Netw. **13**, 368–380 (2014)

37. Nighswander, T., Ledvina, B., Diamond, J., Brumley, R., Brumley, D.: GPS software attacks. In: Proceedings of the 2012 ACM Conference on Computer and Communications Security, pp. 450–461. ACM (2012)

38. Nilsson, D.K., Larson, U.E., Picasso, F., Jonsson, E.: A first simulation of attacks in the automotive network communications protocol FlexRay. In: Proceedings of the International Workshop on Computational Intelligence in Security for Information Systems CISIS'2008, pp. 84–91. Springer (2009)

39. NLC: Successful connection on the model s internal ethernet network, April 2014. https://teslamotorsclub.com/tmc/threads/successful-connection-on-the-model-s-internal-ethernet-network.28185/

40. Ryutov, T., Neuman, C., Dongho, K., Li, Z.: Integrated access control and intrusion detection for web servers. IEEE Trans. Parallel Distrib. Syst. **14**(9), 841–850 (2003)

41. Schneier, B.: Attack Trees - Modeling security threats. Dr. Dobb's Journal, December 1999

42. Schweppe, H.: Security and privacy in automotive on-board networks. Ph.D. thesis (2012)

43. Shameli-Sendi, A., Ezzati-Jivan, N., Jabbarifar, M., Dagenais, M.: Intrusion response systems: survey and taxonomy. Int. J. Comput. Sci. Netw. Secur **12**(1), 1–14 (2012)

44. Stakhanova, N., Basu, S., Wong, J.: A taxonomy of intrusion response systems. Int. J. Inf. Comput. Secur. **1**(1–2), 169–184 (2007)

45. Strasburg, C., Stakhanova, N., Basu, S., Wong, J.S.: A framework for cost sensitive assessment of intrusion response selection. In: 2009 33rd Annual IEEE International Computer Software and Applications Conference, COMPSAC'2009, vol. 1, pp. 355–360. IEEE (2009)

46. Takahashi, J., Aragane, Y., Miyazawa, T., Fuji, H., Yamashita, H., Hayakawa, K., Ukai, S., Hayakawa, H.: Automotive attacks and countermeasures on lin-bus. J. Inf. Process. **25**, 220–228 (2017)

47. Thompson, C.: A hacker figured out a way to almost completely control GM cars with onstar, July 2015. https://www.businessinsider.com/hackers-device-can-take-over-gm-cars-with-onstar-system-2015-7?IR=T

48. Toth, T., Kruegel, C.: Evaluating the impact of automated intrusion response mechanisms. IEEE (2002)

49. Tryfonas, T., Gritzalis, D., Kokolakis, S.: A qualitative approach to information availability. In: Qing, S., Eloff, J.H.P. (eds.) SEC 2000. ITIFIP, vol. 47, pp. 37–47. Springer, Boston, MA (2000). https://doi.org/10.1007/978-0-387-35515-3_5

50. Vöelp, M., Esteves-Verissimo, P.: Intrusion-tolerant autonomous driving. In: 2018 IEEE 21st International Symposium on Real-Time Distributed Computing (ISORC), pp. 130–133, May 2018. DOI: https://doi.org/10.1109/ISORC.2018.00026

Vehicle Data Management System for Scenario-Based Validation of Automated Driving Functions

Lars Klitzke[1]($\boxtimes$) , Carsten Koch[1], Andreas Haja[1], and Frank Köster[2]

[1] Department of Electronics and Informatics, Hochschule Emden/Leer, University of Applied Sciences, Emden, Germany
{lars.klitzke,carsten.koch,andreas.haja}@hs-emden-leer.de
[2] German Aerospace Center (DLR), Institute of Transportation Systems, Braunschweig, Germany
frank.koester@dlr.de

Abstract. Proving the functionality of AI-controlled automated vehicles is a challenging task due to the enormous overall complexity. Although a scenario-based validation approach is widely accepted in the literature, the identification of these scenarios is still an open issue.

Real-world test drives are valuable data sources for this purpose. However, an automated system is required for data management and scenario identification to analyze the vast amount of data in a legitimate amount of time and effort. Therefore, this work proposes a modular multi-tier Vehicle Data Management System for large-scale test campaign management and analysis as the basis for scenario-based validation of automated driving functions. For system demonstration, lane-change maneuvers are identified and extracted, and an onboard DAS is evaluated with a real-world test drive sequence.

Keywords: ADAS validation · Maneuver identification · Real-world test drives · Data enrichment · Scenario mining · Data Management System

1 Introduction

Automakers and suppliers are currently competing fiercely to develop advanced driver assistance systems (ADAS) and to be among the first to launch a fully automated driving solution into the market. In addition to the difficulties of solving technical challenges, the high amount of testing and validation required for such systems poses a serious cost factor for existing players and a high entry barrier for new companies which are planning on entering the ADAS segment. Hence, recent and current research projects aim to provide methodologies, methods and tools [8, 25] to reduce the effort for the validation or, in particular, enable to approve automated driving functions w.r.t to functional safety standards such as the ISO26262.

Technical advances in the field of computer graphics and computer simulation during the last decades paved the way for new testing methods to master the growing complexity of validating driver assistance systems. With more sophisticated models of

© Springer Nature Switzerland AG 2021
M. Helfert et al. (Eds.): SMARTGREENS 2019/VEHITS 2019, CCIS 1217, pp. 342–362, 2021.
https://doi.org/10.1007/978-3-030-68028-2_16

real-world components becoming available, testing shifted from the real to the virtual world. This is due to the fact that simulations allow to conduct risky maneuvers without risking vulnerables such test engineers or other traffic participants [22]. Moreover, they enable to reach a high test coverage more economically [19].

Nevertheless, real-world test drives are still compulsory to finally prove the system functionality since no other certified methods are available [25]. Although simulation-based testing procedures reduce the overall validation effort, they cannot be used for the final system approval. This is due to the fact that they are currently not able to sufficiently represent the extraordinary complexity of the real world. Hence, testing results *"need to be verified and validated on test grounds and in field tests"* [25]. But, since rigorous testing in the real world is economically infeasible, a scenario-driven validation approach aims at reducing the overall effort [1, 13]. Fur that purpose, real-world test drives are mandatory to find relevant or critical scenarios which are the basis for scenario-based validation approaches [4].

However, due to the high mileage that is required to prove the reliability of the system under test (SUT) [9], assessing ADAS functionality in the real world using Field Operations Tests (FOT) or Naturalistic Driving Studies (NDS) is complex, tedious and cost-intensive. Engineers have to process and manage huge amount of recorded data collected during test campaigns to prove the system's functionality or fine-tune the parameter of the SUT by examining and verifying the response of the system in specific scenarios. Furthermore, engineers have to know where to find specific or rather relevant scenarios in the data such as an overtaking sequence on a wet two-lane motorway driving towards sundown.

Discovering such scenarios may become an enormous economic burden and tedious task if analyzing the data without computational assistance. That includes labeling the data with additional information for the identification of scenarios, performance assessment of a system or for providing a comprehensive data basis for machine learning [17]. Apart from that, the vast amount of data gathered during test campaigns must be managed in such a way that it is accessible by multiple project participants. Data Management Systems (DMS) have shown to be the right choice for such data management and analyzing tasks due to their usage in various domains, e.g. medicine [6], finance [20] or ecology [7].

1.1 Research Project FASva

The identification of scenarios in real-world test drives, so-called scenario mining [5], and analyzing the influence of environmental effects on the system performance is still an open research question and the focus of the research project FASva[1]. Besides that, the project aims at conducting and analyzing real-world test drives and propose tools and frameworks supporting scenario-based real-world test drive data analysis. Therefore, test drives of approx. 25,000 km were conducted on motorways, cities and rural roads in mainly northern Germany within the last two years. This data is the basis for addressing

---

[1] Intelligent Validierung von Fahrerassistenzsystemen (*engl.: intelligent validation of driver assistance systems*) of the Hochschule Emden/Leer.

the following open research question within the research project as already pointed out in an earlier work [11]:

1. How to automatically identify scenarios in real-world test drive data efficiently for setting up a rich catalog of general driving scenarios and for enabling scenario search?
2. Which scenarios are relevant for the functional approval process of specific driving functions?
3. Which parameters are system-relevant in certain scenarios?
4. How to evaluate the performance of conducted real-world test drives to ensure conducting test campaigns efficiently?

1.2 Contribution

To help engineers finding scenarios of interest in real-world test-drive data, this work proposes a Vehicle Data Management System (VDMS) that is capable of scenario identification. Hence, this paper addresses the first research question by introducing a system for efficient scenario identification and search. For that purpose, the VDMS presented in an earlier work [11] is extended by a procedure to extract maneuvers as sequences instead of only finding the most likely point in time where the maneuvers occurs, which is the main focus of other works [21,24,26]. The knowledge of the time interval of maneuvers enables to analyze conducted test drives quantitatively in terms of, e.g., total mileage and duration. Apart from that, engineers are able to find sequences in real-world driving data representing a particular maneuver of interest to examine Driver Assistance System (DAS) more efficiently. The feasibility for maneuver extraction is demonstrated and the performance of the approach is evaluated with a motorway sequence of manually labeled lane-change intervals.

1.3 Structure of This Work

This work is structured as follows: Related work and projects are discussed in Sect. 2. Afterwards, requirements on a VDMS are determined in Sect. 3 based on software quality characteristics defined in ISO 25010 and requirements are derived for different users-roles participating in test campaign. For the sake of completeness, the terms scene, maneuver and scenarios are defined in Sect. 4. These definitions are the basis for the proposed processing chain for maneuver identification and extraction presented in Sect. 5. Afterwards, the architecture of the VDMS is described in Sect. 6. To demonstrate the usability of the VDMS and to assess the performance of the proposed maneuver extraction algorithm, a Lane Keep Assist System (LKA) is analyzed with a test-drive on a motorway, and the accuracy of lane-change maneuver extraction is assessed in Sect. 7. The paper concludes with a summary and outlook for further work in Sect. 8.

2 Related Work

Due to the development of AI-driven vehicles, the automotive industry faces new challenges by verifying the functional safety of the systems. Since rigorous testing of the automated driving systems is economically infeasible, a scenario-driven validation app-roach aims at reducing the overall complexity. Due to this, identifying scenarios for the validation of automated driving functions obtained much attention in the last years. In particular, the focus is on the identification of relevant situations [4] in, e.g. databases of traffic accidents [16], field operational tests [3] or naturalistic driving studies [10] aim-ing at setting up a database of relevant traffic scenarios for the validation of automated driving functions [16,27]. However, for the identification of such relevant scenarios, the data of the conducted test drives need to be managed and analyzed.

Schneider et al. utilize a probabilistic approach using a Bayesian network and fuzzy features for the classification of emergency braking situations [18]. Weidl et al. optimize the Bayesian networks to recognize driving maneuver online [24]. In [17] scenario-specific classification algorithms are evaluated for the identification of lane changes, vehicle followings and cut-ins. Sonka et al. [21] propose an approach for lane change and lane keeping detection by combining a probabilistic approach with fuzzy logic.

All of the approaches have in common that they classify scenarios based on the vehi-cle sensor data. Thus, one can argue that they perform multivariate time-series analysis, as already pointed out by [17]. Taking the vast amount of data gathered during test-campaigns into account, reducing the data without high loss of information would, in turn, reduce the required storage capacity, the classification time and thus validation effort. Furthermore, utilizing the definition of the term scenario from [23] stating that a scenario describes a particular time interval with environment and traffic conditions, and including the description of the term scene representing a certain point in time, the vehicle sensor data has to be aggregated to a time-series of scenes for describing scenarios.

Therefore, this work proposes a temporal data discretization approach to aggregate the raw vehicle sensor data to discrete scenes w.r.t to the time using equal width dis-cretization [12] and by applying type-dependent data aggregation functions to reduce the data size [14] while at the same time establishing the foundation for scene-based scenario mining.

To examine the behavior of automated driving functions in specific situations, infor-mation about the occurrence of a maneuver in a certain point in time is helpful. Those data annotations allow test engineers to analyze test drives more efficiently since they know where to find probably relevant situations. Hence, they only need to extract sequences of the drives around those relevant situations.

However, instead of only annotating the point in time with high likelihood for rep-resenting a maneuver, the time interval representing that particular maneuver would further help on assessing certain driving functions in sequences of interest, e.g., the adaptive cruise control (ACC) system in vehicle following scenarios. Moreover, by par-titioning test drives in maneuvers, they can be quantitatively described according to the occurrence of certain maneuvers. For instance, a free driving sequence on a motorway (no vehicle in front of the ego vehicle) may not be relevant for the validation of an ACC system at all. But, if the ACC emits a braking signal in free driving sequences that may require further investigation by the test engineer. Hence, such data annotations enable test engineers to quickly identify sequences of interest.

In the last decades, however, the main focus of other works is on recognizing the presence of a certain maneuver in a specific point in time with high accuracy [21,24], e.g., to predict maneuvers of other vehicles to react accordingly [26]. For that purpose, [21] proposed a method to identify the most probable point in time of a line-crossover by estimating the likelihood for a line crossover for each point in time. The latter serves as the basis for the proposed maneuver extraction approach that is presented in Sect. 5.3.

3 Requirements

Due to the high economic effort of conducting real-world test drives, multiple parties usually plan and perform test campaigns. In this work, however, we focus on the roles working with the VDMS in such projects. A description of these roles is given in this section including role-based functional requirements on the architecture which are the basis for deriving general requirements utilizing software quality characteristics defined in the ISO 25010.

1. The *campaign manager* is responsible for the achievement of the project goals and acts as an interface to the principal or project owner. Consequently, they need up to date status information about the project's progress.
2. On behalf of the *campaign manager*, the *drive planner* plans the conduction of the specific test drives w.r.t to the general campaign goals and the current test drive coverage. They, therefore, require more detailed knowledge about the performed test drives including, for instance, the weather condition on specific trips or the road type distribution.
3. *Test drivers* perform the actual test drives according to the plans of the *drive-planner*. After each drive, they have to verify the fulfillment of drive-specific test requirements. The result may be a report, used by the driver planner to organize follow-up drives.
4. *Test engineers* perform the in-depth validation of the SUT. Based on the defined specification of the system, they verify the performance of the SUT. Hence, they need access to the sensor data collected by the test fleet in case of a system misbehavior.
5. The last role of interest is the *Algorithm engineer*. People with this role either optimize design and develop new system functions or alternative solutions. The former allows adding additional knowledge to the database which may help in the SUT validation whereas the latter allows evaluating a SUT against a reference system, i.e. evaluate the performance of different traffic-sign-detection systems.

Concluding this overview, it is evident that different roles have various functional requirements on the VDMS w.r.t the grad of information detail or how to access the data or even extending the VDMS functionality. Based on the defined role-specific requirements, general characteristics of the architecture are now defined. Therefore, in order to ensure a software-quality driven design approach, a subset of the software quality characteristics defined in the ISO 25010, the successor of the ISO 9126, is employed.

Scaleability. Test drive campaigns typically have a specific duration spanning from several months up to years. Furthermore, the fleet of test drive campaigns typically consists of multiple vehicles and the test drivers may change during the campaign. Thus, the demand on a scalable framework exists in order to gap-free document the progress of the campaign including information about the drivers, e.g. sex, weight and height which might be used for driver behavior or system acceptance analysis, or the configuration of each vehicle used within the campaign, such as the dimension of vehicles or sensor configurations.

Compatibility. Unfortunately, there is currently no standard tool to measure the vehicle sensor data. Conclusively, this also applies to the data format used for storing the vehicle sensor data. Thus, besides the file format of ADTF[2] used within this project, the VDMS should be able to support diverse data file formats. Furthermore, it should be able to manage information of external data sources, such as OpenStreetMap, which may be required for the system analysis.

Maintainable. In order to support multiple data file formats or extend the functionality of the VDMS, adding new modules to the VDMS is vital. Thus, the architecture has to be highly modular – on different levels of the system. On the top level, where drive-related tasks run, adding further modules is required to process drives that were uploaded by test drivers, i.e. import the drive into the database, query the weather database based on the route in the drive or compress the files of the drive after the processing. Whereas on the level, where the processing of the vehicle sensor data takes places, adding new functions is required to add new facts to the database using, e.g. external data sources or developed algorithms, as stated in the previous description of the *Software engineer* role.

Reliability. In order to ensure that failures or non-normative behavior of functions or algorithms added by engineers do not affect the whole system process, each module should run in a dedicated context. In case of an error of a module, the system should log this information and appropriately indicate that error.

4   Scenario Definition

Before presenting the proposed VDMS for scenario mining, the terms *scene, maneuver* and *scenario* used in this work will be briefly described in the following based on a representative sequence. The different terms are illustrated utilizing a hierarchy of timelines depicted in Fig. 1.

The *drive* represents the first timeline. In this work, a drive begins at that moment where the software in the experimental vehicle start recording and ends if the driver stops the recording. A drive may have time gaps caused by the driver pausing and

---

[2] The Automotive Data and Time-triggered Framework (ADTF) of Elektrobit is used for synchronous data measurement and capturing.

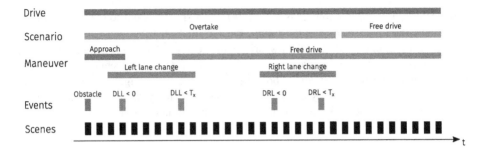

Fig. 1. This figure shows a representative sequence to illustrate the definition of a scenario and scene within this work. The sequence contains an overtaking scenario that consists of multiple subsequence maneuvers, each of which is represented by scenes.

resuming the recording. Each drive consists of multiple consecutive non-overlapping scenarios on the second timeline.

Although different definitions of the term *scenario* exist in the literature, this work employs the one defined by Ulbrich et al. stating that a "scenario describes the temporal development between several scenes in a sequence of scenes. Every scenario starts with an initial scene. Actions & events as well as goals & values may be specified to characterize this temporal development in a scenario. Other than a scene, a scenario spans a certain amount of time." [23]

Such a scenario may be the *overtake* scenario depicted in Fig. 1, where the driver intends to overtake another vehicle. However, this definition of a scenario allows no distinction between a maneuver and a scenario. Maneuvers also span a certain amount of time, and the driver has a specific intention, too. For instance, the driver aims at closing up to a lead vehicle in an approaching maneuver [1]. So, one can argue that maneuvers and scenarios are the same. Due to this, *maneuvers* are, in this work, certain driving actions represented by series of scenes initiated by events such as an obstacle in front of the ego vehicle or the scene where the vehicle crosses a line. Thus, they represent a time interval in which the vehicle performs a particular driving action. Furthermore, the definition of a scenario is extended by the restriction that a scenario consists of at least one maneuver and that it also includes information about the vehicle's environment such as other traffic participants or road infrastructure as in [1].

The smallest time unit is a *scene* representing the state of the vehicle and its environment in a short interval, e.g. seconds, depicted on the last timeline as black bars. Hence, in this work, the restriction of [23] that a scene does not span "a certain amount of time" [23] is relaxed to guarantee that all information are available–even if sensors with different sampling frequencies are used.

5 Processing Chain

Based on the definition of a scene, maneuver and scenario in the previous section, the proposed procedure to process real-world test drive data is presented in the following.

This work extends the three-stage process introduced in [11] for the scene-based identification of scenarios in the real-world test-drive data with a maneuver mining step (see Fig. 2). The data basis for the processing are the raw vehicle sensor data collected during test drives that are transformed to series of scenes. Those scenes will be enriched with additional information from algorithms and external data sources. Based on the enriched scenes, maneuvers are extracted. For the sake of completeness, each stage is described briefly in the following.

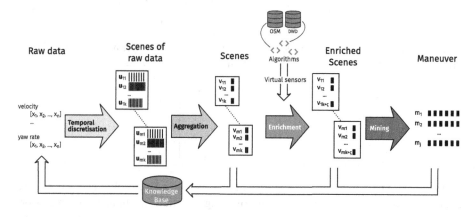

Fig. 2. The four stage process for maneuver identification by transforming the vehicle sensor data to a series of scenes enriched with additional information from algorithms and external data sources.

5.1 Data Discretization and Aggregation

The first step is the temporal data discretization and aggregation utilizing equal width discretization [12] and applying type-depend aggregation operations.

At first, the time series of the available sensors are discretized to a time series of scenes on a per-drive basis. Therefore, let $D = \{t_{start}, S, t_{end}\}$ represent a drive as a set with three elements, whereas $t_{start}^d, t_{end}^d \in \mathbb{N}$ giving the beginning and end time of the drive d as milliseconds since epoch and $S = \{s_1, s_2, \ldots, s_k\}$ as the discretized and aggregated vehicle sensor data as a set of k scenes. Utilizing the definition of multivariate time-series of [2], let $E = \{e_1, e_2, \ldots, e_m\}$ be a set of m vehicle sensors, each of which generates a finite series of n values $x_1, x_2, \ldots, x_n$. Since the vehicle sensors have different sample frequencies and thus the sensor series vary in length denoted in Fig. 2 with the number of black bars per signal in the scene of raw sensor values, the definition of [2] is adapted so that $x_i = [x_1^i, x_2^i, \ldots, x_{n_i}^i]$ represents the time series of the ith sensor with n_i values. Furthermore, the multivariate time series X is defined as a set of vehicle sensor time series with $X = \{x_1, x_2, \ldots, x_m\}$.

For the discretization of the multivariate time series X into a time series of scenes, equal width discretization (EWD) is applied to each sensor series [12]. Hence, using the previous definition of x_i, the time series of the ith sensor is split up into a series of

k scenes $\mathbf{u}_{i1}, \mathbf{u}_{i2}, \ldots, \mathbf{u}_{ik}$ with equal duration Δt so that the jth scene time series of the ith sensor is defined as

$$\mathbf{u}_{ij} = \{x \mid x \in \mathbf{x}_i \wedge \left(t^j_{start} \leq \Phi(x) \leq t^j_{start} + \Delta t\right)\} \tag{1}$$

whereas $\Phi(x)$ giving the time of the sample x in the time series and t^j_{start} stating the beginning of the jth scene s. The number of scenes $k = |S|$ in the drive d is given by

$$k = \begin{cases} \frac{\tilde{d}}{\Delta t} + 1 & \text{if } \tilde{d} \bmod \Delta t > 0 \\ \frac{\tilde{d}}{\Delta t} & \text{if } \tilde{d} \bmod \Delta t \equiv 0 \end{cases} \tag{2}$$

with $\tilde{d}$ stating the duration of the drive d. Then, utilizing the definition of Eq. (1) the series of scenes S of a drive d is formally defined by the $m \times k$ matrix

$$S_d = \begin{bmatrix} \mathbf{u}_{11} & \mathbf{u}_{12} & \cdots & \mathbf{u}_{1k} \\ \mathbf{u}_{21} & \ddots & \ddots & \vdots \\ \vdots & \ddots & \ddots & \vdots \\ \mathbf{u}_{m1} & \cdots & \cdots & \mathbf{u}_{mk} \end{bmatrix}. \tag{3}$$

Aggregation. The next step is to aggregate the sensor series of each scene. Therefore, let $A = \{a_1, a_2, \ldots, a_m\}$ represent a set of m aggregation functions for each sensor, mapping the scene time series $\mathbf{u}_{ij}$ of the ith sensor to an aggregated value v_{ij} with $a \in A : \mathbf{u}_{ij} \rightarrow v_{ij}$. Then, using the Eq. (3), the series of scenes S of a drive d is formally represented by the $m \times k$ matrix

$$S_d = \begin{bmatrix} a_1(\mathbf{u}_{11}) & a_1(\mathbf{u}_{12}) & \cdots & a_1(\mathbf{u}_{1k}) \\ a_2(\mathbf{u}_{21}) & \ddots & \ddots & \vdots \\ \vdots & \ddots & \ddots & \vdots \\ a_m(\mathbf{u}_{m1}) & \cdots & \cdots & a_m(\mathbf{u}_{mk}) \end{bmatrix} \tag{4}$$

where the scene $\mathbf{s}_t$ at time t is represented by the column vector $\mathbf{s}_t = [a_1(\mathbf{u}_{1t}), a_2(\mathbf{u}_{2t}), \ldots, a_m(\mathbf{u}_{mt})]^T$ or in short $\mathbf{s}_t = [v_1, v_2, \ldots, v_m]$.

For the data aggregation, a data-type dependent approach was chosen for selecting the aggregation functions. The supported data types are $T = \{\text{boolean, integer, floating point, string}\}$ and the set of default aggregation functions is $A = \{\text{or, median, mean, concatenate}\}$. The following applies mapping a scene time series $\mathbf{u}_{ij}$ to its aggregated value v_{ij} using the aggregation functions of A:

$$v_{ij} = \begin{cases} \text{mean}(\mathbf{u}_{ij}) & \text{if } \rho(\mathbf{u}_{ij}) \equiv \text{floating point} \\ \text{median}(\mathbf{u}_{ij}) & \text{if } \rho(\mathbf{u}_{ij}) \equiv \text{integer} \\ \text{or}(\mathbf{u}_{ij}) & \text{if } \rho(\mathbf{u}_{ij}) \equiv \text{boolean} \\ \text{concate}(\mathbf{u}_{ij}) & \text{if } \rho(\mathbf{u}_{ij}) \equiv \text{string} \end{cases} \tag{5}$$

with $x = \rho(\mathbf{u}_{ij})$ giving the value type of $\mathbf{u}_{ij}$, whereas $x \in T$. Besides the default aggregation functions, custom ones can be defined for specific signals.

5.2   Data Enrichment

The next step in the processing chain is the enrichment of the scenes with information from various data sources to further describe the vehicle and its environment such as other traffic participants, the weather or road as depicted at the right of Fig. 2. Hence, the previously introduced set E of vehicle sensors is extended with *virtual scene sensors*.

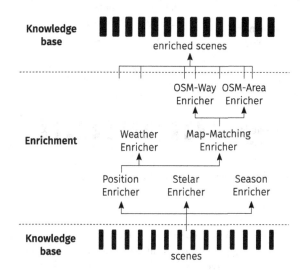

Fig. 3. The enrichment module uses an acyclic graph to manage components and their dependencies for scene enrichment visualized as a tree of components.

Each virtual sensor is a component running as a part of the enrichment module (cf. Sect. 6.2 about modules). Since a virtual sensor may depend on information generated by another sensor, i.e., a map matching algorithm used to map the ego vehicle position to a digital map depends on an accurate ego-position, an acyclic directed graph is used to manage the virtual sensors and the dependencies between them. An overview of the available components is depicted in Fig. 3. Choosing an acyclic graph enables to build up processing chains with components only being run if their dependents finished processing a particular drive. It also allows running independent components concurrently to speed up the processing.

5.3   Maneuver Mining

The last step of the chain is the extraction of maneuvers based on the enriched scenes and depicted in Fig. 4.

Instead of only giving the most likely point in time of the maneuver, the most likely interval is retrieved. Thus, let $M = \{m_1, m_2, \ldots, m_j\}$ be the set of maneuvers in the drive with $B = \{b_1, b_2, \ldots, b_n\}$ as the available maneuver types, and $G = \{(m, b)_1, (m, b)_2\}$ a set of tuples mapping each maneuver $m \in M$ to at least

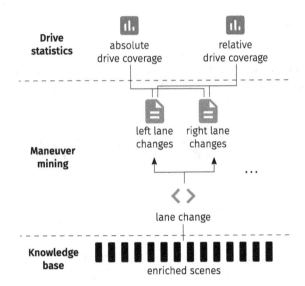

Fig. 4. The procedure for maneuver mining and drive coverage estimation based on the enriched scenes.

one maneuver type $b \in B$. A maneuver m is defined as a series of enriched scenes, $m = s_{t_{start}}, s_{start+1}, \ldots, s_{t_{end}}$ with t_{start} and t_{end} as the start and end of the maneuver. The duration of the maneuver $\tilde{m}$ is estimated by $\tilde{m} = \Delta t * |m|$ with Δt as the chosen scene width in the data discretization step (cf. Eq. (1)). It is assumed that different types of maneuvers (m_{b_i}, m_{b_j}) overlaps, so that $m_{b_i} \cap m_{b_j}$ is not empty in every case. But, maneuvers (m_b^i, m_b^j) of the same type b are distinct, i.e. $m_b^i \cap m_b^j = \emptyset$ which is also represented in Fig. 1. As depicted in Fig. 4 the framework is currently able to identify and extract lane change maneuvers.

For extracting the maneuver interval, a probability-based approach is used based on the *Fine Search* procedure proposed by [21]. The maneuver extraction process is elaborated in the following for the lane change maneuver depicted in Fig. 5.

Let $f(t)$ represent the distance to the right lane of the scene at time t in a moving time window $w = \{t - \Delta t, \ldots, t + \Delta t\}$ with a duration of $2\Delta t$ so that $t \in w$ (see blue line in Fig. 5). The first step is to reduce noise in the signal since this impacts the follow-up steps. Thus, the moving window is smoothed by convolving it with a uniform kernel of size n. Furthermore, let $P(t)$ represent the probability and $P'(t)$ the slope of the probability for a maneuver at time t. For the lane change maneuver, the probability $P(t)$ is defined as

$$P(t) = \frac{|g(t)|}{|g(t)|_{max}} \tag{6}$$

with $g(t)$ as $f(t)$ shifted so that

$$g(t) = f(t) - \tilde{f}(t) \tag{7}$$

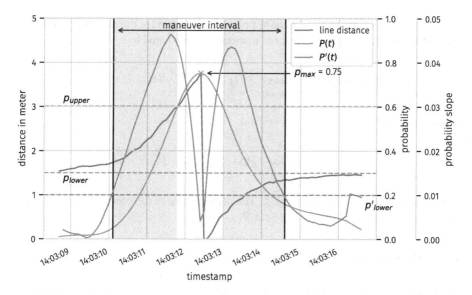

Fig. 5. For maneuver interval extraction, a probability-based approach is utilized and exemplary shown for the lane-change maneuver.

where $\tilde{f}(t)$ is the signal mean in the moving window such that

$$\tilde{f}(t) = \frac{1}{|w|} \sum_{i}^{w} f(i) \tag{8}$$

finally leading to

$$|g(t)| = \left| f(t) - \tilde{f}(t) \right|. \tag{9}$$

To find the start and end time of the maneuver t_{start}, t_{end}, the time and value t_{max}, p_{max} of the signal peak is estimated in the moving window. Afterwards, the signal window is split up into the left and right part. The start of the left $t_{l,start}$ and right $t_{r,start}$ window is the point in times where

$$t_{l,start} = \max \left(\underset{t \in w, t < t_{max}}{\arg\max} \; P(t) < p_{max} \cdot \lambda_{upper} \right) \tag{10}$$

and

$$t_{r,start} = \min \left(\underset{t \in w, t > t_{max}}{\arg\max} \; P(t) < p_{max} \cdot \lambda_{upper} \right) \tag{11}$$

that is the maximum in the left window and minimum in the right window where $P(t)$ is smaller than the upper bound $p_{upper} = p_{max} * \lambda_{upper}$ denoting the start of the gray areas in Fig. 5.

This ensures that the windows do not contain the peak of the signal. This is the requirement for the next step: search the start and end of the maneuver. For that purpose, the thresholds p_{lower} and p'_{lower} are introduced. The first defines the maximum probability and the latter the maximum probability change for the start and end of the maneuver. Hence, the start t_{start} of the maneuver is estimated by

$$t_{start} = \max \left(\underset{t \in w, t < t_{l,start}}{\arg\max} \ P(t) < p_{lower} \wedge P'(t) < p'_{lower} \right) \qquad (12)$$

and the end t_{end} by

$$t_{end} = \min \left(\underset{t \in w, t > t_{r,start}}{\arg\max} \ P(t) < p_{lower} \wedge P'(t) < p'_{lower} \right) \qquad (13)$$

denoted as black vertical lines in Fig. 5. The performance of the presented approach for maneuver extraction is evaluated in Sect. 7.

6 VDMS Architecture

The presented processing chain consists of multiple components each of which is part of the proposed Vehicle Data Management System (VDMS). For the sake of completeness, the modular and event-driven three-tier architecture presented in [11] described, based on the roles and their participation in the project and on the defined general requirements in Sect. 3.

6.1 Data Layer

The bottom layer *Data* contains all types of data in form of files on the file-system that are either generated or from external sources including data in databases. These data files are, for instance, ADTF container collected during test drives by the *test drivers*. Furthermore, the layer also includes files generated by components of the *Modules* layer, such as images extracted from the ADTF container, thumbnails of the images or JSON files representing the decoded CAN data of the ADTF containers.

The CAN signal data are extracted from the ADTF container to a generic JSON file due to the demand to support other measurement tools such as ADTF as well. Because by only supporting a single data format, the usability of the framework is quite limited and thus the flexibility (Fig. 6).

The basic properties of the JSON format provide information about the *vehicle*, *driver* and the *time interval* of the measurements to easily match the conducted test drives to a specific test campaign and driver in the database. The time interval of the record is required since, by design, all signal value timestamps are relative to the start time. That enables to change the reference system even after the campaign, i.e. to synchronize the record times to an absolute reference system. This may be helpful if test drives are conducted in different time zones. The special property *measurements* contains the signal values. Each signal is defined by its minimum and maximum value, its type (e.g. floating point number or integer) and unit (e.g. kilometer per hour). Besides that, it contains all timestamped values of that signal in the property *value* sorted by the signal value timestamps.

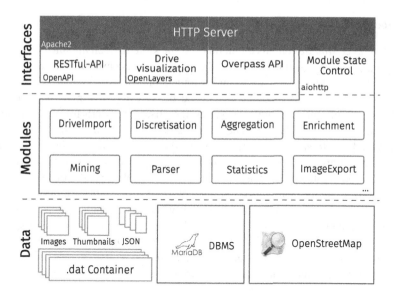

Fig. 6. The architecture of the proposed VDMS for managing large-scale test campaigns consists of three layers: *Data*, *Modules* and *Interfaces* [11].

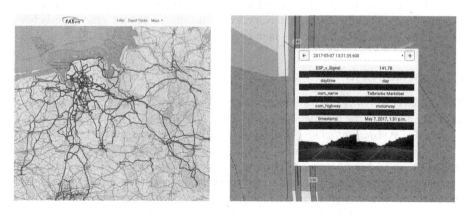

Fig. 7. The *drive visualisation* service provides an interactive web-interface of the conducted test drives including filter capabilities for efficient sequence identification and track selection for scene analysis. *Left:* A map of all conducted test drives. *Right:* The same zoomed-in map showing information of a selected scene [11].

6.2   Modules Layer

The second layer *Modules* entails all modules of the system. Each module has a distinct functional purpose and is independent of the other modules ensuring a loosely-coupled design and thus facilitating a scalable and maintainable software system.

The loose coupling of modules is realized by an event-driven file-system based information passing method and by utilizing the observer pattern for asynchronously notify about module state changes. The latter is used for the *Module State Control* component of the layer *Interfaces* to notify connected clients, e.g. *test engineers*, about the progress of modules via WebSocket connections asynchronously. Whereas the former is used to trigger modules and thus, start the processing of a specific drive. Therefore, all modules have the following three parameters: *source, indicate, destination.*

The *source* parameter defines the directory where the module watches for drives to process. If a module successfully processed a drive, it creates a new symbolic link in one or multiple directories, defined with the parameter *indicate*, to inform all other modules watching for the directory defined in *indicate* about its progress. In the case of modules creating new files, the parameter *destination* defines the location where to put those files.

Having the compatibility in mind, the implementation language of the module functionality is not restricted to the implementation language of the architecture which currently is Python. Instead, the module class merely works as a wrapper or adapter to the actual functionality to save the state of the module's progress in the database and to guarantee the reliability of the framework, i.e. robust the framework against misbehavior or errors in the modules such as memory leaks.

6.3   Interfaces Layer

The last layer *Interfaces* provides access to the VDMS for different project roles with each component of the layer working as a service interconnected by an HTTP server.

The *Drive visualisation* service utilizes OpenStreetMap to show the conducted test drives via an interactive web-based frontend. The left image in Fig. 7 shows the conducted drives within FASva. The purpose of this service is to help *drive planner* by planning test drives since it gives a rough overview about the test drive coverage w.r.t the geolocation and *engineers* by finding sequences of interest. Therefore, the web-interface provides filter and selection capabilities. The former enables to search for sequences with specific characteristics, e.g. test campaign, daytime, region of interest or road type and the latter gives access to specific situations or scenes of a drive. That includes information about the vehicle and its environment either from onboard sensors, e.g. velocity or location or any other external sources such as weather, street type or daytime.

The RESTful-API service provides access to the data of conducted test drives, e.g. sensor data or images of cameras and is used by *test engineers* and *algorithm developers*. The OpenAPI specification is used for the description of the API, allowing to generate client applications for various programming languages. The *drive visualisation* service, for instance, uses the *RESTful-API* to retrieve the meta-information and thumbnails of specific situations and the geolocation of the conducted test drives.

The *Module State Control* service allows *algorithm engineers* to interact with the modules of the Modules layer, e.g. to start the processing of a particular drive or getting notified if a module finished processing.

The Overpass API service grant access to the OpenStreetMap (OSM) server for adding information about the infrastructure. This enables *test engineers* or *algorithm developers* to find sequences that took place on specific road types, e.g. motorway or rural roads. The `Map Matching Enricher` of the *Enrichment* module, for instance, uses the OSM server to retrieve information about the road the vehicle is on, which is used in the maneuver mining step to detect lane-changes on highways.

7   Experiments and Proof of Concept

To evaluate the proposed VDMS architecture and processing chain, the evaluation of driving functions and scenario identification is demonstrated by extracting lane changes and analyze an onboard DAS.

7.1   Dataset

The data basis for the following experiments are two sequences captured with our research vehicle and retrieved via the RESTful API presented in Sect. 6.3.

The first sequence covers approx. 100 km and takes place on a motorway with two to three lanes (see Fig. 9). During the trip, 16 lane changes occurred which were manually labeled using the *drive visualization* interface shown in Fig. 7. The scene duration within this sequence is 1 s, since according to [15], the probability of a lane change duration X being greater two seconds $P(X > 2)$ is approx. 99.52% which is adequate for the analysis since all lane changes are represented in the signal (see black crosses in Fig. 9).

The second sequence is another trip on a motorway with a duration of approx. One hour and total mileage of approx. 55 km. The trip contains 28 left and 30 right lane-changes. For each maneuver, the interval was labeled manually.

7.2   Maneuver Extraction

To evaluate the proposed approach for maneuver extraction, lane changes maneuvers are extracted from the second test sequence since the real maneuver intervals are known.

The prerequisite for maneuver extraction is the identification of the lane crossing event. For that purpose, a sliding window-based approach with a window size of 8 s is utilized to search for dominant peaks in the signals representing the distance to the left and right lane as depicted in Fig. 5. The duration of 8 s is used since [15] shows that the mean lane change duration is $\mu = 6.25$ s with a standard deviation of $\sigma = 1.64$. Although the approach is simple, it correctly identifies all available lane changes but has two false positives for left and right lane changes.

To assess the performance of the maneuver extraction approach, the extracted maneuver are matched against the manually labeled intervals. Therefore, a maneuver is correctly matched if the difference between the estimated and real start and end time

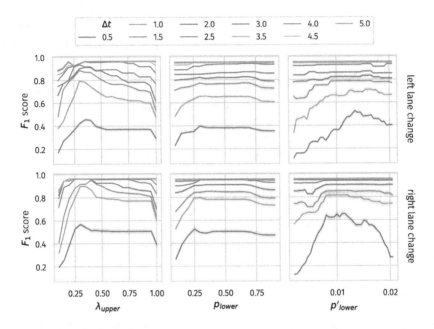

Fig. 8. The performance of the maneuver extraction algorithm depends on multiples thresholds. *Left:* The relative upper bound threshold. *Middle:* The maximum allowed probability p_{lower} for the end and start of the maneuver. *Right:* The maximum allowed probability slope p'_{lower} for the maneuver start and end.

is smaller than a maximum time difference $\Delta t = \{0.5, 1, \ldots, 0.5\}$. To quantify the accuracy, the F_1 score with

$$F_1 = 2 \cdot \frac{\text{precision} \cdot \text{recall}}{\text{precision} + \text{recall}} \tag{14}$$

estimated. The precision and recall is defined as

$$\begin{aligned} \text{precision} &= \frac{t_p}{t_p + f_p} \\ \text{recall} &= \frac{t_p}{t_p + f_n} \end{aligned} \tag{15}$$

where t_p is the number of correctly matched way changes and f_p the number of unmatched maneuvers.

Since the approach depends on multiple thresholds, their influence on the performance is depicted in Fig. 8. It is evident that, the higher the maximum time difference Δt, the more accurate is the approach. Note that the F_1 score cannot be one since the sliding-window approach detected false positives.

Based on the given results, the optimal parameter for each maneuver can be estimated assuming the following requirements.

1. The offset between the extracted and true maneuver intervals should be as small as possible.
2. The computational complexity for finding the start and end of the interval should be minimized.

By applying these restrictions to the preliminary results, the estimated parameters and performance for left and right lane-change extraction are given in Table 1. The extraction of left lane-changes is accurate up to 3.0 s and right lane-changes can be extracted precisely with a maximum difference of 1.5 s. With this method, the parameters for each maneuver can be derived automatically based on ground truth information.

This demonstration shows that accurate maneuver extraction is possible with the proposed approach if the maneuver identification is precise. That enables *test engineers* to assess driving functions in specific sequences more efficiently, since this approach delivers the sequences and not only the point of time of a certain event.

Table 1. The best parameter constellation for each maneuver estimated by maximizing the F_1 score, minimizing the maximum time difference dt and search window.

	Statistics		Parameters		
	Δt	F_1	λ_{upper}	p_{low}	p'_{low}
Left lane-change	3.0	0.9655	0.95	0.075	0.0205
Right lane-change	1.5	0.9642	0.40	0.090	0.0205

7.3   System Evaluation

Besides the identification of scenarios, the assessment of a system under test (SUT) is another typical use-case. A *test engineer* might want to find those situations in which a SUT such as a Lane Keep Assist System (LKA) does not operate. In Fig. 9 the purple line represents the state of the LKA. If the LKA actively assist the driver, the signal is one and zero otherwise. Hence, the situations in which the signal is zero are of special interest. From the Fig. 9 it is evident that on this sequence, the LKA stops operating if the driver performs a lane change (manually marked as black crosses). Hence, this system does not actively assist the driver during lane changes. Besides that, the system is also deactivated in two other cases with no lane-change maneuvers but lane crossing events. Based on this, one can conclude that the system is deactivated fi the vehicle is on multiple lanes and not ultimately conducting a lane-change maneuver.

This demonstration shows that by supporting the addition of algorithms to the VDMS, reference signals with a higher confidence or further knowledge about the vehicle and its environment may help assessing and analyzing onboard DAS.

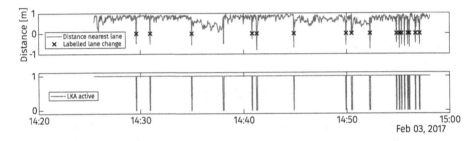

Fig. 9. Sequence of a trip on a motorway with two to three lanes for demonstrating the proof of concept of the proposed VDMS for system evaluation. *Top:* Distance to nearest line and the manually labeled lane changes. *Bottom:* The signal of the onboard Lane Keep Assist System.

8 Summary and Outlook

Test drives in the real world are mandatory to find relevant and critical scenarios for the validation of automated driving functions [4]. However, since the analysis of large-scale test campaigns requires computational assistance for efficient scenario identification, this work proposes a highly modularized three-tier VDMS. That enables to manage and analyses real-world test drives for the scenario-based validation of automated driving functions.

Based on a definition of the terms scene, maneuver, and scenarios, a formal definition of time-series of scenes is given. That is the foundation for the proposed processing chain for maneuver mining. The raw vehicle sensor data are aggregated to time series of scenes enriched with additional information from algorithms or external data sources that may not be available during test drives. The enriched scenes are partitioned into sequences by the maneuver mining component of the processing chain. For that purpose, a novel probability-based maneuver extraction approach is presented. Furthermore, a method is introduced to derive the optimal parameters for the maneuver extraction approach for each maneuver.

That processing chain is a central component of the VDMS, whereas the design of the architecture follows a requirements-driven approach utilizing software-quality characteristics defined in the ISO 25010. Therefore, the needs of particular project roles are analyzed and specific and general requirements on the architecture are derived.

The usability of the VDMS and the performance of the proposed maneuver extraction approach are finally evaluated by assessing an onboard DAS and finding sequences representing lane-change maneuvers. For that purpose, the RESTful API is utilized to retrieve sequences of the conducted test drives and label lane changes based on the images of the front camera.

The evaluation shows that the extraction of left and right lane-changes is accurate up to 3.0 and 1.5 s respectively. That enables test engineers to assess driving functions in specific sequences more efficiently since they can find maneuver sequences instead of only the time a maneuver occurred.

To compile a sophisticated set of scenarios, the focus in follow-up works is to integrate additional algorithms to identify typical maneuver such as vehicle approaching, vehicle following and free driving [17]. Furthermore, the presented method for maneuver interval extraction needs to be validated with other algorithm.

Acknowledgements. We thank LG Electronics, Vehicle Solution Company, Republic of Korea, for supporting this project by cooperating in capturing large-scale test drives and providing valuable measurement equipment.

References

1. Bach, J., Otten, S., Sax, E.: Model based scenario specification for development and test of automated driving functions. In: 2016 IEEE Intelligent Vehicles Symposium (IV), pp. 1149–1155, June 2016. https://doi.org/10.1109/IVS.2016.7535534
2. Baek, S., Kim, D.Y.: Empirical sensitivity analysis of discretization parameters for fault pattern extraction from multivariate time series data. IEEE Trans. Cybern. **47**(5), 1198–1209 (2017). https://doi.org/10.1109/TCYB.2016.2540657
3. Benmimoun, M., Fahrenkrog, F., Zlocki, A., Eckstein, L.: Incident detection based on vehicle can-data within the large scale field operational test "eurofot". In: 22nd Enhanced Safety of Vehicles Conference (ESV 2011), Washington, DC/USA (2011)
4. Damm, W., Möhlmann, E., Peikenkamp, T., Rakow, A.: A formal semantics for traffic sequence charts. In: Lohstroh, M., Derler, P., Sirjani, M. (eds.) Principles of Modeling. LNCS, vol. 10760, pp. 182–205. Springer, Cham (2018). https://doi.org/10.1007/978-3-319-95246-8_11
5. Elrofai, H., Paardekooper, J., Gelder, E.d., Kalisvaart, S., Op den Camp, O.: Streetwise: scenario-based safety validation of connected automated driving. Technical report TNO (2018)
6. Fraenkel, D.J., Cowie, M., Daley, P.: Quality benefits of an intensive care clinical information system. Crit. Care Med. **31**(1), 120–125 (2003)
7. Frehner, M., Brändli, M.: Virtual database: spatial analysis in a web-based data management system for distributed ecological data. Environ. Model. Softw. **21**(11), 1544–1554 (2006)
8. Haja, A., Koch, C., Klitzke, L.: The ADAS swot analysis - a strategy for reducing costs and increasing quality in ADAS testing. In: Proceedings of the 3rd International Conference on Vehicle Technology and Intelligent Transport Systems (VEHITS 2017), pp. 320–325 (2017). https://doi.org/10.5220/0006354103200325
9. Kalra, N., Paddock, S.M.: Driving to safety: how many miles of driving would it take to demonstrate autonomous vehicle reliability? Transp. Res. Part A Policy Pract. **94**, 182–193 (2016)
10. Klauer, S.G., Dingus, T.A., Neale, V.L., Sudweeks, J.D., Ramsey, D.J., et al.: The impact of driver inattention on near-crash/crash risk: An analysis using the 100-car naturalistic driving study data. Technical report National Highway Traffic Safety Administration (2006)
11. Klitzke, L., Koch, C., Haja, A., Köster, F.: Real-world test drive vehicle data management system for validation of automated driving systems. In: Proceedings of the 5th International Conference on Vehicle Technology and Intelligent Transport Systems (VEHITS 2019), pp. 171–180, May 2019. https://doi.org/10.5220/0007720501710180
12. Liu, H., Hussain, F., Tan, C.L., Dash, M.: Discretization: an enabling technique. Data Min. Knowl. Disc. **6**(April), 393–423 (2002). https://doi.org/10.1023/A:1016304305535
13. Menzel, T., Bagschik, G., Maurer, M.: Scenarios for development, test and validation of automated vehicles. In: 2018 IEEE Intelligent Vehicles Symposium (IV), pp. 1821–1827, June 2018. https://doi.org/10.1109/IVS.2018.8500406

14. Moskovitch, R., Shahar, Y.: Classification-driven temporal discretization of multivariate time series. Data Min. Knowl. Disc. 29(4), 871–913 (2014). https://doi.org/10.1007/s10618-014-0380-z

15. Olsen, E.C.B., Lee, S.E., Wierwille, W.W., Goodman, M.J.: Analysis of distribution, frequency, and duration of naturalistic lane changes. In: Proceedings of the Human Factors and Ergonomics Society Annual Meeting, vol. 46, no. 22, pp. 1789–1793 (2002). https://doi.org/10.1177/154193120204602203

16. Pütz, A., Zlocki, A., Bock, J., Eckstein, L.: System validation of highly automated vehicles with a database of relevant traffic scenarios. In: 12th ITS European Congress. ITS European Congress (2017)

17. Roesener, C., Fahrenkrog, F., Uhlig, A., Eckstein, L.: A scenario-based assessment approach for automated driving by using time series classification of human-driving behaviour. In: 2016 IEEE 19th International Conference on Intelligent Transportation Systems (ITSC), pp. 1360–1365, November 2016. https://doi.org/10.1109/ITSC.2016.7795734

18. Schneider, J., Wilde, A., Naab, K.: Probabilistic approach for modeling and identifying driving situations. In: 2008 IEEE Intelligent Vehicles Symposium, pp. 343–348, June 2008. https://doi.org/10.1109/IVS.2008.4621145

19. Schuldt, F.: Ein Beitrag für den methodischen Test von automatisierten Fahrfunktionen mit Hilfe von virtuellen Umgebungen. Ph.D. thesis, Technische Universität Carolo-Wilhelmina zu Braunschweig, April 2017. https://doi.org/10.24355/dbbs.084-201704241210

20. Shavit, E., Teichner, L.: Interactive market management system, US Patent 4.799.156, January 1989

21. Sonka, A., Krauns, F., Henze, R., Küçükay, F., Katz, R., Lages, U.: Dual approach for maneuver classification in vehicle environment data. In: 2017 IEEE Intelligent Vehicles Symposium (IV), pp. 97–102, June 2017. https://doi.org/10.1109/IVS.2017.7995704

22. Stellet, J.E., Zofka, M.R., Schumacher, J., Schamm, T., Niewels, F., Zöllner, J.M.: Testing of advanced driver assistance towards automated driving: a survey and taxonomy on existing approaches and open questions. In: 18th IEEE International Conference on Intelligent Transportation Systems, pp. 1455–1462, September 2015. https://doi.org/10.1109/ITSC.2015.236

23. Ulbrich, S., Menzel, T., Reschka, A., Schuldt, F., Maurer, M.: Defining and substantiating the terms scene, situation, and scenario for automated driving. In: 2015 IEEE 18th International Conference on Intelligent Transportation Systems, pp. 982–988, September 2015. https://doi.org/10.1109/ITSC.2015.164

24. Weidl, G., Madsen, A.L., Kasper, D., Breuel, G.: Optimizing Bayesian networks for recognition of driving maneuvers to meet the automotive requirements. In: 2014 IEEE International Symposium on Intelligent Control (ISIC), pp. 1626–1631, October 2014. https://doi.org/10.1109/ISIC.2014.6967630

25. Winner, H., Lemmer, K., Form, T., Mazzega, J.: PEGASUS—first steps for the safe introduction of automated driving. In: Meyer, G., Beiker, S. (eds.) Road Vehicle Automation 5. LNM, pp. 185–195. Springer, Cham (2019). https://doi.org/10.1007/978-3-319-94896-6_16

26. Wissing, C., Nattermann, T., Glander, K., Bertram, T.: Probabilistic time-to-lane-change prediction on highways. In: 2017 IEEE Intelligent Vehicles Symposium (IV), pp. 1452–1457, June 2017. https://doi.org/10.1109/IVS.2017.7995914

27. Zhao, D., Guo, Y., Jia, Y.J.: TrafficNet: an open naturalistic driving scenario library. In: 2017 IEEE 20th International Conference on Intelligent Transportation Systems (ITSC), pp. 1–8, October 2017. https://doi.org/10.1109/ITSC.2017.8317860

Multi-objective Optimization of Train Speed Profiles Using History Measurements

Achilleas Achilleos[1,3]($\boxtimes$), Markos Anastasopoulos[2,3], Anna Tzanakaki[1,2,3],
Marius Iordache[4,3], Olivier Langlois[4,3], Jean-Francois Pheulpin[4,3],
and Dimitra Simeonidou[2,3]

[1] Institute of Accelerating Systems and Applications, Athens, Greece
aach0765@gmail.com
[2] Department of Electrical and Electronic Engineering, University of Bristol, Bristol, UK
[3] Department of Physics, National and Kapodistrian University of Athens, Athens, Greece
[4] Alstom SA, Saint-Ouen, France

Abstract. The present study focuses on the development of a multi-objective optimization scheme to improve the efficiency of railway systems. This is achieved through the identification of the optimal train speed profiles employing a novel modeling framework based on Data Envelopment Analysis (DEA). Train speed profiles are selected with the objective to transfer more passengers in less time and with less energy under scheduling constraints. Given that DEA is a data oriented, non-parametric method, a large-scale experimental camping has been carried out over an operational tramway system to collect the required inputs/outputs. Numerical results show that when the proposed approach energy consumption can be reduced by 10%.

Keywords: Train speed profiles · Data Envelopment Analysis · Data Collection · Experimental Validation

1 Introduction

According to the International Union of Railways the length of tracks maintained by the European railway sector exceeds 300.000 km operating more than 5 billion train-kilometers and offering services for more than 400 billion passenger-kilometers. A steady increase is expected for the next 30 years making railways a key-asset in the European transportation ecosystem [1]. According to [2], *"railway systems are expected to "increase their share in transportation by expanding and geographical reach and deliver innovative and integrated travel solutions for people and goods meeting the highest service standards in terms of safety and security"*. Besides safety, security and capacity, a key aspect that should be considered during the design of railway systems is environmental sustainability. EU climate actions for sustainable transport mandate that[1] *"greenhouse gas emissions should be reduced by 80–95% below 1990 levels by 2050*

---

[1] https://ec.europa.eu/clima/citizens/eu_en

© Springer Nature Switzerland AG 2021
M. Helfert et al. (Eds.): SMARTGREENS 2019/VEHITS 2019, CCIS 1217, pp. 363–374, 2021.
https://doi.org/10.1007/978-3-030-68028-2_17

whereas by 2030, the goal for transport will be to reduce GHG emissions to around 20% below their 2008 level". It is true to say that if a radically different approach is not adopted, *GHG* emissions will remain at very high levels and congestion costs will further increase.

To avoid these unfavorable scenarios and achieve the 2030 targets for energy efficiency, the introduction of novel concepts for railway systems will be key to lower not only CO2 emissions bus also maximize capacity. Aligned with the flagship initiative *"Resource efficient Europe"* set up in the Europe 2020 Strategy, the paramount goal of European transport policy is to *"help establish a system that underpins European economic progress, enhances competitiveness and offers high quality and scalable mobility services while using resources more efficiently".* Hence, new transport patterns must emerge, according to which greater numbers of travelers are carried to their destination by the most efficient modes. To achieve this goal, future development must address the following topics:

1. *Improvement of the energy efficiency performance through the adoption of electric railway systems. A typical railway system has better energy conservation features than other transportation systems as it is able to transfer passengers with an energy consumption less than 209 kJ per kilometre per person, which is much lower than the energy consumption of cars.*
2. *Optimization of the performance of railways* through the adoption of novel algorithmic approaches.
3. *Coordination and cooperation of the different railway subsystems (rolling stock, stations, substations and the grid etc.) enabling efficient usage of transport and infrastructure.*

The adoption of new technologies and novel software solutions such as the *Internet of Things* (IoT) and Artificial Intelligence (AI) will be key to lower transport emissions. These technologies can be successfully used to address capacity limitations of current railway systems and improve overall system's performance. In response to these challenges, the present study focusing on improving the performance of railway systems through the identification of *optimal driving profiles* adopting the *Data Envelopment Analysis* (DEA) theory extending our previous work in [3]. It is shown that when the proposed approach is adopted better performance can be achieved as the railway system can transfer more passengers in less time and with less energy reducing operational expenditures.

However, to successfully apply this concept in a realistic railway environment an extensive set of measurements covering a broad range of kinematic, energy and environmental parameters needs to be stored, processed and analysed. To address this challenge, an operational data management (ODM) platform has been deployed over an operational tramway system utilizing open source technologies. The installed ODM system was able to monitor the energy flows of the whole railway systems and identify the optimal performance/cost trade-offs on the fly. As discussed in [4], this platform comprises the following core elements:

1. A heterogeneous secure and resilient telecommunication system, consisting of both wireless (e.g. LTE, WiFi, LiFi) and wireline (e.g. optical) technologies converging energy and telecom services. This infrastructure is used to interconnect a plethora of monitoring devices located both on track and at the trackside and end-users to the Operational Control Centre (OCC).

2. A hybrid data storage and processing mechanism combining state-of-the art open source SQL/Non-SQL databases as well as batch and stream processing engines. Based on the characteristics of the collected data and the selected applications, data are dynamically forwarded to the most suitable strage/processing platform. A high-level view of this process is shown in

3. .

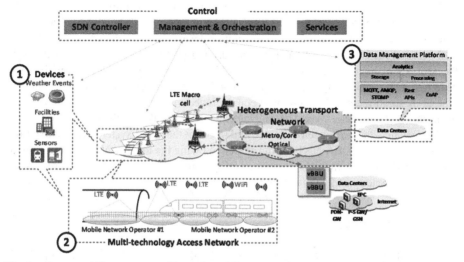

Fig. 1. Converged Heterogeneous Network and Compute Infrastructures supporting railway services: Use case where data are collected from various devices (1) are transmitted over a 5G network (2) to the cloud-based data management platform (3) [3]

The experimental campaign has been carried out over an actual tramway system operating at 750 V. The rest of this study is organized as follows. The definition of the problem is outlined in Sect. 2, Sect. 3 gives a brief overview of the state of the art on the subject. The research methodology along with a description of the proposed scheme is provided in Sect. 4. The results of the study are presented in Sect. 5. Finally, Sect. 6 concludes the paper.

2 Problem Definition

The transportation sector is a major contributor to air pollution and consumer of scarce non-renewable fossil fuels. Electric railway systems and vehicles powered by hybrid energy sources are expected to have high potentials to decrease fuel consumption due to their ability to regenerate kinetic energy in the braking phase. Despite the inherent energy efficient operation of electrified railway systems, reduction of the energy drawn from the power grid is still an overarching problem due to the following reasons:

a) the increasing costs of electric energy in some countries (in particular, where energy produced by non-renewable sources);
b) the increased electric energy demand due to several causes (lifestyle changes, which may be significant in developing countries; the need to supply more railway services, etc.);
c) the increased attention of the public and governments to the environment (air pollution) and to climate changes (greenhouse gas emissions).

A possible solution to reduce the energy consumption of railway systems is the identification of better driving styles. By optimizing the way that a driver accelerates, maintains, slows or brakes, power consumption levels can be reduced. In the present study it is argued that the best performing driving profiles can be identified through the analysis of history measurements. To achieve this an experimental campaign has been carried out collecting data for more than three years over an operational tramway system. A smart metering system has been deployed monitoring energy, kinematic and environmental parameters based on sensing equipment installed both on-board and at the trackside. Once data have been collected and stored at the ODM system, an optimization framework based on DEA has been developed allowing the identification of the optimal driving styles that minimize the consumed energy subject to set of constraints related to scheduling, capacity and environmental conditions.

3 State-of-the-Art

One very effective method of increasing the energy efficiency of railways is the optimized use of braking energy. As discussed in [5], regenerative braking of railway electric vehicles is effective when the electrical load exists near the regenerating train on the same electrified line. So, early in the morning and at midnight, or in the low-density district lines, regeneration cancellation phenomenon often occurs, and the regenerative brake force cannot be operated in accordance with the recommended value. Newly appeared high-performance energy storage devices press the issues of energy storage and reuse technologies on ground and on vehicles. Hybrid energy source is one effective solution especially in DC systems for city trams and urban railways it is not possible to coordinate all vehicle movements in such a way that a complete energy exchange between braking and accelerating phases can be reached. In [6] measurements and calculations have shown that modern vehicles are able to feed up to 40% of the consumed energy back into the grid. This is only possible, however, if the braking phase of one vehicle coincides with the accelerating phase of another vehicle in the vicinity, i.e. not more than one km away. Otherwise the energy must be wasted on the braking resistor. An energy storage unit installed in a DC substation can store the surplus braking energy that cannot be directly supplied to other vehicles and feed the energy back into the grid for subsequent accelerations. It has been proven in several installations that one energy storage unit is able to save up to 340,000 kWh per year [7].

Energy storage units can be installed both in existing and in new substations, whereby track section extensions can be built and operated at lower costs if such units are integrated between the substations as points of supply. The main problem of these methods is that they need some new hardware to be installed on the already existing trams. So, a more efficient and economy approach to reduce the energy consumption is the optimization of driving profiles, speed and timetables. However, the regenerating braking and storing methods can be used in addition to optimized driving profiles. Most other methods provide optimized driving profile in a very different way. They divide tram's route into four steps, acceleration, cruising, coasting and braking. Energy consumption during the cruising and braking is less than during the acceleration phase. Therefore, the key to achieving energy-savings during train operation lies in making the correct choice of transition points for different states, that is, to find the optimal strategies of train operation to minimize energy consumption. The optimal strategies can be derived from the Hamiltonian function and the Pontryagin principle. According to the above two mathematical methods, the optimal strategies were further summarized as follows: maximum acceleration and braking during the beginning and end of a train journey, particle acceleration or braking during cruising, and starting to coast as early as possible. In a method, which have been developed in [8] the speed profile definition module identifies the speed profile that is able to respect some constrains, having fixed the values of cruising speed and average acceleration. The energy consumption estimation module calculates the consumed traction energy corresponding to the defined speed profile. The optimization module operates on the decision variables, on cruising speed and average acceleration, so as to minimize the energy consumed. Evaluation of the objective function requires calculation of the speed profile and the energy consumed. The energy consumed is estimated by an equation, solving the differential equation of the motion by the finite difference approach. In [8] they've made a similar approach with [9] in order to solve the problem. The main difference is that in [9] they've made their own Energy and Running Time Simulator with different describing parameters of the driving operation. In [10] there is a different approach. The purpose of that study is to optimize the energy consumption by adjusting the timetable. As the timetable creation process is based on the predefined running times between stations, the definition of running times will directly impact not only the traffic planning but also the entire energy consumption. Generally, the running time can be adjusted within a certain range by using the running time supplements, which are extra running time on top of the technical minimum running time between every two stations; the longer the running time is, the lower the energy consumption for the same distance as we see in [11]. However, the longer the running time is, the higher the time cost of the railway sector and passengers; thus, a trade-off between the running time and energy consumption is necessary. In addition, the train order may change after adjusting the running time based on energy consumed, and then the train operation needs to be adjusted to maintain safety constraints, and the adjustment of train operation will result in a further change in energy consumption.

Table 1. Sample of the collected dataset [3].

Timestamp	External temp	Speed	Current HVAC C2	Voltage (catenary)	Current (Ventilation)	Voltage HVAC	Total energy pantograph
	°C	km/h	A	V	A	V	kWh
1442729913	10.8	43	15.6	892	38.7	449.32	37.0573402
1442729914	10.8	40.8	15.6	891	37.9	449.28	37.00736674
1442729915	10.7	38.9	15.6	869	38.2	449.55	36.95579201
1442729916	10.7	36.9	15.6	874	38.2	449.64	36.90263086
1442729917	10.8	35.1	15.6	855	39.5	449.73	36.85689206

4 Proposed Approach

4.1 Data Collection Process

To improve energy efficient operation of railway systems, initially, an ODM platform has been deployed enabling data collection and processing of information obtained from a variety of sensors and devices. This platform comprises a communication segment that relies on a set of optical and wireless network technologies to interconnect a variety of end-devices and compute resources. Through this approach, data obtained from various sources (monitoring devices, users and social media) can be dynamically and in real-time directed to the OCC for processing. The wireless technologies comprise cellular WiFi, LiFi and LTE networks to provide the on-board and on-board to trackside connectivity. For the trackside the to the OCC segment, information is transferred over an optical network. The overall solution is shown in Fig. 1. As mentioned above, this platform is used to monitor a variety of parameters. An indicative sample of the collected measurements is provided in Table 1. Sample of the collected dataset This dataset includes information related to the geographic location of the rolling stock, on-board $CO2$ levels that is used to estimate the number of passengers, internal and external temperature that is important for the evaluation of the Heating Ventilation and Air-conditioning system's (HVAC) performance, kinematic parameters (including acceleration and speed) etc.

The smart metering solution also comprises an Information Technology (IT) segment that is responsible for the storage and processing of the measurements. Storage is accommodated by hybrid mechanism combining state-of-the-art open source SQL/NoSQL databases while processing is executing based on Apache Spark. Using purposely developed algorithms, knowledge can be extracted from the dataset which can assist railway system operators to identify optimal train driving and scheduling profiles.

4.2 Analytical Model

In the present study, identification of the optimal driving profiles is performed using DEA. DEA is a very powerful service management and benchmarking technique originally developed by Chames, Cooper and Rhodes (1978) to evaluate non-profit and public sector organizations [12]. This is achieved by measuring the productive efficiency of the construction elements of these organizations, namely, decision-making units (DMUs). DEA can measure how efficiently a DMU uses the resources available to generate a set of outputs. The performance of DMUs is assessed using the concept of efficiency or productivity defined as a ratio of total outputs to total inputs. Note that efficiencies estimated using DEA are relative, that is, relative to the best performing DMU or DMUs (if multiple DMUs are the most efficient). The most efficient DMU is assigned an efficiency score of 1, and the performance of other DMUs vary between 0 and 1 relative to the best performance.

Table 2. Sample of the collected dataset. Sample of 10 routes used for the identification of the optimal driving profiles [3].

Style ID	Inter-station travelling time (sec)	Total energy (KW)	HVAC (KW)	CO2 (Average ppm)	Temperature °C
1	73	3139.2726	44.872627	47.979189	11.301351
2	77	2665.796	47.293833	38.555385	13.503846
3	73	4601.6475	29.122982	42.172973	14.404054
4	74	3397.467	45.642488	41.707368	14.797368
5	73	3146.8157	44.755127	45.322297	14.97973
6	77	3549.4091	307.04326	42.435443	15.134177
7	78	3334.6836	48.084032	42.387342	14.173418
8	75	3090.6305	45.894299	54.406974	13.892105
9	68	4883.8277	41.379654	46.720725	13.031884

To apply DEA in railway environments, driving styles are treated as DMUs. Now, let S be the set of driving styles extracted from the dataset with $\mathbf{X}_i, i \in S$, being the vector of inputs of style i, with N elements $x_{ij}, j \in N$. Let $\mathbf{Y}_i, i \in S$ be corresponding vector of outputs with size M ($\mathbf{Y}_i = [y_{i1}, y_{i2}, \ldots, y_{iM}]$. Let also $\mathbf{X}_0 = [x_{01}, \ldots x_{0N}]$ be the inputs of the driving style that we want to evaluate and $\mathbf{Y}_k = [y_{01}, \ldots, y_{0M}]$ the output vector. Introducing parameter λ_i indicating the weight given to driving style i in its attempt to dominate Style 0, the measure of efficiency θ of Style 0 is determined through the solution of the following optimization problem:

$$Min\theta$$

Subject to

$$\sum_{i \in S} \lambda_i x_{ij} \leq \theta x_{0j}, \forall j \in N \tag{1}$$

$$\sum_{i \in S} \lambda_i y_{ij} \geq y_{0j}, \forall j \in M \tag{2}$$

$$\lambda_i \geq 0 \forall i \in S$$

Constraint (1) limits the inputs of all other driving styles below the inputs used by the reference model 0, while Eq. (2) selects the driving styles that outperform style 0. The above problem is solved for all driving styles to identify the most efficient one.

In the present study, the optimal driving styles have been calculated taking as inputs parameters related to the in-cabin CO_2 levels, the external temperature, the total driving time between adjacent stations, the total power consumption as measured by the pantograph and the power consumed by the HVAC system. An indicative sample of the parameters characterizing the driving styles is provided in Table 2, while the corresponding linear programming (LP) formulation considering only the first two styles is given below:

- *LP for evaluating Style 1:*

$$\min \theta$$

subject to

$$47.979189\lambda_1 + 38.555385\lambda_2 + 42.172973\lambda_3 \geq 47.9791890\theta \qquad (3.1)$$

$$11.301351\lambda_1 + 13.503846\lambda_2 + 14.404054\lambda_3 \leq 11.3013510\theta \qquad (3.2)$$

$$3139.2726\lambda_1 + 2665.796\lambda_1 + 4601.6475\lambda_3 \leq 3139.2726 \qquad (3.3)$$

$$44.872627\lambda_1 + 47.293833\lambda_2 + 291.22982\lambda_3 \leq 44.872627 \qquad (3.4)$$

$$73\lambda_1 + 77\lambda_2 + 73\lambda_3 \leq 73 \qquad (3.5)$$

$$\lambda_1, \lambda_2, \lambda_3 \geq 0$$

- *LP for evaluating Style 2:*

$$\min \theta$$

subject to

$$47.979189\lambda_1 + 38.555385\lambda_2 + 42.172973\lambda_3 \geq 38.5553850\theta \qquad (4.1)$$

$$11.301351\lambda_1 + 13.503846\lambda_2 + 14.404054\lambda_3 \leq 13.5038460\theta \qquad (4.2)$$

$$3139.2726\lambda_1 + 2665.796\lambda_1 + 4601.6475L3 \leq 2665.796 \qquad (4.3)$$

$$44.872627\lambda_1 + 47.293833\lambda_2 + 291.22982\lambda_3 \leq 47.293833 \qquad (4.4)$$

$$73\lambda_1 + 77\lambda_2 + 73\lambda_3 \leq 77 \qquad (4.5)$$

$$\lambda_1, \lambda_2, \lambda_3 \geq 0$$

5 Results

Solving the LP model for the styles shown in Table 2, the efficiency scores can be readily determined. The relevant results are provided in Table 3. A preliminary set of results indicating the driving styles obtained when the DEA approach is adopted is illustrated in Fig. 2. When the system is optimized for energy efficiency (green curve) the obtained driving style is smooth. On the other hand, when the system is optimized for shorter travelling times a higher average speed and steeper acceleration levels are observed.

A similar set of results is given in Fig. 3 where the optimal profile that minimizes the power consumption under end-to-end scheduling and passengers' constraints is illustrated. When the proposed method is applied, a 10% reduction in the overall power consumption can be achieved.

In the method followed, the fastest routes were compared, those with the highest consumption and those with the slowest routes, respectively. In addition, the similar time

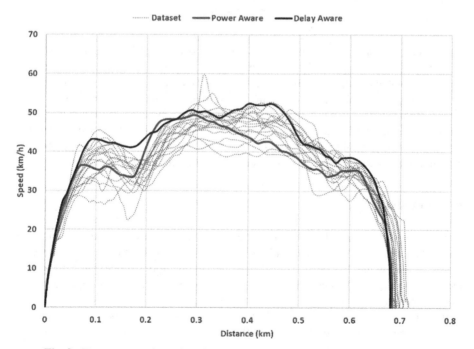

Fig. 2. Tramway speed as a function KM distance for various driving profiles [3].

Table 3. Efficiency scores for the driving styles shown in Table 2 [3].

Style ID	Efficiency score
1	0.8099
2	0.7312
3	0.6887
4	0.6902
5	0.7649
6	0.6746
7	0.67
8	0.8975
9	0.819

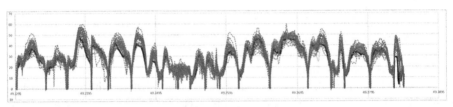

Fig. 3. Optimal driving profile obtained when the DEA method is applied (red line) and comparison with styles obtained from measurements (grey lines) [3].

routes were compared to each other to arrive at the above results. For example, we notice that routes 1 and 5 reach their destination at the same time and have almost the same consumption, total and ventilation. However, CO_2 levels in the cabin are higher in the case of the first route, so more passengers are transferred. Therefore, it is reasonable to get the result that route 1 is more efficient than route 5. Additionally, we notice that route 8 is more efficient than route 1. Also, in these routes the consumptions are similar, but we observe a considerable increase CO_2. As a result, the tramway on route 8, with more passengers and lower consumption, arrived later to the station compared to route 1.

6 Conclusions

In this paper, the problem of optimal train speed identification has been analyzed adopting for the first time the concept of Data Envelopment Analysis (DEA). DEA is a nonparametric technique that has been originally applied in operations research to empirically measure productive efficiency of decision-making units. Inspired by this approach, this study adopts DEA as a tool to measure efficiency in railways. Efficiency has been defined as the ratio of weighted sum of outputs to a weighted sum of inputs which for the rail scenario inputs/outputs are associated with the number of passengers' transferred, the energy consumption of the train, the inter-station travelling time, the internal and external conditions etc. Our objective is to identify driving policies that can transfer more passengers with less power and in less time.

To solve this problem, in the first stage of the research, a smart energy metering platform has been deployed on an actual tramway system monitoring system parameters such as energy, speed, acceleration, temperature etc. Once data has been collected, a linear programming model has been formulated aiming at identifying the optimal train speed profiles. Numerical results show that when the DEA method is applied, the energy consumption in railway systems can be reduced by 10%. A main limitation of this approach is related to its increased computational complexity as large number of measurements are required. To address this, in our future work the DEA method will be coupled with machine learning techniques to reduce the complexity of the ILP formulations.

Acknowledgement. The present study has received funding from the European Union's Horizon 2020 research and innovation programme IN2DREAMS under grant agreement No: 777596 and IN2STEMPO under grant 777515.

References

1. https://uic.org/support-activities/statistics/#UIC-statistical-indicators
2. CYbersecurity in the RAILway sector, D2.1 – Safety and Security requirements of Rail transport system in multi-stakeholder environments, cyrail.eu
3. Achilleos, A., et al.: Optimal Driving Profiles in Railway Systems based on Data Envelopment Analysis. VEHITS 2019, pp. 254–259 (2019)
4. Anastasopoulos, M., Tzanakaki A., Iordache, M., Langlois, O., Pheulpin, J.-F., Simeonidou, D.: ICT platforms in support of future railway systems. In: Proceedings of TRA 2018, Vienna, 16–19 April 2018
5. Ogasa M.: Energy saving and environmental measures in railway technologies: example with hybrid electric railway vehicles. IEEJ Trans. Electr. Electron. Eng. 304–311, May 2010
6. Gunselmann, W.: Technologies for increased energy efficiency in railway systems. In: European Conference on Power Electronics and Applications, Dresden (2005)
7. Gunselmann, W., Godbersen, C.: Double-layer capacitors store surplus braking energy. In: Railway Gazette International, November 2001 S. 581 ff
8. Gallo, M., Simonelli, F., De Luca, G., De Martinis, V.: Estimating the effects of energy-efficient driving profiles on railway consumption. In: 2015 IEEE 15th International Conference on Environment and Electrical Engineering (EEEIC), pp. 813–818, Rome (2015)
9. Lukaszewicz, P., Allan, J., Brebbia, C.A., Hill, R.J., Sciutto, G., Sone, S.: Energy saving driving methods for freight trains. Div. Railway Technol. KTH (Royal Inst. Technol.), Sweden Computers in Railways IX, © 2004 WIT Press (2004). www.witpress.com, ISBN 1-85312-715-9
10. Zhang, H., Jia, L., Wang, L., Xinyue, X.: Energy consumption optimization of train operation for railway systems: algorithm development and real-world case study. J. Clean. Prod. **214**, 1024–1037 (2019)
11. Scheepmaker, G.M., Goverde, R.M.P., Kroon, L.G.: Review of energy-efficient train control and timetabling. Eur. J. Oper. Res. **257**(2), 355–376 (2017)

12. Charnes, A., Cooper, W.W., Rhodes, E.: Measuring the efficiency of decision making units. Eur. J. Oper. Res. **2**(6), 429–444 (1978)
13. De Martinis, V., Gallo, M., D'Acierno, L.: Estimating the benefits of energy-efficient train driving strategies: a model calibration with real data
14. Mensing, F., Trigui, R., Bideaux, E.: Vehicle trajectory optimization for application in ECO-driving. In: Vehicle Power and Propulsion Conference (VPPC), pp. 1–6 (2011)
15. Powell, J.P., Palacín, R.: A Comparison of Modelled and Real-Life Driving Profiles for the Simulation of Railway Vehicle Operation, NewRail – Centre for Railway Research. Newcastle University, Newcastle upon Tyne, UK (2014)
16. Strössenreuther, H.: Energy Efficient Driving -DB AG. 2nd UIC Railway
17. Energy Efficiency Conference UIC, Paris 4–5 February 2004
18. Lukaszewicz, P.: Driving techniques and strategies for freigth trains. Computers in Railways VII. COMPRAIL 2000 Bologna
19. Lukaszewicz, P.: Energy Consumption and Running Time for Trains. KTH Stockholm 2001, p. 25. TRITA-FKT 2001 ISSN 1103-470X
20. Cornuejols, G., Trick, M.: Quantitative Methods for the Management Sciences, Course Notes, Chapter 12, Data Envelopment Analysis (1998). https://mat.gsia.cmu.edu/classes/QUANT/
21. Toledo, T., Lotan, T.: In-Vehicle data recorder for evaluation of driving behavior and safety". transportation research record. J. Transp. Res. Board, 112–119, January 2006
22. Chang, C., Sim, S.: Optimising train movements through coast control using genetic algorithms. IEEE Proc. Electr. Power Appl. **144**, 65–73 (1997)

Correction to: Making CCU Visible: Investigating Laypeople's Requirements for a Trusted, Informative CCU Label

Anika Linzenich, Katrin Arning, and Martina Ziefle

Correction to:
Chapter "Making CCU Visible: Investigating Laypeople's
Requirements for a Trusted, Informative CCU Label"
in: M. Helfert et al. (Eds.): *Smart Cities, Green Technologies*
*and Intelligent Transport Systems***, CCIS 1217,**
https://doi.org/10.1007/978-3-030-68028-2_3

In the originally published version of the chapter 3, the link "CCU-Label – www.ccu-reduction.org" in Fig. 5 was missing. To enable a proper understanding of the content the link has been added.

The updated version of this chapter can be found at
https://doi.org/10.1007/978-3-030-68028-2_3

Author Index

Printed in the United States
By Bookmasters